lonely planet

Melbourne | Oakland | London

Charles Rawlings-Way &
Natalie Karneef

917.13

Toronto

Introducing Toronto

Facing-off against New York State, far across the slate-grey waters of Lake Ontario, Toronto walks the line between American cultural osmosis and staunch northern independence. Masters of this balancing act, Torontonians embrace both worlds with verve and open-mindedness. Enlightened, multicultural and uniquely Canadian – welcome to T.O.!

Once an earnest 'icebox' town, Toronto has thawed through waves of European, Latin American, Asian and Caribbean immigration. One in two Torontonians was born somewhere else, their transplanted cultures creating an effervescent patchwork of neighborhoods. Typically laconic, Toronto is both unpretentious and complex.

Toronto's big-ticket sports teams rarely deliver, but fans remain optimistic. Creativity provides solace, the arts community thriving on suburb-to-suburb evolution. This is a literary, artistic, musical town – symphony seats sell as fast as hockey tickets (well, almost…).

As September hints at winter, the Toronto International Film Festival (TIFF) provides a cultural Indian Summer. When the red carpets recede, street festivals, rock concerts, exhibitions and dance extravaganzas take the stage.

Hungry? Toronto's kitchens are as multicultural as its population. Korean walnut cakes, Italian espresso, Malaysian laksas and face-melting Indian curries – all in a day's dining.

Shopping here is wonderful, too. Rummage through the racks with the sharp-dressed locals. If shopping's not your bag, escape into the city's leafy ravines – full of raccoons and sweaty joggers – or day-trip down to Niagara's vineyards.

Air pollution and homelessness are big-city headaches, but 'Toronto the Good' isn't a menacing place. Courtesy prevails, but there's no shortage of sexy subculture here: 'Clubland' gyrates towards the dawn, wine lists impress, bar stools wobble until 2am.

Sound appealing? Believe it! Underwhelmed Montrealers sneer, 'Is diversity enough to hang your hat on?' Calgary's boomtown rats say, 'Why define your city by a lack of consistency?' Torontonians smile wryly, knowing that in this age of tinderbox international relations, their recipe of good-hearted tolerance may be the answer to all our problems.

1 *Crest poles carved by First Nations Tribes, Royal Ontario Museum (pp66–7)* **2** *Toronto's lush parklands at dusk* **3** *Statue of Winston Churchill watching over City Hall (pp60–1)* **4** *Toronto's Provincial Legislature buildings and gardens (p69)*

Previous Pages (left) *Caribana carnival parade (p14)* **(right)** *The CN Tower (p51), Flatiron (Gooderham) Building (p57) and skyscrapers, Front St East*

1 *Sassafraz restaurant, Bloor-Yorkville (p103)* **2** *Interior of Hôtel Le Germain (p169)* **3** *Sculpture in Chinatown (pp62–4)* **4** *Madison Avenue pub, The Annex (p120)*

1 *Sam the Record Man shop, Yonge Street (p154)* 2 *Vintage clothing shop in Kensington Market (pp158–9)* 3 *Toronto Maple Leafs ice hockey team (p142) playing at the Air Canada Centre (p50)* 4 *Fancy footwear of Elton John and Justin Timberlake at the Bata Shoe Museum (p66)*

1 *Frozen edges of Niagara Falls (pp181–6) in winter* 2 *The 19th-century Niagara Apothecary in Niagara-on-the-Lake (p193)* 3 *Niagara Peninsula Wine Country (pp186–90) in spring* 4 *Whirlpool Aero Car over the Niagara River (p185)*

Following Page *Reflection of the CN Tower (p51)*

Contents

Published by Lonely Planet Publications Pty Ltd
ABN 36 005 607 983

Australia Head Office, Locked Bag 1, Footscray,
Victoria 3011, ☎ 03 8379 8000, fax 03 8379 8111,
talk2us@lonelyplanet.com.au

USA 150 Linden St, Oakland, CA 94607,
☎ 510 893 8555, toll free 800 275 8555,
fax 510 893 8572, info@lonelyplanet.com

UK 72–82 Rosebery Ave, Clerkenwell, London,
EC1R 4RW, ☎ 020 7841 9000, fax 020 7841 9001,
go@lonelyplanet.co.uk

© Lonely Planet Publications Pty Ltd 2007
Photographs © Corey Wise and as listed (p217) 2007

Printed by SNP Security Printing Pte Ltd
Printed in Singapore

The Authors

Charles Rawlings-Way

Charles first made Toronto's acquaintance when he was eight, flying in from Tasmania to assess the squirrels and his uncle's croissants. He's since cultivated a Toronto habit, shifting focus towards baseball, bookshops and beer. He's been snowed-in by blizzards, bamboozled by microbrews, rocked earless in grungy bars and overwhelmed by global culinary delights. A meek decision to avoid the giant trampoline at Ontario Place in 1978 haunts him to this day…

A lapsed architect, underrated guitarist and fearless home renovator, Charles greased the production wheels at Lonely Planet's Melbourne HQ for many years before becoming a freelance travel writer in 2005.

Natalie Karneef

Natalie's love of style has taken her through Indian bazaars, up London high streets, around Parisian markets and into boutiques in her hometown of Montréal. She spent two years living, and shopping, in Toronto, and returned there to write the Shopping and Excursions chapters of this book. She also interviewed John Moore (p19) and wrote the Fashion section in the City Life chapter.

CONTRIBUTING AUTHOR
MONICA BODIRSKY

Monica wrote the 'First Nations Foundations' box (p40) in the History chapter. She is the coordinator of 'Getekindaswingamig' Native Community History Program at the Native Canadian Centre of Toronto (p69).

PHOTOGRAPHER
Corey Wise

For photographer Corey Wise, a stint in Europe unleashed a hopeless case of travel addiction that led to multi-month forays around the Middle East, Asia and South America. Toronto was a change of venue, but surprisingly exotic, thanks to the city's diverse population.

Charles' Top Toronto Day

I can't get started without a kick-ass coffee, so it's straight to **Jet Fuel** (p124) or **Moonbean Coffee Company** (p124) for a fix. After the Andy Warhol exhibition at the **Art Gallery of Ontario** (p64) I boot it into **Baldwin Village** (p99) for a street café brunch. Plunging into the subway, I rumble into grandiose **Union Station** (p54) – the **Toronto Islands** (p75) ferry isn't far away. The bike I rented keeps slipping gears, but the Islands sure do look good. My jealousy is thinly veiled as I trundle past some **Ward's Island** (p77) hippies snoozing in the boardwalk sunshine. Back on the mainland I slurp down some $3 noodles in **Chinatown** (p99) then rummage around **Kensington Market** (p158) for a new *toque* (winter hat). I wonder if the **Royal Ontario Museum** (p66) extensions are finished? Somehow I doubt it… There's time for a quick pint at the **Distillery District** (p120) before the Blue Jays (p53) baseball game tonight. The indie street-press *Now* coughs up a cool band at the **Cameron House** (p125) later on, but I'll keep my appreciation low-key – tomorrow I'll drive down to the **Niagara Peninsula** (p186) to stock up on wine and check climate change hasn't evaporated the falls.

City Life

City Life

TORONTO TODAY

Toronto is an ebullient town – the economy has recovered from setbacks in the early '90s, the shopping scene is vibrant as ever and regular festivals bring smiles to people's faces. Food-lovers continue to count their blessings, and politically (locally at least) things are on a relatively even keel.

The soul of contemporary Toronto, however, seems to be split in two: on one side the bohemian descendants of Yorkville's '60s folk scene drift hazily around Kensington Market and West Queen West, admiring each other's tattoos, puffing on joints and indulging their artistic passions. In the opposite corner, the pinstriped 'Bay St Boys' exchange business cards, work long stock-market hours then buy city girls dinner at **Bymark** (p94). And never the twain shall meet. Caught in between, middle Toronto attempts to lasso the best of both worlds.

Meanwhile, astute Toronto real estate agents continue to play 'Follow the Artists.' It's a familiar phenomenon: young artists move into a cheap neighborhood and get busy with spoken word, painting, music, sex and drugs, hanging out in lofts and generally being cool.

Then the yuppies decide they want to live somewhere cool too – the money moves in, and the real estate magnates make a killing. Pretty soon there's a Starbucks where the pawn shop used to be and the artists can't afford the rent, so they pack their paintbrushes and move somewhere else. In Toronto, 'somewhere else' has been Yorkville in the '60s, The Annex and Kensington Market in the '70s and '80s, Queen West in the '90s, and West Queen West in the 2000s. Where next? Leslieville? Corktown? Our money's on West Bloor Village, where the crack dealers enjoy excellent public transportation, affordable rent and a distinct absence of yuppies.

CITY CALENDAR

Peak summer season runs from Victoria Day (the Monday preceding May 24) to Labour Day (the first Monday in September), during which time accommodations fill to overflowing (and charge accordingly) and queues at major attractions extend toward the horizon. Everywhere stays open later during summer; neighborhood street festivals happen most weekends. Other busy times are Easter, Thanksgiving, Christmas and New Year's, as well as during major events like **Caribana** (p14) and the **Toronto International Film Festival** (p15).

During July, the hottest, most humid month, many Torontonians escape to the Harbourfront, Toronto Islands or The Beaches where, even if the air temperature is only a few degrees cooler, lakefront breezes make life more tolerable. Subarctic winds howl through the city in January and February, when sensible folks descend into Toronto's underground PATH system (p215). But regardless of the weather, there's always something going on in T.O.!

See p201 for a list of Toronto's public holidays.

JANUARY & FEBRUARY
WINTERCITY FESTIVAL
☎ 416-395-0490; www.toronto.ca/special_events
From late January through mid-February, the city pulls out all stops to urge folks to defy the cold, offering free outdoor concerts, fireworks, arts and cultural events, special tourist packages and even a barbecue outside City Hall (p60). WinterCity Passport coupons offer discounts to city attractions.

WINTERLICIOUS
☎ 416-395-0490; www.toronto.ca/special_events
The early February version of Summerlicious (p14).

MARCH & APRIL
CANADA BLOOMS
☎ 416-447-8655, 800-730-1020; www.canada blooms.com
Heralding the arrival of spring, this is one of the most florid horticultural expos in North America.

TORONTO TASTE
☎ 416-408-2594; www.torontotaste.ca
Tasty T.O. at its charitable best (p112).

MAY
DOORS OPEN TORONTO
☎ 416-205-2670; www.doorsopen.org
Architectural treasures creak open their doors to let the public sneak a peek (p34).

MILK INTERNATIONAL CHILDREN'S FESTIVAL OF THE ARTS
☎ 416-973-4000; www.harbourfront.on.ca/milk
Around Victoria Day weekend, hundreds of kids take over the Harbourfront Centre (p52) for international puppetry, theatre, dance and musical performances, as well as deliciously messy art workshops, outdoor games and storytelling events. Day passes cost $12.50.

JUNE & JULY
TORONTO INTERNATIONAL DRAGON BOAT FESTIVAL
☎ 416-595-0313; www.torontodragonboat.com
Adhering to 2000-year-old Chinese traditions, these hefty, luridly decorated 'dragon' canoes froth up the lake around the Toronto Islands (p75) in mid-June. Crowds yell enthusiastically as over 120 teams compete to represent Canada internationally.

NORTH BY NORTHEAST (NXNE)
☎ 416-863-6963; www.nxne.com
An independent music and film festival to rival South by Southwest (SXSW) in Austin, Texas. A $25 wristband (likely to cost more from 2007) gets you in to any of 400 new music shows at over 30 clubs, all squeezed into one long, boozy weekend in mid-June.

NATIONAL ABORIGINAL DAY
☎ 416-392-5583; www.toronto.ca/diversity /events.htm
Although not a statutory holiday, Canada's heritage of First Nations, Inuit and Métis cultures is celebrated on June 21 (the summer solstice), including a cultural arts fair outside City Hall in Nathan Phillips Square (p60). Politicians fall over themselves to attend.

PRIDE TORONTO
☎ 416-927-7433; www.pridetoronto.com
Larger and more flamboyant than ever, Pride Week climaxes in late June with an out-of-the-closet Dyke March and Pride Parade, with the festival's G-spot in the Church-Wellesley Village (p64). See *Xtra!* (p203) for a schedule of free LGBTTIQ (lesbian, gay, bisexual, transsexual, transgender, intersex and queer) events.

DOWNTOWN JAZZ FESTIVAL
☎ 416-928-2033; www.tojazz.com
For 10 days in late June and early July, jazz blazes through Toronto's city streets, clubs and concert halls, with musical workshops, film screenings and harbor cruises. Expect anyone from Wynton Marsalis to gospel choirs, with blues and world beat influences thrown into the mix.

SCREAM IN HIGH PARK
☎ 416-466-8862; www.thescream.ca
Sit on a blanket under the stars and listen to local poets, novelists, storytellers and random wordsmiths from across Canada perform on the Dream in High Park (p129) stage, as well as at events around town. The culmination of the broader Scream Literary Festival, the High Park event happens one night in mid-July.

TORONTO: A DAY IN THE LIFE

A random sampling of a few days' worth of Toronto events as listed in the free weekly street-press *Now* (p203):

- Big Rude Jake plays ragtime guitar in the Melody Bar at the **Gladstone Hotel** (p119).
- *Counting Sheep*, a 15-minute film featuring sheep wandering around a field, screens at the **Nuit Blanche** festival (opposite).
- The **Canadian Opera Company** (p133) warbles through a free lunchtime Mussorgsky concert.
- Dharma discussions and walking meditation transpire at **Tengye Ling Tibetan Buddhist Temple** (p143)
- Public forums on improvements to Toronto's garbage disposal occur across the city.
- Toronto's largest adult store ramps up advertising for its line of saucy Halloween costumes.
- **Yuk Yuk's** (p133) comedy lounge presents Amateur Night – Tuesday night stand-up for the fearless, thick-skinned or talented.
- Fly Fridays at **Government** (p131) features hip-hip, old school, house and reggae with DJs Boza, Wristpect and Brian Bliss.
- **CanStage** (p128) conducts auditions for mid- to large-sized dogs for their upcoming production of *Of Mice and Men*.
- Las Vegan charisma-rockers The Killers blitz into town and lift the roof off the **Koolhaus** (p131).

TORONTO FRINGE FESTIVAL

☎ 416-966-1062; www.fringetoronto.com

The promoters' slogan for Toronto's stand-out theatre festival is 'Unjuried. Unexpected. Unforgettable.' Happening over two weeks in early July, dozens of stages host dozens of plays ranging from utterly offbeat to deadly serious, plus a program of kids' plays too.

GRAND PRIX OF TORONTO

☎ 416-922-7477; www.grandprixtoronto.com

Formerly the Molson Indy, T.O.'s Grand Prix in mid-July sees drivers from the international circuit competing in front of massive crowds, two practice days building to the big race on the third day. Whining engine noise fills the air as cars top 300km/h along Lake Shore Blvd.

SUMMERLICIOUS

☎ 416-395-0490; www.toronto.ca/special_events

For two weeks in mid-July, 130 of Toronto's top eateries throw financial prudence to the wind, plating up three-course prix-fixe lunches ($15 to $20) and dinners ($25 to $35) for all-comers. You can experience the likes of **North 44°** (p113), **Auberge du Pommier** (p113) and **Canoe** (p94) without breaking the bank. **Winterlicious** (p13) is the same but different.

BEACHES INTERNATIONAL JAZZ FESTIVAL

☎ 416-698-2152; www.beachesjazz.com

Going strong for almost 20 years, this high-caliber, free, three-day jazz festival in late July fills stages along Queen St E, at **Kew Gardens** (p75) and in the **Distillery District** (p56) with classy zah-bah-dee-dah. Jazz, big band, trad R&B and soul are the names of the games.

AUGUST

CARIBANA

☎ 905-799-1630; www.caribana.com

This energetic carnival is North America's largest Caribbean festival, running from late July into early August. The finale is a weekend of reggae, steel drum and calypso mayhem, a huge carnival parade featuring ornate and skimpy costumes à la Rio. It takes five hours to gyrate past – damn, that's some party!

TASTE OF THE DANFORTH

☎ 416-469-5634; www.tasteofthedanforth.com

Modeled on the Taste of Chicago, this multicultural food-and-music festival takes over the streets of Greektown in early August. Look for beer gardens, food stalls, cooking demos, fashion shows and the Danforth Dash bed race.

TORONTO INTERNATIONAL DANCE FESTIVAL

☎ 416-214-5854; www.ffida.org

'Where the world comes to dance!' is the catch-cry here, and they ain't kidding. For two weeks in mid-August, the Distillery District erupts with groovers and shakers from all over the globe, performing, conducting workshops and exchanging ideas. Some shows are free; most cost around $20.

CANADIAN NATIONAL EXHIBITION
☎ 416-393-6300; www.theex.com
Dating from 1879, 'The Ex' claims to be the world's oldest and largest annual exhibition. Over 700 exhibitors conduct agricultural shows, lumberjack competitions, outdoor concerts, carnival games and rides at Exhibition Place (p51). The air show and Labour Day fireworks take the cake.

TORONTO BUSKERFEST
☎ 416-964-9095; www.torontobuskerfest.com
For three days in late August, a rag-tag troupe of Canadian and international buskers descends on St Lawrence Market to perform and raise money for Epilepsy Toronto. Expect sword-swallowers, jugglers, musicians of unpredictable merit and more unicycles than you've ever seen in one place.

SEPTEMBER
TORONTO INTERNATIONAL FILM FESTIVAL (TIFF)
☎ 416-968-3456; www.bell.ca/filmfest
Toronto's prestigious 10-day film fest is one of the world's best (p27).

CABBAGETOWN FESTIVAL
☎ 416-921-0857; www.oldcabbagetown.com
A family-focused celebration held the first weekend after Labour Day, featuring corn roasts, pancake breakfasts, a minifestival of film and performing arts and historic home tours. Elvis impersonators and jazz and blues acts grace various stages.

VIRGIN MUSIC FESTIVAL
☎ 888-999-2321; www.virginfestival.ca
In 2006 Dick Branson brought his musical extravaganza to the Toronto Islands, with predictable success. Thirty-six bands (The Flaming Lips, Sam Roberts, Muse etc) rubbed up against 15 DJs over two mid-September days, just late enough in the season to avoid the Centre Island crowds.

NUIT BLANCHE
☎ 416-338-0338; www.livewithculture.ca
Loosely translated it means 'sleepless night.' Over 140 free, zany, urban art experiences – from 24-hour Three Stooges film

marathons to nocturnal pool parties and ballroom dancing sessions run by 10-year-old DJs – keep Toronto awake for one night (7pm to 7am) in late September.

OCTOBER
INTERNATIONAL FESTIVAL OF AUTHORS
☎ 416-954-0366; www.readings.org
Part of the Harbourfront Reading Series (p132), the Authors' festival delivers over 100 acclaimed writers from Canada and abroad (including big names like Margaret Atwood) to the Harbourfront Centre for readings, panel discussions, lectures, awards and book signings.

AFTER DARK FILM FESTIVAL
☎ 416-967-1528; www.torontoafterdark.com
New to the Toronto festival circuit, After Dark is a cinematic celebration of international sci-fi, horror and fantasy cinema, timed appropriately to coincide with Halloween. Also on the cards are animated, action and short-film offerings from local film-makers.

NOVEMBER & DECEMBER
CANADIAN ABORIGINAL FESTIVAL
☎ 519-751-0040; www.canab.com
Open to everyone, this multiday celebration held at the Rogers Centre (p53) in late November involves dancing, drumming, artisan crafts, new films and traditional teachings, as well as a lacrosse competition. This is Canada's biggest Aboriginal festival.

CHRISTMAS & NEW YEAR'S EVE
☎ 416-392-8674; www.city.toronto.ca/culture
In the weeks leading up to Christmas, traditional celebrations light up Casa Loma (p68), Mackenzie House (p61), Black Creek Pioneer Village (p77) and other cultural venues. The Church of the Holy Trinity (p60) runs a not-to-be-missed musical nativity pageant. Over three days leading up to the New Year, First Night Toronto (☎ 416-603-4778; www.firstnighttoronto.ca) organizes wonderful family-friendly entertainment at the Distillery District (p56). Pray for snow – Torontonians are not happy if they don't get a white Christmas.

CULTURE

IDENTITY

Like most Canadians, Toronto residents usually define themselves by what they are *not* (not Americans, not Québécois etc), rather than positively defining who they actually are. This habit changed during the 2006 soccer World Cup, when every Torontonian suddenly became patriotically Italian, French, Portuguese, Brazilian or English, delving into family trees to unearth distant genetic ties to whichever team was winning at the time!

The English modernist Wyndham Lewis said of Toronto, 'O for a half-hour of Europe after this sanctimonious icebox!' The long-standing tag of 'Toronto the Good' has been hard to shake. Initially a safe haven for Loyalists fleeing the American Revolution, Toronto was ruled by a conservative British colonial society, led by politically savvy Anglican clergy. In 1906 the Lord's Day Act (p41) was passed, which forbade working and socializing on Sundays.

Free from the binds of history, modern Toronto has swapped dour sanctimoniousness for indulgent good-times – this is a party town, infatuated with theatre, live music, sports, festivals, fine food and wine. It's Canada's most culturally diverse city, with more than 70 resident ethnic groups and over 100 languages spoken. Half the city's residents were born outside Canada. The urban sprawl of the Greater Toronto Area (GTA), accounts for one in seven Canadians, and continues to swell as new immigrants arrive from around the globe. Torontonians insist on identifying their city as 'world class' – and rightly so!

Canadians are more lax about religion than their US counterparts, and generally don't mix religion with politics. Tolerance is a way of life, with a high number of 'affirming' congregations that ordain, marry and welcome the lesbigay community. At pious places like downtown's **Church of the Holy Trinity** (p60), the congregation comes more for the social activism than the Sunday service. Historically, Toronto has maintained a strong Jewish presence. Buddhism predominates among Asian communities, including a small Tibetan Buddhist community.

Toronto's Aboriginal population, comprising mostly of First Nations people, nudges over 10,000 people. A 1997 Canadian Supreme Court ruling stated that, based on oral history, Aboriginal people have legitimate title to their lands and that provincial governments have a 'moral duty' to negotiate with them. Frustratingly, this ruling hasn't helped Aboriginal groups without a land base, like those in urban Toronto. The nearest established Aboriginal community is Brantford's Six Nations of the Grand River Territory, near the Niagara Peninsula. *Back on the Rez: Finding the Way Home* (1996) by Brian Maracle is an account of one Torontonian's return to life on the reserve after 40 years away.

LIFESTYLE

In general, Torontonians are a mannerly bunch, if sometimes a little too earnest. They think long and hard about how to live their lives, ruminating over everything from recycling to the Blue Jays' prospects. Sincerity aside, there's no shortage of irony or wryness in the local sense of humor, which at its most potent can strip paint.

HOT CONVERSATION TOPICS

- With plumes of **air pollution** drifting in from the south and Canada's conservative government making anti-Kyoto Protocol mutterings and procrastinating over new environmental measures, it seems Toronto's asthmatic fog is unlikely to dissipate anytime soon. Wheeze…
- Toronto's eyesore **Gardiner Expressway** conveys 180,000 motorists every day, but it's perpetually congested and needs constant expensive maintenance. A recent report from the Toronto Waterfront Revitalization Corp suggested demolishing it and building a 10-lane, $758 million 'Great Street' – who'll be paying for *that*?
- Toronto is proud of its long-standing 'safe city' reputation, but gun crime is on the rise. Everyday there's at least one gun-related incident somewhere in the GTA, and locals are getting edgy. What the hell is this, Detroit?
- Still no action down at **Maple Leaf Gardens** (p65), eh? After malingering on the auction block for a while, this classic Toronto landmark, where the Leafs played from 1931 to 1999 and Elvis crooned, was bought by grocery chain Loblaws in 2004. History-sensitive redevelopment is scheduled for late 2007.

IT'S A DOGS LIFE

Dogs enjoy an elevated social status in Toronto. Unlike many western cities where hounds are tied up on the sidewalk, Toronto's mutts can freely access shopping malls, supermarkets, cafés, the PATH network and the subway. Affluent Yorkville ladies parade pedigree pooches along Bloor St, shop attendants not batting an eye as wet noses sniff through racks of YSL and Prada. A crop of downtown doggy boutiques (p162) ensure that Toronto's canines are groomed to the nines. Thankfully, city dogs have trained their owners to stoop and scoop the poop – unfortunate footwear encounters are rare. Woof!

The work ethic in the Financial District on Bay St (Toronto's version of Wall St), is intense. *Waaay*-too-young stockbrokers do their best to convince themselves that Toronto is actually New York, but most people here know how to clock-off and relax too. Eating and drinking are major pursuits, with life lived outdoors as much as possible, especially during summer.

Torontonians are more likely to speak their mind than other Canadians (especially when anyone mentions George Bush), but tolerance remains a virtue. Most embrace multiculturalism, especially with its festivals, thriving arts scene and fusion cuisine.

Quiet residential blocks scattered throughout the city centre boast shady trees, one-way streets (called 'Traffic Calming Zones') and Victorian row houses, interlinked by the efficient TTC public transport system. Despite the grim winter and the critical issue of homelessness, general living standards are high – Torontonians know that they've got it good.

FOOD & DRINK

When you're on the road, you want to try the local cuisine, right? Except in Canada, because what's there to try? A bit of charred moose? Maple syrup pie? Once there was only Québécois cuisine, but all that has changed. New Canadian cuisine combines unusual, fresh (often organic) local ingredients with classic French stylings and daring fusion techniques from Asia. It's similar to Californian cuisine, but fleshed out with northern game and continental-inspired sauces. That said, Yukon Gold potatoes are still just potatoes, and Prince Edward Island seafood isn't necessarily anything special. Our advice: order internationally and adventurously and see what arrives!

Most Torontonians are real 'foodies,' the names of local chefs rolling off their tongues as easily as those of movie stars. People here are as comfortable plunging chopsticks into a bowl of *pho* (Vietnamese soup) at **Phô' Hu'ng** (p100) as they are polishing the silver during tea at the **Windsor Arms** (p172). The city's high-flying restaurants have some of the top tables in North America, including **Canoe** (p94) and **Auberge du Pommier** (p113). The **Summerlicious** (p14) and **Winterlicious** (p13) festivals increase your chances of being able to afford to eat at these kinds of places.

Weighing in on the local cuisine scene are the fecund Niagara Peninsula vineyards (p186), which take enormous steps forward with every vintage. The Niagara Peninsula enjoys a quirky microclimate (it almost never snows), allowing the world-famous Niagara ice wines to flourish. Also on offer are excellent bottles of pinot noir, cabernet sauvignon, merlot, cabernet franc and pinot grigio – wine tasting is a mandatory experience if you're touring the Peninsula. If you're city-bound, most decent Toronto restaurants proffer healthy wine lists, usually peppered with Niagara classics.

Wine not your thing? You'll be relieved to hear that microbrew culture is alive and kicking in Toronto, many pubs and bars like **C'est What?** (p119) and **Smokeless Joe** (p123) serving small-batch Ontarian, Québécois and British Columbian beers. Don't miss a tour of **Steamwhistle Brewing Company** (p54)

TORONTO THE (STILL) GOOD

Describing Toronto in 1984, Jan Morris wrote that Torontonians were 'incoherently polite.' Indeed, during your visit you might wonder, 'What the hell did I do to deserve all this courteousness?' Those unlikely to earn a knighthood will enjoy the standard 'Sir' and 'M'am' salutations, while riding the punctual TTC with its charter of 'Respect & Dignity' is an oddly calming experience. Subway notices say, 'Be courteous – do not rush doors'; street-crossings are adorned with signs saying, 'Pedestrians obey your signals.' Walking from A to B, Torontonians stick religiously to the right of the sidewalk, conditioned by years of driving. This absence of chaos might drive you nuts, but don't complain – you'll always get where you're going on time.

TOP FIVE TORONTO CHEFS

Torontonians worship their celebrity chefs, some of whom flit from restaurant to restaurant, their reputations and clientele tagging along for the ride. Scan the fine (or sometimes not-so-fine) print on the menu to see if you're feasting on the inventive creations of the following:

- David Chrystian – a serial success story, Chrystian skipped through the kitchens of Cafe Societa, Patriot, Accolade and the Drake Hotel to his current domain, **Joy Bistro** (p110). He's passionate about Canadian wines, and founded **The Centre for Wine and Food Experimentation** (www.thecentreforwineandfood.com).
- Susur Lee – welcomed home like a prodigal son after a stint in East Asia, this pony-tailed Hong Kong chef reigns supreme, serving up classy, imaginative cuisine at **Susur** (p109). He's even had a book written about him.
- Mark McEwan – world-wise McEwan blew people's minds in 1990 with **North 44°** (p113), which remains one of Toronto's top tables. He followed up with super-slick **Bymark** (p94), and now has a TV show called *The Heat*, and a new restaurant opening in 2007.
- Pascal Ribreau – after languishing in middling French kitchens, Ribreau struck out on his own with sparkling **Celestin** (p113), a success made all the more triumphant after a paralyzing car accident in the late '90s. He rates Toronto above Paris in the food stakes.
- Dufflet Rosenberg – Toronto's 'Queen of Cake' started her pastry biz at home in 1975. Today, **Dufflet Pastries** (p107) – a 31-year-old pioneer Queen West business – sells her divine (and reasonably priced) delights.

if you're at a loss for something to do around Harbourfront. If you're more of a cocktail fiend, Toronto's love affair with the martini remains undiminished – you'll have no trouble pickling yourself with countless interpretations of the classic recipe.

Outside of European restaurants, decent coffee can be hard to find in Toronto. Humongous North American chains proliferate, serving watery, overheated, oversized caffeine monstrosities to the ill-educated masses. But weed around the back blocks and you'll be able to find a decent latte (p123).

FASHION

With two internationally renowned Fashion Weeks, a glittering selection of big name designer boutiques, and an inspired selection of vintage and antique clothiers, Toronto is at the centre of the Canadian fashion stage. Some of fashion's most recognized labels were born here: twin brothers Dean and Dan Caten, brainchildren behind the catwalk favorite DSquared, are from Toronto. So is Alfred Sung, father of Club Monaco, and Arthur Mendonca, whose bold designs have grazed the backs of countless celebrities. Eco-forward Preloved, groundbreaker in the use of recycled fabric, was born on Queen West, and cosmetic giants MAC makeup, known for their support of AIDS research and their use of big-name spokespeople (which have included Lisa Marie Presley, Elton John and Mary J Blige) originated in T.O.

Meanwhile, Toronto continues to produce a steady hum of young, up-and-coming independent designers ready to provide the next big thing. Local creations are featured at eclectic boutiques such as **Propaganda** (p154), **Courage My Love** (p158), **Fresh Collective** (p158) and sister store **Fresh Baked Goods** (p158), while **Secrets From Your Sister** (p157) provides a comfortable setting for proper bra-fitting and a wide range of sizes. Trendsetters will head straight to one of the Fiorio salons, or to **Coupe Bizarre** (p145) for of-the-moment hairstyling.

SPORTS

Toronto is utterly sports mad. Media burgeons with the latest headlines, while before big hockey games, TTC buses display 'Go Leafs!' messages instead of route numbers. Despite the fact that the **Toronto Maple Leafs** (p142) haven't won the Stanley Cup since 1967, the city is rabid with hockey fever all winter long. Tickets to Leafs games are expensive and hard to come by, but the atmosphere is unforgettable.

When the **Toronto Blue Jays** (p140) won back-to-back World Series in 1992 and '93, they became the only non-US team ever to claim Major League Baseball's holy grail. Less fortunate have been the **Toronto Raptors** (p141), who belong to the Atlantic Division of the National Basketball League's Eastern Conference. Since Vince Carter packed his bags for New Jersey in 2004, it's been slim pickings for the Raps. Emerging star Chris Bosh might pick up the pieces.

First observed by a Jesuit missionary during the 1600s, when teams of hundreds of First Nations warriors placed goals miles apart and competed from sunrise to sundown, lacrosse is often called 'the fastest game on two feet.' Modern matches are played on indoor hockey rinks. The blazing **Toronto Rock** (p142) dominate in the National Lacrosse League.

The Canadian Football League is an odd duck, considered to be 'longer, wider and faster' than its American counterpart. The **Toronto Argonauts** (p142) are the winningest team in CFL history.

On the back of the 2006 World Cup, soccer is staking a claim as Toronto's (and indeed North America's) fastest growing sport. **Toronto FC** is poised to join America's Major League Soccer (www.nslnet.com) competition in 2007.

For golf information see p139; horseracing p142.

MEDIA

Toronto is Canada's English-language publishing centre. Publishing houses abound – major internationals like Random House, Harper Collins and Penguin have offices here. Although newsstands aren't generally found on the street (they're usually inside subway stations where it's warmer), the city has an abundance of magazine shops to satisfy residents' voracious appetites for news. Free street-press dailies, weeklies and quarterlies – available pretty much everywhere – fill the cultural gaps and keep locals informed about upcoming concerts, exhibitions, shows and lectures. See p203 for an essential list of newspapers and magazines.

Toronto is also a major centre for TV, film and radio production. Downtown you'll find the English-language headquarters of the **Canadian Broadcasting Corporation** (p58), as well

LOCAL VOICES: JOHN MOORE

Born and raised in Montréal, **John Moore**, 40, is best known for his freewheeling, acerbic entertainment reports on radio stations around the country. On TV, John has hosted, voiced, written, directed and been featured on a dozen shows. He currently hosts the cleverly named *John Moore Show* on Toronto radio station CFRB 1010, and lives in both Toronto and Montréal.

What do you love most, or think is unique about Toronto?
Toronto is a city of neighborhoods. You can easily live, shop and eat without a car which means that even if you live in the core of the city (which I do) it's a bit like being in a small town. I like Toronto because it's still trying to figure out what it wants to be when it grows up, which means everyone who lives here has a stake in the future of this city.

What's your favorite eatery around town?
I have so many. There's a sushi joint (Sushi Inn) I love in Yorkville that cares so little about what you think that it's like being in New York. But I have a thing for outrageously over the top dinning so I like **Canoe** (p94), **Bistro 990** (p102) and **Scaramouch** (p113). **The Drake Hotel** (p121) is a great hang out but what a lot of people don't know is that it's a terrific place to eat. For cheap and cheerful eats you can't beat **The Rivoli** (p126).

What's Toronto's best-kept secret?
I love the residential streets on the Toronto Islands. There is no other place like this in North America. You can spend a couple of hours on a summer's afternoon walking along the pathways and taking in homes of iconoclasts who have opted out of urban life.

What key controversial issue does the city face today, and what are your thoughts on it?
Toronto needs to quit obsessing over what the rest of the world thinks and to merely build one of the world's greatest cities in which to live. Toronto is like a microcosm of Canada: it worries too much about how it's perceived. The irony is that when cities are built for their citizens, they immediately become interesting to visitors.

YOU KNOW YOU'VE BEEN IN TORONTO TOO LONG IF:

- You wouldn't be seen dead in a toque (winter hat) anywhere above 0°C.
- You think purple cabbages are an acceptable form of floral decoration.
- You're used to public washroom soap that smells like marzipan (or is it Dr Pepper?).
- You named your goldfish after a former Maple Leafs goalie.
- You can tell the difference between a subway token and a dime in the dark.
- You call six inches of snow a 'dusting.'
- You don't wear a watch anymore because the clock towers around town actually work.
- You obey the 'Move just a little farther back please' signs on buses when there's no one else standing up.
- You're considering stitching a Canadian flag on your backpack so people don't think you're American.
- You won't eat anywhere that doesn't have an omelette on the menu.

as Citytv (p60), Toronto's first independent TV station founded by media innovator Moses Znaimer. Most Toronto homes have cable TV which offers around 70 stations – enough to keep dedicated channel-surfers occupied for days. Sports, movies, current affairs and chat-shows proliferate, but you'll struggle to find much arts coverage. Keep an eye out for charismatic Toronto culture jammer George Stroumboulopoulos and his CBC show *The Hour*, which delivers a left-field, alternative take on the day's news.

Walking around Toronto's streets you'll regularly see film crews in action, powdering starlets' noses and yelling '*Cut!*'. Favorable exchange rates, excellent infrastructure and 'this could be any town' architecture make Toronto (aka Hollywood of the North) an appealing place to shoot a movie.

Perhaps because of civic pride, graffiti culture isn't really something downtown Toronto has embraced, but ride the subway to the end of the line and you'll start to see some expressive pieces.

See p204 for a snapshot of local radio stations.

LANGUAGE

We challenge you to name a language that isn't spoken in the GTA! City Hall notices are printed in Chinese, English, French, Greek, Italian, Polish, Portuguese, Spanish, Tagalog and Tamil. Unlike the rest of Canada, most of Toronto's bilingual signs are written in English and Chinese, not French. Most of the French signs are near the US border, as if Ontario wants to hit arriving Americans with the message, 'We are Canadian! We are bilingual!'

In practice, Toronto is predominantly Anglophone. Residents don't exactly speak the Queen's English, but many British terms and spellings (eg 'centre' instead of 'center') endure. The proper pronunciation of the city's name troubles visitors. You can pick out the newbies by how they enunciate each syllable of 'Toh-*ron*-toh,' while natives dissolve the second 't' and slur the word into 'Tuh-*rah*-noh.'

A quick glossary of Canuck (Canadian) slang: 'ski-doo' means snowmobile; a 'toque' (rhymes with duke) is a winter hat; 'peameal bacon' is cured (not smoked) pork; a 'Newfie' is someone from Newfoundland (a source of much amusement to many Canadians); a 'hoser' is a beer-guzzling fool; if you're tired, you're 'bagged'; a 'patio' is a terrace, courtyard or deck; the word 'all' adopts an 's', becoming 'alls.' To summarize: 'Alls I did was ride my ski-doo to Newfie to buy a toque, but I'm totally bagged. You hosers wanna eat some peameal bacon on the patio?'

For a full explanation of the famous Canadian 'eh?,' check out Will and Ian Ferguson's book *How to Be a Canadian: Even if You Already Are One* (2001).

ECONOMY & COSTS

From its colonial fur trade roots, Toronto has grown to be pivotal in Canada's economy. The Toronto Stock Exchange, which opened in 1937, conducts over $100 billion worth of business annually from its high-rise tower off Bay St. Canada's five largest banks are headquartered in the Financial District. The city has the nation's busiest airport, is an important Great Lakes port, and straddles two industrial powerhouses: the 'Golden Horseshoe' (along Lake Ontario from Niagara Falls to Hamilton), and the Québec–Windsor corridor.

At the beginning of the 20th century, Britain was Canada's strongest trading partner, but in the 21st century the USA has snapped up more than three-quarters of Canada's exports, especially raw materials. Since the passage of the Free Trade Agreement (what Americans call NAFTA), the border has become even more porous. Alarmists decry the 'brain drain' of educated Canadians leaving for higher-paying jobs in the south.

After the 1995 referendum rejected Québec's independence, Toronto absorbed much of Montréal's nervous business exodus, but the 2003 SARS outbreak cost the city a billion dollars in lost revenue. Things have recovered since then, but boomtown Calgary is starting to erode Toronto's mantle as Canada's business *numero uno*.

Thanks to the soaring Canadian dollar, Toronto is the most expensive city in Canada (and is on the world's '50 Priciest Cities' list), but for US and European visitors it'll still seem affordable. The most expensive item will be a plane ticket, followed by accommodations. Couples traveling together should count on spending around $200 per day on a B&B room, neighborhood restaurant meals and splashing some entertainment cash.

HOW MUCH?

Airport shuttle $16.50

Bottle of water $2.50

B&B room with private bathroom $100

Cheap ticket to a Blue Jays game $9

Crappy 'I Love T.O.' T-shirt $12

Glass of Niagara wine $6

Litre of gasoline 80¢

Return ferry to Toronto Islands $6

Short taxi ride $10

Slice of pizza $3

GOVERNMENT & POLITICS

Once the Canadian capital, Toronto is now the just capital of the province of Ontario (national capital Ottawa is a short flight away). Relations between the three levels of government – municipal, provincial and federal – are positively Byzantine with overlapping responsibilities, as well as gaps where no one seems to be minding the store.

When Charles Dickens visited the city in the 1840s, he decried its 'rabid Toryism.' The Union Jack still appears on the provincial flag, but the Tories were long out of power until Mike Harris' promises of tax cuts and reduced social spending returned them to provincial power in 1995. Post-election, the Tories slashed government jobs, shut down hospitals and mental health services and weakened labour laws. Toronto's politics have been traditionally progressive, but these right-wing tactics shifted the political climate and the resultant wave of mad homeless people yelling at themselves in the streets has changed the face of Toronto.

Locally, Toronto's mayor presides over the city council, the primary municipal legislature, with 44 members hailing from the city's different wards. The council in session can resemble a Shakespearean drama, with agitated ravings and fools letting the insults fly. In 1997 the amalgamation of the Megacity (p38) created a strong new suburban voting bloc that swept North York mayor Mel Lastman into the city mayoral seat. Although mayors traditionally aren't required to announce a party affiliation, Lastman was clearly comfortable with the Tories.

But Torontonians weren't comfortable with him. Shortly after Premier Dalton McGuinty (aka Mr Ontario) and his Liberals were returned to provincial power in 2003, voters elected Harvard-educated David Miller, a former High Park councilman, as their new mayor. Proving popular, Miller was re-elected in 2006, pledging to pursue a 1% share of existing goods and sales taxes from the federal and provincial governments to improve Toronto's public transit, housing, child care and family services.

Cynical Torontonians suspect that if they gain 1% here, they'll lose it somewhere else just as fast.

ENVIRONMENT

THE LAND

Ontario is separated from western Canada's prairies by the massive Canadian Shield, a stretch of Precambrian rock over 1600km long formed by a prehistoric glacier. Toronto was once under the waters of Lake Iroquois, an ancient sea lapping up against the escarpment roughly traced by today's St Claire Ave, upon which Casa Loma (p68) resides. The old shore cliffs have eroded over millennia but are still visible. The rest of Toronto is pretty flat, making for easy walking.

Modern Toronto sits beside Lake Ontario, part of the chain of Great Lakes shared between Canada and the USA.

The Toronto Islands (p75), originally a 9km-long sandbar peninsula, were created when a violent 19th-century storm blasted away an isthmus connecting them to the mainland. The sandbar itself was formed by drifting material eroded from the Scarborough Bluffs (p79) further east along the lakeshore – gnarly cliffs formed over five different glacial eras.

GREEN TORONTO

On the streets of Toronto, recycling bins are as common as garbage cans – residents have taken a shine to sustainable living practices, going to great lengths to separate organic waste from bottles and cans.

Toronto is no Los Angeles, but CN Tower (p51) visitors will get a smoggy eyeful of the city's air pollution problem. Helping the cause, City Hall enacted a bylaw to prevent motorists from idling their cars more than a few minutes. Meanwhile, American car-sharing company Zipcar (p212) set up shop in Toronto in 2006, and Pedestrian Sundays have become a fixture at Kensington Market.

Although many Torontonians own bicycles, there are still too many vehicles on the streets – competing with them on two wheels can be hazardous. As a result, most cyclists stick to the ravines and established parkland bike trails.

Torontonians love their lakefront beaches, boardwalks and recreational paths (see the Green Ravine Scene walking tour, p85). Gradually, old shipping quays are being converted along the Harbourfront, creating spaces like the Toronto Music Garden (p54). Almost every downtown block has at least some green space, whether it's a tree-lined residential street or a small conservatory tucked between skyscrapers. Toronto's ravines remain largely untouched.

IT'S NOT EASY BEING GREEN

...but here's a handful of leafy T.O. places that'll restore your faith in sustainability:

- Community Vehicular Reclamation Project (Map pp240–1) – Kensington Market's kooky car-becomes-greenhouse street installation on Augusta Ave.
- High Park (p77) – acres of unkempt scrub, stands of oaks and Grenadier Pond. This is what Toronto looked like before Europeans arrived.
- Spadina Quay Wetlands (p53) – a former parking lot transformed into a sustainable ecosystem for birds, frogs and fish.
- Todmorden Mills Wildflower Preserve (p80) – nine hectares of wildflowers, reclaimed from industrial wasteland.
- Tommy Thompson Park (p74) – a man-made green refuge for snakes, turtles, foxes and even coyotes!

URBAN PLANNING & DEVELOPMENT

Toronto was tinkering with its environment well before it decided to push the Don River around during the Don Valley Parkway construction in the '50s. In recent decades, the Toronto & Region Conservation Authority has based its acts on sounder ecology, evidenced by the astounding success of **Tommy Thompson Park** (p74) and the regeneration of natural wetlands at **Grenadier Pond** (p78) and **Spadina Quay** (p53).

Community groups play an active role in fighting ill-planned urban development, largely driven by explosive population growth. Most development battles focus on the Harbourfront: City Hall's optimistic 'Making Waves' plan proposed thousands of new high-rise lakeside condos (without much green space), while the future of the Gardiner Expressway fuels ongoing debate (p16).

One of the city's recurring environmental nightmares is toxic water conditions along the Lake Ontario shoreline. Sudden, heavy rains cause sewage treatment plants to overflow, sending garbage and bacteria (such as *E. coli*) straight into the lake. Summer beach closures and bacteria blooms in ravine creeks are regularly announced on TV.

Arts

Arts

Like anywhere with a chilly climate, Toronto's internal arts scene is a going concern. The city's heritage of world-class fine arts stretches back to its early years as the colonial town of York, but T.O. is best known for its celebration of a 20th-century phenomenon – cinema. The **Toronto International Film Festival** (opposite) has grown into a wildly popular event, tickets selling like hotcakes for the myriad short films, feature-length spectaculars and documentaries that flicker across city screens every September.

Toronto is a furtive, book-clutching, introspective kind of town – essential indicators of the wellspring of literature and poetry seeping through the city's urban fabric. Regular spoken word open-mic nights keep the beery local student body entertained and provide an invaluable sounding board for urban poets and aspiring novelists. More formal (but no more important) highlights of the literary calendar include international and local authors' festivals.

Musically, Toronto has it all: grungy, sweaty rock rooms, refined orchestral chambers, raucous blues bars, a spanking-new opera house, indie music festivals, touring world musicians and hip jazz joints bee-bopping toward the dawn. Not an especially talkative bunch, Torontonians sure know how to listen.

The theatre scene here is overshadowed only by those in New York and London, the local cache of gorgeous old-time venues attracting big shows from the US and UK. These are complemented by a gaggle of modern theatre groups producing off-the-wall, city-centric works and more stately Canadian plays from all over the country.

The city's architecture is a work of art unto itself, sometimes haphazard but often featuring beautifully restored gems or innovative new designs. Aside from the CN Tower, the downtown skyscrapers don't offer much in the way of creative form – instead, look for dazzling museum and gallery designs and superbly maintained districts of historic housing.

Dance in Toronto often gets overlooked, out-yelled by the film and theatre industries' media mouthpieces. Regardless, Toronto's citizens love to watch dance, and love to dance themselves even more! The city swells with multicultural dance troupes offering lessons in everything from salsa to tango, tap and hip-hop (see p199).

Meanwhile, visual artists have resurrected a few Victorian-era industrial complexes around town, filling them with stylish contemporary galleries and studios. The less moneyed of their clan continue to generate wild works in areas like West Queen West and Kensington Market. Masterpieces from decades past watch on approvingly from major gallery walls.

CINEMA & TELEVISION

Toronto is unquestionably the Hollywood of the North, despite the fact that Torontonians tend to favor more independent cinema. The Toronto International Film Festival has a booming reputation and draws an international slew of good-looking LA types to the city. Importantly, and unusually, Ontario's provincial government is a key sponsor of the festival, as is the federal cultural agency Telefilm Canada, whose mandate is the development and promotion of the Canadian audiovisual industry. This is no flash-in-the-pan, small-town shindig – it's a momentous international event with an impact reaching far beyond Toronto's city limits.

Just like their Vancouver and Montréal cousins, locals have become used to tripping over film sets and TV trailers as they go about their daily business. On any given summer day you'll find as many as 40 movies, TV shows and music videos shooting around town. Entire blocks are cheerily roped off and traffic rerouted, the bean counters at City Hall recognizing the gigantic contributions film crews and the **Toronto Film and Television Office** (TFTO; www.city.toronto.on.ca/tfto) make to the city's economy. Almost everyone you meet will know someone (if not themselves) who's been cast as a silent, one-of-a-crowd extra in a film, TV show or advertisement. In the same way the city manages to substitute for any city, so too can Torontonians resemble anyone else in the world. It's a strangely reversed cult of personality.

TORONTO INTERNATIONAL FILM FESTIVAL (TIFF)

Every September as autumn winds start to gust, the film world begins its annual migration to the Great White North and the Toronto International Film Festival (TIFF). For 10 days, the city is turned into a cinephile's paradise. Red carpets roll out for the stars (everyone from Sean Penn to Sofia Coppola), the paparazzi angling for photo ops and stalking the limo drivers outside the Sutton Place Hotel (p172). Almost a dozen cinemas show films nonstop, from early-morning shows through to 'Midnight Madness' screenings. Film critics dart around to a dozen movies a day, while wide-eyed traveling movie buffs stare at their ticket books, looking a tad lost, yet ecstatic just to be here.

It all started off as an idea tossed around over lunch nearly three decades ago by two unlikely candidates: a lawyer and a mayoral assistant. They weren't the first to dream up a potent media cocktail of Toronto and movies, but it wasn't until 1976 – when their 'Festival of Festivals' opened with *Cousin, Cousine* at Ontario Place's Cinesphere (p52) – that an embryonic international festival got rolling. Running on a hope and a prayer, the festival's early films were delivered by bicycle, as debt-collectors were appeased and the town ran rife with wild rumors of stars who never showed up. Back then it cost $150 for the VIP treatment. Nowadays, gold packages including invites to star-studded galas cost around $3000 – and they sell out!

Critics and the film industry acknowledge that Toronto's festival has grown into one of the most prestigious and influential in the world, perhaps second only to Cannes. In 2006 two-thirds of the 352 films from 61 countries screened over the festival's 11 days were premieres, including 22 full-length Canadian flicks. TIFF films have won hundreds of Academy Awards over the years, launching local directors like Atom Egoyan and reviving the entire Canadian film industry along the way. Plans have been unveiled for Festival Tower, a condo/entertainment complex at King and John Sts in the Entertainment District, which will have a film library and year-round screening rooms.

Each year over 1000 volunteers help make it all happen. Festival themes change, but popular series include 'Contemporary World Cinema,' 'Real to Reel' documentaries, boundary-breaking 'Visions' and the cult favorite, 'Midnight Madness.' **Tickets** (☎ 416-968-3456; www.bell.ca/filmfest) go on sale in early July by phone or online, or in person at box offices around town once the festival commences. A 50-film Festival Pass costs $498; a 25-film Daytime Pass costs $192 (for films starting before 5pm). Coupon books for 10 ($155) or 30 ($399) are also available. You can buy single tickets ($18) in advance, or if a film isn't sold out, they go on sale at theatre box offices one hour before screening. Rush tickets are sold five minutes before show time, but don't guarantee a seat and you'll usually have to queue up. Check the free weeklies and major newspapers for film festival miniguides, or shell out for the festival program book ($32).

In the interests of getting the most bang for your buck, here are some TIFF tips:

- Give your retinas a rest – don't watch more than three movies a day.
- Feast on the buffet – don't settle for just one genre or one world region.
- Support indie filmmakers by avoiding films that are going into wide release anyway.
- You don't need to read 'The Bible' – only film geeks read the festival program book cover to cover.
- You're not a superhero – don't schedule back-to-back screenings at cinemas across town.
- No one can live on popcorn alone. Bring some trail mix, Red Bull, chocolate bars – whatever it takes to sustain you through the *loooong* movie-viewing day.
- Even if it's your 35th film of the week, please don't yap through it.

ON LOCATION

Toronto has been a cinematic stand-in for dozens of cities in the United States, as well as being an on-screen substitute for several towns in Europe. To cover the hundreds of titles filmed on location here would take a guidebook of its own, but following are a few highlights.

The US TV series *Queer as Folk* was based in the Church-Wellesley Village (p64), with scenes shot at the Art Gallery of Ontario (p64) and Seduction sex shop on the Yonge Street Strip. When Minnie Driver and Matt Damon go shopping in *Good Will Hunting* (1997), they're at the **Ontario Specialty Co** (Map pp232–3; 133 Church St) – ask to see the autographed movie stills under the front counter.

More recently, scenes from *Chicago* (2002) were shot in the Distillery District (p56). In *Cinderella Man* (2005), Russell Crowe grunted around **Leslieville** (Map pp244–5), which passed admirably as Depression-era New York City. Parts of David Cronenberg's *A History Of Violence* (2005) were also shot in T.O., while much of *The Sentinel* (2006) was filmed in Mississauga and Etobicoke, with cameos from City Hall (p60) and the McMichael Collection (p189). Xavier's academy from *X-Men* (2000) was filmed inside Casa Loma (p68).

Keanu Reeves sped through Allan Gardens (p73) and Union Station (p54) in *Johnny Mnemonic* (1995), while the Elgin & Winter Garden Theatre Centre (p61) appeared in *Blues Brothers 2000* (1998). Even further into the past, *The Black Stallion* (1979), with Francis Ford Coppola as the executive producer, was set at the Woodbine Racetrack (p142).

LOCAL HEROES

More international film and TV stars and directors come from Toronto than you might think, though many of them have completely assimilated into the Hollywood culture south of the border, losing whatever it was that made them distinct in the first place. Check out www.northernstars.ca to unmask a few.

Among those who still call Toronto home are David Cronenberg, the director of far-out films like *Videodrome* (1983), *The Fly* (1986), *Naked Lunch* (1991), *eXistenZ* (1999) and more recently (and less weirdly) *A History Of Violence* (2005). Toronto born and bred, he's a University of Toronto graduate with a penchant for playing quirky bit-parts in TV series, most recently a surgeon on the spy drama *Alias*.

Atom Egoyan, another renowned Canadian director, started making movies while a U of T student. His works, including *Exotica* (1994), *Ararat* (2002) and *Where the Truth Lies* (2005), offer big doses of bitter reality. In 2006 he started lecturing at U of T in theatre, film, music and visual studies. And yes, he was named in honor of a nuclear reactor built in Egypt, from where his Armenian family immigrated.

Another U of T graduate, Toronto-born Norman Jewison worked as a director and producer at the CBC during TV's 'Golden Age' before moving to the US to launch *Your Hit Parade* and make feature films. He got his big break when he was called in to finish Sam Peckinpah's *The Cincinnati Kid* (1965), but his crowning achievement was directing the Academy Award–winning *In the Heat of the Night* (1967). His success helped revive the flagging Canadian film industry. Jewison's recent titles include *The Hurricane* (1999), a biographic drama starring Denzel Washington, and *The Statement* (2003), a thriller about a hunted Nazi war criminal and the Catholic church.

When it comes to comedians and actors, Toronto churns them out by the dozen. Getting their start at legendary Second City (p133) were Gilda Radner, Dan Aykroyd and Mike Myers, all of whom moved on to New York's *Saturday Night Live* TV show. Myers grew up in suburban Scarborough and remains a die-hard Toronto Maple Leafs fan. Jim Carrey launched his career here too, with open-mic performances at Yuk Yuk's (p133) comedy club. His physical slapstick and wild impersonations went over so well that he was persuaded to give LA a try, which was where Rodney Dangerfield finally 'discovered' him. The enduringly popular Kiefer Sutherland spent his teens here, while Toronto's dirty little secret is that Keanu Reeves, born in Beirut, Lebanon, grew up in T.O. too.

TOP FIVE TORONTO FILMS

Innumerable films have been shot in Toronto, but very few movie storylines are set here (with a few bizarre exceptions). Torontonian directors, on the other hand, are pretty prolific.

- *Hollywood North* directed by Peter O'Brian (2003) – a satirical look at the Canadian film industry and its tangled Hollywood love affair; north-of-the-border viewers will dig the insider gags.
- *Last Night* directed by Don McKellar (1998) – a bizarre end-of-the-world fantasy, with Toronto denizens going on a violent rampage, overturning TTC streetcars and making suicide pacts; David Cronenberg has a bit part.
- *M Butterfly* directed by David Cronenberg (1993) – often called a depraved 'baron of blood,' Toronto-born director David Cronenberg occasionally reaches for higher ground, such as this beautiful failure starring Jeremy Irons and John Lone.
- *The Sentinel* directed by Clark Johnson (2006) – adopted Torontonian Kiefer Sutherland stars in this treacherous political thriller which is both filmed *and* set in Toronto (how refreshing!).
- *The Sweet Hereafter* directed by Atom Egoyan (1997) – another poignant film from T.O. resident Egoyan, this one is loosely based on a true story, focusing on the aftershocks of a fatal school bus accident that devastates a small town.

THE SMALL SCREEN

Although addicted to the silver screen, Torontonians are also enamored of their TV sets, a shimmering blue tele-glow emanating from suburban street windows every evening. Imported cable TV means there's an endless supply of stuff to watch, but as the Bruce Springsteen song of the same name goes, it's often a case of '57 channels and nothin' on...' (actually, in most homes it's closer to 73). But just like everyone else when they're bored, tired or looking for distraction, Torontonians will watch just about anything. It would be interesting to study what depths the city's TV viewing standards slide to once the long, dark winter rolls around.

A diamond is the TV rough is the continually expanding Citytv network, which includes over a dozen specialty channels. It's downtown Chum/Citytv Complex (p60) is home to MuchMusic (a sort of Canadian MTV) and the *Bravo!* arts channel. Citytv itself bravely broadcasts outtakes from Speakers Corner (p60). The public Canadian Broadcasting Corporation (CBC), whom you'll often see filming around the city, has its English-language radio and TV production headquarters downtown as well, and offers moments of mainstream quality.

CRITICAL MASSAGE

One of the great critics to hail from the University of Toronto, Marshall McLuhan (1911–80) was a cultural commentator who preached about the 20th-century explosion of electronic media and its ability to hypnotize us into passivity. His famous book, *The Medium is the Massage,* propelled him to the forefront of 1960s counterculture. Various pilgrims visited him during his tenure as director of U of T's Centre for Culture and Technology, including John Lennon and Yoko Ono after they climbed out of their eight-day Montréal 'bed-in' protest in 1969. He's also famed for his pithy wordplay (eg 'The future of the book is the blurb') and his prediction that TV would unite us all in a global village.

LITERATURE

As the English-language capital of Canada, Toronto has been fertile ground for as many homegrown writers as it has authors in exile. Each year the Harbourfront Readings Series (p132) puts together the International Festival of Authors (p15), a veritable who's-who of Canadian letters. If you're here in mid-July, catch some local literati at the Scream in High Park (p13). The spoken word scene is fired-up year-round, mixing freely with sketch comedy, video and performance art. Cabarets and bars are the venues of choice (see p132).

More than a few Canadian literary giants have studied at U of T, including Margaret Atwood (1939–) and Ceylon-born Michael Ondaatje (1943–). Ondaatje became famous for his Man Booker Prize–winning novel *The English Patient,* but his earlier fiction and poetry are equally moving for their tales of lyrically broken lives, postcolonial cultural clashes and the loss of identity. Literary lioness Atwood, for better or for worse, has become synonymous with modern Canadian literature. A long bibliography of novels, short fiction, poetry, children's books and screenplays includes *The Handmaid's Tale,* an allegedly feminist story set in a future world of straw men. It is now quite dated, but remains her most famous work. Atwood won the esteemed Man Booker Prize in 2000 for *Blind Assassin.*

On the pop fiction front, 'Toronto the Good' was the original publishing home of none other than the Harlequin Romance series. Modern historical fiction by Rosedale boy Timothy Findley (1930–2002) is set mostly in Toronto. The beloved children's writer and city poet laureate Dennis Lee (1939–) penned the lyrics to the theme song for the TV show *Fraggle Rock* here. And don't miss the visual ('concrete') poem by bpNichol (1944–88) and yes, that's the correct spelling) drilled into bpNichol Lane, running north off Sussex Ave between Huron and St George Sts. It's inscribed beside the historic Coach House Press, which was associated with the avant-garde *Open Letter* poetry journal of the 1970s and '80s. Today the press publishes much of its catalogue online (www.chbooks.com), where you can leave tips for authors.

William Gibson (1948–), although South Carolinan by birth, now lives in Canada and has spent years in Toronto, especially around Kensington Market (p70). In earlier times the city hosted Dickens, Yeats, Arthur Conan Doyle and Walt Whitman, who thought Toronto 'a wild dashing place.' More critical guests included Oscar Wilde, who lambasted

TOP 10 TORONTO BOOKS

Although Toronto is a place where great works are frequently penned, not too many great works of literature actually feature the city. Our favorite works either about Toronto or by Torontonians:

- *Alligator Pie* by Dennis Lee (1974) – these magical rhyming nonsense poems have wormed their way into the brains of two generations of youngsters.
- *The Blind Assassin* by Margaret Atwood (2002) – this richly layered tale of two Canadian sisters in the aftermath of WWII won Atwood the prestigious Man Booker Prize.
- *Cabbagetown* by Hugh Garner (1950) – a classic reminiscence of growing up in Toronto's working-class Irish neighborhood during the Depression.
- *The Chef's Table* by Lucy Waverman (2000) – beautifully records the creations of top chefs during the annual Toronto Taste (p22), with superb background color on the city's culinary scene.
- *Doors Open Toronto: Illuminating the City's Great Spaces* by John Sewell (2002) – an illustrated guide to beloved buildings and secret places, with text written by a former mayor of Toronto.
- *Headhunter* by Timothy Findley (1993) – a reinterpretation of Joseph Conrad's *Heart of Darkness*, with Kurtz as a psychiatrist who 'goes native' in Toronto's urban jungle.
- *In the Skin of a Lion* by Michael Ondaatje (1987) – working-class life and love in Toronto during the construction of the Palace of Purification (p75) and the Bloor Street Viaduct (p72), with glimpses of *The English Patient* characters.
- *The Martyrology* by bpNichol (1972–92) – a nine-book poem written over two decades, it brings the interplay of text, context and design to the forefront of meaning, and a quest for selfhood.
- *Lost Toronto* by William Dendy (1993) – a bittersweet guide to demolished and disappeared buildings, with some photographs, by a noted architectural scholar.
- *This Ain't No Healing Town: Toronto Stories* edited by Barry Callaghan (1995) – two dozen dark, macabre and seamy short stories by famous Canadians and local authors.

the city's architecture in 1882 during his 'The House Beautiful' North American tour, but was welcomed anyway because he was Irish. The English artist and writer Wyndham Lewis got stranded here during WWII and had nary a good word to say about the city he considered 'a sanctimonious icebox.'

Ernest Hemingway got his start as a cub reporter with the *Toronto Star,* where he penned such smartly titled masterpieces as 'Before You Go on a Canoe Trip, Learn Canoeing.' After joining Hemingway and other expatriates in Paris, local writer Morley Callaghan (1903–90) returned home to Toronto to write several acclaimed novels. His novels often wrestle within a framework of Roman Catholicism to find meaning in modern urban life. He won the Governor General's Literary Award in 1951.

MUSIC

Toronto's classical-music scene is thriving. The Toronto Symphony Orchestra (p134) is truly world class, but the city also has a jewel box of small chamber orchestras and choirs, the most critically acclaimed of which is Tafelmusik (p134). Others perform downtown at the Glenn Gould Studio (p134), which spotlights young musicians and offers free noontime concerts. Meanwhile the respected Canadian Opera Company (p133) is tuning its pipes at the new Four Seasons Centre for the Performing Arts.

Switching to a completely different genre, folk artists Joni Mitchell and Gordon Lightfoot performed (or before that, washed dishes and served) at the 1960s bohemian coffeehouses of Yorkville. Neil Young, the Band and Rush all started in the Toronto area, as did the Tragically Hip (aka 'The Hip,') who some say are the definitive Canadian rock band, the Cowboy Junkies, modern rockers Our Lady Peace and renegade indie collective Broken Social Scene. The Barenaked Ladies (two of whose members started out playing in a Rush tribute band in suburban Scarborough) were once barred from performing in Nathan Phillips Square (p60) because of their 'scandalous' name. All was forgiven when they were symbolically handed the keys to the city after being invited back to give a concert in 2000.

Downtown you can often catch free local rock shows in Dundas Square (p59), while bigger international acts blast out the city's earwax at Koolhaus (p131), the Air Canada Centre (p50), and the Rogers Centre (p53). Every year, the North by Northeast (NXNE; p13) festival is Canada's answer to the famous Austin indie music festival, South by Southwest. Rockin' the Toronto Islands, the Virgin Music Festival (p15) is the new kid on the block, and might give NXNE a run for its money.

Local live acts favor smaller venues: pubs, bars and legendary neighborhood rock clubs. Around bohemian Queen West (p71), classic boom rooms like Lee's Palace (p126) and Cameron House (p125) often give local bands their first shot at the title. Toronto also has some famous venues for folk, jazz and blues, including Healey's (p126), owned by Canadian blues-rock guitarist Jeff Healey. After going blind when he was a young kid, Healey invented his trademark technique of slinging his axe across his lap. Elsewhere there's the jazzy Rex (p127); blues at the Silver Dollar Room (p127); punk, metal and Brit-pop at the Bovine Sex Club (p125); and live Celtic fiddle-dee-dee at Allen's (p118). For a more detailed rundown of the city's best music rooms, see p125.

Everyone seems to know someone who's a DJ here, and Toronto's club scene (p130) both grows and imports some heavy-hitting sounds. Dance clubs are popping up along Queen West, while a night out in the more mainstream Entertainment District, aka Clubland (p62), is an essential, surreal and amusing T.O. experience.

So relax, it's not all Céline Dion 'round here (she's from Québec). But backed into a corner, Ontarians will shamefully admit their responsibility for brassy country twanger Shania Twain, tear-jerk rock balladeer Bryan Adams and black-eyed skater-punk darling Avril Lavigne.

TOP FIVE TORONTO CDS

- *Broken Social Scene* by Broken Social Scene (2005) – the eponymous, and many say definitive, album from Toronto's prolific muso super-collective, which at last count featured 17 regular members.
- *Glenn Gould: A State of Wonder,* Sony Classical (1955 and 2002) – both of Gould's *Goldberg Variations* albums, recorded 25 years apart in the same NYC studio, plus a rare interview with GG just before his premature death.
- *In Violet Light* by the Tragically Hip (2002) – a solid return to the band's original sound of idiosyncratic poetry and manic emotion, with gorgeous cover art to boot.
- *Stunt* by the Barenaked Ladies (1998) – showing more strains of pop and less biting sarcasm than the band's earlier releases, but the rapid-fire single 'One Week' was a global hit.
- *The Trinity Sessions* by Cowboy Junkies (1988) – this haunting album of ballads was recorded inside Toronto's Church of the Holy Trinity (p60) in just one day using a single microphone.

GLENN GOULD

One musical star Toronto can proudly claim as its own is Glenn Gould. Born in The Beaches community in 1932, this eccentric piano genius started composing at the age of five, took lessons at the Royal Conservatory of Music just five years later and debuted with the Toronto Symphony Orchestra before his 16th birthday.

But Gould despised the cult of the virtuoso, believing that young musicians should not have to compete against one another, and that live performances would quickly become outmoded in the modern age. After his famous 1955 recording of JS Bach's *Goldberg Variations*, he toured in Europe, including the Cold War–era Soviet Union. He retired from public performance a few years later, abruptly pulling the pin after a concert in Los Angeles. He was 32.

Gould never considered himself to be just a pianist. His real fascination was with sound technology, and he spent the rest of his life writing, composing music, recording albums and making radio documentaries for the Canadian Broadcasting Corporation (CBC). *The Idea of North* (1967), part of Gould's *The Solitude Trilogy* albums, was originally a 60-minute CBC radio broadcast. It featured an 'oral tone poem' of documentary interviews that Gould conducted with Canadian train passengers about the romance, reality and uncertainty of life in the nation's northern lands.

Shortly before his death in 1982, Gould made another recording of the *Goldberg Variations*. He had come to think differently about Bach's music over the years, and also wanted to take advantage of modern sound-recording technology. He always believed that recording artists, rather than live performers, could achieve the most intimate connection with audiences. Today, Gould's *Goldberg Variations* have become his legacy, which perhaps proves his point.

LOCAL VOICES: NOEL DITOSTO

Noel DiTosto, 26, was born and raised in North York, Toronto, and has been playing live music gigs around the city since he was 16. Passionate about world music, he plays nine different stringed instruments including guitar, banjo, sitar, mandolin, oud, the Japanese *koto* and Chinese *gu zheng*. Along the way he's played in rock bands The Kinetics, Silvertongue Records and Sir. More recently he wrote the score for *The Magic Paintbrush* – a Chinese-directed play at the Toronto Fringe Festival (p14). No doubt about it, Noel rocks.

Which rooms around town do you like to play?
I really like the Cameron House (p125). Of all the clubs in Toronto, that's the place I've played the most. It feels really homey, and I like the atmosphere. It's not a huge room, but I like playing there. The Rivoli (p126) is pretty nice. I've played at El Mocambo Lounge (p125) a few times and it's awesome – the stage is really big, with cool Moroccan lamps everywhere.

Where do you usually go to see bands?
The best venue for world music or jazz is Massey Hall (p62). The acoustics there are awesome. In terms of rock venues for bigger bands, I like the Koolhaus (p131), it's a good size. The Rogers Centre (p53) is too big. The Air Canada Centre (p50) is OK when they do a semiarena thing, but you just get lost if it's too big.

How about jazz venues?
Toronto jazz clubs don't get a lot of recognition. The Rex (p127) is pretty good – it's like 'poor man's jazz.' There's another place on Queen St E called Dominion On Queen (p127) – that's really nice. There are a lot of posh jazz clubs around too.

Does Toronto have a happening music-festival scene?
The Virgin Music Festival (p15) was pretty cool this year, which was two days on Centre Island in September. Broken Social Scene do a one-day festival there too.

Any favorite Toronto bands?
Broken Social Scene. Some of them are from Montréal, but they're based in Toronto. I like one of my buddies' bands – Marathon – they're probably going to be signed pretty soon. Another band called Dala – they're a folk duo, kind of like a female Simon & Garfunkel.

How does the music scene here compare with other Canadian cities?
In a lot of cities you have to 'pay to play' – you have to rent out the venues – but here you don't. For some of the bigger venues like the Horseshoe Tavern (p126), you have to be established and able to draw a crowd, but you don't have to make a down-payment or guarantee X-many dollars be made at the bar. It's all pretty friendly between bands too, and Toronto is really diverse, so you can get a real mish-mash of stuff going on.

So there's not really a 'Toronto Sound'?
No, not really. If you go to any random club, you can hear blues, jazz, rock, hip-hop, and we get a lot of big-name world-music acts coming through Toronto. It's really diverse.

Do you think Toronto's multiculturalism influences the local music, or is the American influence stronger?
I guess it depends on the artist. A friend of mine plays sitar and mixes it with electronic music, with drum beats, samples and stuff – kind of unique. So there is a multicultural influence. The American influence is more 'corporate rock,' like Nickelback or something more radio friendly. There's also a Brit Pop influence. There's a Toronto band called Pilot Speed, they're really Brit Pop. Because there's such diversity in clubs here, you get a bit of everything – heavy metal, punk, ska – and some bands just mish-mash it all together, which is really cool. There's a lot of musical freedom in Toronto.

THEATRE

After London and New York, Toronto lays claim to the third-largest theatre scene in the English-speaking world. Although at times overshadowed by prestigious festivals in Stratford (p190) and Niagara-on-the-Lake (p193), the city keeps a full house of productions running, averaging 75 per month. That's enough to satisfy any theatrical taste, whether you're into Broadway musicals, international premieres or provocative contemporary Canadian works. Over seven million people attend plays in Toronto each year – about half are visitors.

Toronto's theatrical history is mirrored by the topsy-turvy fortunes of the double-decker Elgin & Winter Garden Theatre Centre (p61). In the heyday of live vaudeville acts, the likes of George Burns and Gracie Allen, Milton Berle and Sophie Tucker all performed here. Patrons would pay only 15¢ to stay all day if they liked. But the advent of 'talkies' in the 1920s closed the fantastic Winter Garden theatre and saw the Elgin converted into a movie house. After TV was invented, even the Elgin went into a tailspin, later declining further through incarnations as a kung-fu dojo and a porn cinema. In the '80s the Ontario Heritage Trust bought the theatres and launched a full-scale restoration, re-opening them in 1989 with an all-Canadian production of *Cats*. It was sold out for months.

When 'Honest Ed' Mirvish renovated the Royal Alexandra Theatre (p129) in the 1960s and courted big musical productions with international casts, such as *Godspell* and *Hair,* live theatre in Toronto got a real shot in the arm. The Broadway musical trend gained momentum with Mirvish's building of the Princess of Wales Theatre (p129) two decades later. Then the Mirvish cartel joined forces with big business to save another venue, the old Pantages vaudeville theatre, just down the street. Renamed the Canon Theatre (p128), it now hosts sell-out, big-ticket shows like *The Producers* and *Wicked.*

Toronto audiences don't just favor big-time musicals. Since the 1970s, new and experimental dramatic works by Canadian playwrights have captured the public's imagination. Many groundbreaking small theatres have made their home here, including Theatre Passe Muraille (p130); the Factory Theatre (p129), with 100% Canadian content; and queer-oriented Buddies in Bad Times Theatre (p128). Contemporary company CanStage (p128) and the companies at the Young Centre for Performing Arts (p130) present Canadian and international premieres. The ever-popular Dream in High Park (p129) is always worth a look.

ARCHITECTURE

When the town of York was founded in 1793, colonials constructed many of their churches and mansions in the solid Georgian style. Warehouses and factories cropped up along Front St; one of these processed pigs, giving rise to the nickname Hogtown. Brewing and distilling whiskey were also popular, with the famous Gooderham and Worts Distillery (1832) anchoring today's Distillery District (p56).

Toronto's wealthier Victorian citizens built fanciful Italianate and Romanesque villas, Gothic manors and grand Queen Anne row houses. Also appearing at about this time was the city's distinct 'bay-and-gable' style, which typically consisted of two semidetached dwellings, each with a round bay window and a pointy Victorian gable, sharing a front garden. The city's best-preserved collection of Victorian houses and bungalows is in Cabbagetown and Rosedale (see p82 for an architectural walking tour).

Around the beginning of the 20th century, the great civic buildings of a burgeoning Edwardian metropolis were constructed, including Old City Hall (p62), the Royal Ontario Museum (p66) and Union Station (p54). Many were designed by EJ Lennox, aka the 'Architect of Toronto,' who also designed the Provincial Legislature (p69) and Casa Loma (p68). These were part of a 'City Beautiful' scheme that envisioned parkways radiating from downtown, but the city managed to build only University Ave before the Depression hit.

The great fires of 1849 and 1904 didn't destroy as many city buildings as they might have otherwise done, seeing as earlier legislation had mandated that buildings should made of brick. Strict zoning limitations were finally lifted in 1905, and at last taller buildings began to rise on the city's horizon. Most mid-century skyscrapers were molded in the pragmatic 'form follows function' international style, popular throughout the 1950s.

DOORS OPEN TORONTO

Ever wanted to open the door of some snazzy, eye-catching building and walk right in? That's what **Doors Open Toronto** (☎ 416-205-2670; www.doorsopen.org) is all about. It's based on a wildly successful festival that started in Glasgow over a decade ago, an idea that's now spread to more than 40 countries.

In May 2000 Toronto was the first city in North America to adopt the festival – the doors of its architectural gems, both famous and forgotten, were flung open to the public. Now, during one weekend every spring, over 200,000 enthusiastic (and voyeuristic) locals and tourists queue to peek inside the Cadbury Chocolate Factory or to hear the Italian Consulate's tales of hidden mosaics and a secret passageway leading to the house of the ex-ambassador's mistress.

Who knew that Torontonians had an appetite for architecture? The city has largely shown a lack of respect for its architectural heritage. Many of its finest historic buildings have been torn down since the 1950s, when the Guild Inn (p79) started collecting chunks of discarded urban architecture on its front lawn. Those venerable buildings left standing often have private citizens such as 'Honest Ed' Mirvish or nonprofit groups to thank for their survival, not the government, even though City Hall's sponsorship of Doors Open Toronto is a boost.

This extremely popular festival's two days in May seem all too short, but take heart, it's now part of the much larger **Doors Open Ontario** (☎ 800-668-2746; www.doorsopenontario.on.ca) celebrations from April to October, which include a bi-national event in the Niagara Falls region. In Toronto, each year's selection of buildings is bigger and more intriguing than the last. If you're lucky, maybe the city will open the ghostly subway station rumored to still exist underneath Bay St.

The most stimulating contemporary architecture in Toronto is being produced by the firm **Moriyama & Teshima** (www.mtarch.com). Cofounded by Vancouver-born Raymond Moriyama, the M&T creed is 'healthy' architecture that's both harmonious and ecologically sound, involving community cooperation at the design stage. Much of the firm's work shows the elegance and clarity of Japanese influences, reminiscent of Frank Lloyd Wright's Prairie School, but these designs are more dynamic, less predictable. Public projects include the Bata Shoe Museum (p66); the Ontario Science Centre (p79), which has great glass windows overlooking the Don River ravine; and the Toronto Reference Library (p67).

Recently, Toronto's Royal Ontario Museum (p66) and Art Gallery of Ontario (p64) have launched into ambitious renovation projects. The revamped ROM's 'crystal galleries' should be eye-popping when they're finished (late 2007), while the AGO has recruited famous Canuck architect Frank Gehry – designer of the Guggenheim museum in Bilbao, Spain – to spearhead its transformation. It's Gehry's first Canadian project, even though the AGO is just a short walk from his childhood home. The city's top architecture-focused gallery is the University of Toronto's Eric Arthur Gallery (p70), named after a U of T professor and cofounder of the Architectural Conservancy of Ontario.

The **Ontario Heritage Trust** (☎ 416-325-5000; www.heritagefdn.on.ca) has been instrumental in restoring the city's 19th- and 20th-century treasures, notably the Elgin & Winter Garden Theatre Centre (p61) and the Niagara Apothecary (p193) in Niagara-on-the-Lake. The St Lawrence Hall (p57) now houses the offices of **Heritage Toronto** (☎ 416-338-0684; www.heritagetoronto.org), which also promotes historical site preservation, cosponsors Doors Open Toronto (above) and runs tours (p49). Also useful is the Ontario Heritage Connection Society website, www.ontario heritageconnection.org.

CONDOMINIUM MANIA

Over the last decade, Toronto has weathered a boom in towering condominium developments, particularly in areas of inner-city consolidation like the **Harbourfront** (p50) district and around Spadina Ave and Bathurst St to the west of the Financial District. In 2005, 17,000 new condos were sold here, more than double the amount in any comparable city in North America.

Why is everyone clambering to live on top of each other? Well, it has a lot to do with the price of housing. After the recent global boom (the real estate equivalent of an atomic bomb), an average (often very average) Toronto house in the outer suburbs now costs almost $350,000. Anywhere closer to downtown and you're looking at half a million. This dire situation, coupled with government land release restrictions and the desire for downtown convenience presents condos as a viable alternative: cheaper, less maintenance, and right in the heart of the action. But now condos are experiencing growth of around 10% per annum, outstripping houses. Where are people going to live next – in the lake?

VISUAL ARTS

Toronto doesn't seem to quite grasp the importance of public art. In the 1960s when the new City Hall was being built, the English sculptor Henry Moore offered to practically donate his work to the city, but the city council (at first) turned him down. Apart from a few abstract sculptures in the Financial District and the murals adorning the Flatiron (Gooderham) Building (p57) and the St Lawrence Market (p57), the city barely has any outdoor art installations, even today. Halfhearted attempts at city-funded art projects are limited to projects like the metalwork sculptures along the Spadina streetcar line.

It probably has something to do with the weather, but graphically, Toronto can be accused of the same lack of vision. Graffiti (as a medium beyond school-kid marker-pen tags on the subway), is relegated to the outer suburbs, while the sedate-looking local street-press looks like it's been left out to bleach in the sun. Downtown signage is utterly demure – look no further than the blink-and-you'll-miss-them TTC signs, for example.

Indoors, however, it's an entirely different story. Toronto has an active contemporary art-gallery scene, mostly focused in converted industrial buildings around downtown, including the labyrinthine 401 Richmond (p58) and the revitalized Distillery District (p56). Further north, more upscale art galleries cash-in on affluent passers-by in the Bloor-Yorkville backstreets.

When it comes to First Nations art, you'll be hard-pressed to find anything apart from museum exhibits, mostly imported from British Columbia and Arctic Inuit nations. An exception is the McMichael Collection (p189) in suburban Kleinburg, one of the country's finest museums for both traditional and contemporary Aboriginal art. A handful of shops around the city also sell high-quality First Nations art and crafts, including the Bay of Spirits Gallery (p150), Arctic Nunavut (p149) and the Cedar Basket at the Native Canadian Centre of Toronto (p69).

Contemporary Canadian artisans are thriving in Toronto, the studios at York Quay Centre (p199) and in the Distillery District (p56) providing mainstream impetus. The Museum of Contemporary Canadian Art (p72) is reveling in it's new West Queen West location. Shops for contemporary crafts, many of them Ontario-centric, include The Canadian Naturalist (p150) and the Guild Shop (p155).

> ## TOP FIVE ART MUSEUMS AND GALLERY COMPLEXES
>
> Art Gallery of Ontario (p64)
>
> 401 Richmond (p58)
>
> Museum of Contemporary Canadian Art (p72)
>
> McMichael Collection (p189)
>
> Gardiner Museum of Ceramic Art (p66)

DANCE

Just like the local food and music scenes, dance in Toronto is driven by multiculturalism. A vibrant international presence has emerged on contemporary dance stages, the exchange of ideas and techniques between groups leading to a sometimes bizarre fusion of styles.

> ## THE GROUP OF SEVEN
>
> This gung-ho, all-male group of Canadian landscape painters first came together in the 1920s. Fired by an almost adolescent enthusiasm, they spent a lot of time rampaging through the wilds of northern Ontario, capturing the rugged Canadian wilderness through the seasons in all kinds of weather. The energy they felt joyfully expressed itself in vibrant, light-filled canvases of mountains, lakes, forests and provincial townships.
>
> Painter Tom Thompson died before the group was officially formed, but the other members – Arthur Lismer, JEH MacDonald, Frank Johnston, Frederick Varley and Franklin Carmichael – considered him their leading light. An experienced outdoorsman, Thompson drowned in 1917 just as he was producing some of his most powerful work. His deep connection to the land is obvious in his works hanging at the Art Gallery of Ontario (p64). His rustic cabin has been moved onto the grounds of the McMichael Collection (p189), the best place to view esteemed Group of Seven creations.

In this way, most of the ethnic and cultural dance troupes around town are considered contemporary rather than traditional – progressive groups founded in, but not bound to, traditional styles of dance. A similar conceptual crosspollination has occurred between theatre and dance in Toronto, choreographers proving themselves adept at shuffling their deck of influences.

The Toronto ballet community has been active for around 100 years. The National Ballet of Canada (p135) first tottered onto the stage back in 1951, but, despite the talented pool of local dancers available to directors, it developed a reputation for traditional, somewhat staid productions. Tutus and tiaras were the order of the day. Things have been looking up, however, since Ontarian dancer and choreographer James Kudelka was appointed Artistic Director in 1996. Classically-trained Kudelka is considered something of a maverick, managing to buck the tired confines of tradition and approach dance as an expressive art, full of emotional potency with recurrent themes of love and death weaving through his productions.

On the other hand, modern dance in Toronto is a relatively young beast. Small schools teaching modern styles first emerged during the 1950s, but citizens had to wait until 1968 for the Toronto Dance Theatre (p135) to arrive and really start shaking the foundations. The '70s was a progressive decade for Toronto dancers, but in the '80s the city followed the global conservative trend, more interested in shoveling cocaine up its nose than supporting broad-minded, creative dance endeavors. Conversely, Montréal was burgeoning with new, forward-thinking choreographers and troupes. But by the time the mid-'90s post-grunge era rolled around, things were back on track, and Toronto was brimming with new dance hustle. Small new troupes and independent companies began experimenting in diverse, full-bodied styles, feeding off each other and revitalizing the city dance scene. This trend continues today, with dozens of dance schools (see p199) spreading the gospel.

Check out www.danceumbrella.net for listings and background on dance troupes around the city.

History

History

THE RECENT PAST

THE MEGACITY

In 1998 five sprawling Toronto suburbs – York, East York, North York, Etobicoke and Scarborough – were corralled under the City of Toronto's municipal umbrella. The Greater Toronto Area (GTA) 'Megacity' was born, the largest city in Canada and the fifth largest in North America – certainly a long way from its beginnings as 'Muddy York,' Ontario's second-choice town after Niagara.

Yet the Megacity was not a wildly popular proposition. Many residents felt that amalgamation would result in threadbare city services, especially in outlying neighborhoods that would now have to shoulder more than their fair share of City Hall's financial burdens. When a referendum was held in 1997, voters in the proposed Megacity municipalities soundly rejected the plan. But former Ontario Premier Mike Harris introduced legislation that forced the Megacity merge through anyway, making an awful lot of folks unhappy.

Overnight the population of Toronto jumped from 650,000 to somewhere closer to four million people. Millionaire 'bad boy' appliance salesman Mel Lastman, formerly the mayor of North York, assumed the mayoral reins at City Hall. He was a flamboyant character, known for stunts like riding a fire truck in Toronto's Pride Parade and begging Ginger Spice to rejoin the Spice Girls. Lastman accurately reflected the schizophrenia of the new Megacity: ruthlessly prodevelopment with a guilty social conscience.

Despite having an annual operating budget greater than that of some Canadian provinces, Toronto had a recession in the 1990s that led to social spending cuts resulting in increased homelessness and environmental neglect. Meanwhile, development was pushed forward – condominium projects (p34) were promoted ahead of increasingly pricey established housing stocks, new subway lines were built (never mind that they don't go anywhere useful) and historic structures suffered the swing of the wrecking ball.

Considering what was about to happen, a salesman mayor like Lastman may have been exactly what was needed to help the Megacity cope with the 21st century.

THE 21ST CENTURY

Although Toronto is still 'The City That Works,' a geeky nickname acquired for its urban planning successes, the new millennium has delivered a lot of headaches so far.

First, Toronto lost its bid to host the 2008 Summer Olympics. Then it was smacked in the head by successive outbreaks of West Nile Virus and Severe Acute Respiratory Syndrome (SARS). The Great Blackout of 2003, when power plants failed across northeastern US and Canada, left Torontonians in the dark for days. Chinatown vendors quickly began selling 'Toronto Survivor' T-shirts as barflies joked about 'Toronto the Bad' becoming 'The City That Works You Over.' Undeterred, the tourist board embarked on an optimistic new ad campaign, 'Toronto: You Belong Here.'

Ousting Lastman from the mayor chair in 2003, David Miller was comfortably re-elected in 2006. His initial platform was a vision of returning Toronto to its roots as a patchwork city of neighborhoods. Other big plans included the consolidation of Dundas Square as a public space worthy of NYC's Times Square, cleaning up City Hall corruption and pushing environmental healing to the front of the city's agenda. Highlighting his 2006 campaign was a scheme to secure 1% of provincial and federal GST taxes to put toward improving

TIMELINE

1615	1649
Voyageur Etienne Brûlé arrives at the Humber River	League of the Iroquois attacks local Huron tribes

38

local services. He's also promised to ramp up gun-control measures, court big business and improve policing. Time will tell if he's successful…Miller is also an advocate for civil rights for minorities, including the disabled, gay and lesbian citizens, and various ethnic groups. He's also established a Racial Diversity Secretariat, a crucial step for a city where interethnic gang violence is becoming a real problem.

And so, as the CN Tower turns 30, it seems there is every reason for enthusiasm about Toronto's future. Today 50% of Torontonians have immigrated from somewhere else, bringing fresh ideas, perspectives and the riches of diversity to the city. More than 100 languages ricochet through the streets of an experimental city that's almost found its feet. The only constant is change – Toronto is a city in evolution.

FROM THE BEGINNING

ABORIGINAL HISTORY

Before Europeans showed up, the Toronto area was home to indigenous tribes for 11,000 years. See the First Nations Foundations boxed text on p40 for some background.

ARRIVAL OF THE FRENCH

In 1615 Etienne Brûlé arrived at the mouth of the Humber River on a mission for French explorer Samuel de Champlain, who had already founded a settlement at Québec. This site, at the convergence of several key trading and portage routes, became known as Toronto, a name possibly derived from a Mohawk name for a sacred fallen tree. The trade routes running north from here were historically used by First Nations tribes and later by French fur traders as shortcuts between Lake Ontario and Georgian Bay or the upper inland lakes. It wasn't until around 1720, however, that the French were able to establish a permanent fur-trading post and mission near the Humber River. In 1750 they built Fort Rouillé – also known as Fort Toronto, on the site where Exhibition Place (p51) now stands – one in a series of forts set up to control navigation on the Great Lakes and links with the Mississippi River.

MUDDY YORK

After years of hostility with the dastardly French on both sides of the Atlantic, the British took over all of New France, including the area around Toronto, under the 1763 Treaty of Paris. Montréal had already been captured three years earlier. However, it wasn't until after

---

STILL HANGING AROUND

Even as things evolve in the Megacity, Toronto's famous ghosts have chosen to remain. As you amble about town, you're likely to visit more than a few of the city's most haunted sites. It's said that on certain nights at the Mackenzie House (p61), the 19th-century-style print shop machines in the basement can be heard working when no one is around. The hand-operated elevators in the Elgin & Winter Garden Theatre Centre (p61) have also been known to move of their own accord. Poltergeist activity has been reported in the Distillery District (p56), where one of the distillery's original owners drowned in a well (by accident or suicide, no one's really sure) shortly after his wife died during childbirth. On the islands, the Gibraltar Point Lighthouse (p76) is haunted by the malingering ghost of its first keeper, a bootlegger allegedly murdered for his stash. Red-coated guards are still seen patrolling the grounds of Fort York (p51), while elegantly dressed apparitions float through The Grange (p64). The souls of the last men hanged in Canada are said to be heard moaning inside Old City Hall (p62); the former jail cells in the basement of the Courthouse Market Grille (p96) are almost as chilling. BOO!

1813	1849
Americans invade during the War of 1812 (which actually lasted until 1815)	First great fire starts in the stables behind Covey's Inn on King St E

FIRST NATIONS FOUNDATIONS *Monica Bodirsky*

Chances are, anywhere you step in Toronto, you are walking on the bones of First Nations ancestors. Toronto has been continually occupied by Aboriginal people for the past 11,000 years, and beneath its towers of concrete and steel, the foundations of this city may lie obscured, yet not eradicated.

Several place-names that travelers encounter are clues to the true history of our sprawling Megacity and continue to honor its First Nations origins. Mississauga scholar AR Bobiwash interpreted 'Toronto' as a Wendat (Huron) word for a fishing weir, a group of sticks placed together at the mouth of a river to gather fish. It is this etymological understanding that gives Toronto its description as 'The Gathering Place.' An equally valid Aboriginal perspective on the meaning of the city's moniker is offered by Mohawk historian and architect William Woodworth of Ontario's Six Nations of the Grand River Territory. Woodworth understands that 'Toron:to' (pronounced Delondo) is derived from the Mohawk word for log. He believes that the name may refer to a fallen log that had a deep spiritual and ceremonial purpose. 'Trees grew to heights that defy our imagination,' he says. 'There were white pines as tall as 100m then.' Interpretations of language, as with many other things, are subjective. In keeping with the Aboriginal concept of all perspectives being equal, and the practices of tolerance and respect, the important thing to remember is that the name 'Toronto' is Aboriginal.

Spadina Ave, which runs from Lake Ontario north to Bloor St and continues as Spadina Rd up to Roselawn Ave, was originally known as 'Ishpaadiina' (ish-*pah*-dee-nah), which is an Anishnawbe word meaning 'to go up the hill.' The hill being referred to is still part of the city's landscape and today leads to Casa Loma (p68). Five thousand years ago, the original shoreline of Lake Ontario reached the top of that same hill. At that time it was a campground for Iroquois people. When the glacier receded, what is now known as Davenport Rd became a lakefront trail. Instead of being moved, this trail was just paved over. As many travelers will notice, it meanders off Toronto's typical urban grid.

St George St and its subway station are generally thought to have been named after St George, the patron saint of England and famed dragon slayer. However, they were actually named after Clinton St George, an Aboriginal fur trader who did business regularly between Toronto and Rama, north of the city off Lake Huron. He was involved with the influential Baldwin family, who gained much of their wealth through the fur trade. One of the Baldwin family's houses, the Spadina Museum (p69; located next to Casa Loma) still stands to this day, and has been turned into a museum.

Not far from Spadina Ave is Queen's Park, home of the Provincial Legislature (p69). It has been noted with some irony that this was the original site of the city's first insane asylum. Unfortunately, at the time of construction, no consideration was given to the Mississauga people who had been using the grounds at Queen St to hold council. An appeal was made to the governor with no resolution, and the Mississauga land claim is still being resolved today.

The Toronto Islands remain a sacred part of Aboriginal history in Toronto. With a spectacular view of Lake Ontario and the city skyline, the islands have long been used as a spa by Aboriginal people, who came here to camp seeking solitude and rest. Dr Peter Martin (Oronyatek:ha) was a noted Six Nations physician who lived in a house north of Allan Gardens, just east of downtown. He was a renowned 19th-century philanthropist. When he passed away in 1907, his body lay in state in Massey Hall (p62) for three days. A newspaper account at the time noted, 'The drawn blinds, the bared heads and the sorrowful faces formed a tribute of respect such as is paid to few men in either life or death.'

Stop by the Native Canadian Centre of Toronto (p69) to get a better understanding of what lies beneath Toronto's towers of concrete and steel. The 'Great Indian Bus Tour of Toronto' is now accessible online at www.firststory.ca, along with First Nations stories and back issues of the monthly newspaper the *Native Canadian*.

Monica Bodirsky is the coordinator of Getekindaswingamig (Native Community History Program) at the Native Canadian Centre of Toronto. This article was written in memory of Mississauga scholar and historian A Rodney Bobiwash (Wacoquaakmik, 1959–2002). Chi miigwetch (thank you) Rodney.

the American Revolution that Loyalists fleeing the United States arrived and settlement began in earnest. The British paid £1700 to the Mississauga nation for the Toronto Land Purchase of 1787, although the 'official' deed was suspiciously left blank. Four years later the provinces of Upper Canada (now Ontario) and Lower Canada (Québec) were created.

Soon afterwards, in 1793, John Graves Simcoe, the new Lieutenant Governor of Upper Canada, moved the provincial capital from Niagara-on-the-Lake to a more defensible position at Toronto, officially naming the new settlement York. This colonial town was laid out on a

1904	1920
Second great fire starts at the C&S Currie neckwear factory on Wellington St W	Group of Seven exhibits paintings at the Art Gallery of Toronto

10-block grid with patriotic street names like King, Queen, George and Duke. The lieutenant governor's men also constructed a trail, which later became Yonge St, leading 48km straight north through the wilderness to the borders of the original Toronto Land Purchase. Incidentally, the *Guinness Book of World Records* officially lists Yonge St as the longest road in the world. It winds over 1800km north along Hwy 11, terminating at Rainy River, Ontario.

The perennial muddiness of the new capital gave rise to the unflattering nickname 'Muddy York,' but Simcoe figured this made York even less likely to be attacked should the Americans decide to invade. Which, of course, they did anyway during the War of 1812. On April 27, 1813, American forces reached Fort York and after a short struggle overcame the British and Ojibwa troops. The Americans looted and razed York but hung around for only six days before leaving of their own volition. Canadian troops followed them all the way back to the US political headquarters in Washington and attempted to burn down the White House when they got there (allegedly so named for the white paint that was used to cover up the charred bits afterwards).

After the 1814 Treaty of Ghent ended the hostilities between the USA and Canada, the British no longer saw the Iroquois nations as valuable allies and quickly subjected them to increased government control. At the same time, the city of York began to expand and, in 1828, the first stagecoach service began on Yonge St. British and then Irish immigrants started to arrive in Upper Canada in increasing numbers, quadrupling the population to around 10,000 people.

FROM REBELLION TO UNITY

By 1824 firebrand William Lyon Mackenzie had started publishing his *Colonial Advocate,* an outcry against the oligarchic Tory government that ruled York. Termed the 'Family Compact,' these Loyalist families, including the Jarvises, Baldwins and Strachans, had come to power as advisers to Lieutenant Governor Simcoe, who before departing Upper Canada had limited the province's legislative powers as a means of avoiding an American-style revolution.

During 1834 Mackenzie got himself elected as the first mayor of the new city of Toronto, but the Family Compact's continuing political influence proved much too strong for him. Finally out of options, Mackenzie initiated the shortest-lived rebellion in Canadian history on December 5, 1837. He and an assorted band of around 600 disgruntled citizens marched down Yonge St and confronted the Loyalist troops that were directed by Sheriff Jarvis. Shots were volleyed, confusion and panic ensued and both sides broke and ran. Mackenzie went into temporary exile in the USA while unluckier rebels were hanged.

Another newspaperman, George Brown, the publisher of the *Globe* since 1844, became a key political player in Toronto politics in Mackenzie's absence. Brown forged a new liberal party and was also a driving force behind the confederation of Canada during 1867, to which most voters agreed more out of fear of another US invasion than out of any nationalistic ideals. Their fears were not unfounded, considering that Fenian raids (p42) were still being launched across the border. By the time of confederation, the railway had already brought the coalescing nation much closer together. Toronto gained prominence as the capital of the newly renamed Ontario, even though the city was still in the economic shadow of Montréal.

TORONTO THE GOOD

Throughout the Victorian era of the late 1800s, there was seemingly nothing but progress for Toronto. Eaton's and Simpson's department stores opened their doors on Yonge St, the city was wired for electricity and the first national exhibition was held. By the end of the century, more than 200,000 folks called Toronto home. Masterpieces of Edwardian architecture emerged downtown, and the first Italian and Jewish immigrants arrived. Following the

1967	1976
Toronto Maple Leafs win the Stanley Cup for the 13th (and most recent) time	The CN Tower opens its elevators to the public

world trend, Toronto had a 'Great Fire' in 1849, but proceeded to have another one on 19 April, 1904. Starting at the C&S Currie neckwear factory at 58 Wellington St W, the blaze charred through 20 inner-city acres, leveling 100 buildings. Amazingly, no one died.

Around this time the city became known as 'Toronto the Good,' a tag that only began to fade a few decades ago. Conservative politicians voted for prohibition (outlawing the production and sale of alcoholic beverages) and strong antivice laws (it was illegal to rent a horse on Sunday) that culminated in the Lord's Day Act of 1906. Eaton's department store drew its curtains to guard against 'sinful' window shopping, and city playgrounds were locked up. These antivice laws remained on the books until 1950.

Meanwhile, businessmen like Sir Henry Pellat of Casa Loma fame were amassing their fortunes, and by the 1920s Bay St was booming, partly because gold, silver and uranium mines had been discovered in northern Ontario. Everything stopped short during the Depression era, sparking ethnic hostilities. Chinese immigration was banned, anti-Semitic riots exploded in Christie Pits Park and during WWII, Canada interned citizens of Japanese ancestry in camps, as did the USA. Widespread prejudice against African Canadians was all the more lamentable for Ontario having been a safe haven for Harriet Tubman and other slaves via the famous Underground Railroad escape route.

THE WHOLE WORLD IN A CITY

After WWII the city breathed a huge sigh of relief. Thousands of European immigrants rolled into town, gifting the city with an influx of new tongues, customs and food. Enclaves like Kensington Market began showing signs of the cultural diversity that has become Toronto's trademark, while the Yonge St subway line opened in 1954 to shunt the burgeoning population from A to B. Toronto spread out in all directions (except south, of course), but in the 1960s people started moving back into the innercity and began restoring gracious old Victorian homes. Bohemian folk-music coffeehouses opened in Yorkville, patronized not least by US conscientious objectors looking to evade the clutches of the Vietnam War draft.

The building of the controversial new City Hall in 1965 really gave Toronto a boost into modernity. In the 1970s Portuguese, Chilean, Greek, Southeast Asian, Chinese and West Indian immigrants surfed into the city in waves, the redevelopment of the Harbourfront

---

O BROTHER, WHERE ART THOU?

What do Irish Republicans, African Americans, Mohawk tribes and Québec radicals have in common? They all hate the British – or at least they did during the mid-19th century. Although the resultant raids by the Fenian brotherhood (tacitly approved but not acknowledged by the US) are a side note to Canadian history, their epic ambitions are worth recounting.

A series of border incursions organized by the Fenian brethren, made up of Irish Americans loyal to the Republican cause, were aiming to harangue British forces and eventually capture Canada's major cities, Toronto and Montréal. Why? The fiendish Fenians planned to hold both cities hostage until Britain agreed to free Ireland – a cunning plan that had veteran fighters from the US Civil War, including a company of African American soldiers, along with 500 Mohawk warriors and French sympathizers in Montréal, rallying to the cause.

Everything went tragicomically awry when the raids began in 1866. One detachment of Fenians quickly overran Fort Erie, but a lethal combination of fever outbreak, poor planning and laziness among the brotherhood – along with efficient spying by British military scouts – stymied the impassioned brunt of the attack. When the Fenians at Fort Erie tried to retreat across the Niagara River, they were arrested by a US warship, then convicted and sentenced in a New York court. Later on, when all the fuss had died down, they were quietly released. Prisoners of war taken to Toronto fared far worse – nearly two dozen were executed. Nevertheless, the Fenian border raids continued sporadically into 1871, but had little success.

1993	1999
Toronto Blue Jays win the baseball World Series for the second year in a row	City council legalizes 'clothing optional' status of Hanlan's Point beach

TOP FIVE TORONTO HISTORY BOOKS

- *Accidental City: The Transformation of Toronto* by Robert Fulford (1995) – an engaging interpretation of how modern architecture, lakefront development and natural ravine lands conspire to create one of North America's most livable cities.
- *A Magical Place: Toronto Island and Its People* by Bill Freeman (1999) – takes readers effortlessly through the islands' turbulent history, historic sites and lighthouse ghosts.
- *Muddy York Mud: Scandal and Scurrility in Upper Canada* by Chris Raible (1992) – dishes the dirt on key players in the old town of York – the Baldwins, the Mackenzies et al.
- *Niagara: A History of the Falls* by Pierre Berton (1992) – for all the tales of tightrope walkers and daredevils in barrels.
- *Toronto Then and Now* by Mike Filey (2000) – a photographic portrait of the city's evolution from virgin woods to thriving 'hoods.

district began and new skyscrapers sprang up. Toronto finally overtook Montréal's population, becoming one of the fastest-growing cities in North America.

The city's optimism and civic pride expressed themselves in the building of the funky CN Tower (p51) in 1976, continuing right through the 1980s economic boom on Bay St and the city's sesquicentennial in 1984. However, not everyone shared the 'progressive' outlook of City Hall. In 1980 the 'Sandbar Bohemians' on Toronto Islands stood their ground against eviction by the municipal government, and won. And of course, the economy had to go bust sometime, which it did with a bang during the mid-'90s.

2003	2006
Toronto legalizes same-sex marriage, survives an outbreak of SARS and the Great Blackout	CN Tower turns 30

Sights ∎

Sights

A jigsaw puzzle of distinctly flavored neighborhoods, Toronto only really makes sense when you view it as a whole. But who wants to do that? Half the fun of being here is pretending you're eating noodles in Macau, wandering along a leafy Dublin backstreet or sipping ouzo in Athens. This is a city that takes the best of world cultures and delivers it to you in compact, neighborhood-sized pieces. We suggest you graze from 'hood to 'hood, focusing on the parts without trying to define the whole. There'll be plenty of time for that once you get home!

A gently undulating plain sliding down to Lake Ontario, Toronto is an easy-walking city, but if your stamina gives out, the subway is quick, safe and simple to navigate. So too are the old-fashioned streetcars that rumble through the city grid. Each of the following neighborhood sections contains transportation details; the Transportation chapter (p210) has further information.

Downtown Toronto is bounded to the west, north and east by a hodgepodge of bohemian, ethnic and historic neighborhoods, with the city's southern edge crisply defined by Lake Ontario. Just offshore are the Toronto Islands. The Harbourfront district lies between the lake and Union Station, the gateway to the skyscraping Financial District and historic Old York. The Theatre Block congregates around King St W, butting up next to the nocturnal Entertainment District (aka Clubland). Further north, Queen St parades east past City Hall towards the Eaton Centre and Dundas Square.

Toronto's main east-west streets are labeled 'East' or 'West' on either side of Yonge St, the main north-south artery, which rolls north from the lake into chichi Bloor-Yorkville. The Church-Wellesley Village is a gay parallel universe a few blocks to the east. East Toronto extends from here through Cabbagetown, Greektown (The Danforth) and The Beaches community.

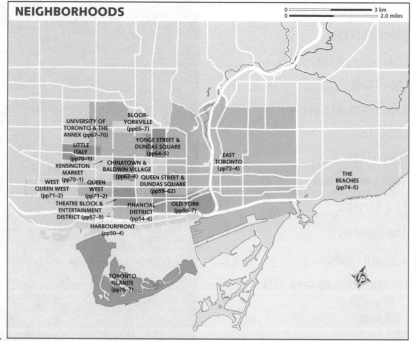

Over on the west side, low-key Baldwin Village and frenetic Chinatown bump into Kensington Market and the main University of Toronto (U of T) campus. The Annex is a student-dominated 'hood northwest of U of T, adhering to Bloor St W. A short stroll along College St from Kensington Market is Little Italy, paralleling the artsy Queen West and West Queen West strips further south.

ITINERARIES

Two Days

After a heart-starter coffee in Cabbagetown (p123) jump on the subway to Union Station (p54) and take a rocket ride up the CN Tower (p51) – as high as Torontonians get without wings or drugs. Back at ground level, shuffle over to St Lawrence Market (p95) for lunch then head up to Bloor-Yorkville (p155) to splash some afternoon cash in the shops. Compensate with a thrifty dinner in Chinatown (p99) that night.

Dedicate the morning of day two to a major sight – maybe the Royal Ontario Museum (p66), Hockey Hall of Fame (p55), Art Gallery of Ontario (p64) or Casa Loma (p68) – then chow down with lunch at Baldwin Village (p99). Afterwards, stroll through the Harbourfront (p50) district then take the ferry over to the Toronto Islands (p75) where you can hire a bike and wheel away the afternoon. Back on the mainland, grab dinner in Little Italy (p105) then a see rockin' live gig (p125) or have a few drinks to cap off the night.

Four Days

If you're in town for a few more days, sleep late then rummage through the secondhand boutiques at Kensington Market (p158). Roam through the University of Toronto (p70) campus, aiming for lunch in The Annex (p104). Spend the afternoon rambling along one of our walking tours (p82), or take the streetcar east to explore The Beaches (p74). Dinner and drinks in the Distillery District (p96) is the perfect way to cap off the day.

On day four, peruse the hip/hippie shops, bars and eateries along Queen West and West Queen West (p71). Make plans to catch some dance (p135), classical music (p133) or theatre (p128) that night, perhaps with dinner beforehand in Little India (p110) or The Danforth (p110). If you're feeling more like hotdogs-and-beer, catch a baseball game at the Rogers Centre (p53) or ice-hockey at the Air Canada Centre (p50). A trashy night club-hopping through the Entertainment District (p131) makes a fitting last hurrah.

One Week

With more time up your sleeve, you'll have the chance to explore some highlights beyond the downtown area. Check out the Scarborough Bluffs (p79), Tommy Thompson Park (p74) or the McMichael Canadian Art Collection (p189). Some kid-friendly options include the Ontario Science Centre

ESSENTIAL TORONTO

CN Tower (p51) Turned 30 in 2006 – old enough to be retro, young enough to be cool.

Kensington Market (p70) Funky secondhand clothes stalls, good coffee and multicultural eats.

Toronto Islands (p75) Embrace your inner hippie on these chilled-out, leafy isles.

Toronto Maple Leafs at the Air Canada Centre (p142) Hard-headed Toronto on ice – yell loudly and try not to spill your beer.

Niagara Falls (p181) More amazing than any of the pictures you've seen.

(p79), **Black Creek Pioneer Village** (p77) and **Paramount Canada's Wonderland** (p79). Further afield, **Niagara Falls** (p181) are just as spectacular as ever, while the **Niagara Peninsula Wine Country** (p186) makes a worthy/woozy excursion.

If you'd rather stay downtown, spend some time digging up Toronto's historic roots in **Old York** (p56), bag yourself a bargain along the **Yonge Street Strip** (p64) or see what's going on in **Dundas Square** (p59). Whatever you do, eat well and eat often – this town is a food-lover's delight!

ORGANIZED TOURS
Boat Trips

Several companies run boat tours around the harbor and Toronto Islands between May and September. Most boats set sail from the Harbourfront beside Queen's Quay Terminal or further west beside York Quay Centre. For shorter harbor excursions, you can often just show up and buy a ticket at the quay, though reservations are recommended for brunch and dinner cruises.

Keep in mind that the ferries to and from the **Toronto Islands** (p213) offer spectacular city views – cheaper than taking a private tour, but minus the commentary and insight.

GREAT LAKES SCHOONER COMPANY
Map pp234-5

☎ 416-203-2322; www.tallshipcruisestoronto.com; 90min cruise adult/child/senior $20/11/18; ☺ 1-3 departures daily Jun-Labour Day; ♿ ; ☒ 509, 510
The dashing, black three-master *Kajama*, a 1930 trading schooner launched in Germany, towers 55m above water. It's moored behind the Power Plant at the foot of Lower Simcoe St, but there's usually a summer ticket kiosk beside Queen's Quay Terminal. Food and drinks are available onboard.

MARIPOSA CRUISES Map pp234-5
☎ 416-203-0178, 866-627-7672; www .mariposacruises.com; Queen's Quay Terminal, 207 Queens Quay W; 1hr cruise adult/child/concession $18/13/16.50; ☺ 5 departures daily May-Sep; ♿ ; ☒ 509, 510
Narrated harbor tours are the standard offering here, but they also run two-hour buffet lunch (adult/child $40/20) and Sunday brunch (adult/child $45/24) cruises, plus three-hour dinner-and-dance evening cruises ($70). Check the website or call for times and dates.

TORONTO TOURS Map pp234-5
☎ 416-868-0400; www.torontotours.com; Pier 6, Queens Quay W; 1hr cruise adult/child/concession $18/13/16.50; ☺ 11am-5pm Apr-May, 10am-6pm Jun-Aug, 10am-5pm Sep-Oct; ♿ ; ☒ 509, 510
Narrated harbor cruises depart hourly in April, May, September and October; every 30 minutes between June and August. This is a great way to check out the Toronto Islands if you're not visiting them under your own steam, and they also run various city/harbor tour combos (some including the CN Tower). The departure dock is at the foot of York St. Online booking discounts available.

Bus Tours

Bus tours are convenient, but with TTC day passes (p215) being so cheap, a do-it-yourself tour makes perfect sense.

GRAY LINE TOURS Map pp232-3
☎ 416-594-3310, 800-594-3310; www.grayline.ca; departs Metro Toronto Coach Terminal, 610 Bay St; 3-day pass adult/child/senior/family $34/18/30/95; ☺ departures hourly 9am-4pm; Ⓜ Dundas
Ever-reliable Gray Line runs basic two-hour, double-decker bus tours looping around central Toronto. You can start your hop-on, hop-off tour at the bus station, or buy tickets onboard the bus where it pulls up outside **Nicholby's Sports & Souvenirs** (Map pp234–5; ☎ 416-955-8893; 123 Front St W), one of the points along the loop. Passengers who book in advance can request pick-ups from downtown hotels and hostels. Also on offer are day tours to Niagara Falls.

ROMBUS Map pp238-9
☎ 416-586-5797; www.rom.on.ca; 100 Queen's Park; full-day tours $85-95; ☺ 9am-5pm; Ⓜ Museum
The **Royal Ontario Museum** (p66) puts the keys in the ignition of monthly bus tours, arranged around historical, architectural and cultural themes – perhaps surveying

stained glass at the University of Toronto, art deco heritage or trawling past the architectural offerings of Cabbagetown. Advance reservations required; tours depart the ROM.

TORONTO HIPPO TOURS Map pp234-5

☎ 416-703-4476, 877-635-5510; www.toronto hippotours.com; 151 Front St W; 90min tour adult/child/concession/family $38/25/33/110; ⏰ 11am-6pm May-Nov, office from 9am; ♿ ; 🚇 Union

How can you spot the Hippo bus? It's the big yellow thing with seaweed dipping off its axles (well, lake weed perhaps…). These amphibious buses take families on goofily narrated tours of downtown before plunging into the harbor; your driver is also a marine captain.

Walking & Cycling Tours

By far the easiest way to experience Toronto is on foot – you'll see more, meet more people and get fit in the process! Cycling tours allow you to cover a bit more territory. See our dedicated walking and cycling tours on p82.

A TASTE OF THE WORLD

☎ 416-923-6813; www.torontowalksbikes.com; 2-3½hr tours $20-39; ⏰ year-round

Quirky, well-qualified guides lead off-beat walking and cycling tours of Toronto's nooks and crannies, usually with a foodie focus. Recent expeditions have delved into the culinary secrets of Chinatown and Kensington Market, while others have harassed the ghosts of Yorkville and traced Charles Dickens' 1842 Toronto footsteps. Departure points vary, as do prices depending on whether or not bike rental and food are included. Reservations essential.

CIVITAS CITY WALKS

☎ 416-966-1550; city.walks@sympatico.ca; 1½-2hr walks $15; ⏰ May-Oct

Civitas walks focus on the people, places and events that dapple the history of Toronto, taking in the architecture and conjuring up the atmosphere of Old York. Along the way you'll check out old town icons like Union Station, St Lawrence Market and St James Cathedral. Tours run on request, usually departing from the corner of Jarvis and Front Sts.

HERITAGE TORONTO

☎ 416-338-0684; www.heritagetoronto.org; 1½-3hr tours free-$5; ⏰ usually weekends May-Sep

Over three dozen historical, cultural and nature walks are led by museum docents and neighborhood historical society members. Each uniquely designed tour is given only once during the summer. Recent walks have taken inquisitive groups around The Beaches, chewed through the history of St Lawrence Market and hiked the city's ravines and wilderness parks. Check the website for a schedule; reservations usually not required.

Sights

ORGANIZED TOURS

WINTER IN THE CITY

Cold out, eh? From November to March the wind whips off the lake and slices up Bay St, crystallizing your breath and freezing your bones. Many shops, restaurants and attractions reduce their winter hours; some even close. Still, even the coldest day can be redeemed with a fireside pint or a hearty meal, and don't forget, it's hockey season (as if you could avoid it…). **Ice-skating** (p139) is another favorite pastime, while Victorian-style Christmas celebrations abound at various attractions. When the gas lamps are lit on Toronto St during a snowfall, romantic souls will be transported to another century. After New Year's, the **WinterCity Festival** (p13) comes alive during the subzero months, while **Winterlicious** (p13) lets you beat the freeze and dine in style for not much cash at all.

On days when the wind-chill factor sends temperatures to ungodly lows, frostbite can become a possibility. But don't worry, you'll hear all about it – everybody discusses the freezing cold, and radio stations broadcast warnings stating exactly how many minutes it's safe to expose your skin. That's your cue to scuttle below ground into the PATH system (p215) or whittle away the hours in one of the city's museums, galleries, tropical conservatories, the enclosed **St Lawrence Market** (p57) or a rejuvenating **spa** (p144).

Many locals refuse to wear heavy down jackets, even when it's 30°C below zero outside, just so they still look hip, although snazzy winter hats (called *toques*, pronounced 'tukes') have evolved into a fashion statement unto themselves. Even in winter, pack a bathing suit for heated indoor pools and saunas. Bring a good, sturdy pair of walking shoes that won't slip on the ice. And remember, this *is* the Great White North – rug up and get psyched to brave the elements and you'll be just fine.

ROMWALKS

☎ 416-586-8097; www.rom.on.ca; 2hr tours $10;
☺ usually Wed & Sun afternoons May–mid-Sep
Volunteers from the Royal Ontario Museum (p66) lead happy punters on historical and architectural walking tours with a neighborhood focus. Tours run rain or shine; no advance reservations necessary for most tours. Check current schedules online or pick up a brochure at the museum.

SIGHTS ON BIKES

☎ 416-274-8784; www.sightsonbikes.com; 2-4hr tours incl helmet & bike $30-50; ☺ 10am & 3pm daily May-Oct
These free-wheelin' two-wheelers run bike tours of the city (northern and southern areas), the Toronto Islands, The Beaches and west along the lakeshore to the Humber River. There's lighthearted, informative commentary along the way, and the pace is leisurely enough to accommodate all levels of fitness. Most tours depart St Lawrence Market, but it's best to confirm when you book.

HARBOURFRONT

Map pp234–5; Eating p93; Shopping p149; Sleeping p167

The Harbourfront district was once a run-down area of warehouses, factories and docklands lapping on the shores of Lake Ontario. Some people, frustrated with the pace and quality of redevelopment, say not much has changed: ugly condo constructions have been given the green light while well-considered pedestrian-friendly developments have seemingly been put on hold. The current state-of-play is a lakeshore that may seem underutilized to visitors from great waterside cities like Chicago or Sydney, but any further progress has been stymied by wrangling among governmental bodies.

Regardless, once redevelopment commenced along Queens Quay W, the area gained galleries, cultural centres and sports and entertainment venues, most of them springing up between Yonge St and Spadina Ave. On weekends the Harbourfront is popular for walks and harbor cruises that take advantage of fresh lakeshore breezes. A few ex-shipping terminals now contain shopping malls and indoor/outdoor performing and visual arts venues, and of course, the CN Tower

(opposite) isn't too far from the shore. The area is well worth a visit, especially combined with a ferry trip over to the Toronto Islands (p75). Attractions for families abound, especially beyond the quays at Fort York (opposite) and Ontario Place (p52), with special events at Exhibition Place (opposite). A laidback stroll, cycle or skate along the waterfront Martin Goodman Trail (p138) is another option.

Don't expect much action east of Yonge St – this is still part of Toronto's functioning docklands, with container ships shunting into port and a sugar mill filling the air with caramel scents. After dark the odd nightclub fires up here, while street drag-racers exploit wide lanes and minimal traffic lights along Queens Quay E.

Orientation

The main Harbourfront area centres around the foot of York St, a short walk south from Union Station. Most of the foot traffic follows Queens Quay W either west towards the Rogers Centre and the CN Tower or east towards the Toronto Islands ferry terminal and Yonge St. Outlying attractions are a 15-minute streetcar ride west of the main quay area, beyond Bathurst St.

AIR CANADA CENTRE Map pp234-5

ACC; ☎ 416-815-5982; www.theaircanadacentre .com; 40 Bay St; 1hr tour adult/child/concession $13/9/11; ☺ tours May-Sep; ♿ ; Ⓜ Union
Guided 'inner workings' tours of the home of the Toronto Maple Leafs (hockey; p142) and Toronto Raptors (basketball; p141) take you where the players go, even into the dressing room sans players. But you'll enjoy the hi-tech arena more if you can actually score tickets to a game. Tours run hourly, events permitting, highlighting remnants of the 1941 *moderne* Toronto Postal Delivery Building incorporated into the structure of the ACC, which opened for business in 1999.

AMSTERDAM BREWING CO Map p231

☎ 416-504-6886; www.amsterdambeer.com; 21 Bathurst St; 30min tour $6; ☺ tours 1:30pm daily, 5pm Mon-Sat; 🚋 511
Steam Whistle's poor relation hangs out in a seedy redbrick building under the Gardiner Expwy. But without Amsterdam, Toronto's first microbrewery (1986), the local microbrew scene would never have scaled such light-headed heights! House specials include a

Dutch Amber Lager, a seasonal Spring Bock brew, a lighter Summer Wheat Beer and a British-style Nut Brown Ale. Tour reservations essential; pay an extra $2 and get a pint glass to take home and enshrine.

CN TOWER Map pp234-5

Canadian National Tower, La Tour CN; ☎ 416-868-6937; www.cntower.ca; 301 Front St W; Observation Deck adult/child $22/15; ☼ 10am-10pm, later in summer; ⬤ ⬤ ; ⬤ Union

Having recently turned 30, this funky spike remains every bit as cool and iconic as it was when it opened in 1976. Its primary function is as a radio and TV communications tower, but relieving tourists of as much cash as possible seems to be the second order of business. Sure, it's expensive, but riding the great glass elevators up the highest freestanding structure (553m) in the world is one of those things in life you just *have* to do. On a clear day, the views from the Observation Deck are absolutely astounding; if it's hazy, you won't be able to see a thing. For extra thrills, tread lightly over the knee-trembling Glass Floor deck, or continue climbing an extra 101m to the uppermost SkyPod viewing area. Alternatively, if you're feeling chipper, you might want to enter the annual CN Tower Stair Climb – a heart-thumping dash to the top of the tower's 1776 steps that happens every October.

Various tour packages allow access to different combinations of the various decks (see 'relieving tourists of cash' above), but all you really need to buy is a basic ticket to the Observation Deck. Beware: two million visitors every year means summer queues for the elevator can be up to two hours long – going up *and* coming back down. For those with reservations and bags full of cash, the award-winning revolving restaurant, 360° (p93) awaits (the elevator ticket price is waived for diners).

EXHIBITION PLACE Map p231

☎ 416-263-3600; www.explace.on.ca; off Lake Shore Blvd W, btwn Strachan Ave & Dufferin St; ☼ event schedules vary; ⬤ ⬤ ; ⬤ 511

Each year these historic grounds are revived for their original purpose: the Canadian National Exhibition (p15). During 'The Ex' millions of visitors enjoy carnival rides, lumberjack competitions and more good, honest, homegrown fun than a Sunday School picnic in June. Presiding over the main

entry is the beaux-arts Princes' Gate – one of the few buildings in Toronto that will make you stop and say 'Wow!'. Built in 1927 in celebration of Canada's 60th birthday, the gate consists of a fabulously ornate grand arch with carved rose coffers and hefty Corinthian columns, topped by a winged, wreath-clutching Victory angel.

Other special events held at Exhibition Place throughout the year include the Grand Prix of Toronto (p14), the Royal Agricultural Winter Fair and an effervescent variety of sports and design shows. Otherwise the grounds are often spookily bereft of visitors, apart from conventioneers dutifully plodding to their next meet-and-greet session and die-hard historians visiting Toronto's oldest building, the humble Scadding Cabin. Built around 1795 by an estate clerk of Colonial Lieutenant Governor John Simcoe, the cabin isn't open to the public, but often participates in Doors Open Toronto (p34).

FORT YORK Map p231

☎ 416-392-6907; www.toronto.ca/culture/fort_york.htm; 100 Garrison Rd, off Fleet St W, east of Strachan Ave; admission & tour adult/child/concession $6/3/3.25; ☼ 10am-5pm Jun-Aug, to 4pm Sep-May, closed mid-Dec–early Jan; ⬤ ; ⬤ 509, 511

Established by the British in 1793 to protect the town of York, as Toronto was

TRANSPORTATION

Subway & Streetcar From Union Station, take either the underground 509 Harbourfront or 510 Spadina streetcars which emerge at ground level on Queens Quay W. For destinations further west, the 509 Harbourfront streetcar joins up with the 511 Bathurst streetcar at Bathurst St.

Bicycle & Skates The Martin Goodman Trail is a paved recreational path connecting all of the Harbourfront sights. In the Queen's Quay area, pedestrians share the trail.

Walking On a still, sunny day, the Harbourfront can be divine for walking, but in winter you might wish you'd stayed in bed.

Car Harbourfront parking is a drag. Private lots charge at least $10 per day (no hourly rates). The municipal lot at 10 York St normally charges $1.50 per half-hour (daily maximum $9); rates jump during special events.

then known, Fort York was almost entirely destroyed during the **War of 1812** (p39), when a small band of Ojibwa warriors and British and local troops couldn't halt the US incursion. The Americans went on to raze and loot the city but left of their own accord after just six days. The fort was rebuilt between 1813 and 1815.

Today, beneath the growl of trucks on the Gardiner Expwy, a handful of the original log, stone and brick buildings have been restored. In summer, men decked out in 19th-century British military uniforms carry out mildly preposterous marches and drills, firing musket volleys into the sky. Kids feign interest or run around the fort's embankments with wooden rifles. Included in the admission price, tours run hourly from May to September – watch out for goose poo on your shoe!

HARBOURFRONT CENTRE Map pp234-5
☎ 416-973-4000; www.harbourfrontcentre.com; York Quay, 235 Queens Quay W; events free-$10; 🕑 box office 1-6pm Tue-Sat; ♿ ; 🚋 509, 510
Throughout the summer, especially during the weekends, the Harbourfront Centre (see also Entertainment, p135) puts on a kaleidoscopic variety of performing arts events at the **York Quay Centre**; many are aimed at kids, some are free. Performances sometimes take place on the covered outdoor Concert Stage beside the lake. Also outside are a lakeside **ice-skating rink** (p139) where you can learn to slice up the winter ice, and a ramshackle series of **Artists' Gardens** – seasonally rotating raised planter beds constructed by local artists in a spirit of 'guerilla gardening.' The idea here is to inspire people to reclaim abandoned corners of the city with native species and heritage food plants. Sculptural elements include everything from smashed crockery to broken hockey sticks and caved-in televisions.

Also at York Quay are a series of free galleries including the Photo Passage and a functioning **Craft Studio** (p199) which runs courses in ceramics, jewelry, glass-blowing and textiles. The Harbourfront Centre also maintains the **Toronto Music Garden** (p54) and incorporates the **Power Plant (right)** and the **Premiere Dance Theatre** (p135) in the Queens Quay Terminal building. The **Harbourfront Readings Series** (p132) is a Toronto literary stalwart which runs from September to June.

ONTARIO PLACE Map p231
☎ 416-314-9900, 866-663-4386; www.ontario place.com; 955 Lake Shore Blvd W; day pass adult/ child $22/12, grounds admission only $13/7, Cine-sphere per person $8; 🕑 10am-8pm late Jun-early Aug, Sat & Sun only May & Sep; ♿ 🛗 ; 🚋 511
Built in 1971 on three artificial islands offshore from Exhibition Place, this 40-hectare recreation complex is an easy way to beat the summer heat. It is starting to feel a little dated, but Ontario Place still offers something for everybody. A 'Play All Day' pass entitles you to most of the thrill rides and attractions, including Soak City waterpark, with its waterslide towers visible from a mile away, and walk-up seating at the **Cinesphere**, a spiky, space-age gooseberry where 70mm IMAX films screen on a six-storey curved screen. Parents watch a movie while kids go berserk at soft-play areas like the H2O Generation Station and the Atom Blaster.

Additional attractions, like the human-sized MegaMaze and House of Blues concerts at the **Molson Amphitheatre** (☎ 416-260-5600; www.hob.com/venues/concerts /molsonamp), must be paid for separately. Discounted passes may be available after 5pm and for grounds-only admission. On rainy days, many of the rides, activities and restaurants shut up shop.

You can catch a streetcar to Exhibition Place then trudge over the Lakeshore Bridge to Ontario Place, or take the free shuttle bus from Union Station. The shuttle runs daily from June to August, and on weekends in May and September, departing every half-hour between 9am and 7pm.

POWER PLANT Map pp234-5
☎ 416-973-4949; www.thepowerplant.org; Harbourfront Centre, 231 Queens Quay W; adult/child/ concession $4/free/2, admission free 5-8pm Wed; 🕑 noon-6pm Tue-Sun, to 8pm Wed; 🚋 509, 510
Under the protective umbrella of the **Harbourfront Centre** (left), the Power Plant is a big-reputation art gallery celebrating contemporary Canadian art. The focus is on sculpture and large-scale installations, with live performances, lectures and Power Kids art sessions thrown into the formula. Free talks by visiting artists happen occasionally; free tours roll out at 2pm and 4pm on weekends. The gallery occupies a

renovated ice house and coal store next to the Harbourfront Theatre, which is inside an old power generator.

QUEEN'S QUAY TERMINAL Map pp234-5

☎ 416-203-0342; www.queens-quay-terminal .com; 207 Queens Quay W; admission free; ⊙ 10am-6pm; ⧖ ; ⎕ 509, 510

Start your morning Harbourfront constitutional with a diversion into this refurbished 1926 warehouse, now filled with skylights, arts-and-crafts shops, ritzy boutiques, cafés and galleries, revolving around an eight-storey atrium. Renovated in 1983, this was one of the first Harbourfront buildings to emerge from lakeside dereliction. The Premier Dance Theatre (p135) is also on-site; loud-mouthed ticket sellers hawk harbor cruises outside.

REDPATH SUGAR MUSEUM

Map pp234-5

☎ 416-933-8341; richard.feltoe@tateandlyle.com; 95 Queens Quay E; self-guided tour free; ⊙ 10am-noon & 1-3:30pm Mon-Fri; ⎕ 6

The working Redpath sugar refinery, a descendant of Canada's oldest refinery which opened in Montréal in 1854, wafts delicious sugary smells along Queens Quay E. Inside, a small museum tackles a variety of topics related to the social development and modern refining of sugar, with biographic information on founder John Redpath. A 15-minute film explains the modern refining process. Enter via the west gate near the foot of Yonge St, sign in at the security desk and follow the museum signs (watch out for trucks!).

ROGERS CENTRE Map pp234-5

☎ 416-341-3663; www.rogerscentre.com; 1 Blue Jays Way; 1hr tour adult/child/concession $13.50/8/9.50; ⊙ tour schedules vary; ⧖ ⧗ ; ⊕ Union

As technically awe-inspiring as the CN Tower, the Rogers Centre (formerly the Sky-Dome – people still confuse the two) sports stadium opened in 1989 with the world's first fully retractable dome roof. Made mostly of concrete, this engineering spectacular moves at a rapid 22m per minute, taking just 20 minutes to completely open. That sure beats Montréal's Olympic Stadium, which opened once but failed to ever do so again.

Tours include a brain-scrambling video wall featuring footage of past sporting glories, concerts and events, a sprint up to a box suite, a detour through a locker room (sans athletes) and a newly renovated memorabilia museum. Did you know that eight 747s would fit on the playing field and that the stadium uses enough electricity to light the province of Prince Edward Island? Betcha didn't…

A budget seat at a Blue Jays baseball (p140) or Argonauts football (p142) game is the cheapest official way to see the Rogers Centre. In between times the centre hosts everything from wedding expos to Disney On Ice, dirt-bike demonstrations and Wiggles concerts. When there isn't a game happening, the Hard Rock Café (p119) upstairs runs as a regular sports bar; you can go in for a hamburger and a beer and check out the playing field through huge windows. During games, tables with views must be booked and paid for. Rooms overlooking the field can also be rented at the Rogers Centre's own hotel, the Renaissance Toronto (p167).

While you're here, check out Michael Snow's hysterical *The Audience* sculptures high up on the building's northeast and northwest corners. Look familiar?

SPADINA QUAY WETLANDS & WATERFRONT CHILDREN'S GARDEN

Map pp234-5

☎ 416-392-1111; www.toronto.ca/harbourfront /spadina_quay_wet.htm; 479 Queens Quay W; admission free; ⊙ dawn-dusk; ⧖ ; ⎕ 509, 510

This 0.28-hectare former parking lot is now a thriving, sustainable ecosystem full of frogs, birds and fish. When lakeside fishermen noticed that mature Northern Pike were spawning here each spring – a pattern probably (and remarkably) unchanged for centuries – the city took it upon itself to create this new habitat. Complete with flowering heath plants, poplar trees and a birdhouse modeled on former industrial architecture, it's a little gem leading the way in the Harbourfront district's redevelopment. Aside from the pike, look for Monarch butterflies, Mallard ducks, Goldfinches, dragonflies and Red-winged Blackbirds.

Adjoining the wetlands is the modest but equally rewarding Waterfront Children's Garden, where city kids can plant veggies, do some weeding and generally get a feel for something green among the concrete.

STEAM WHISTLE BREWING

Map pp234-5

☎ 416-362-2337, 866-240-2337; www.steamwhistle .ca; 255 Bremner Blvd; 45min tour $8; ☉ noon-6pm Mon-Sat, to 5pm Sun; ☒; ◉ Union ⓡ 509, 510

Bubbling away in a 1929 steam train repair depot at the foot of the CN Tower, this microbrewery specializes in a hugely popular, crisp European-style Pilsner. In fact, that's all they make! (A policy of 'Do one thing, but do it really, really well' prevails). During snappy, punny tours of the premises, guides explain the brewing process in great detail and let you blow the railway roundhouse's historic steam whistle (thrilling for kids, annoying for staff). Tours depart hourly from 1pm and include tastings at the brewery's retail store. Alternatively, you can pay $13 and get a six-pack with your tour, or $23 with a 12-pack. Before you wobble off towards the horizon, check out the local art displays in the tasting area, which change on a monthly basis.

TORONTO MUSIC GARDEN

Map pp234-5

☎ 416-973-4000; www.harbourfrontcentre.com; 475 Queens Quay W; admission free; ☉ dawn-dusk; ☒ ☒; ⓡ 509, 510,

Delicately strung along the western Harbourfront, this sculpted garden was designed by Julie Moir in collaboration with famed cellist Yo-Yo Ma. It aims to express Bach's *Suite No 1 for Unaccompanied Cello* through landscape. An arc-shaped grove of conifers introduces a treble-clef-shaped path through a meadow and a grass-stepped amphitheatre where free concerts are held from June to September (usually 7pm Thursday and 4pm Sunday). Contact the Harbourfront Centre box office in the York Quay Centre for performance schedules. Free garden tours are run by volunteers during summer (usually 11am Wednesday and 5:30pm Thursday), or you can take a self-guided 70-minute musical audio tour available from the Marina Quay West office (Map pp234-5; ☎ 416-954-5596; 539 Queens Quay W; rental $5; ☉ 10am-8pm) on the pier immediately south of the garden.

FINANCIAL DISTRICT

Map pp234-5; Eating p93; Shopping p150; Sleeping p167

The area to the north of Union Station hustles night and day with fast-paced young executives, lost tourists trying to find the CN Tower and fresh-faced suburbanites waiting for the hockey to start at the Air Canada Centre. This is where Toronto gets vertical – towering monoliths scrape the sky and create wind tunnels at street level. Newspapers blow past countless hotdog stalls, city girls shimmy from doorway to doorway and smokers shiver in the shadows. There's a crop of great restaurants here, but apart from that there's not much going on. On weekends skateboarders roll through the streets.

Designed in part by the famous Montréal architects Ross and MacDonald, Union Station adopted a classical revival style to signify progress and prosperity. After a decade of WWI and bureaucratic construction delays, the station finally opened in 1927. Standing opposite in regal splendor is the Fairmont Royal York (p167), one of a slew of formidable, chateau-like hotels across Canada built by the Canadian Pacific Railroad to accommodate rail passengers.

From Union Station, walk the windy corridor of Bay St, Canada's premier Financial District where about $100 billion worth of stocks are bought and sold each year. The high-tech Toronto Stock Exchange relocated to King St's Exchange Tower during Toronto's boom years, not too long before the big market crash of 'Black Monday' on October 19, 1987. Dominating the district are the three stark, black towers of the Toronto-Dominion Centre, designed in the International Style and overseen by Ludwig Mies van der Rohe, the famed German modernist. When IM Pei, who also designed Paris's Pyramide du Louvre and the Rock & Roll Hall of Fame in Ohio, drew up plans for Commerce Court across the street, he gleefully made it one storey taller than the TD Centre.

Banks make up the bulk of the Financial District's other landmarks. Dignified Scotia Plaza has art deco bas reliefs and is the city's second-tallest skyscraper after First Canadian Place. Elegantly constructed from ribbed arches that make you feel like you're inside the belly of a whale, the glass atrium connecting the two towers of BC Place is the handiwork of Spanish architect Santiago Calatrava. Inside stands a restored 1845

Bank of Montréal building facade from Kingston, a town in eastern Ontario that once dreamed of being Canada's capital of commerce. Nearby the triangular towers of the **Royal Bank Plaza** echo Trump Tower in New York City. With 2500 ounces of 24-carat gold baked into the glass, they're a golden corporate bedazzlement in the sunlight.

Orientation

Union Station is the city centre's transport hub, standing on Front St just north of the Harbourfront. The Financial District gobbles up much of the downtown core, taking up over a dozen city blocks between the subway lines along Yonge St and University Ave. It stops short at Queen St, which defines the district's northern edge.

CLOUD FOREST CONSERVATORY

Map pp234-5

☎ 416-392-7288; btwn Richmond & Temperance Sts, east of Yonge St; admission free; ☾ 10am-3pm Mon-Fri; ☒ ☒ ; ☺ Queen

This unexpected downtown sanctuary is a steamy tropical greenhouse, crowded out with enormous jungle leaves, vines and palm trees. Built vertically as a 'modernist ruin,' it features exposed steel, a waterfall and a mural depicting the trades of construction workers. Information plaques answer the question 'What Are Rainforests?' for temperate Torontonians, distracting financial workers from their spreadsheets and sums for a few minutes. It's a great place to warm up during winter, but avoid the area after dark – the adjacent park attracts some pretty lewd types. This would no doubt annoy the original land owner Jesse Ketchum, a Methodist who prohibited 'nauseous or offensive behavior' around Temperance St in the 1840s.

DESIGN EXCHANGE Map pp234-5

DX; ☎ 416-363-6121; www.dx.org; 234 Bay St; admission free, surcharge for special exhibitions; ☾ 10am-5pm Mon-Fri, from noon Sat & Sun; ☺ King

The streamlined *moderne* Design Exchange building served as the original Toronto Stock Exchange from 1937, its grand opening pushing Toronto ahead of Montréal as Canada's financial centre. Check out the art deco stone friezes and the medallions on the stainless steel doors detailing

stern-faced communist pick-wielders and jack-hammer operators. Inside there's a gift shop and eye-catching temporary exhibits of contemporary and retro industrial design (everything from record players to kettles).

HOCKEY HALL OF FAME Map pp234-5

☎ 416-360-7765; www.hhof.com; BC Pl, 30 Yonge St, lower concourse; adult/child/concession $10/9/9; ☾ 10am-5pm Mon-Fri, 9:30am-6pm Sat, 10:30am-5pm Sun, to 6pm in summer; ☒ ☒ ; ☺ Union

Inside an ornate, gray stone rococo Bank of Montréal building (c 1885), this shrine to the great game gives hockey fans everything they could possibly want. Check out the collection of *Texas Chainsaw Massacre*-esque goalkeeping masks, attempt to stop Wayne Gretzky's virtual shot or have your photo taken with hockey's biggest prize – the hefty Stanley Cup (no trifling shield or pint-sized urn for these boys, oh no, no, no...). Even visitors unfamiliar with this superfast, ultraviolent sport will be impressed with the interactive multimedia exhibits and nostalgic hockey memorabilia, and might begin to comprehend Canada's passion for hockey.

TORONTO DOMINION GALLERY OF INUIT ART Map pp234-5

☎ 416-982-8473; Maritime Life Tower, 79 Wellington St W, ground fl & mezzanine; admission free; ☾ 8am-6pm Mon-Fri, 10am-4pm Sat & Sun; ☒ ; ☺ St Andrew

A fourth Toronto-Dominion Centre tower stands on the other side of Wellington St

---

TRANSPORTATION

Subway & Streetcar Union subway and streetcar station is adjacent to Union train station.

Walking The underground PATH system (p215) connects Union Station with many of the surrounding sights.

Car Parking lots and garages are plentiful, but expensive. Most charge at least $2.50 per hour, although early-bird specials (in before 7:30am) keep the daily maximum around $10 to $15. The municipal garage at 40 York St charges $2.50 per half-hour (daily maximum $17), but only $7 on evenings and weekends. Daily maximum rates are lower at the St Lawrence Garage at 2 Church St and other municipal lots along Lakeshore Blvd W, which are further away.

from the original trio of skyscrapers. In a corner of the lobby is an exceptional gallery of post WWII Aboriginal carvings and sculptures in stone and bone, worthy of display in any museum, and free for public viewing. A succession of glass cases displays otters, bears, eagles and carved Inuit figures in day-to-day scenes.

OLD YORK

Map pp234–5; Eating p95; Shopping p150; Sleeping p168

A few blocks east of Union Station along Front St, many of the city's oldest and best-preserved buildings come into view. Old York holds the keys to Toronto's past – don't miss it! There are plenty of pubs and decent eateries here too, so spend some time ogling the antiquities then retreat to a cozy booth somewhere.

Established by Captain John Simcoe in 1793, the historic town of York was bounded by Duke, Front, George and Berkeley Sts. Although a few of the street names have changed, this neighborhood still boasts the city's greatest concentration of historic sites dating from early colonial times. In 1834 York was officially engulfed by the newly established city of Toronto, but remained the social, political and economic centre, especially around St Lawrence Market (opposite).

Over the centuries, the district has maintained a weird mix of posh and run-down areas. The first parliament buildings of Upper Canada, which were burned to the

---

TRANSPORTATION

Subway Both Union and King subway stations are about a 500m walk from the old town of York.

Streetcar The 504 King streetcar runs along King St, stopping within a block or two of every sight. The 503 Kingston Rd streetcar line makes a useful loop onto Wellington St E, just east of Yonge St, but only runs during weekday morning and evening rush hours.

Walking Old York was a small town – walking is no problem.

Car Metered on-street parking is rarely available, except during the early morning and late evening. Fortunately, pay lots and garages abound. The municipal St Lawrence Garage at 2 Church St charges $1.50 per half-hour (daily maximum $8).

---

ground by American troops during the War of 1812, were built here, as were the homes of many a highbrow colonial citizen. But Old York was also the province's first red-light district, the festering source of cholera epidemics and the ignition point of the city's first great fire in 1849.

During the 1960s, when a shortsighted fit of urban renewal swept through North America, many of Old York's grand Victorian and Edwardian structures were torn down. Fortunately, a handful of fine buildings dodged the wrecking ball, including the Flatiron (Gooderham) Building (opposite), St Lawrence Hall (opposite), the Le Royal Meridien King Edward (p168) hotel, the Courthouse Market Grille (p96) and the buildings along Toronto St. Further east, some of the old warehouses still stand vacant, but the Distillery District (below) has been given the facelift to end all facelifts.

Orientation

Historically speaking, the old town of York comprised just 10 square blocks. But today the district extends east of Yonge St all the way to the Don River, and from Queen St south to the waterfront Esplanade.

DISTILLERY DISTRICT Map pp244-5

☎ 416-866-1177; www.thedistillerydistrict.com; 55 Mill St; admission free; ☉ 10am-6pm, later in summer; ⴴ ; ⬛ 503, 504

Emerging phoenix-like from the 1832 Gooderham and Worts distillery – at one time the largest distillery in the British Empire – this slick, 13-acre arts complex features Victorian industrial warehouses converted into soaring galleries, artists' studios, pricey design shops, coffeehouses, restaurants, the new Young Centre for Performing Arts (p130) and the Mill Street Brewery (p120). Wedding parties shoot photos against a backdrop of redbrick and cobblestone; clean-cut Mediterranean couples shop for leather lounge suites beneath charmingly decrepit gables and gantries. In summer expect live jazz, exhibitions and food-focused events.

ENOCH TURNER SCHOOLHOUSE

Map pp244-5

☎ 416-863-0010; www.enochturnerschoolhouse.ca; 106 Trinity St; admission free; ☉ 10am-5pm Mon-Fri; ⬛ 503, 504

Dating from 1848, this restored one-room classroom is where local kids are shown what the good ol' days were like. Wealthy brewer Enoch Turner opened it as Toronto's first free school so poor children could learn the three Rs. Gothic church-style windows emphasize the seriousness of it all. Visitors are only allowed inside when school tours aren't scheduled.

FLATIRON (GOODERHAM) BUILDING

Map pp234-5

49 Wellington St E; 🚇 **503, 504**
Originally the headquarters of the Gooderham family's distillery in the 1890s, the redbrick Flatiron is famous for its wacky triangular floorplan, dictated by the angle at which Old York's grid system intersects the waterfront. An exterior trompe l'oeil mural by Derek Besant mimics the restored 19th-century warehouses with their cast-iron facades across Front St. Inside are private offices, so unless you're in town for **Doors Open Toronto** (p34) you'll have to make do with an exterior viewing.

ST JAMES CATHEDRAL Map pp234-5

☎ **416-364-7865; www.stjamescathedral.on.ca; 65 Church St; admission free;** 🕙 **7:30am- 5:30pm Sun-Fri, 9am-3pm Sat, services daily, museum & archives 1-4pm Tue & Wed;** 🚇 **503, 504**
Erected after the Great Fire of 1849, this venerable Gothic Revival cathedral is graced by Tiffany stained glass, a grand organ, lovely gardens and bells pealing out from the tallest spire in Canada. You will find a small historical museum is tucked away in the parish house. Check the website for details on free **Music at Midday** and **Twilight Recitals** concerts.

ST LAWRENCE MARKET & HALL

Map pp234-5

☎ **416-392-7120; www.stlawrencemarket .com; South Market, 95 Front St E; admission free;** 🕙 **8am-6pm Tue-Thu, 8am-7pm Fri, 5am-5pm Sat;** ♿ 🚻 ; 🚇 **503, 504**
Old York's sensational market has been a neighborhood meeting place for over two centuries. The restored, high-trussed 1845 **South Market** (p95) building houses more than 50 specialty food stalls : cheese vendors, fishmongers, butchers, bakers and pasta makers with lots of action and yelling of prices in silly voices. Inside the old council chambers upstairs, the **St Lawrence Market Gallery** (☎ 416-392-7604; admission

free; 🕙 10am-4pm Wed-Fri, 9am-4pm Sat, noon-4pm Sun) is now the city's exhibition hall, with rotating displays of paintings, photographs, documents and historical relics. Hordes of school kids laugh it up, perhaps not as enthralled as you might be.

On the opposite side of Front St, the dull-looking **North Market** is redeemed by a Saturday **farmers' market** and a Sunday **antique market** (p150). After being sadly neglected, it was rebuilt around the time of Canada's 100th birthday in 1967. A few steps further north, the glorious **St Lawrence Hall** (1849), topped by a mansard roof and a working, copper-clad clock tower that can be seen for blocks, is considered one of Toronto's finest examples of Victorian classicism.

TORONTO'S FIRST POST OFFICE

Map pp244-5

☎ **416-865-1833; www.townofyork.com; 260 Adelaide St E; admission free;** 🕙 **9am-4pm Mon-Fri, 10am-4pm Sat & Sun;** ♿ ; 🚇 **503, 504**
Dating from the 1830s, the old post office is now a living museum. After you've written your letter with a quill and ink, seal it with wax and send it postmarked 'York-Toronto 1833' for a small fee. Famous folks like William Lyon Mackenzie and the Baldwins once rented postal boxes here. At the back is an old-fashioned reading room with historical displays and a model of Toronto c 1833. Self-guided tour pamphlets are available at the door. Look for the British and Canadian flags flying out front, just west of the Bank of Upper Canada building.

THEATRE BLOCK & ENTERTAINMENT DISTRICT

Map pp234–5; Eating p96; Shopping p150; Sleeping p168

West of the Financial District along King St W is Toronto's theatre district, called the **Theatre Block**. In the 19th century, the corner of King and Simcoe Sts was nicknamed 'Education, Legislation, Salvation and Damnation' – Upper Canada College, the Lieutenant Governor's house, **St Andrew's Presbyterian Church** (p59) and a bawdy tavern faced off on opposite street corners. Today, only salvation remains. The focal point of the Theatre Block is the beaux-arts **Royal Alexandra Theatre** (p129). Nicknamed the 'Royal Alex,' it was built by Toronto's youngest millionaire, Cawthra Mulock, in 1907. Fred Astaire, Humphrey Bogart and Edith Piaf cracked the boards before the stage lights started to flicker out. It was saved from demolition in the 1960s by entrepreneur 'Honest Ed' Mirvish. Mirvish restored the Royal Alex's velvet, brocade and crystal Edwardian luxury and bankrolled productions of *Hair* and *Godspell* that woke up the entire district. Two decades later Mirvish and his son David commissioned the **Princess of Wales Theatre** (p129) for *Miss Saigon*. Princess Di attended the opening in 1983. 929 square meters of Frank Stella murals adorn the walls.

The Theatre Block is part of the ever-expanding galaxy of the **Entertainment District** (aka Clubland, p62), where nightclubs and pizza stalls compete for drinkers' dollars. It's quiet here during the day, but at night the scene descends into hedonistic mayhem that makes Sodom and Gomorrah look like a kiddie's birthday party. Also here is the legendary **Second City** (p133), a comedy venue sharing its name with a sister club in Chicago. The common moniker wryly refers to how Chicago is seen to play second fiddle to New York City, as Toronto does to Montréal (in the proud eyes of Montrealers, that is).

Orientation

The Theatre Block occupies two blocks of King St W between John St and Simcoe St. Most of the Entertainment District's bars and clubs are further north, on a few square blocks of Adelaide St W and Richmond St W, between John St and Spadina Ave.

TRANSPORTATION

Subway St Patrick and Osgoode stations on the University line are a short walk east of the neighborhood.

Streetcar The 504 King streetcar runs through the Theatre Block. The 501 Queen and 510 Spadina lines border Clubland.

Walking This compact area is easily tackled on foot.

Car Avoid driving here, especially at nights and on weekends when private lots charge extortionate rates. Fees vary at the underground garage at Roy Thomson Hall, open 6am to 12:30am, excluding holidays.

---

401 RICHMOND Map pp234-5
☎ 416-595-5900; www.401richmond.net; 401 Richmond St W; admission free; ☽ most galleries 11am-5pm Tue-Sat; ☝ ; ☒ 510

Inside an early 20th-century lithographer's warehouse, restored in 1994, the 200,000 sq foot 401 Richmond bursts forth with 130 diverse contemporary art and design galleries displaying the heartfelt works of painters, architects, photographers, printmakers, sculptors and publishers. The original floorboards creak between the glass elevator, ground-floor café, leafy courtyard and rooftop garden.

ART AT 80 Map pp234-5
☎ 416-504-3690; 80 Spadina Ave; admission free; ☽ 8:30am-10pm Mon & Wed, to 7pm Tue, Thu & Fri, 10am-4pm Sat; ☒ 504, 510

Across the road from 401 Richmond, this small gallery complex houses six contemporary galleries – Albert White, Leo Kamen, Moore, Ryerson, Trias and Toronto Image Works – spread over four levels. Photography and painting are the focus here.

CANADA'S WALK OF FAME
Map pp234-5
☎ 416-367-9255; www.canadaswalkoffame.com; cnr King & Simcoe Sts; admission free; ☽ 24hr; ☝ ; ◉ St Andrew

True to its nickname 'Hollywood of the North,' Toronto has its own walk of fame, with a collection of subdued red granite stars set into the concrete sidewalk beside Roy Thomson Hall. You'll see a few names you recognize (and some you wish you didn't), though not many of those honored were actually born in Toronto. On the roll call are chameleon comedian Mike Meyers, high-pitched singer Alanis Morissette, brooding guitarist/songwriter Robbie Robertson, supermodel Linda Evangelista and self-deprecating grandmaster William Shatner.

CANADIAN BROADCASTING CENTRE
Map pp234-5
CBC; ☎ 416-205-3311; ww.cbc.ca; 250 Front St W; admission free; ☽ museum & theatre 9am-5pm Mon-Fri, noon-4pm Sat; ☝ ; ◉ Union, ☒ 504

Toronto's enormous Canadian Broadcasting Centre (CBC) is the headquarters for English-language public radio and TV programming across Canada. The French-language production facilities are in Montréal, which leaves the president, in a truly Canadian spirit of compromise, stranded in an executive office in Ottawa.

You can take a peek at the radio newsrooms anytime or attend a free noontime concert in the world-class **Glenn Gould Studio** (p134). For a dose of Canadian pop-culture nostalgia, visit the miniature-sized **CBC Museum** with its great collection of antique microphones, sound effects machines, tape recorders and puppets from kids' TV shows. Next door the **Graham Spry Theatre** screens classic TV show excerpts.

GOETHE-INSTITUT GALLERY
Map pp234-5

☎ 416-593-5257; www.goethe.de/toronto; 163 King St W; admission free; ⏰ 10am-5pm Mon-Thu, to 4pm Fri & Sat; ♿ ; 🚇 St Andrew

This esteemed German cultural centre presents temporary exhibitions of contemporary fine arts emphasizing the avant-garde from Europe and across Canada. German language courses, German film screenings with English subtitles ($5 per person), concerts and dramatic readings are also on the agenda. Check the online schedule.

ROY THOMSON HALL
Map pp234-5

☎ 416-872-4255; www.roythomson.com; 60 Simcoe St; shows $30-120; ⏰ box office 10am-6pm Mon-Fri, noon-5pm Sat, 2hr preshow Sun; ♿ ; 🚇 St Andrew

Looking like an inverted ballerina's tutu, this concert hall's controversial design has been called neo-expressionist, deconstructionist, and a whole lot of other rude words we can't repeat here. Inside it's another story, the superb acoustics more than good enough for the **Toronto Symphony Orchestra** (p134) and touring acts like Ladysmith Black Mambazo and Ravi Shankar.

ST ANDREW'S PRESBYTERIAN CHURCH Map pp234-5

☎ 416-593-5600; www.standrewstoronto.org; 75 Simcoe St; admission free; ⏰ 8am-3pm Mon-Sat, services Sun; 🚋 504

Built in 1876, rock-solid Romanesque Revival-style St Andrew's encourages stressed-out city workers to come inside

and 'find a quiet moment.' It's a peaceful place indeed, its tranquility only shattered when the multipiped Karl Wilhem Organ on the 2nd floor starts pumping. Pick up a self-guided tour pamphlet by the entrance.

QUEEN STREET & DUNDAS SQUARE
Map pp232-3; Eating p98; Shopping p151; Sleeping p169

The area between Queen Street and Dundas Square isn't geographically distinct, architecturally consistent or socially significant, but it does contain three of the city's best-known landmarks – City Hall, Dundas Square and the Eaton Centre – as well as Toronto's main hospitals and the **Metro Toronto Coach Terminal** (p212).

In 1869 historic Eaton's department store was established on Yonge St by enterprising Timothy Eaton. His dry-goods business succeeded with the 'revolutionary' sales policies of fixed prices, cash only and refunds for dissatisfied customers. Eaton's went bankrupt in 1999, but the gargantuan **Eaton Centre** (p153) shopping complex remains. You'd be forgiven for thinking it's still under construction – renovations are ongoing and no attention has been paid whatsoever to the exterior – but inside it's all sweetness and light, with trees and sculpted Canada geese by Michael Snow suspended from the ceiling.

Just northeast of here, **Dundas Square** aspires to be the city's civic heart, with an outdoor concert stage, big-screen media, snazzy red umbrellas and kids splashing around in fountains. Local radio station Q107 broadcasts classic rock from inside a ground-floor window across the street at the Hard Rock Café – unflappable DJs manage not to be distracted by the teenagers licking the glass. Further south on Yonge St, well-heeled patrons tend to mill around outside the restored **Canon Theatre** (p128) and venerable **Elgin & Winter Gardens Theatre Centre** (p129). This half-block has become Toronto's second theatre district, after the Theatre Block (p57).

To the east, the brave modern architecture of **City Hall** (p60) still irritates conservative locals, but it's actually an exquisite piece of architectural mastery.

Orientation

The Queen Street & Dundas Square area sits between Dundas St to the north and Queen St to the south, roughly around Dundas Square and the Eaton Centre on Yonge St. Both sit south of the main Yonge Street Strip and east of the Queen West shopping district.

CAMPBELL HOUSE Map pp232-3

☎ 416-597-0227; www.campbellhousemuseum.ca; 160 Queen St W; tour adult/child/concession/family $4.50/2.50/3/10; ☷ 9:30am-4:30pm Mon-Fri, plus noon-4pm Sat & Sun Jun-Sep; ⬚; ◉ Osgoode

This formal Georgian mansion dating from 1822 was one of the city's first brick buildings, belonging to Chief Justice William Campbell. It's been beautifully refurbished in 19th-century style by the Advocates' Society, which uses the premises as its clubhouse. Tours are run by friendly costumed guides. In 1972 the whole house was shifted here from its original location on Adelaide St, 1.5km away – a slow six-hour voyage.

CANADA LIFE BUILDING Map pp232-3

☎ 416-597-6981; www.canadalife.ca; 330 University Ave; admission free; ☷ 9am-5pm Mon-Fri; ◉ Osgoode

Push through the huge doors of the megalithic stone Canada Life building and front up to the lobby desk where you can collect a weather card that explains the mysteries of the 1950s beacon on top of the building. If it's flashing white, get ready for a big dump of snow.

TRANSPORTATION

Subway Queen and Dundas stations are on the Yonge subway line. A few blocks further west, Osgoode (at Queen St W) and St Patrick (at Dundas St W) are stops on the University line.

Streetcar 501 Queen and 505 Dundas streetcars roll through the area.

Walking Eaton Centre and City Hall are part of the underground PATH system.

Car The municipal garage at 25 Dundas St E charges $2 per half-hour (daily maximum $15). Parking at Nathan Phillips Sq or the municipal garage at 37 Queen St E costs $5 maximum after 6pm weekdays or before 6pm on weekends.

CHUM/CITYTV COMPLEX Map pp232-3

☎ 416-591-5757; www.chumlimited.com; 299 Queen St W; speakers cnr $1; ☷ 7am-11:30pm Mon-Fri, from noon Sat & Sun; ⬚ 501

Inside the historic industrial gothic Wellesley Building (1913), the progressive Citytv network films its foibles and broadcasts outtakes from their infamous Speakers Corner on the John St corner. Here, anyone can step inside the public video booth, drop a loonie ($1) in the slot, wait for the five-second countdown then record themselves saying or doing pretty much anything for two minutes. At the adjacent studios of MuchMusic (www.muchmusic.com), the Canadian version of MTV, pop stars dash inside from their limos as teen fans cheer à la Beatlemania. Above the east parking lot, a CityPulse news truck spins its wheels as it explodes out of the Citytv studio walls.

CHURCH OF THE HOLY TRINITY

Map pp232-3

☎ 416-598-4521; www.holytrinitytoronto.org; 10 Trinity Sq; admission free; ☷ 11am-3pm Mon-Fri, services 9am & 10:30am Sun, 12:15pm Wed; ◉ Dundas

On the west side of the Eaton Centre is the oasis-like Trinity Square, named after this welcoming Anglican church. When it opened in 1847, it was the first church in Toronto not to charge parishioners for pews, thanks to an anonymous English benefactress who was reportedly quite taken with the bishop. Today it's a cross between a house of worship, small concert venue (p134) and a community drop-in centre – everything an inner-city church should be. Don't miss the Christmas pageant if you're in town in December.

Also in the square is a labyrinth and Henry Scadding House (1862), which some believe is haunted by the benign ghost of the first rector. Unfortunately it's not open to the public, so you can't go inside and flush him out.

CITY HALL Map pp232-3

☎ 416-338-0338; www.toronto.ca; 100 Queen St W; admission free; ☷ 8:30am-4:30pm Mon-Fri; ⬚ ◉ Queen

Much-maligned City Hall was Toronto's bold leap of faith into architectural modernity. Its twin clamshell towers, flying

TORONTO FOR KIDS

Special events for children happen regularly throughout the year – two of the best are the **Milk International Children's Festival of the Arts** (p13) and the **Canadian National Exhibition** (p15). During summer it's easy (if a little expensive) to keep 'em occupied at **Ontario Place** (p52) or **Paramount Canada's Wonderland** (p79) amusement parks. In any season, the interactive exhibits at the **Ontario Science Centre** (p79) and **Royal Ontario Museum** (p66) are winners. For entertainment, drop by story time at the **Toronto Public Library – Lillian H Smith Branch** (p69) or catch a performance at the innovative **Lorraine Kimsa Theatre for Young People** (p129). The **Gardiner Museum of Ceramic Art** (p66) runs regular children's clay classes. Specialty stores include **Kidding Awound** (p155) and cozy **Parentbooks** (p157).

Outside in the sun, explore the **Harbourfront** (p50), **Toronto Islands** (p75), **The Beaches** (p74) or **High Park** (p77). Take them ice-skating in winter at the **Harbourfront Centre** or **Nathan Phillips Square** (p139). Little city slickers can get a taste of rural life at **Riverdale Farm** (p73), **Black Creek Pioneer Village** (p77) or the **Spadina Quay Wetlands & Waterfront Children's Garden** (p53). On a muggy summer's day, the fountains in **Dundas Square** (p59) will extinguish flaming four-year-olds in quick time.

See p138 for more outdoor activity ideas, p96 for kid-friendly restaurants and p198 for an overview of traveling with kids in Toronto.

saucer-like central structure, sexy ramps and funky '60s mosaics were completed in 1965 to Finnish architect Viljo Revell's award-winning design. An irritable Frank Lloyd Wright had called it a 'headmarker for a grave,' and in a macabre twist of fate, Revell died before construction was finished. When sculptor Henry Moore offered to sell *The Archer* (1966) to the city at a low price, the city council (unbelievably) refused, but later changed its mind. Collect a self-guided tour pamphlet at the info desk; don't miss the charmingly geeky 1:1250 Toronto scale model in the lobby.

Out the front is **Nathan Phillips Square**, a meeting place for skaters, demonstrators and office workers on their lunch breaks. In summer, look out for **Fresh Wednesdays** farmers' market (10am to 2:30pm), free concerts and special events. Canadian rock band the Barenaked Ladies were once banned from playing here but were later invited back in a conciliatory gesture. The fountain pool becomes a popular **ice skating rink** in winter (p139). Don't feel intimidated if you're a novice – you won't be alone. Immigrants from around the world are out there gingerly making strides (or slides) towards assimilation.

ELGIN & WINTER GARDEN THEATRE CENTRE Map pp232-3

☎ 416-314-2871; www.heritagefdn.on.ca; 189 Yonge St; tours adult/child $7/6; ☯ tours 5pm Thu & 11am Sat; ☺ Queen

A restored masterpiece, the Elgin & Winter Garden is the world's last operating double-decker theatre. Built in 1913, the stunning Winter Garden was built as the flagship for a vaudeville chain that never really took off, while the downstairs Elgin theatre was converted into a movie house in the 1920s.

The Ontario Heritage Foundation saved both theatres from demolition in 1981. During its $29-million restoration effort, bread dough was used to uncover original rose-garden frescoes, the Belgian company that made the original carpeting was contacted for fresh rugs, and the beautiful foliage hanging from the Winter Garden ceiling was replaced, leaf by painstaking leaf. Seats were trucked in from Chicago's infamous Biograph Theatre. Public tours run by passionate volunteers are worth every cent. See p33 for more history; p129 for box office information.

MACKENZIE HOUSE Map pp232-3

☎ 416-392-6915; www.toronto.ca/culture /mackenzie_house.htm; 82 Bond St; adult/child/ concession$4/2.50/2.75; ☯ noon-4pm Tue-Fri, to 5pm Sat & Sun, weekends only Jan-Apr; ☺ Dundas

Built in 1858, this brown brick rowhouse was owned by William Lyon Mackenzie, the city's first mayor and the leader of the failed Upper Canada Rebellion of 1837. Inside is a museum, a recreated printshop and a gallery featuring changing exhibitions. Check out the brass door knocker, presented to Mackenzie in 1859 after his return from exile in America. Handmade 'Mackenzie: Rebel with a Cause' T-shirts and reproductions of the 'ye olde' variety are sold in the gift shop.

ADVENTURES IN CLUBLAND

Toronto's 'Clubland' convenes around Richmond St W and Adelaide St W at John St, where dozens of nightclubs come to life after dark. Nondescript doorways creak open, thick-necked bouncers cordon off sidewalks and queues of scantily clad, shivering girls start to form. Hip-hop guys from the 905 suburbs drive hotted-up cars past the girls, hissing come-ons from wound-down windows. The air hangs thick with clearly defined gender roles and anticipation…

Later in the night, things get messy. Drunk girls stagger and wipe vomit from their hair, guys swing apocalyptic fists and hotdog-cart owners struggle to maintain order among the condiments. It's quite a scene.

Despite the human circus, there are some world-class clubs here, and if you can sidestep the flailing masses of underage boozers, you can catch some top-notch DJs. Clubs come and go with alarming frequency, falling into favor then disappearing just as fast, but do some research (p130) and you'll be able to cut the rug with a minimum of hassles.

MASSEY HALL Map pp232-3

☎ 416-872-4255; www.masseyhall.com; 178 Victoria St; shows $25-80; ☾ box office from noon on show days; ⓞ Queen

Landmark redbrick Massey Hall, festooned with fire escapes, was given to the city in 1894 by industrial baron Hart Massey. Orators, explorers and other famous faces (including Oscar Wilde, George Gershwin, Charlie Mingus and the Dalai Lama) have all appeared on its stage. The acoustics are superb, a fact not lost on occasional performers the Toronto Symphony Orchestra (p134).

OLD CITY HALL Map pp232-3

☎ 416-327-5614; www.toronto.ca/old_cityhall; 60 Queen St W; admission free; ☾ 8am-9pm Mon-Thu, to 5pm Fri, 8:30am-3pm Sat; ⓞ Queen

Across Bay St from City Hall is the Romanesque Old City Hall (1899), the definitive work of architect EJ Lennox, who also built Casa Loma (p68). Lennox was chastised for inscribing his name just below the eaves, tainting what was the largest municipal building in North America. Now housing legal courtrooms, the hall has a bell tower, interesting murals, grimacing gargoyles and an allegorical stained-glass window.

OSGOODE HALL Map pp232-3

☎ 416-947-3300; www.osgoodehall.com; 130 Queen St W; admission free; ☾ tours usually 1:15pm Mon-Fri Jul & Aug; ⓞ Osgoode

Built in phases through the Victorian era, this august classic (named after Ontario's first Chief Justice) became a showcase for elite colonials, many of whom were lawyers. Inside a grand staircase rises from a gorgeous tiled atrium to the Ontario Court of Appeal and the Great Library, with miles of books, twisting stairways and 12m-high vaulted ceilings. The peculiar wrought-iron 'cow gates' out front were put up to keep out wandering bovines, a common problem in the 1860s. Free tours are conducted by law students.

TEXTILE MUSEUM OF CANADA
Map pp232-3

☎ 416-599-5321; www.textilemuseum.ca; 55 Centre Ave; adult/concession/child/family $10/6/6/22, admission free 5-8pm Wed; ☾ 11am-5pm, to 8pm Wed, tours 2pm Sun; ⓖ; ⓞ St Patrick

Obscurely located at the bottom of a condo tower in an otherwise cultureless corner of town, this small museum's exhibits draw upon a permanent collection of 10,000 items from Latin America, Africa, Europe, Southeast Asia and India, as well as contemporary Canada. Workshops teach batiking, weaving, knitting and all manner of needle-stuff.

CHINATOWN & BALDWIN VILLAGE

Map pp232–3; Eating p99; Sleeping p170

Toronto's principal Chinatown is right in the city centre, milling around the junction of Spadina Ave and Dundas St W. The whole area looks more like Little Saigon or Bangkok every year, as Vietnamese and Southeast Asian immigrants continue to arrive. Like its counterparts around the world, Chinatown is a culturally immersive experience. Forget you're in the middle of North America and swim into a graphically overloaded sea of foot-reflexology practitioners, Canto-pop twang, $4 haircuts, cheap restaurants, lousy digitally accompanied buskers, people sucking on coconuts and traditional medical shops selling ginseng, shriveled squid and dried chili by the bucketful.

GOOD TIMES FOR FREE

Here's a quick rundown of things to do when your wallet is running on empty! See the City Calendar (p12) for free-for-all festivals and celebrations. Most architectural sights, cemeteries and cathedrals are also free, as are gardens, conservatories and parks. For more on outdoor activities, see p138.

Most Days

401 Richmond (p58; ☯ closed Mon & Sun)

Allan Gardens Conservatory (p73)

Arabesque Academy (p199) Free introductory bellydancing class.

CBC Museum (p54)

City Hall (p60; ☯ closed Sat & Sun)

Cloud Forest Conservatory (p54; ☯ closed Sat & Sun)

High Park (p77)

St Lawrence Market Gallery (p57)

Police Museum & Discovery Centre (p65)

Museum of Contemporary Canadian Art (p72)

Provincial Legislature (p69)

Redpath Sugar Museum (p53; ☯ closed Sat & Sun)

Riverdale Farm (p73)

Scarborough Bluffs (p79)

Spadina Quay Wetlands & Waterfront Children's Garden (p50)

Tengye Ling Tibetan Buddhist Temple (p143) Dharma talk and walking meditation.

Tommy Thompson Park (p74)

Toronto Dominion Gallery of Inuit Art (p55)

Toronto Music Garden (p54)

Toronto's First Post Office (p57)

University of Toronto Campus (p70)

Zen Buddhist Temple (p143) Free public meditation.

Wednesday

Art Gallery of Ontario (p64; ☯ 6-9pm)

Power Plant (p52; ☯ 5-8pm)

Textile Museum of Canada (opposite; ☯ 5-8pm)

Thursday

Bata Shoe Museum (p66; ☯ 5-8pm)

Friday

Gardiner Museum of Ceramic Art (p66; ☯ 4-9pm & all day 1st Fri of month)

Special Events & Exhibitions

Eric Arthur Gallery (p70)

Glenn Gould Studio (p134)

Heritage Toronto (p49)

Nuit Blanche (p15)

Osgoode Hall (opposite)

U of T Art Centre (p70)

TRANSPORTATION

Streetcar 510 Spadina streetcars run from Spadina subway south through Chinatown, while the 505 Dundas line cuts east-west. The 506 College or 501 Queen streetcars are within walking distance of Baldwin Village and Chinatown.

Subway Baldwin Village is 500m from St Patrick station.

Walking Tackling the area on foot is the best way to go.

Car Driving around Chinatown is a real drag, but if you have to, the municipal garage at 40 Larch St is the best value in town: $1 per half-hour; $6 daily maximum. Dragon City garage at 521 Dundas St W charges slightly more. Residential streets around Baldwin Village are either metered or restricted, but you might find space to park for an hour or two.

Another fabulous place for food is shady **Baldwin Village**, a short stroll north of the **Art Gallery of Ontario** (below). The village has Jewish roots, with a bohemian air instilled by counterculture US exiles who decamped here during the Vietnam War. Today, discovering Baldwin St feels like stumbling into a Greenwich Village Manhattan movie set, complete with Italian sidewalk cafés, maple trees and school kids on bicycles. Spillover from Chinatown keeps things multicultural, with Malaysian, South Asian and Chinese eateries joining in. During summer, restaurants fill to bursting with neighborhood denizens, first-date couples and a few lucky tourists.

Orientation

Chinatown was originally restricted to Dundas St W, but today Spadina Ave between College and Queen Sts is just as busy. Baldwin Village is one short block of Baldwin St between Beverly and McCaul Sts, about 300m east of Spadina Ave.

ART GALLERY OF ONTARIO
Map pp232-3

AGO; ☎ 416-979-6648; www.ago.net; 317 Dundas St W; adult/concession/child/family $8/5/5/20, admission free 6-9pm Wed, surcharge for special exhibitions; ❤ 10am-9pm Wed-Fri, to 5:30pm Sat & Sun; ♿; ◻ 505

The AGO's art collections are excellent and extensive – unless you have a lot of stam-

ina, you'll need more than one trip to take it all in. This dilemma may be solved by the gallery's ongoing renovations, overseen by famed architect **Frank Gehry** (p33), which continue to require the temporary closure of various wings and exhibits. When work finishes in summer 2008, the AGO's exhibited collection will grow from 33,000 to 43,000 pieces – a hefty expansion incorporating Australian Aboriginal art and a huge photographic collection. Existing highlights include rare Québécois religious statuary, First Nations and Inuit carvings, major Canadian works by Emily Carr and the Group of Seven, the Henry Moore sculpture pavilion, and a restored Georgian house called **The Grange**. Prices will almost certainly rise once renovations are complete. Check the website for updates.

While you're in the 'hood, note that **Cinematheque Ontario** (p117) screens movies at the AGO's Jackman Hall, which may escape renovation closures.

YONGE STREET STRIP & CHURCH-WELLESLEY VILLAGE

Map pp238–9; Eating p101; Shopping p154; Sleeping p170

Often called the 'longest road in the world,' **Yonge St** actually seems to be the start of the world's longest strip of porn theatres, exotic-dance venues and XXX lingerie boutiques. Once a humble oxcart trail, it roughly traces the route taken by First Nations tribes and colonial traders as they portaged their canoes north, avoiding the exposed waters of the Great Lakes. Turning a blind eye to the sleaze, you'll also find a few good record stores here, plus cheap eateries, bookstores, electronics shops and cavernous shoe stores.

If Toronto is the whole world in one city, then the **Church-Wellesley Village** is a whole world of queer culture unto itself. Often referred to simply as 'Church St' or the 'Gay Village,' Toronto's gay quarter features leafy streets of elegant brownstone terraces with rainbow flags flying proudly everywhere you look. Quality cafés, restaurants, bars and clubs keep the big-city energy flowing, while the social scene focuses squarely on the parade of well-groomed, mustachioed men cruising up and down the street. A focal point of the community is the **519 Community Centre** (p201) next to Cawthra Square Park, where community health vans dole out food to the homeless. The park itself is part gay beat, part junkie hangout, and contains a simple yet poignant **AIDS Memorial**.

Orientation

Although another interesting pocket of Yonge St shops crops up around the Eaton Centre and Dundas Square, the main Yonge Street Strip falls between College and Bloor Sts. One long block to the east is Church St, where the Gay Village has its epicentre at the intersection of Church and Wellesley Sts.

MAPLE LEAF GARDENS Map pp238-9
60 Carlton St; ⊖ **College**
The hallowed Maple Leaf Gardens hockey arena was built in an astoundingly quick five months during The Depression, and was home to the **Toronto Maple Leafs** (p142) for over half a century. The Leafs lost their first game to the Chicago Blackhawks in 1931, but went on to win 13 Stanley Cups and play countless sold-out seasons before relocating to the **Air Canada Centre** (p50) in 1999. Over the years, Elvis Presley, Frank Sinatra and the Beatles all belted out tunes at the Gardens.

Rumors that this much-loved piece of city history was going to be demolished were only partly true. The Gardens were bought by grocery chain Loblaws in 2004, with a shopping complex redevelopment scheduled to begin in late 2007. Some of

---

TRANSPORTATION

Subway Useful stops along the Yonge St line are College, Wellesley and Bloor-Yonge.

Streetcar The 506 College (westbound) and 506 Carlton (eastbound) streetcars run along the area's southern edge, but aren't as handy as the subway.

Walking Sure, it's the longest street in the world, but you're not walking all of it! Get to steppin' folks.

Car On-street parking is either metered or severely restricted. You may find a free spot for an hour or two on residential side streets east of Yonge St. The municipal lot at 15 Wellesley St E charges $2 per half-hour (daily maximum $13).

---

the original art deco facade will remain, and a hockey souvenir shop is likely to open inside.

POLICE MUSEUM & DISCOVERY CENTRE Map pp238-9
☎ 416-808-7020; www.torontopolice.on.ca /museum; 40 College St; admission free; ⏱ 8:30am-4pm Mon-Fri; ⏳ ♿; ⊖ College;
Inside the monumental Toronto Police HQ, this nonprofit museum has a small but diverting collection of equipment, uniforms, vehicles and crime-related paraphernalia from 1834 to the present day. Aspiring CSIs can learn how to trace a murderer's DNA from a cigarette butt, while an antique (if a little morbid) billboard clocks traffic deaths in Toronto and A/V exhibits convey the evils of narcotics. Displays attempting to humanize parking inspectors are less effective.

BLOOR-YORKVILLE

Map pp238–9; Eating p102; Shopping p155; Sleeping p171
The colonial village of **Yorkville** was founded by brewer Joseph Bloor and Sheriff William Jarvis in the 1830s. In the 1960s it became Toronto's version of Greenwich Village or Haight-Ashbury, full of penny-pinching rooming houses, Vietnam draft-dodgers and smoky cafés where Joni Mitchell and Neil Young started a singer/songwriter revolution. These days Yorkville has become a playground for Toronto's rich and glamorous, dolled up with expensive boutiques, up-market salons, art galleries, glitzy nightspots and exclusive restaurants. Modern Yorkville is all about being seen: cashed-up ladies parade ridiculously shaven poodles along sidewalks (see It's A Dog's Life p17), while skinny models flit between passing Ferraris, glancing up at billboards advertising 'Plastic Surgery For All!' Well-preserved Victorian houses and the atmospheric **Old York Lane** provide glimpses of yesteryear, as does the 650-ton Precambrian rock sitting in the park off Cumberland St.

Present-day **Bloor St** is a gold-card shopper's paradise with high-end international chains like Chanel, Tiffany's and MAC, plus Canada's own upscale Holt Renfrew department store. Also stationed here are several embassies and some of Toronto's top museums.

SPACE CADETS

On any given Yonge St corner in any given season, you're likely to bump into at least one clean-cut young Air Cadet attempting to sell a tray full of red charity buttons. Clad in polished black shoes, starchy blue uniforms and nifty little caps, these guys suffer an endless barrage of rejection as locals ignore them as a matter of course. Naïve and a little pathetic, perhaps, but you'll never see them crack under the weight of their social penance, and they remain achingly polite at all times. You don't have to buy a button, but give them a sympathetic smile – if nothing else, you've got to admire their resilience.

Orientation

Yorkville officially stretches from Yonge St west to Avenue Rd, just north of Bloor St. In practice, the neighborhood extends a few blocks further west along Bloor St W into the Annex. The neighborhood's northern edge is Davenport Rd.

BATA SHOE MUSEUM Map pp238-9

☎ 416-979-7799; www.batashoemuseum.ca; 327 Bloor St W; adult/child/concession/family $8/4/6/20, free 5-8pm Thu; ☽ 10am-5pm Tue, Wed, Fri & Sat, to 8pm Thu, noon-5pm Sun; ⛛ ⛾; ⊙ St George

It's important in life to be well shod, a stance this museum obsesses over. Designed by famed architect **Raymond Moriyama** (p33) to resemble a stylized shoebox, the museum displays over 10,000 'pedi-artifacts' from around the globe, collated by Sonja Bata of Canada's famous Bata shoe family. Peruse some 19th-century French chestnut-crushing clogs, Aboriginal Canadian polar boots or famous modern pairs worn by Elton John, Indira Gandhi and Pablo Picasso. Permanent exhibits cover the evolution of shoemaking, as well as human footwear, both gruesome or gorgeous, with a focus on how shoes have signified social status throughout human history. Rotating exhibitions on special topics are thoughtfully curated.

FIREHALL NO 10 Map pp238-9

22 Yorkville Ave; ⊙ Bay

Yorkville's historic 19th-century fire hall (1876) is still putting out fires. Beneath its impressive turret, a coat-of-arms relocated from the old town hall depicts the occupations of elected councilors: brewer, brick-maker, carpenter, blacksmith and butcher, united under a Canadian beaver. It's not open to the public, but the firemen don't mind if you stare at them from the street.

GARDINER MUSEUM OF CERAMIC ART Map pp238-9

☎ 416-586-8080; www.gardinermuseum.on.ca; 111 Queen's Park; adult/child/student/senior $12/free/6/8, admission free 4-9pm Fri & all day 1st Fri of month; ☽ 10am-6pm, to 9pm Fri; ⛛ ⛾; ⊙ Museum

Opposite the Royal Ontario Museum, this compact, recently renovated museum was founded by philanthropists who were passionate collectors themselves. The external esthetic is late-20th-century modern, but inside the collections cover several millennia. Spread over three floors, various rooms focus on 17th- and 18th-century English tavern ware, Italian Renaissance majolica, ancient American earthenware and blue-and-white Chinese porcelain designed for export to European markets. Special exhibits rotate regularly, and there's a rigorous program of activities, talks, tours, demonstrations and screenings on offer – check the website for schedules. If you're feeling peckish, there's a handy restaurant upstairs.

JAPAN FOUNDATION Map pp238-9

☎ 416-966-1600; www.japanfoundationcanada .org; 131 Bloor St W, 2nd fl; admission usually free; ☽ 11:30am-4:30pm Mon-Wed & Fri, 2-7pm Thu, 1-5pm 1st Sat of month; ⊙ Bay

Jostling for respect amongst the Bloor St embassies, this Japanese cultural centre offers temporary multimedia exhibitions, special events (like dramatic readings of medieval Japanese comedies and film retrospectives) and artistically inspired rest rooms that deserve design awards. The library drifts between arts, literature, history, geography and Manga. Reservations required for some events.

ROYAL ONTARIO MUSEUM

Map pp238-9

ROM; ☎ 416-586-8000; www.rom.on.ca; 100 Queen's Park; adult/child/concession $18/12/15, surcharge for special exhibitions; ☽ 10am-6pm Sat-Thu, to 9:30pm Fri; ⛛ ⛾; ⊙ Museum

The multidisciplinary ROM was already Canada's biggest natural history museum, even before embarking upon the 'Renaissance ROM' building project due for completion in late 2007. The main building work involves a magnificent explosion of architectural crystals on Bloor St, housing an array of new galleries. The museum remains open, but certain galleries and wings are closed during construction. To avoid disappointment, check the website for updates.

ROM's collections bounce between natural science, ancient civilization and art exhibits. The Chinese temple sculptures, Gallery of Korean Art and costumery and textile collections are some of the best in the world. Kids file out of yellow school buses chugging by the sidewalk and rush to the dinosaur rooms, Egyptian mummies and Jamaican bat cave replica. Don't miss the cedar crest poles carved by First Nations tribes in British Columbia; the largest pole (85m) was shipped from the West Coast by train, then lowered through the museum roof, leaving only centimeters to spare. The on-site Institute of Contemporary Culture explores current issues through art, architecture, lectures and moving image. There are free museum tours daily – call or check the website for times.

TORONTO HELICONIAN CLUB
Map pp238–9

☎ 416-922-3618; www.heliconianclub.org; 35 Hazelton Ave; admission free; ☻ 9am-4pm Mon-Fri; ◉ Bay

Nudged between art galleries and salons on Hazelton Ave, the former Olivet Congregational Church (1875) is constructed in 'Carpenter Gothic' style – boards, battens and intricate trim with a carved rose window and wooden spire. The hall was taken over in 1923 by the Heliconian Club, an association for women in the arts that hosts exhibitions, book launches and arts functions.

TORONTO REFERENCE LIBRARY
Map pp238-9

☎ 416-395-5577; www.torontopubliclibrary .ca; 789 Yonge St; admission free; ☻ 10am-8pm Mon-Thu, to 5pm Fri & Sat, 1:30-5pm Sun; ♿ ; ◉ Bloor-Yonge

More cultural centre than somber reading room, this snappy modern space was designed by architect Raymond Moriyama (p33). Among millions of books, the library runs writers' workshops, storytelling sessions, film studies, drawing classes, open-mic 'face-offs' and 'How to do graffiti' classes. Oh, and there are some somber reading rooms too.

YORKVILLE LIBRARY Map pp238-9

☎ 416-395-5505; www.torontopubliclibrary.ca; 34 Yorkville Ave; admission free; ☻ 10am-6pm Mon, Wed & Fri, to 8:30pm Tue & Thu, 9am-5pm Sat; ◉ Bloor-Yonge

One of 99 library branches around town, this one is 100 years old – the oldest, and definitely the best looking. A sandstone Palladian facade leads into a lofty lemon-and-white interior housing many shelves, a theatre, gay and lesbian resource centre, 130 magazine titles and small gallery at the back exhibiting local artists' work.

UNIVERSITY OF TORONTO & THE ANNEX
Maps pp238–9 & pp242–3; Eating p104; Shopping p156; Sleeping p172

Founded in 1827, the prestigious **University of Toronto**, or **U of T** for short, is Canada's largest university, with around 65,000 full-time students, over 10,000 faculty and staff members and a whopping annual budget of a billion bucks. A wander through the central St George campus quadrangles – calm, composed and venerable – will make even the most hardcore of Animal House frat slobs pull themselves into line.

U of T has long been a wellspring of Canadian literature and the arts, counting authors

---

TRANSPORTATION

Subway Convenient stations include Bloor-Yonge, St George and Museum. Bay station has a confusing number of entrances, so read the exit signs carefully before emerging to save yourself some walking, especially in winter.

Walking As per almost everywhere else in T.O., walking here is the way to go.

Car On-street parking is metered or restricted. Spaces are rarely available, except maybe on Scollard St. The municipal garage at 9 Bedford Rd charges $1.50 per half-hour (daily maximum $12), cheaper than the 125 Yorkville Ave lot.

Margaret Atwood and Michael Ondaatje and filmmakers David Cronenberg and Atom Egoyan among its alumni. Meanwhile, back in the lab, Dr Charles Herbert Best and Sir Frederick Banting discovered insulin here in 1921. They received a Nobel Prize for their efforts, and the university has been endlessly bragging about it ever since.

West and north of U of T is **The Annex**, a residential neighborhood that assumed the mantle of Toronto's artistic epicentre in the '70s and '80s after the Yorkville folk scene had played itself out. These days the streets run rich with students, learned professors, pubs, organic grocery stores, global-minded eateries, pool halls, futon stores, sushi bars, second-hand CD shops and spiritual venues like **Trinity-St Paul's United Church** (p134) and the **Tengye Ling Tibetan Buddhist Temple** (p143). Orbiting The Annex like satellite moons are eclectic and ethnic communities like **Markham Village** (right), **Koreatown**, **Chinatown** (p62), **Kensington Market** (p70) and **Little Italy** (p70), all within easy walking distance.

Orientation

U of T's principal St George campus is on University Ave north of College St, continuing north to Bloor St W and east to Queen's Park and the Provincial Legislature buildings. West of Spadina Ave, Bloor St W is the main drag of The Annex, although Harbord St also has a few restaurants and shops. The Annex is bounded by Dupont St to the north and Bathurst St to the west. Markham Village is a short block of Markham St, south of Bloor St W. Koreatown begins west of Bathurst St, stretching west to Christie St.

CASA LOMA Map p231

☎ 416-923-1171; www.casaloma.org; 1 Austin Tce; adult/child/concession $16/8.75/10; ⏰ 9:30am-5pm, last entry 4pm; ♿ ☗ ; Ⓜ Dupont

Literally the 'House on a Hill,' this mock medieval castle towers above The Annex on a cliff that was once the shoreline of the glacial Lake Iroquois, from which Lake Ontario derived. Climb the 27m **Baldwin Steps** up the slope from Spadina Ave, north of Davenport Rd, past flowering gardens and benches.

The eccentric 98-room mansion – a crass architectural orgasm of castellations, chimneys, flagpoles, turrets and Rapunzel balconies – was built between 1911 and 1914 for Sir Henry Pellat, a wealthy financier

TRANSPORTATION

Subway Spadina and Bathurst stations are handy to U of T, while the Bloor-Danforth line parallels Bloor St W.

Streetcar The subway connects to the 510 Spadina and 511 Bathurst streetcars, while the 506 College streetcar runs along the south side of campus.

Walking Walking around campus is the way to go, but Bloor St W is a *loooong* street – take the subway.

Car Metered on-street parking is rare. Parking on residential side streets is usually free, but strict time limits apply. Private lots on Spadina Ave north of Bloor St charge around $9 per day. The municipal parking lot at 465 Huron St charges $1.50 per half-hour (daily maximum $10).

who made bags of cash from his exclusive contract to provide Toronto with electricity. He later lost everything in land speculation, the resultant foreclosure forcing Hank and his wife to move out. The castle briefly reopened as a luxury hotel, but its big-band nightclub attracted more patrons than the hotel ever did, and it too failed.

During the Depression, the charitable Kiwanis organization bought the castle and has operated it as a tourist site ever since. Self-guided audio tours (available in eight languages) lead you through the sumptuous interior. The conservatory where the Pellats entertained is lit by an Italian chandelier with electrical bunches of grapes. Rugs feature the same patterns as those at Windsor castle. The original kitchen had ovens big enough to cook an ox, and secret panels and tunnels abound. The stables were used by the Canadian government for secret WWII research into anti-U-boat technology.

MARKHAM VILLAGE Map pp242-3

Markham St, south of Bloor St W; Ⓜ Bathurst

Not to be confused with the town of Markham north of Toronto, this downtown enclave entails a couple of blocks of classy shops, bookstores, eateries and galleries along **Markham St**. Nearby on the corner of Bloor and Bathurst Sts, **Honest Ed's** (p157) is a gaudy discount-shopping emporium owned by theatre impresario Ed Mirvish. You might think you've teleported down to Las Vegas as giant multiglobe signs flash corny messages like 'Don't just stand there, buy something!' and 'Honest Ed's a nut, but look at the cashew save!' Comedy gold... The queues before opening time have to be seen to be believed.

NATIVE CANADIAN CENTRE OF TORONTO Map pp242-3

☎ 416-964-9087; www.ncct.on.ca, www.firststory .ca; 16 Spadina Rd; admission free; ⌚ 9am-8pm Mon-Thu, to 6pm Fri, noon-4pm Sat; ◉ Spadina

As well as managing the onsite Cedar Basket gift shop, this community centre hosts Thursday night drum socials, seasonal powwows and elders' cultural events that promote harmony and conversation between tribal members and non-First Nations peoples. You can also drop by the Toronto Native Community History Project, or ask about their occasional 'Great Indian Bus Tours' of Toronto which give you a better understanding of the area's Aboriginal history (p39).

PROVINCIAL LEGISLATURE

Map pp238-9

☎ 416-325-7500; www.ontla.on.ca; Queen's Park, north of College St; admission free; ⌚ tours 10am-4pm Mon-Fri, also 9am-4pm Sat & Sun Jun-Aug, legislature usually in session Mon-Thu Mar-Jun & Sep-Dec; ♿ ; ◉ Queen's Park

The seat of Ontario's Provincial Legislature resides in a fabulously ornate 1893 sandstone building in Queen's Park. Hospital employees lunch on the lawns as a few stray demonstrators write up sandwich boards and picket the front steps. Formidable oils of early colonials like Simcoe, Brock and Wolfe hang in the lobby, alongside Ontario's first parliamentary mace. For some homegrown entertainment, head for the visitors' gallery when the adversarial legislative assembly is in session. Viewing is free, but security regulations are in full force. You can't write, read or applaud as the honorable members

heatedly debate such pressing issues as ski-doo safety. Free tours depart from the information desk – call or check the website for exact times, which are subject to change.

SPADINA MUSEUM Map p231

☎ 416-392-6910; www.toronto.ca/culture /spadina; 285 Spadina Rd; adult/child/concession $6/4/5, grounds admission free; ⌚ noon-4pm Tue-Fri, to 5pm Sat & Sun, grounds 9am-4pm Mon-Fri, noon-5pm Sat & Sun; ◉ Dupont

More low-key than neighboring Casa Loma (opposite), this gracious mansion was built in 1866 as a country estate for financier James Austin and his family. Cream-painted brickwork is complimented by gloriously ornate wrought-iron portico and blue timber shutters. Lit by Victorian gaslights, the interior contains three generations of furnishings, art and fabrics. The working kitchen hosts seasonal cooking demonstrations by costumed workers, while Edwardian Teas ($20 per person; ⌚ most Sundays; call for bookings), strawberry festivals and summer concerts happen in the apple orchard. If you're not really a history buff, the beautiful gardens are perfect for a stroll or a sunny snooze.

TORONTO PUBLIC LIBRARY – LILLIAN H SMITH BRANCH Map pp238-9

☎ 416-393-7746; www.torontopubliclibrary.ca; 239 College St; admission free; ⌚ 10am-8:30pm Mon-Thu, 10am-6pm Fri, 9am-5pm Sat, also 1:30-5pm Sun Sep-Jun; ♿ ; 🚊 506, 510

Architecturally speaking, this children's library is worth a peek for its fairy-tale interior and bronze griffins flanking the front door. Special collections archive precious picture books, sci-fi novels, original artwork and manuscripts, poetry, letters and early movable (pop-up) books. Storytime and puppet shows are free.

COLLEGE JUST AIN'T WHAT IT USED TO BE

You go to university to expand your horizons, challenge your preconceptions, engage in rigorous political and social debate, read poetry, smoke pot and get laid, right? Not anymore you don't. In what seems to be a national trend, today's U of T students tend to be a conservative bunch, drinking more Red Bull than beer and paying big bucks to study here. Politically indignant? Forget about it! Voting in Canada isn't compulsory, and in the 2006 federal elections, student voter turnout bottomed out somewhere south of 20%. It seems students no longer quest for social justice, preferring to concentrate on how they're going to earn a crust after they graduate. My how things have changed since the heady days of protest, incense and acoustic ballads in the '60s Yorkville coffeehouses.

UNIVERSITY OF TORONTO –
ST GEORGE CAMPUS Map pp238-9

☎ 416-978-5000; www.utoronto.ca; Nona Macdonald Visitors Centre, 25 King's College Circle;
admission free; ⏰ 1hr campus tours 11am & 2pm
Mon-Fri, 11am Sat & Sun; ♿; Ⓜ Queens Park,
Museum, 🚋 506, 510

Campus life rotates around the grassy/
muddy expanse of **King's College Circle**, where
students study on blankets, kick soccer
balls around and dream of graduation day
in domed **Convocation Hall**. Dating from 1919,
sociable **Hart House** (☎ 416-978-2452; www
.harthouse.utoronto.ca; 7 Hart House Circle;
⏰ 6:45am-midnight) is an all-purpose art
gallery, music performance space, theatre,
student lounge and café. **Soldiers' Tower** next
door is a memorial to students who lost
their lives during WWI and WWII ('Vic College Rules!' graffiti is a little insensitive).

The nearby Romanesque Revival building
houses the **U of T Art Centre** (☎ 416-978-1838;
www.utoronto.ca/artcentre; 15 King's College
Circle; adult/student $5/3; ⏰ noon-5pm Tue-
Fri, to 4pm Sat), a contemporary art gallery
for Canadian and world cultures.

If you're architecturally bent or have
an inclination for urban planning, check
out the **Eric Arthur Gallery** (☎ 416-978-5038;
www.ald.utoronto.ca; 230 College St, 2nd
fl; admission free; ⏰ 9am-5pm Mon-Fri,
noon-5pm Sat), curated by the Faculty of
Landscape, Architecture and Design.

The most famous U of T college is the
ultratraditional **Trinity College** (☎ 416-978-
2651; www.trinity.toronto.edu; 6 Hoskin
Ave), where entering collegians are anach-
ronistically required to wear academic robes
to meals. It's worth looking around the
traditional quadrangle and the **Anglican Chapel**,
which was designed by Sir Gilbert Scott, the
same man responsible for Britain's ubiqui-
tous red telephone booths. Pick up a self-
guided tour pamphlet from the rack near the
door. The leafy **Philosopher's Walk** leads north
along the east side of Trinity College towards
the stone-and-iron **Alexandra Gates** on Bloor St
W, just east of the **Royal Conservatory of Music**.

Free university walking tours of the
historic St George campus visit these sights
and more. Student tour guides shed light
on the haunted stonemasons love triangle
at the neo-Romanesque **University College**, and
point out how the campus' old cannons aim
toward the **Provincial Legislature** (p69) a stone's
throw (or one good shot) east of campus.

KENSINGTON MARKET & LITTLE ITALY

Map pp240–1; Eating p105; Shopping p158; Sleeping
p174

Tattered around the edges, elegantly wasted
Kensington Market is multicultural Toronto at
its most authentic. Jewish merchants arrived here in the early 1900s from rural
Orthodox communities in Eastern Europe
and Russia. After WWII, immigrants from
Hungary, Italy, Portugal and Ukraine rolled
into the 'hood. In the 1970s waves of Chinese arrived, followed by Latin Americans,
East and West Indians, Koreans, Vietnamese, Malays and Thais.

Predictably, eating here is an absolute
joy. Shopping here is also a blast; local
specialties including fresh produce, baked
goods, vintage duds and discount clothing. Wander through on a busy Saturday
morning, when the open-air vendors crowd
the sidewalks and shops throw their doors
open to the day. Army surplus jackets, retro
lounge-pants, imported cheeses, sticky Na-
naimo bars – you'll find them all here.

Lining the underbelly of Kensington Market is a seamy bohemian element. The streets
are full of artists, urban hippies, punks, pot-
heads, junkies, dealers, bikers, goths, musicians and anarchists. Shady characters on
bicycles whisper their drug menus to you
as they slide slowly past; hooch and Hendrix
waft through the air. Graffiti says, 'Resist-
ance is Fertile!'; T-shirts decry, 'FUCK WAR.'
The streets simmer with a mildly menacing,
hung-over vibe, but it's rarely unsafe.

TRANSPORTATION

Subway Spadina station is close to Kensington
Market.

Streetcar The 506 College and 510 Spadina lines
border the Kensington Market area, the 506
continuing through to Little Italy.

Walking By far the best way to explore both areas
is on foot.

Car On-street parking in both areas is metered;
spaces are rarely available. The municipal garage at
20 St Andrews St in Kensington Market charges $1
per half-hour (daily maximum $6). You'll have more
of a chance finding a park in Little Italy the further
west you go.

Further along College St, **Little Italy** is an established trendsetting strip of outdoor cafés, hip bars and stylish restaurants that are almost always changing hands – the affluent clientele is notoriously fickle. The further west you go, the more traditional things become, with aromatic bakeries, sidewalk *gelaterias* and fine *ristoranti*. There are no 'sights' here as such – the attraction here is the intangible quality of life Italians manage to conjure up wherever they go. There's another Italian area north of downtown called **Corso Italia** on St Clair Ave W, west of Dufferin St. You'll find Italian cinemas, espresso cafés and pool halls. When Italy won the 2006 soccer World Cup, the place went berserk.

Also nearby is **Portugal Village**. Many of the houses here are decorated with traditional painted ceramic tiles, and the bakeries, fish shops and markets are enticing. The old guys inside the sports bars don't appear to have moved much since the day they arrived from the old country.

Orientation

Kensington Market's shops line a few narrow streets west of Spadina Ave, bounded by College St on the north and Dundas St W on the south side, where the neighborhood merges into Chinatown. The main drags are Baldwin St, Augusta Ave and Kensington Ave, the last of which has the majority of vintage clothing shops. Little Italy follows College St west from Bathurst St, all the way to Ossington Ave. Portugal Village is south of College St and north of Queen St, running along Dundas St W all the way to Dufferin St.

ANSHEI MINSK SYNAGOGUE

Map pp240-1

☎ 416-595-5723; www.theminsk.com; 10 St Andrew St; admission free; ⏱ daily prayer 7:30am, kosher dinner 7:30pm Fri; ⓢ Spadina, 🚃 510

This 1930 Russian Romanesque masterpiece will once again be a real gem after restoration work is complete. Sadly, the synagogue was vandalized by arson in early 2002, when thousands of holy books were damaged. Restoration is ongoing, but you may be able to sneak a peek inside if the doors are unlocked. Orthodox Jewish services are held daily, while shared Friday-night kosher meals attract everyone from long-time market stalwarts to travelers and U of T students.

QUEEN WEST & WEST QUEEN WEST

Map pp240–1; Eating p107; Shopping p159; Sleeping p175

Although Queen West and its extension, West Queen West, may not have many dedicated sights to speak of, they effect a siren's call nonetheless. This is where the wild things are, Toronto's funkiest 'hoods – shop avariciously, dine deliciously and rock into the wee small hours.

Queen West started to emerge from its blue-collar background in the early 1990s, gradually shedding its shaky reputation as artists moved in followed by more moneyed residents. These days it's almost mainstream, with big-name coffee and fashion chains setting up shop next to the grungy bars and tattoo parlors. It's not entirely gentrified though (throw a quarter in any direction and you'll hit a homeless person in the head), and it's still a really funky neighborhood. If you like your 'alternative' delivered in a manageable package, this is the place for you.

Further west is the similar but much edgier **West Queen West** district. Based around Toronto's old garment district, this is a Toronto's version of NYC's SoHo, although nowhere near as affluent. Driven ever westward from Queen West, impecunious artists have retreated here, spawning a swathe of creative, upstart restaurants, hip boutiques, industrial design shops, cool bars and galleries. What really put West Queen West on the map was

TRANSPORTATION

Subway Osgoode station is just to the east of Queen West.

Streetcar The 501 Queen streetcar runs all the way along Queen St through both districts.

Walking Explore both areas on foot, but take the streetcar if you're traversing Queen St from end to end.

Car On-street parking in both areas is metered. Spaces are rare, but become more likely the further west you drive. In Queen West the private lot on the corner of Portland St charges $3 per half-hour (daily maximum $8). In West Queen West the municipal lot at 1119 Queen St W charges $1 per half-hour (daily maximum $5).

the renovation of the **Drake Hotel** (p175) after 2001. It's something of a bohemian beacon for the district, though it's stealthily aligning itself with a more upmarket clientele. Unimpressed, freshly tongue-pierced punks struggle with their 's' sounds and sip beers at the **Gladstone Hotel** (p119) down the street.

Orientation

Yeah, we know, it's confusing. Where does Queen West end and West Queen West begin? Queen West can be defined as Queen St W west of Spadina Ave as far east as Strachan Ave and Trinity Belwoods Park. West Queen West is west of here, as far as Landsdowne Ave.

MUSEUM OF CONTEMPORARY CANADIAN ART Map pp240-1

MOCCA; ☎ 416-395-0067; www.mocca.toronto
.on.ca; 952 Queen St W; admission free; ⏰ 11-6pm
Tue-Sun; ♿ ; 🚋 501

The new MOCCA, recently relocated from far northern Yonge St, is the city's only museum mandated to collect and promote works by living Canadian visual artists. It says a lot about West Queen West's consolidation as an arts and design strip that the museum chose this district for its new facility. The permanent holdings only number about 400 works, curated since 1985, but award-winning exhibitions focus on new artists from Nova Scotia to British Columbia.

EAST TORONTO

Map pp244–5; Eating p109; Shopping p162; Sleeping p175

The district east of Parliament St to the Don River was settled by Irish immigrants fleeing the potato famine of 1841. It became known as **Cabbagetown** because the area's sandy soil proved ideal for growing cabbages. These days proud residents fly green-and-white Cabbagetown flags from their windows, similar to the Canadian flag but with a fat green cabbage instead of a maple leaf. Since the 1970s the gentrification broom has swept through, restoring Cabbagetown's Victorian houses. See the Cabbagetown & Rosedale Architecture Walk, p82.

To the north of Cabbagetown is **Rosedale**, arguably the city's wealthiest suburb, first settled by Sheriff William Jarvis who built

THE BLOOR STREET VIADUCT

In his 1987 novel *In The Skin Of A Lion*, Michael Ondaatje describes the torturous man-versus-steel construction of Toronto's **Bloor Street Viaduct** (Map pp244–5). Completed in 1918, the 490m bridge soars 40m above the Don River, linking east and west Toronto. Structural engineer Edmund Burke cunningly included a lower deck for future rail transport in his design, a controversial move due to the extra costs involved, but a decision that would later see him hailed as a genius. When the TTC opened the Bloor-Danforth subway line in 1966, they rolled their trains straight across Burke's bridge without any structural modifications at all, saving the city millions.

Farsighted, yes, but what Eddie-baby didn't plan on was the hundreds of miserable Torontonians who would use his bridge to hurl themselves into oblivion. At a peak rate of one every 22 days, around 500 folks decided to end it all here, making it the second-most fatal structure in the world (after San Fran's Golden Gate Bridge). The solution? A very expensive barrier of closely spaced steel rods called the 'Luminous Veil,' installed in 2003.

his country villa here. The local subway station was named after **Castle Frank**, the summer residence of Toronto's founder, Lieutenant Governor John Simcoe, and his artistic wife Elizabeth. Their majestic riverbank house burned down two centuries ago, but the area still boasts some of Toronto's most luxurious homes. It's the kind of place where perfectly good refrigerators are left out on the sidewalk with 'Free – just needs cleaning' signs stuck to them.

Across the **Bloor Street Viaduct** (above) spanning the Don River is Danforth Ave, the centre of **Greektown**. Often called just 'The Danforth,' this is one of Toronto's most popular restaurant districts, full of Greek street signs, ouzo bars and muttering old men playing with worry beads. Further south by the river is **Chinatown East**, a small pocket of Chinese merchants and restaurants. Also out this way is **Little India**, with great curry joints, ravishing sari shops and Bolly-rock music stores. Hip young Indian dudes slap backs in the street among the rich scent of spices.

A miscellany of eclectic neighborhoods lines Queen St E en route to The Beaches, including industrial **Leslieville**, which has some ace restaurants, antiques stores and design shops (and is also home to Toronto's Hells Angels).

Orientation

Cabbagetown's main drag is Parliament St, running north from Gerrard St E up to Bloor St E. Cabbagetown extends east to the Don River, dividing Rosedale and Greektown (The Danforth).

Rosedale lies north of Bloor St E sprawling west to Sherbourne St, although the main business strip is Yonge St, north of Bloor St. Greektown bustles around Danforth Ave, east from Broadview Ave to Coxwell Ave.

Little India is further south on Gerrard St E, west of Coxwell Ave, while Chinatown East centres on the Gerrard St E and Broadview Ave intersection. Leslieville lies along Queen St E, roughly from Carlaw Ave east to Coxwell Ave.

ALLAN GARDENS CONSERVATORY
Map pp244-5

☎ 416-392-7288; www.toronto.ca/parks/parks _grdens/allangdns.htm; 19 Horticultural Ave; admission free; ☷ 10am-5pm; ⬤ ⬤ ; ⬤ 506

The jewels of this scruffy city park are its six early-20th-century greenhouses, filled with huge palms and trees from around the world divided into arid, cool and tropical plantings.

On a cold day it's a great place to warm up – check out the spiky golden barrel cacti in the arid garden and pretend you're in Death Valley. Speaking of which, death is something you might come a little closer to if you walk through the park after dark… Limited free parking is available off Horticultural Ave.

RIVERDALE FARM Map pp244-5
☎ 416-392-6794; www.friendsofriverdalefarm .com; 201 Winchester St; admission free; ☷ 9am-5pm, farmers' market 3-7pm Tue May-Oct; ⬤ ⬤ ; ⬤ 506

The 7.5-hectare Riverdale Farm was once the Toronto Zoo, where prairie wolves howled at night. It's now run as a working farm museum, with two barns, a summer wading pool and pens of sundry fowl and animals (geese, goats, pigs, rabbits, turkeys etc). Kids follow the farmer around as he does his daily chores, including milking the cows daily at 10:30am. The Farmers' Market features hippies selling organic goods and buskers playing Appalachian mountain dobros.

ST JAMES CEMETERY Map pp244-5
☎ 416-964-9194; www.stjamescathedral.on.ca; 635 Parliament St; ☷ 8am-5pm Nov-Mar, 8am-8pm Apr-Oct; ⬤ ; ⬤ Castle Frank

Many of Toronto's founding families are pushing up daisies at this historic cemetery, which belongs to St James Cathedral (p57).

TRANSPORTATION

Subway From Rosedale's Castle Frank station, walk south into Cabbagetown. Stops along the Bloor-Danforth line near Greektown are Broadview, Chester and Pape.

Streetcar The 506 College line heads east of downtown into Cabbagetown then across the river to Chinatown East and Little India. The 504 King and 505 Dundas lines turn north after crossing the Don River, running through Chinatown East en route to Broadview subway station. The 501 Queen line runs from downtown to The Beaches via Leslieville, as do the 502 Downtowner and 503 Kingston Rd (weekday rush hours only) lines.

Bus TTC bus lines run north-south along most major streets; useful routes include 65 Parliament, 72 Pape and 75 Sherbourne.

Car Metered on-street parking isn't difficult to find; you might even score a free spot in a Cabbagetown side street. Municipal lots along Danforth Ave, on Broadview Ave near Queen St E, at 51 Aberdeen Ave in Cabbagetown and at 405 Sherbourne St near Allan Gardens charge 75¢ to $1 per half-hour (daily maximum $6).

Ancient gravestones slowly succumb to gravity and disappear beneath the lawn. Its beautifully proportioned little Gothic Revival Chapel of St James-the-Less (1860) – a national historic site – has justifiably been called one of the prettiest buildings in Canada.

TOMMY THOMPSON PARK Map p231

☎ 416-661-6600; www.trca.on.ca; Leslie St, off Lake Shore Blvd E; admission free; ⏰ 9am-4:30pm Sat & Sun Nov-Mar, 9am-6pm Apr-Oct; ♿ ⛟; 🚋 501, 502, 503 then 🚌 83

A 5km-long man-made peninsula between the Harbourfront and The Beaches, Tommy Thompson Park (named after a former Toronto Parks commissioner) juts further into Lake Ontario than the Toronto Islands. Managed by the Toronto & Region Conservation Authority (TRCA), this 'accidental wilderness' – constructed from Outer Harbour dredgings and fill from downtown building sites – has become a phenomenal wildlife success. It's one of the world's largest nesting places for ring-billed gulls, and is a haven for terns, black-crowned night heron, turtles, owls, foxes, even coyotes!

The park is open to the public on weekends and holidays; vehicles and pets are prohibited. Summer schedules offer interpretive programs and guided walks, usually with an ecological theme. At the end of the park there's a lighthouse and some awesome city views.

To get here on public transport, take any streetcar east along Queen St to Jones Ave, then jump on the 83 Jones bus southbound. Get off at Commissioners St, from where it's a 500m walk south to the park's main gate (the bus doesn't run on Sunday or some holidays). Call the TRCA for information on shuttles from the gate into the park (May to mid-October). Alternatively, hire a bike or some in-line skates and follow the Martin Goodman Trail (p138) all the way here.

TORONTO NECROPOLIS Map pp244-5

☎ 416-923-7911; www.mountpleasant groupofcemeteries.ca; 200 Winchester St; admission free; ⏰ 8am-5:30pm; ♿; 🚋 506

The remains of 984 of Toronto's colonists, including the city's first mayor William Lyon Mackenzie, were transferred to this wickedly named cemetery in the 1850s when the old Potter's Field burial ground near Todmorden Mills (p80) started to contaminate the town. A road leads off Winchester St through the gates of the Necropolis, passing a Victorian Gothic chapel with a multicolored slate roof.

THE BEACHES

Map p246; Eating p111; Shopping p162; Sleeping p177

To residents, 'The Beach' is a neighborhood of wealthy professionals down by the lakeshore. To everyone else, it's part of 'The Beaches' – meaning the neighborhood, the beaches and the parklands along Lake Ontario. The area was first settled in the late 18th century by the Ashbridge family, loyalists who fought on the British side during the American Revolution (and lost). Today the bay is still named after them.

Development took off here during the '70s and the onslaught of beachfront construction hasn't stopped since. Fortunately, the side streets east of Woodbine Ave still have gardens bursting with color and quaint lakeside houses. The three beaches themselves – Woodbine, Kew and Balmy – are good for sunbathing and picnicking, though at times

LAKE ONTARIO

It's a bit like ignoring the elephant in the corner of the room, but Torontonians consistently fail to appreciate or even think very much about their lake. It's probably not their fault – lousy urban planning means it's usually impossible to even see the water from the city, and public access to the lakeshore has only really opened up in recent decades. Industrial chemicals, sewage and fertilizer run-off have traditionally fouled the waters, and, although the situation is improving, only the brave and stupid dare to swim at the city beaches. For most citizens, Lake Ontario simply a big, grey, cold thing that stops the Americans from driving up Yonge St.

For the record, Lake Ontario is the fourteenth largest lake in the world and the smallest and most easterly of the five Great Lakes: 311km long, 85km wide and 244m deep, with 1146km of shoreline and 1639 cubic kilometers of water. The name 'Ontario' derives from *Skanadario*, an Iroquois word meaning 'sparkling water,' and, despite the bad planning and pollution, it still sparkles. Take a trip to the Toronto Islands or Tommy Thompson Park and you'll soon see the lake for what it really is – stoic, powerful and very beautiful. Be sure to tell the locals all about it.

the sand here is more like sticky grey mud. A 3km **boardwalk** follows the shore and fills with cyclists, joggers, dog walkers and school kids running cross-country races.

Travelers should think twice before hurling themselves into Lake Ontario. Although it's happening less and less frequently, every summer the city periodically closes its public beaches due to toxic pollution levels. Closures aren't well signposted, so if you miss the TV news and go swimming you might be headed for a nasty result. When in doubt, keep out.

After a sunny day by the lakeshore, there are plenty of places to dine, drink and shop along Queen St E.

Orientation

The Beaches neighborhood extends from Woodbine Ave east to Victoria Park Ave, along the Queen St E spine. Most of the recreational areas are along the lakefront, one long block south of Queen St E. The streetcar ride east to The Beaches from downtown takes about 30 minutes.

BEACHES & PARKS Map p246

☎ 416-392-8186; www.toronto.ca/parks; admission free; ☽ dawn-dusk; ☒ ☒ ; ☒ 501
Kew Beach is the most popular stretch of sand, the boardwalk running east to **Balmy Beach** and west to **Woodbine Beach**. Adjacent **Kew Gardens** offers rest rooms, snack bars, a skating rink, lawn bowls, **tennis courts** (p140) and benches for kicking back; at the west end there's an Olympic-size public **swimming pool** (p140). The **Martin Goodman Trail** (p138) leads past Ashbridge's Bay Park. Off Queen St, the sunken **Ivan Forrest Gardens** leads to **Glen Stewart Ravine**, a wilder patch of green running north to Kingston Rd.

RC HARRIS FILTRATION PLANT

Map p246
☎ 416-392-2934; www.beachestoronto.com/tour/harris.html; 2701 Queen St E; ☒ 501
Commanding heavenly views of the lakefront on a priceless slab of real estate, the elegantly proportioned RC Harris Filtration Plant is a modern art deco masterpiece that has appeared in countless movies and TV shows, as well as in Michael Ondaatje's *In The Skin Of A Lion* (p30). Originally residents disparagingly dubbed it the 'Palace of Purification,' due to hefty construction

costs during the Depression. It's currently closed to the public, but hardcore Ondaatje fans should call to see if tours are back on the agenda.

TORONTO ISLANDS

Map p247; Eating p112; Sleeping p177
Once upon a time, there were no Toronto Islands. There was only an immense sandbar made from material eroded from the Scarborough Bluffs, stretching 9km out into the lake from the foot of present-day Woodbine Ave. Early colonials flocked here to take advantage of stiff lakeshore breezes, as did First Nations peoples, who had been coming here for centuries. Later the sandbar was simply called 'The Peninsula,' a name adopted by a Victorian resort hotel that stood here in the 1850s. On April 13, 1858, a hurricane blasted through the sandbar, swallowed the hotel and created the gap now known as the Eastern Channel. Toronto's jewel-like islands were born – nearly two-dozen isles covering 600 acres.

Present-day **Centre Island** draws hundreds of visitors each weekend, but has no residents. During the 1960s the city began steadily evicting all of the 'sandbar bohemians' who had been living here for more than a generation. The remaining residents on other islands struggled for over 20 years to keep their homes and unique way of life. It all boiled down to a dramatic standoff in 1980, after which the city granted 99-year leases for year-round residents under a land trust administration arrangement. When you visit the close-knit, 800-strong artistic communities on **Algonquin Island** and **Ward's Island**, expect pangs of jealousy. They've got a peaceful, trusting, kid-safe community,

Sights

TORONTO ISLANDS

little pollution, photogenic clusters of cottages among tall maples and incredible city skyline views. Bring along a picnic lunch, as most of the islands' fast-food outlets are overpriced.

Orientation

Most ferries dock at Centre Island Park, which has the majority of outdoor amusements and hosts the Islands' major events, including June's **Toronto International Dragon Boat Festival** (p13) and September's **Virgin Music Festival** (p15). Beaches along the southern shores of the main islands are popular for picnicking, beach volleyball and lizard-like sunbathing.

If you only plan to explore one island, you can get around on foot easily enough. Otherwise, you'll need to rent a bicycle. For general information on the Islands, contact **Toronto Parks and Recreation** (☎ 416-397-2628; www.toronto.ca/parks) or stop by the seasonal tourist information booth on Centre Island. The **community website** (www.toronto island.org) is a flavorful slice of island life.

CENTREVILLE AMUSEMENT PARK
Map p247

☎ 416-203-0405; www.centreisland.ca; day pass adult/child/family $28/19/80, grounds entry free; ☯ 10:30am-8pm daily Jul-Aug, 10:30am-5pm Mon-Fri & 10:30am-8pm Sat & Sun Jun, 10:30am-6pm Sat & Sun May & Sep; ☒ ☷ ; ☗ Centre Island
From the **Centre Island** ferry terminal, wander past the information booth and first-aid station to quaint Centreville. Squeezed together on a few hundred acres are an antique carousel, goofy golf course, miniature train rides and a sky gondola. **Far Enough Farm** zoo presents kids with plenty of opportunities to cuddle something furry and step in something sticky.

South over the Centreville bridge is a well-over-head-high **hedge maze** and ticket booths for Toronto Islands **tram tours** (☎ 416-392-8192; 35min ride adult/child/concession $5/2/4; ☯ 1-5pm Mon-Thu, to 6pm Fri-Sun). Further south are changing rooms, snack bars, **bicycle rentals** (p138) and a pier jagging out into the lake. Just to the east is a **boathouse** (☎ 416-392-8192; rentals $15-25 per hr; ☯ 11am-5:45pm Mon-Thu, to 6:45pm Fri-Sun) where you can rent canoes, kayaks or paddleboats and explore the Islands' lagoons.

ST ANDREW-BY-THE-LAKE CHURCH
Map p247

☎ 416-813-6198; www.torontoisland.org/church; admission free; ☯ services 10am Sun; ☒ ; ☗ Centre Island
Indeed, it is by the lake! This white weatherboard Anglican church (1884), often referred to simply as 'The Island Church,' holds heart-warming traditional Christmas celebrations each year and harbor boat blessings every June.

GIBRALTAR POINT Map p247
☗ Centre Island
Gibraltar Point, as per Gibraltar in the Mediterranean, was the most easily defensible point in the harbor. Captain John Simcoe ordered a British fort built here in 1800. It was destroyed just 13 years later during the American raid on York.

Not far inland stands the photogenic Gibraltar Point Lighthouse (1809), just 25m tall, built with grey limestone quarried at Queenston on the Niagara escarpment. The lighthouse was the first of its kind on the Great Lakes, using sperm-whale oil to fuel its lamp. Its first keeper, JP Radan Muller, disappeared mysteriously in 1815. Years later human bones were unearthed nearby, supporting the theory that Muller was knocked off by American soldiers for refusing to share his bootleg whiskey.

HANLAN'S POINT Map p247
☗ Hanlan's Point
At the west end of Centre Island by the Toronto City Centre Airport is sporty Hanlan's Point, named after world-champion sculler 'Ned' Hanlan (1855–1904), a member of the first family to permanently settle here. Babe Ruth hit his first professional home run here in 1914 while playing minor-league baseball – the ball drowned in Lake Ontario, and made no one rich. The sport of ice-boating atop the frozen lake was at its peak until the 1940s; thanks to climate change, winters nowadays are too mild for it.

Beyond the free **tennis courts** and a fragile ecosystem of low-lying dunes sustaining rare species, the not-so-rare *nekkid humanus* roams free on the grey sand of **Hanlan's Point Beach**. Popular with gay men, the beach's 'clothing optional' status was finally legalized in 1999. Officially the beach is only supervised during July and August.

lonelyplanet.com

TRANSPORTATION

Ferry From the foot of Bay St near the Westin Harbour Castle hotel, catch a ferry (p213) to Centre Island, Hanlan's Point or Ward's Island – quick rides which are as good as harbor tours.

Walking Of course you can explore the islands on foot, but from Ward's Island to Hanlan's Point is a deceptively long way.

Bicycle & Skates Bicycles are allowed on some ferries, but not all (call the Toronto Islands Ferry Terminal ticket booth ☎ 416-392-8193). Bicycle rentals are available on Centre Island (p138). You can also rent bicycles and in-line skates along the Harbourfront (p138) before boarding the ferry.

WARD'S ISLAND Map p247

🚇 Ward's Island

At the western end of Ward's Island is an 18-hole **Frisbee Golf Course** (☎ 416-203-0807; www.discgolfontario.com; admission free; ⏰ dawn-dusk). An old-fashioned boardwalk runs the length of the south shore of the island, passing the back gate of the **Rectory Café** (p112).

GREATER TORONTO AREA (GTA)

Map p230 & Map p231; Eating p112; Shopping p163; Sleeping p177

Many of the towns surrounding Toronto have been incorporated into the Megacity (p38), which is just as monstrous as it sounds, at least when it comes to navigating your way around. But this is where the majority of Torontonians live, work and play. Exploring these areas can be rewarding, but it'll take a chunk out of your day if you don't have a car. There's plenty to see; the following selection is the pick of the bunch. While some attractions are almost 'must-dos,' especially for families, just one of the historic sites is probably enough for anyone who isn't a complete history fiend.

Orientation

It would take an encyclopedia to list all of the suburbs, towns and communities comprising the GTA, but visitors will only need a few reference points. East of downtown

and The Beaches are Toronto's quieter lakefront communities, like Scarborough. Affluent neighborhoods north of downtown are an entirely different story, with vast amounts of wealth concentrated in North York and at the intersection of Yonge St and Eglinton Ave, nicknamed 'Young and Eligible.' Multicultural neighborhoods crowd the western outskirts of the city, including communities near High Park, Bloor Village on Bloor St W west of Keele St, and Eastern European Roncesvalles Village (pronounced 'Ron-cess-vaal'), running along Roncesvalles Ave between Queen St W and Dundas Ave W. Suburban Etobicoke (pronounced 'Ee-toe-bee-coe') lies further west towards the airport.

GTA WEST

BLACK CREEK PIONEER VILLAGE

Map p230

☎ 416-736-1733; www.blackcreek.ca; 1000 Murray Ross Pkwy, Downsview; adult/child/concession $12/8/11; ⏰ 10am-4pm Mon-Fri, 11am-5pm Sat & Sun May-Dec; ♿ 👶 ; 🚇 Finch then 🚌 60

Toronto's most popular historical family attraction re-creates rural life in 19th-century Ontario. Workers in period costume care for the farm animals, play fiddlin' folk music and demonstrate country crafts and skills using authentic tools and methods. Shops sell the artisans' handiwork – everything from tin lanterns to fresh bread to woven rugs. Souvenir postcards can be mailed from the old-fashioned post office. Holidays are often the best time to visit; traditional Victorian 'Christmas Remembered' celebrations start in mid-November. The village is on the southeast corner of Steeles Ave and Jane St, a 40-minute drive northwest of downtown.

HIGH PARK Map p231

☎ 416-392-1111; www.highpark.org; 1873 Bloor St W; admission free; ⏰ dawn-dusk; ♿ 👶 ; 🚇 High Park, 🚋 501, 506, 508

Delightfully unkempt, Toronto's biggest park (398 acres) is a heavenly escape – unfurl a picnic lunch, cycle around, ice-skate or just sit amongst great stands of oaks and watch the sunset. Near the north gates are **tennis courts** and an outdoor **swimming pool** (p140). The main road weaves south through the park; another road branching to the east

GRENADIER POND

The story behind the naming of High Park's **Grenadier Pond** goes back to the War of 1812. Apparently, a gallant troupe of British Grenadiers from the King's 8th Regiment who were stationed at Fort York struck out across the frozen pond in pursuit of American renegades. The Americans made it across, but the ice cracked and some of the Grenadiers fell through and drowned. The pond looks innocuous enough, but fishermen and boaters often report a creepy feeling of being watched from underwater, while winter skaters report a similar sense from beneath the ice.

takes you to the **Dream in High Park** (p129) stage. Further south are the **Hillside Gardens** overlooking **Grenadier Pond** (above) where people ice-skate (p139) in winter. The road continues downhill past the **animal paddocks** (a small children's zoo) to **Colborne Lodge** (☎ 416-392-6916; www.toronto.ca/culture/colborne .htm; Colborne Lodge Dr; adult/child/concession $5.50/3.50/4; ☷ noon-4pm Tue-Sun Oct-Dec, noon-5pm May-Sep, Sat & Sun only Jan-Apr), a Regency-style cottage built in 1836 by the Howard family, who donated much of High Park to the city in 1873.

High Park's north entrance is off Bloor St W at High Park Ave. Bus 30B picks up at High Park subway station, then makes a loop through the park on weekends and holidays from mid-June to Labour Day. Otherwise it's a 200m walk to the north gates. The 506 High Park streetcar drops off on the east side of the park. If you exit the park by Colborne Lodge at the south gates, walk down to Lake Shore Blvd W and catch any streetcar back east to downtown.

MONTGOMERY'S INN Map p230

☎ 416-394-8113; www.montgomerysinn.com; 4709 Dundas St W, Etobicoke; adult/child/concession/family $3/1/2/8; ☷ 1-4:30pm Tue-Fri, 1-5pm Sat & Sun; ◉ Islington then ▦ 37

Montgomery's Inn was built in 1832 by an Irish military captain of the same name, and its gracious stone symmetry is a fine example of Loyalist architecture, restored to its late-1840s heyday. It was a hotel for 25 years then a farm until the 1940s. Staff in period dress answer questions and serve afternoon tea (p95). Contemporary and traditional art exhibits, cooking classes and wine-and-cheese tastings are often hosted here.

GTA NORTH
DAVID DUNLAP OBSERVATORY
Map p180

☎ 416-884-9562; www.astro.utoronto.ca/DDO; 123 Hillsview Dr, Richmond Hill; 50min tour adult/senior/child $6/4/4; ☷ 7:30pm Sat Jun-Oct, also 7:30pm Fri Jul-Aug

Just north of the Toronto city limits, the David Dunlap Observatory – a major player in the cut-throat world of international stargazing – presents introductory talks on modern astronomy, followed by interplanetary voyeurism through Canada's biggest optical telescope (the reflector measures 1.9m). If the skies are clear, tickets are sold on a first-come, first-served basis (cash only). Call ahead to check weather conditions. Kids under seven years old aren't permitted for safety reasons. On some clear-sky nights, the Royal Astronomical Society of Canada brings its own telescopes and sets up informal (and free!) viewing for the public outside, too.

To reach the observatory, drive 30 minutes up Bayview Ave past 16th Ave to Hillsview Dr, turn left onto Hillsview Dr and drive 1km west until you see the sinister white dome on your left. Alternatively take the TTC subway north to Finch station. Walk underground to a nearby transit terminal and catch the 91 Bayview bus operated by **York Region Transit** (☎ 905-762-2100, 866-668-3978; www.yorkregiontransit.com). This bus stops on request at Hillsview Dr, from where it's a 1km walk to the observatory. The entire trip costs $2.75, with a free transfer from the subway station.

GIBSON HOUSE Map p230

☎ 416-395-7432, events line ☎ 416-338-3888; www.toronto.ca/culture/gibson_house.htm; 5172 Yonge St; adult/child/concession $3.75/1.75/2.25, extra 50¢ Nov-Dec; ☷ noon-5pm Tue-Sun Oct-Aug, closed Sep; ◉ North York

Scottish immigrant David Gibson, a successful surveyor and politician, built this refined Georgian-style house in 1851 after his return from an 11-year exile in the USA, the unfortunate result of his role in the Upper Canada Rebellion of 1837. Costumed workers run house tours between 11am and 3pm, as well as occasional weekend hearth cooking demonstrations. Gibson House is north of Sheppard Ave, next to a small park. If you're driving, limited parking is accessible via a small laneway off southbound Yonge St.

MT PLEASANT CEMETERY Map p231

☎ 416-485-9129; www.mountpleasant groupofcemeteries.ca; 375 Mt Pleasant Rd; admission free; ⏰ 8am-8pm in Jun-Aug, 8am-5:30pm Sep-May; ♿; Ⓜ Davisville

'Rest assured, we have space' is the slogan here, and indeed, it's hard to imagine a more pleasantly assuring place for the ultimate rest. Since the 19th century, many of Toronto's brilliant and best (or at least richest) citizens have concurred, including classical musician Glenn Gould, former prime minister William Lyon Mackenzie, Eaton's founder Timothy Eaton, Titanic survivor Arthur Godfrey Peuchen, and Foster Hewitt, Canada's 'Voice of Hockey,' who coined the phrase, 'He shoots, he scores!'

The cemetery is north of Moore Ave, between Yonge St and Bayview Ave. Guide maps are available from the office near the south gate on the east side of Mt Pleasant Rd, which cuts through the middle of the cemetery.

PARAMOUNT CANADA'S WONDERLAND Map p180

☎ 905-832-8131; www.canadas-wonderland .com; 9580 Jane St, Vaughan; day pass adult/concession/child $52/30/30; ⏰ 10am-10pm Jun-Aug, Sat & Sun only late Apr-late May & early Sep-early Oct; ♿ 🚼

Wonderland is a state-of-the-art amusement park with over 60 rides, including some killer rollercoasters with lunch-losing names like 'The Cliffhanger,' 'Drop Zone' and 'Sky Rider.' There's also an exploding volcano, a 20-hectare Splash Works water park (bring your bathing suit), Jimmy Neutron's Brainwasher, and the Fantastic World of Hanna-Barbera for the young 'uns. Queues can be lengthy, except on overcast days; most rides operate rain or shine.

Wonderland is a 45-minute drive northwest of downtown Toronto on Hwy 400. Exit at Rutherford Rd, 10 minutes north of Hwy 401. Alternatively, from Yorkdale or York Mills subway stations catch the GOTransit Wonderland Express Bus (☎ 416-869-3200; www.gotransit.com; per person $4.25; ⏰ hourly 9am-5:30pm).

GTA EAST

GUILD INN Map p230

☎ 416-410-2755; www.guildwood.on.ca; 201 Guildwood Parkway, off Kingston Rd; admission free; ⏰ dawn-dusk; Ⓜ Kennedy then 🚌 116

A 15-minute drive east of the Scarborough Bluffs is the quirky Guild Inn, an Arts & Crafts–style mansion dating from 1914 set among quiet lakefront parklands. An artists' colony formed here during the Depression; the garden contains a collection of sculptures, Ionic columns and gargoyles rescued from condemned city buildings during the '50s. Plans are afoot to build a $56 million hotel here, so don't be surprised if it's off limits. Call or check the website to avoid disappointment.

ONTARIO SCIENCE CENTRE Map p231

☎ 416-696-1000; www.ontariosciencecentre.ca; 770 Don Mills Rd; Science Centre adult/child/concession $17/10/12.50, Omnimax $12/8/9, combined ticket $25/15/19; ⏰ 10am-5pm; ♿ 🚼; Ⓜ Eglinton then 🚌 34, or Ⓜ Pape then 🚌 25

Climb a rock wall, catch a criminal with DNA fingerprinting and race an Olympic bobsled – this excellent, interactive museum (designed by innovative architects Moriyama & Teshima, p33) lets you do it all. Over 800 high-tech exhibits and live demonstrations wow the kids (and the adults at the back, pretending not to be interested).

Don't miss the hair-raising Van de Graaff Generator, the terrifying Aging Machine, and the alarming exhibits in the Human Body section (analyze spit and figure out what's inside a zit). Also here is the giant domed Omnimax Cinema. Check the website for family events, including theme-night sleepovers ($49, reservations required). The science centre is located in a small ravine on the corner of Eglinton Ave E and Don Mills Rd.

SCARBOROUGH BLUFFS Map p230

☎ 416-392-1111; www.toronto.ca/waterfront /tour/scarborough_bluffs.htm; off Kingston Rd (Hwy 2), Scarborough; admission free; ⏰ dawn-dusk; 🚼; Ⓜ Victoria Park then 🚌 12

A few kilometers east of The Beaches, this gnarly 14km stretch of glacial cliffs jags up from the lakeshore. When Elizabeth Simcoe came here in 1793, she named the spot

TRANSPORTATION

Subway & Bus TTC subway lines will take you to many outlying sights, although a free transfer to a local bus may be required to reach your destination.

Car If you want to really explore, rent a car. Parking at most attractions is plentiful, although it can be surprisingly expensive. The fastest routes out of the city centre are the Don Valley Pkwy north to Hwy 401, or take the Gardiner Expwy west to Hwy 427, then head north.

Scarborough after the town in Yorkshire, England, also famed for its cliffs. Several parks provide access to clifftops, from where views sweep across the Bluffs to Lake Ontario.

From Kingston Rd (Hwy 2), turn south at Cathedral Bluffs Dr to reach an excellent vantage point, **Cathedral Bluffs Park**. It's the highest section of the bluffs (at 65m) and once belonged to the Sisters of St Joseph, whose property extended from Kingston Rd to the lake. Erosion has created cathedral spire–like formations, exposing evidence of five different glacial periods. You can also access the shore at Galloway Rd further east. Below this section of Bluffs off Brimley Rd, landfill has been used to form **Bluffer's Park**, a private marina and recreational area.

Unless you have wheels, getting to the Bluffs can be a drag, and if you do have a car, parking is severely limited. One option is to take the subway to Victoria Park, then bus 12 along Kingston Rd. Ask the driver to let you off near Cathedral Bluffs Dr, east of the St Clair Ave E intersection.

TODMORDEN MILLS Map p231

☎ 416-396-2819; www.toronto.ca/todmorden; 67 Pottery Rd; adult/child/concession $3.50/1.50/2.25; ⊗ 11am-4pm Tue-Fri, from noon Sat & Sun May-Dec; ♿ ♿ ; Ⓜ Broadview then 🚌 8, 62, 87, 100
Quietly set by the Don River, this unique industrial relic housed a late-18th-century gristmill turned sawmill, then brewery and distillery, then paper mill. Historical exhibits are housed inside the Brewery Gallery, where guides show visitors around old millers' houses and the Don train station, relocated here in the 1960s. Nature paths start near the bridge and wind back to the secluded **Todmorden Mills Wildflower Preserve** (www.hopscotch .ca/tmwpl), 9.2 hectares of wildflowers growing on former industrial wasteland, complete with boardwalks and viewing platforms.

The Mills make a great detour if you're exploring The Danforth. For urban hikers, one of the city's **Discovery Walks** (p139) runs by here. Otherwise from Broadview subway station, take any bus northbound a few blocks to Mortimer Ave, then walk 1km west.

Walking & Cycling Tours

Walking & Cycling Tours

The best way to explore Toronto's neighborhoods, compact downtown area and revitalized Harbourfront is to strike out on your own. We've included a range of options here, from historical and architectural walks to beachfront bike rides, even an underground Toronto tour for when the weather turns nasty, but nothing will beat your own random explorations. So get out there and get walking – you don't need us to hold your hand! For organized group tours, see p48.

CABBAGETOWN & ROSEDALE ARCHITECTURE WALK

On the corner of Metcalfe and Winchester Sts is the former St Enoch's Presbyterian Church, now the **Toronto Dance Theatre & School 1** (p135) – a grandiose redbrick Romanesque Revival building (1891). South at 37 Metcalfe is an **Italianate Villa 2**, which once belonged to the president of the Brilliant Sign Company. When an apartment complex was built next to his home in 1910, he transferred all of its finest details, including classical Ionic columns, to the Metcalfe St façade.

Dogleg south along Dermott Pl to the **Trinity Mews 3**, at 41 Spruce St. Once part of Trinity College Medical School (1859), the old building is infinitely more appealing than the modern mimics in the courtyard behind. Continue east then turn left towards the unloved-looking **Shields House 4**, at 377 Sackville St, typical of the mansard-roofed Second Empire buildings in the neighborhood. At the end of the block, turn right towards **320 Carlton St 5**, a plump example of Toronto's quintessential 'bay-and-gable' architecture (see p33).

Continue east, loop past the consistent working-class-style **Geneva Ave Cottages 6**, then trudge up Sumach St next to Riverdale Park. On the left at 384 Sumach St is the **Witches' House 7**, nicknamed for its gingerbread appearance and gruesome gargoyle (modeled on HRH Prince Charles?). Veer right towards **Riverdale Farm 8** (p73), across from which are the impressive **Toronto Necropolis 9** (p74) gates. Backtrack to Sumach St, then truck north to Wellesley St E for a sampler of Cabbagetown's various architectural styles. The hidden **Alpha Ave Cottages 10** and on Wellesley St E, the **Wellesley Cottages 11** are pint-sized brick rowhouses with steep roofs built for 19th century workers, but now full of yuppies. Further west, **314 Wellesley St 12** is a whimsical delight of terracotta and carved Victorian excess, including keystone gargoyles and a lizard carved under the highest gable.

Turn right on Parliament St toward the well-fertilized lawns of **St James Cemetery 13** (p73). Continue north to Bloor St E, then walk east past the former site of **Castle Frank 14** (p72). From here, cross into wealthy Rosedale. Trundle north up Castle Frank Rd, stopping to assess the terracotta turret and circular porch on the **James Ramsey House 15**, the Dr Seuss–like hedges outside **65 Castle Frank Rd 16**, and the 'clinker brick' walls of **43 Castle Frank Rd 17**, made of misshapen rejects.

The road wiggles around to redeveloped cul-de-sac **Hawthorn Gardens 18**, where a sign points to the sunny lawns, oaks and benches of **Craigleigh Gardens 19**. Castle Frank Rd leads to Elm Ave – most houses here are listed by the Ontario Heritage Foundation as being architecturally or

WALK FACTS

Best time Any morning or afternoon

Start Toronto Dance Theatre & School (🚋 506)

End Branksome Hall (Ⓢ Sherbourne)

Distance 4.5km

Time 2–3 hours

Food en route Chapter Eleven (p110), Raashna (p109), Town Grill (p111)

Drinks en route Beers at Brass Taps (p119), caffeine at Jet Fuel (p124)

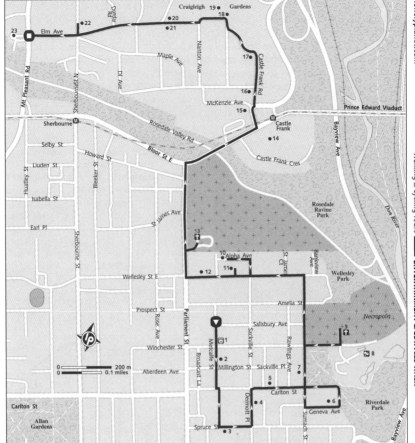

historically significant. Particularly impressive are the 1921 prize-winning **88 Elm Ave 20**, for sale at the time of research (got a spare $9 million?), and **93 Elm Ave 21**, with its ornamental iron porch.

Turn north onto Sherbourne St towards the stately Georgian **Edward Gooderham House 22** at No 27, built for the famous brewing family that had its offices in the Flatiron (Gooderham) Building (p57) and Distillery District (p56).

Finally, backtrack and walk to the western end of Elm Ave past the original houses of Rosedale. At the end of the street, just over Mt Pleasant Rd, a group of Victorian manors comprises the impressive private school **Branksome Hall 23**. From here it's a 10-minute walk south to Sherbourne subway station.

ENTERTAINMENT & EDIFICES WALK

To glimpse Toronto in all its glory, kick off in the late afternoon or just before sunset, as the city neons start to flicker and ghosts come out of the woodwork. Hop off the 504 King streetcar in the Theatre Block (p57) at the corner of John St and King St W. Shimmy east under the bulb-lit awnings of the **Princess of Wales Theatre 1** (p129) and the **Royal Alexandra Theatre 2** (p129). Check the billboards for upcoming spectaculars, then shoot a glance right for a perfect view of the CN Tower (p51), before you reach the famous Simcoe St/King St W corner of 'Education, Legislation, Salvation and Damnation' (see p57). At Simcoe St, cross over to 'intimately powerful' **Roy Thomson Hall 3** (p59) and **Canada's Walk of Fame 4** (p58) – tilt your hat to hockey royalty Mario Lemieux and goofball Jim Carrey. If it's still early, sneak a peek inside **St Andrews Presbyterian Church 5** (p59), or continue west past the **Goethe-Institut Gallery 6** (p59). Turn right at York St then left onto Wellington St W for the **Toronto Dominion Gallery of Inuit Art 7** (p55) – scrimshaw and sculpture oddly disenfranchised in a sterile office lobby.

WALK FACTS

Best time Any afternoon or evening

Start Theatre Block (🚋 504)

End City Hall (🚋 501)

Distance 3km

Time 1½ hours

Food en route Bymark (p94), Terroni (p98), Wayne Gretzky's (p96)

Drinks en route The Charlotte Room (p124), Smokeless Joe (p123)

Turn north onto Bay St, Canada's Wall St, and shuffle along to the **Design Exchange 8** (p55). Continue north, gasping in capitalist awe at powerhouses like **First Canadian Place 9** (p54) and the **Scotia Plaza 10** (p54), with its anatomically impressive carvings. As you approach Adelaide St E, the **Canada Permanent Building 11**, another art-deco skyscraper, is on your left. Cross Temperance St and Richmond St E then sneer up at the gargoyles on **Old City Hall 12** (p62). Walk east on Queen St W, then up Yonge St to the **Elgin & Winter Garden Theatre Centre 13** (p61).

Detour right onto Shuter St to sonic temple **Massey Hall 14** (p62), built with bricks

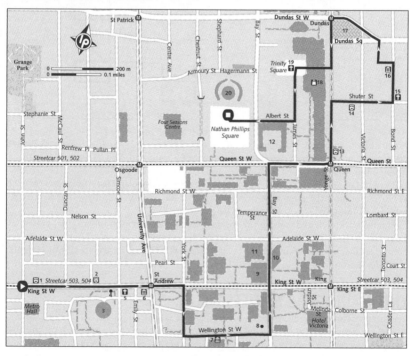

from the Don Valley Brickworks (below). At Bond St, turn left by **St Michael's Catholic Cathedral 15** and visit **Mackenzie House 16** (p61), haunted by a printing press operator (see p39). Cross the rear carpark then jag right around **Dundas Square 17** (p59). Cross Yonge St then through the **Eaton Centre 18** (p153) to Trinity Square's **Church of the Holy Trinity 19** (p60) and its labyrinth. **City Hall 20** (p60) is just a wiggle away, as is the 501 Queen streetcar running west into cool Clubland (p62).

GREEN RAVINE SCENES WALK

Toronto is sliced through by a web of leafy, oxygenated ravines, full of wildlife, babbling brooks and locals looking for some serenity – the perfect diversion from downtown's clash and throb. Keep an eye out for cardinals, blue jays, raccoons, chipmunks and even eagles along the way.

WALK FACTS

Best time Any morning or afternoon
Start Mt Pleasant Cemetery (Davisville)
End St Clair
Distance 5.5km
Time 3 hours
Food & drinks en route Bring a picnic!

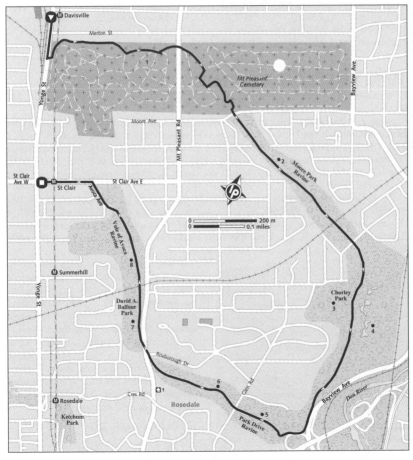

Exit Davisville subway onto Yonge St and head south, crossing east at Merton St. Head up the stairs south of the green-painted overpass, turn right and dive into verdant **Mt Pleasant Cemetery 1** (p79). A sign board illustrates a blue-dotted trail – follow it through to Moore Ave, crossing the street into the cool depths of **Moore Park Ravine 2**. Amble along the boulder-dashed bed of Mud Creek through a forest of finger-straight Manitoba maple, crack willow and staghorn sumac trees, below fortunate houses up on the ridgeline.

Struggle to remember you're in the middle of a huge city as you pass beneath concrete flyovers and railway bridges. **Chorley Park 3** was once the site of the grandiose home of the lieutenant governor of Ontario, until it was demolished in 1961. Further along are the **Don Valley Brickworks 4**. Plain, fancy and enameled bricks made here until 1989 found their way into the walls of Massey Hall, Casa Loma's stables, Osgoode Hall and Old City Hall. After a century of industrial pollution and dereliction, it's now a symbol of the Don River Valley's regeneration.

Back on the track, ignore some ugly roads and arc around to the right into forest again. At the fork in the trail, head left for Cabbagetown and further Don Valley Discovery Walks (p139), or take the right-hand fork into **Park Drive Ravine 5** along Rosedale Creek, a route once used by local milkmen. Beyond the Glen Rd overpass, stop and check the progress of environmental restoration at **Yellow Creek Butterfly Meadow 6**. Cross Mt Pleasant Rd at Roxborough Dr into manicured **David A Balfour Park 7** then the **Vale of Avoca Ravine 8**. Pass under one more bridge, cross the creek over a wooden bridge, turn right and head up the slope to re-enter the city on Avoca Ave. St Clair Ave is straight ahead – turn left toward the subway.

ROYAL YORK TO OLD YORK WALK

Overshadowed by the downtown skyscrapers, you can almost feel the streets of 'Muddy York' slipping beneath your feet.

Begin at **Union Station 1** (p54), exiting from the grand lobby onto Front St W. Cross over to the **Fairmont Royal York 2** (p167) – wink at the crimson-clad bellhops, enter the opulent lobby then turn around to admire the cheesy/romantic Canadian history fresco above the doors: tall ships, arctic Inuit, soaring white peaks and quizzical-looking deer. Walk east over the lobby's mosaic floors, past the squatting stone lions and down the stairs onto Front St W.

On your left **Royal Bank Plaza 3** (p54) glimmers like a giant gold concertina. Cross Bay St, walk a few steps north then duck into stunning **BC Place 4** (p54). Catch a glimpse of the comparatively austere **Dominion Public Building 5** (p54) through the southern windows. Emerging on Yonge St, check out the whimsical 1886 stone façade of the **Hockey Hall of Fame 6** (p55 – such a brutal game, such refined architecture).

WALK FACTS

Best time Any morning or afternoon, except Monday and Sunday when St Lawrence Market is closed

Start Union Station (Ⓜ Union)

End Toronto's First Post Office (🚋 504)

Distance 2.5km

Time 1½–2 hours

Food en route Nami (p96), St Lawrence Market (p95), Sultan's Tent & Café Maroc (p95)

Drinks en route C'est What? (p119), Foundation Room (p121)

Resume walking east along Front St E. At Scott St, a small park affords decent views of the trompe l'oeil mural on the **Flatiron (Gooderham) Building 7** (p57). Stroll along the south side of Front St E to **St Lawrence Market 8** (p57), then cross to the north side of the street into Market Lane Park along the west wall of the North Market building. Next on the list are the site of **York's first well 9**, **St Lawrence Hall 10** (p57) and **St James Cathedral 11** (p57), with its copper-sheathed spire and beautiful gardens.

Across the street, the **Toronto Sculpture Garden 12** doesn't contain much art worth looking at, but sit on the rainbow seat and

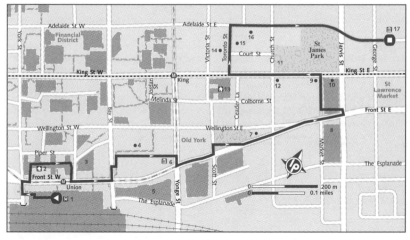

chill out for a minute or two. Heading west on King St E, spin through the revolving doors and scan the lofty lobby of **Le Royal Meridien King Edward 13** (p168), then pay your respects to Old York along **Toronto St 14**, a narrow thoroughfare of noble, triple-storey 19th-century office buildings. Spy the heraldic lion and unicorn atop 10 Toronto St and the flickering gas lamps outside the **Rosewater Supper Club 15** in the old Consumers' Gas Co Ltd building.

Turn right into Adelaide St E for the rusty lamps and somber façade of **Courthouse Market Grille 16** (p96). Three blocks further east on Adelaide St E, beyond St James Park, is **Toronto's First Post Office 17** (p57), now a museum, and just a block north of the 504 King streetcar line.

SUBTERRANEAN TORONTO BLUES WALK

When the weather outside gets depressing, sink into Toronto's underground PATH system (p215), an accidental 27km labyrinth of subterranean corridors connecting downtown sights, skyscrapers and shops.

From the coffered brick void of **Union Station 1** (p54), follow the tubular SkyWalk over the railroad tracks to the giddying heights of the **CN Tower 2** (p51), next to the **Rogers Centre 3** (p53). Retrace your steps to Union Station, cross beneath Front St and spiral up the staircase into the salubrious **Fairmont Royal York 4** (p167). Back inside the basement concourse of Union Station, follow the signs to the **Air Canada Centre 5** (p50) – home of the Toronto Maple Leafs (p142) and Toronto Raptors (p141) – and check out the architectural conservation displays near the Bay St doors.

Retrace your steps to Union Station, dashing through the outside air into Union Station's TTC section below Front St W. Turn sharply right just inside the doors and follow the color-coded arrows to **BC Place 6** (p54) and the **Hockey Hall of Fame 7** (p55).

WALK FACTS

Best time Weekday winter mornings

Start Union Station (Union)

End Trinity Square (Dundas)

Distance 5km

Time 3 hours

Food en route Mercatto (p94), Richtree Market Restaurant (p94), Vertical (p94), countless food courts

Drinks en route Beer Bistro (p94), Turf Lounge (p123)

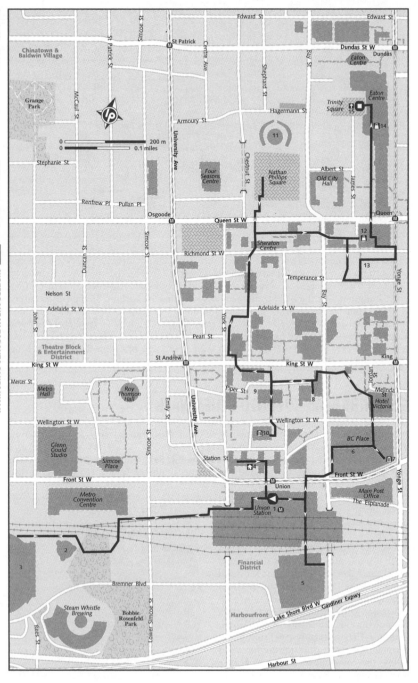

Wander through Commerce Court, turning left beyond the digital stock-market displays and taking the stairs up to the **Design Exchange 8** (p55). Back downstairs continue towards the **Toronto-Dominion Centre 9** (p54). Follow the signs south to visit the **Toronto Dominion Gallery of Inuit Art 10** (p55). Backtrack to the TD Centre and chase the signs towards the Standard Life Centre, the Exchange Tower then the Richmond-Adelaide Complex, which seems to be one enormous foodcourt. The Sheraton Centre Hotel is next, before **City Hall 11** (p60) – pop your head above ground to see the ice-skaters in Nathan Phillips Square (p139), the weather beacon on the Canada Life Building (p60) to the west and the Old City Hall (p62) clock tower further east.

Back underground on the PATH, follow the signs for **the Bay 12** (p155) department store. Shuffle through the basement, diverting right through a striped corridor and up the stairs onto Temperance St. It's a quick sprint from here to the **Cloud Forest Conservatory 13** (p55). Warm up inside, then cross the street and enter the Bay again, reconnecting with the PATH downstairs. Pursue the signs to the **Eaton Centre 14** (p153), window-shop your way to the north end of the mall, then take the escalators up two levels. Outside is Trinity Square, in the welcoming shadows of the **Church of the Holy Trinity 15** (p60).

TORONTO ISLANDS CYCLING CIRCUIT

A short sail from the Harbourfront brings you to paradise, the Toronto Islands (p75), a vehicle-free escape from the crush of downtown. Whether you come for an afternoon or the whole day, it's sure to be a highlight of your trip.

Getting here is part of the fun: jump on the ferry at the Toronto Islands Ferry Terminal (p213) at the bottom of Bay St and enjoy a minicruise over to Centre Island. From the Centre Island ferry terminal, follow the crowd past **Centreville Amusement Park 1** (p76), over the bridge by the **Hedge Maze 2** (p76) to the south shore, where you'll find **Toronto Islands Bicycle Rental 3** (p138). Hop on your trusty metal steed and turn left onto the paved recreational path, cycling parallel to Centre Island Beach all the way to **Hanlan's Point 4** (p76). There's a string of curious historical plaques to read along the way.

Before you reach the ferry terminal near Toronto City Centre Airport, loop back past to the clothing-optional **Hanlan's Point Beach 5** (p76). Next on the right is missable Gibraltar Point (p76), but keep your eyes peeled for the **Gibraltar Point Lighthouse 6** (p76), haunted by the original lighthouse keeper (see p39). Keep going east, wave as you zoom by Centre Island Bicycle Rental and follow the paved shoreline path onto the boardwalk. Trace the lakeshore for a little over a kilometre to the back gate of the **Rectory Café 7** (p112). Or, if you've been clever enough to bring a picnic, sweet little **Ward's Island Beach 8** isn't far away.

Continue along the boardwalk all the way east, then cut back onto 1st St. At the corner of Channel Ave is a photogenic spot with perfect **Toronto skyline views 9** (the CN Tower is one big baby, ain't it just?). From here, it's a short cruise west to the Ward's Island Ferry Terminal, where you pick up Bayview Ave – follow it west past the bridge to residential Algonquin Island and the **Frisbee golf course 10** (p77). Veer right as the Royal Canadian Yacht Club comes into view, following a smaller paved path to the picturesque white gothic **St-Andrew-by-the-Lake Church 11** (p76). Cycle past the **boathouse 12** back to the pier at Centre Island Beach and, with a flush of self-satisfaction, return your bicycle.

TOUR FACTS

Best time Sunny summer weekdays

Start Toronto Islands Ferry Terminal (p213)

End Centre Island Pier

Distance 11km

Time 2 hours

Food & drinks en route Rectory Café (p112), or pack a picnic

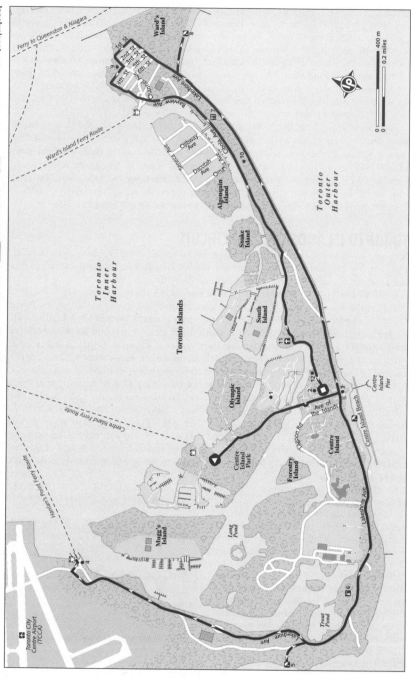

400 m

0.2 miles

Eating

Eating

If you've come to Toronto expecting a morass of tepid hotdogs and sickly hamburgers, think again pal. Nowhere is the city's multiculturalism more obvious, potent and thrilling than on the plates of its restaurants. Eating here is an absolute delight – ponder your profoundest cravings, identify your neighborhood of choice, then dive right in. You'll find everything here from Korean walnut cakes to sweat-inducing Thai curries, New York steaks and good ol' Canuck pancakes with peameal bacon and maple syrup. Stick with the classics, or immerse yourself in fusion food – Toronto's chefs have mastered the art of taking traditional recipes from the West, throwing in handfuls of zingy Eastern ingredients and cooking the whole lot with lashings of pan-Asian flare. Lingering British influences are hard to shake, but who wants to? Fizzy lunchtime pints and formal afternoon high teas remain much-loved traditions. Meanwhile, out on the streets, locals linger in the last rays of summer, dining out on rooftops, in shady backyards and on effervescent sidewalk patios. In winter, they beat a retreat to crackling fireside dinners and hearty pub meals.

Executive diners file into classy restaurants in the Financial District and Old York, while eclectic, affordable eateries fill Baldwin Village, Kensington Market, Queen West and the Yonge Street Strip. More ethnically consistent are Little Italy, Greektown (The Danforth), Little India and Chinatown.

Opening Hours

Restaurants are usually open for lunch on weekdays from 11:30am until 2:30pm and serve dinner daily from 5pm until 9:30pm, usually later on weekends. Many also serve weekend brunch, usually from 11am to 2:30pm. Breakfast time in restaurants is usually around 7:30am until 10am. If restaurants take a day off, it's Monday. Some restaurants may close early or on additional days in winter, then stay open later during summer.

How Much?

For American and European visitors, eating in Toronto will be an entirely affordable experience. Stretch your budget even further by eating well at lunch, when many restaurants charge about two-thirds as much for meals as they do at night – often from exactly the same menu. Otherwise at dinner, expect to pay $15 to $20 (before taxes and tip) for main courses at midrange eateries, with main-course prices sometimes nudging over $40 at top-end restaurants. Many coffeehouses (p123) and pubs (p118) also serve great food. See the Price Guide boxed text (opposite) for further fiscal guidance.

Booking Tables

As a general rule, the higher the menu prices, the more strongly reservations are advised. Without a reservation, the best approach is to show up for an early or late seating, say, before 6pm or after 9pm. Free tables are generally at their most scarce in the Financial District, Old York, the Theatre Block and the Entertainment District, as well as trendy neighborhoods like Little Italy and The Beaches.

Taxes & Tipping

Toronto's feast of tables and cuisines is only soured by taxes. A hamburger and beer priced at $9.95 on the menu will actually cost you $13, including taxes and a tip of 15% (equal to the total amount of tax on your bill, or calculate 20% for excellent service). Either discreetly leave the tip behind on the table or hand it directly to your server. A few restaurants may include a service charge for large parties; you don't need to tip in these situations.

Groceries

The aisles at St Lawrence Market (p95) and the delis around Kensington Market (p105) are great sights as well as providers of take-out meals and picnic goodies. Big chain supermarkets crop up in most neighborhoods. For vegetarian, vegan and nondairy eats, natural food stores and organic grocers are the best bet, often including hot and cold buffets; here are a few worth trying:

Baldwin Naturals (Map pp232–3; ☎ 416-979-1777; Baldwin Village, 16 Baldwin St; ☾ 10am-7pm Mon-Fri, to 6pm Sat, 11am-5pm Sun; ⓡ 501, 506) Fruit, vitamins, cosmetics, organic bread and dreadlocked staff.

Big Carrot (Map pp244–5; ☎ 416-466-2129; Greektown, 348 Danforth Ave; ☾ 9am-9pm Mon-Fri, to 8pm Sat, 11am-6pm Sun; ⓞ Chester) Organic juice bar, holistic dispensary, healthy cooking classes and organic groceries. The carrots are of normal size.

Lennie's Whole Foods (Map pp244–5; ☎ 416-967-5196; Cabbagetown, 489 Parliament St; ☾ 10am-7pm Mon-Fri, 9:30am-6pm Sat, noon-5pm Sun; ⓡ 506) Vitamins, minerals, protein powders, yoga mats and inflatable fitness balls.

Noah's Natural Foods (Map pp242–3; ☎ 416-968-7930; The Annex, 322 Bloor St W; ☾ 10am-8pm Mon-Wed, to 9pm Thu & Fri, to 7pm Sat, 11am-6pm Sun; ⓞ Spadina) Vitamins, food supplements, organic fruit and vegetables, juices and sandwiches.

Wholesome Market (Map p246; ☎ 416-690-9500; The Beaches, 2234 Queen St E; ☾ 9:30am-8pm Mon-Fri, to 7pm Sat; ⓡ 501) Fruit, vegetables, packaged nuts and well-dressed couples debating lettuce.

HARBOURFRONT

Oddly, given the prospect of superb lake views, there's not a whole lot going on in the Harbourfront food scene. There are a couple of decent options though.

PIER 4 RESTAURANT

Map pp234-5   Comfort Food $

☎ 416-203-1440; 245 Queen's Quay W; mains patio $5-10, restaurant $15-35; ☾ noon-10:30pm; ⓖ ; ⓡ 509, 510

Sit inside if you want to, but the place to be on a muggy summer day is on Pier 4's lakeside patio, strewn with timber-topped tables like God's spilled Scrabble board. Patio food offerings are cheap and cheerful (burgers, wings, salads, sourdough chowder etc). Inside the faux-nautical restaurant – a landlubber's spoil of wicker and wood – the menu includes pastas, soups, steaks and seafood.

HARBOUR SIXTY STEAKHOUSE

Map pp234-5   Steakhouse/Seafood $$$

☎ 416-777-2111; 60 Harbour St; mains $29-52; ☾ 11:30am-1am Mon-Fri, 5pm-1am Sat & Sun; ⓡ 509, 510

Inside the strangely isolated 1917 Toronto Harbour Commission building, this opulent baroque dining room glows with brass lamps and plush booths. Indulge yourself in an eminent variety of steaks, sterling salmon ($32) or seasonal Florida stone-crab claws and broiled Caribbean lobster tail. Side dishes seem pricey but are big enough for two people. Arrive early to start on an award-winning wine list of European and New World vintages, then stay late and linger over chocolate soufflé with Grand Marnier *crème anglaise* ($17). Book ahead.

360° Map pp234-5   International $$$

☎ 416-362-5411; 301 Front St W; mains $32-65; ☾ 11am-10pm; ⓞ Union

You don't need to tell us that dining at the top of the CN Tower is an obvious cliché, and it's damn pricey too, but come on, how can you compete with those views?! Even if the food was ordinary (which it most certainly isn't), there would be no better place in Toronto, if not Canada, for a high-class meal and a conversation about mankind's magnificent achievements. And the elevator ride is free!

FINANCIAL DISTRICT

High-powered and traditional restaurants populate the Financial District, convenient for shoppers and downtown hotel guests.

SPICES CAFÉ Map pp234-5   Indian $

☎ 416-364-6276; 4 Temperance St; mains $5-10; 🕑 11am-8pm Mon-Fri, noon-6pm Sat; 🚇 Queen

Lost in a realm of fat wallets and million-dollar deals closed with the snap of a cell phone, Spices presents an incongruously affordable and atmospheric option for lunch or an early city dinner. A sitar soundtrack twangs seductively, and there's a home-made feel to the food, served buffet-style or packaged up for a quick-fire take-out. Grab some *samosas*, a butter chicken curry and a mango *lassi* and head for the Cloud Forest Conservatory (p55) down the street.

RICHTREE MARKET RESTAURANT

Map pp234-5   International/Late Night $

☎ 416-863-0108; BC Pl, street level, 42 Yonge St; mains $6-10; 🕑 7:30am-2am; 👶 ; 🚇 Union

Inside the skeletal BC Place, this rainbow-flag-dappled market-style eatery plates up generous serves to satisfy every whim – cakes, freshly made soups, pizza slices, pasta dishes, roast chicken, fried rice, baked goods, fresh juices and coffee. Contemporary adult Brit-rock (Sting, Clapton et al) lends an air of affluent self-satisfaction to themed eating areas. Most of the pot-plants are real; the parrot in the cage isn't. There's another branch in the Eaton Centre (Map pp232–3; ☎ 416-351-8783; Queen St & Dundas Square, 220 Yonge St, lower level; 🚇 Queen).

MERCATTO Map pp234-5   Italian Café $$

☎ 416-306-0467; 330 Bay St; meals $8-14; 🕑 7am-8pm Mon-Fri; 🚇 King

One of an effervescent string of Italian deli cafés, Mercatto serves up creative panini, pasta, risotto, frittata and pizza dishes at a central dining bench beneath entirely out-of-place chandeliers. No one's much concerned with what's above them though – faces are focused on the plates. A cappuccino bar and toasty patio nook sit off the sidewalk. Another branch is in Old York (☎ 416-366-4567; Old York, 15 Toronto St; 🚇 King).

BEER BISTRO Map pp234-5   Bistro $$

☎ 416-861-9872; 18 King St E; mains $8-24; 🕑 11:30am-1am Mon-Wed, to 2am Thu & Fri, 4pm-2am Sat; 🚇 King

Packed to the gills with city lunchers during the day and boozy, flush-faced suits after dark, this stylish bistro offers sensational sandwiches, salads, meat and seafood dishes, each with a suggested beer pairing. Descriptions of the alcoholic experience include 'spicy,' 'bold,' 'robust' and 'sociable.' Try the grilled lamb loin niçoise with a pint of 'appetizing' Petrus Oud Bruin ($22). Avoid the side patio unless it's balmy beer weather.

VERTICAL Map pp234-5   Modern European $$

☎ 416-214-2252; First Canadian Pl, 100 King St W, Upper Level; mains lunch $15-24, dinner $17-44; 🕑 11:30am-3pm & 5-10pm Mon-Fri; 🚇 King

Vertical hangs off the side of an upmarket downtown foodcourt (protected from the proletariat by double doors and a sassy maître d').Chef Tawfik Shehata scales lofty lunch-time heights, his seasonal specials spinning off a core menu of pasta dishes and meaty mains. Dinners are a little more adventurous with mains like potato-wrapped tuna with roasted eggplant and salsa *rossa* ($33). Wines sluice from California to Italy, Australia and the Niagara Peninsula.

BYMARK

Map pp234-5   Contemporary Canadian/Fusion $$$

☎ 416-777-1144; street level, Toronto-Dominion Centre, 66 Wellington St W; mains $34-50; 🕑 11:30am-11pm Mon-Fri, 5-11pm Sat; 🚇 St Andrew

Celebrity chef Mark McEwan of North 44° (p113) brings his sophisticated menu of continentally-hewn cuisine to this hip, bilevel downtown room, a favorite with the 'Bay St Boys.' His crew of genuinely creative kitchen operators whip seasonal regional ingredients (wild truffles, Niagara quail, the season's first soft-shell crab) into sensational combinations, each with its own suggested wine or beer pairing. Keep an ear to the ground for the 2007 opening of McEwan's new restaurant, tentatively called 'One.'

CANOE

Map pp234-5   Contemporary Canadian $$$

☎ 416-364-0054; 54th fl, Toronto-Dominion Centre, 66 Wellington St W; mains $36-42; 🕑 11:45am-2:30pm Mon-Fri, 5-10:30pm daily; 🚇 St Andrew

Toronto's definitive dining space may still be Canoe, and what a space it is! Sweeping views of choppy Lake Ontario and the Toronto Islands extend from the dining room, about half-mast to the CN Tower. Intriguing regional Canadian haute cuisine is on offer

HIGH TIME FOR TEA

Remember, Canada was once British territory – old-world tea and cake is a tradition Torontonians seem unwilling to forget.

For a straight-laced Victorian afternoon tea, the **Windsor Arms** (p172) has all the whistles and bells: tinkling ivories, starched tablecloths, overstuffed chairs and crackling fireplaces. Call for times and reservations. Meanwhile, **Epic** (Map pp234–5; ☎ 416-860-6949; Financial District, 100 Front St W; ⏰ 2:30-4pm Mon-Fri, 1-4pm Sat, 3-4pm Sun; Ⓤ Union) restaurant, just off the lobby of the **Fairmont Royal York** (p167), offers variations like 'Tea and Tarot' and special caffeine-free kids' teas. Expect to pay $20 to $30 per person at both these venues.

On Queen West, the **Red Tea Box** (p108) serves pan-Asian afternoon teas (from $15) inside its small shop, which has more in common with a Malaysian tea plantation bungalow than Olde England. At The Beaches, whimsy abounds at **La Tea Da Salon de Thé** (Map p246; ☎ 416-686-5787; 2305 Queen St E; afternoon tea $15; ⏰ 11am-6pm Tue-Sun; 🚋 501), where a medley of fresh-baked scones, jam, cream and sandwiches is served. Further-flung **Montgomery's Inn** (p78) has a tea room full of history, open from 2pm to 4:30pm Tuesday to Sunday.

Phone ahead to book Edwardian teas at the **Spadina Museum** (p69), afternoon tea tours of the **Provincial Legislature** (p69) and glorious operatic teas sponsored by the **University of Toronto Faculty of Music** (p134).

---

here. Find your sea legs after the elevator ride then tuck into a plate of pan-seared Yarmouth scallops ($23) or Nunavut caribou hind ($44). Reservations essential.

OLD YORK

The streets of Old York offer a broader range of eateries than those in the neighboring Financial District – less flash for less cash. St Lawrence Market is an absolute must-see.

ST LAWRENCE MARKET

Map pp234-5   Specialty/Take-out $
☎ 416-392-7120; South Market, 95 Front St E; ⏰ 8am-6pm Tue-Thu, 8am-7pm Fri, 5am-5pm Sat; 🚻 ; 🚋 503, 504

Buskers and classical trios provide an acoustic backdrop at the city's beloved indoor market, offering a mouth-watering range of quality produce, baked goods and imported foodstuffs. Crowds pack lunch counters outside Everyday Gourmet, Quik Sushi ('Free meal for primadonna!'), St Urbain for Montréal-style bagels and Mustachio's for chicken sandwiches which are 'about as big as your head.' The Farmers' Market (since 1803) livens up the North Market from 5am Saturdays.

SPRING ROLLS

Map pp234-5   Pan-Asian $$
☎ 416-365-3649; 85 Front St E; mains $8-16; ⏰ 11am-11pm; 🚋 503, 504

One of five Spring Rolls around town, the Old York dining space is a cool mod room cast-

ing its culinary net from Vietnam to China. Bowls of Vietnamese *pho* (noodle soup) mingle with spicy Sichuan wok dishes, classic *pad thai* (stir-fried noodles), curries and banana fritters. And yes, they have spring rolls too (two for $4).

BIFF'S

Map pp234-5   French Bistro/Pre-theatre $$
☎ 416-860-0086; 4 Front St E; mains $11-25, oysters $1 4-7pm Mon-Fri; ⏰ noon-2:30pm Mon-Fri, 5-10pm Mon-Sat; 🚋 503, 504

A short flight from the Hummingbird Centre for the Performing Arts, Biff's is a welcoming place for all occasions: a high-stakes business lunch, a pre-theatre supper or a romantic full-course meal spent lingering over champagne on the sidewalk patio. Chef Basilio Pesce's specials include roast wing of skate with sauce *vierge* and preserved lemon ($22).

SULTAN'S TENT & CAFÉ MAROC

Map pp234-5   Moroccan $$
☎ 416-961-0601; 49 Front St E; mains $12-25; ⏰ noon-3pm Mon-Fri, 5-10:30pm Mon-Sat; 🚋 503, 504

Arabic, Spanish, French, English and Berber influences have swept through Morocco over the centuries, the culinary fallout from which can be sampled at this atmospheric room, replete with stained-glass lanterns, candles, slow-spinning ceiling fans, fringed cushions, and a bar to rival Rick's Café. Try the *harira* soup (chickpeas, lentils and spices, $5), followed by zesty crab cakes ($11) and the splendid Couscous Royale ($22). Belly-dancers may or may not help you digest.

CYRANO'S

Map pp234-5   Steakhouse Grill $

☎ 416-362-4342; 73 King St E; mains $12-27; ⏰ 11am-11pm Mon-Fri, from 5pm Sat; Ⓜ King

Follow your nose in Cyrano's, an enduring (since 1959) downtown bistro with red leather seats and a portrait of the nasally well-endowed Monsieur de Bergerac on the wall. Order reliably good salads, ribs or seafood offerings, or launch into the signature 16oz rib steak. If you're in a hurry, sit at the bar and graze through a quick-fire menu of burgers, wings and oysters, washed down with Creemore Springs on tap.

NAMI Map pp234-5   Japanese $$

☎ 416-362-7373; 55 Adelaide St E; mains $16-33; ⏰ 11:45am-2.30pm Mon-Fri, 5:30-10:30pm Mon-Sat; Ⓜ King

The name means 'wave' (as in tsunami) – look for the curly neon version on the sign out the front. Bustling about the sleek, black lacquered interior are kimono-clad matrons and intense-looking sushi chefs, who make only small concessions to North American palates. *Robatayaki* grilling is a specialty.

COURTHOUSE MARKET GRILLE

Map pp234-5   Steakhouse Grill $$

☎ 416-214-9379; 57 Adelaide St E; mains $17-27; ⏰ 11:30am-10pm Mon-Wed, to 11pm Thu, to midnight Fri, 5pm-midnight Sat; Ⓜ King

You mightn't want to dedicate much thought to it over your sirloin, but Toronto's last public execution took place here. It's a distinguished 1853 building with fireplaces, leather chairs and marble floors – downstairs the bathrooms are inside old jail cells. Expect perfectly grilled meats and whole fish, and a wine list which, unlike the architecture, is cleverly cleft into 'Old World' and 'New World.'

TOP FIVE RESTAURANTS FOR KIDS

Bright Pearl (p100)

Duke of York (p103)

Richtree Market Restaurant (p94)

St Lawrence Market (p95)

Wayne Gretzky's (right)

PURE SPIRITS

Map pp244-5   Oyster House & Grill $$$

☎ 416-361-5859; Distillery District, 55 Mill St; mains $22-31; ⏰ 11:30am-3pm & 5-11pm; 🚋 503, 504

The best of the upmarket eateries in the Distillery District, Pure Spirits' superb brick-lined vault fills with theatre-goers, international tourists and affluent locals enjoying plates of oysters on ice ($2 to $3 each) and delicious seafood and meat meals, like the Arctic Char – a mussel and clam *bourride* (soup) with toasted pine nuts, basil, vegetables and pesto tapenade ($27). Free live jazz on the patio in summer aerates the mood; reservations essential.

THEATRE BLOCK & ENTERTAINMENT DISTRICT

These overlapping districts feature plenty of affordable pre-theatre dining options around King St W, though service here can be surprisingly abrupt (we suspect a bad case of 'I want to go to the theatre too!' blues). In the Entertainment District, eateries tend to fall on the fast-food side of the culinary tracks, but there are a few gems here too.

BURRITO BOYZ

Map pp234-5   Mexican/Take-out $

☎ 416-593-9191; 120 Peter St; mains $4-8; ⏰ 11:30am-11pm Mon-Thu, to 4am Fri & Sat, noon-9pm Sun; 🚋 501, 502

Club-hounds who haven't got lucky pile into this basement booth to assuage their disappointment with a hefty Mexican injection of chili, sour cream and salsa. There's hardly enough room in here for both you and your burrito, so grab one to go.

WAYNE GRETZKY'S

Map pp234-5   Family Restaurant $$

☎ 416-979-7825; 99 Blue Jays Way; mains $11-25; ⏰ 11:30am-1am Mon-Thu, to 2am Fri & Sat, to 11pm Sun; 👶 ; 🚋 503, 504

Named after the Canadian hockey deity, Wayne Gretzky's is a sports bar, restaurant and rooftop patio serving fairly

LOCAL VOICES: SUSIE READING

Having grown up in Cabbagetown, Susie Reading, 41, is a true downtown Torontonian. Graduating from George Brown College (Toronto's famous hospitality school), she served an apprenticeship at the **Fairmont Royal York** (p167) and became its sous chef. Now as **Claphalon Cooking Academy's** (p199) executive chef, she runs classes and plans the Academy's delicious recipes.

What makes Toronto such a great city for dining?
It's the diversity of the food – especially through multiculturalism in the last 30 years. If you walk up Spadina Ave, within 10 minutes you'll be in Chinatown – all Asian restaurants and markets. Then you cut across into Kensington Market which is really bohemian, then you'll hit the old Italian district on College St – it's all restaurants and bars. Then you continue up to Bloor St through the University area to Koreatown. And this is literally 30 minutes' walk.

So multiculturalism has only really influenced Toronto's cuisine in the last 30 years?
I think so. I've had instructors that say when they arrived in Toronto in the '50s, the only real food available was English food, and ethnicity went about as far as spaghetti. That's about it. Probably from the '70s things started to change.

How do you think Toronto's food scene stacks up against the other Canadian cities?
I think Montréal might have a leg up on a few items – the French-based foods. Québec City too, but I think Toronto is a bit more daring. Vancouver has a fantastic restaurant scene, but they're more fickle than we are. They're always looking for the next 'hot' thing, but here if we have a great restaurant, we stick with it. I don't know about the east coast – they have bountiful seafood, but I don't know if they have the melting pot that demands the different cuisines that we do here.

Where do you shop for your ingredients?
Usually **Kensington Market** (p105) which is nearby. I live in Riverdale on the other side of Cabbagetown, and there's an Asian market there. For produce, definitely Asian markets. **St Lawrence Market** (p95) is also a great spot.

Where do you like to eat out on your nights off?
I think I'm doing it more and more! A cook's life is usually, A) you don't have any nights off, and B) you don't have any money, but now that's changing a little bit. I like very simple food, easily prepared, and somewhere without a line-up. I hate waiting. I usually go up to **Kensington Market** (p105) or **Baldwin Village** (p99) – within half a block there's about 10 choices, all really diverse.

Yeah, there's that little Malaysian place, some Chinese…
And **John's Italian Café** (p100) – good pizza. If it's too busy I walk up to **Little Italy** (p105).

Do you use maple syrup in your cooking for anything other than pancakes?
Absolutely, I love it! Maple syrup and scallops! If you add a touch of olive oil to the scallops then a touch of maple syrup on top in a hot pan and sear it, it caramelizes and it's a little crunchy – beautiful. And maple-glazed salmon, of course!

innocuous pastas, salads, steaks and burgers. But the food is almost a secondary concern – a lot of sports fans are here on a pilgrimage to view the hockey memorabilia, emblazoned with the famous No 99. Grandma Gretzky's 'heirloom classic' meatloaf is a real gap-filler.

URBAN Map pp234-5   Eclectic/Pre-theatre $$
☎ 416-598-5656; 303 King St W; mains lunch $13-27, dinner $18-40; ⏱ 11:30am-11pm; 🚊 504

Drawing more than its fair share of diners to this stretch of King St W, Urban's secret is its cool rooftop patio where a mature crowd lingers over dishes like the daily risotto ($18) and halibut saltimbocca with herb and mascarpone polenta, ratatouille and olive oil ($28). If you have to ask what saltimbocca is, staff are knowledgeable without smugness. Exactly how do they roll the serviettes to create a replica of City Hall?

Eating   **THEATRE BLOCK & ENTERTAINMENT DISTRICT**

KIT KAT Map pp234-5 — Italian/Pre-theatre $$

☎ 416-977-4461; 297 King St W; mains $14-28; ☽ 11:30am-10:30pm Mon-Fri, 4-11pm Sat, to 11pm Sun; ◻ 504

A saving grace near the Theatre Block is Kit Kat, where the vibe manages to stay low-key (dare we say, bohemian) despite the surrounding glitz. It's a cute Italian shopfront restaurant, complete with red-and-white checked tablecloths, serving traditional southern Italian pasta and meat dishes like *osso buco Milanese* ($22) and spaghetti *pescatore* ($20).

AUTOGRILL Map pp234-5 — Modern Italian $$

☎ 416-599-0961; 345 Adelaide St W; mains $17-23; ☽ 11am-11pm Mon-Fri, 5pm-midnight Sat; ◻ 510, 504

Wow, this substreet room is *so* sexy! Leave the uncool you at the door, slink downstairs and order a martini at the bar. Cream leather dining booths await, from which friendly staff receive orders for 10-inch stone-baked pizzas, rigorously re-interpreted pasta favorites and magical risottos (try the Risotto Barolo – smoked pancetta and spring onions sautéed in Barolo wine and topped with shaved parmigiano cheese, $17).

SPOON

Map pp234-5 — Contemporary Canadian $$

☎ 416-599-7000; 391 King St W; mains lunch $11-19, dinner $17-35; ☽ 11:30am-2:30pm Tue-Fri, 4:30-10pm Tue & Wed, to 11pm Thu-Sat; ◻ 504, 510

Impressive Spoon spoons out a dose of style among an otherwise dated row of restaurants. It's a long, thin room with voluminous wine glasses, spoon-shaped chairs, lulling urban jazz and walls almost as white as the teeth of the picture-perfect clientele. Start with some PEI mussels in green tea, lemongrass, lime leaf and coconut broth ($12), before moving on to the braised lamb shank with sweet potato mash, sprouts and pomegranate reduction ($23). Wines by the glass or bottle.

MONSOON

Map pp234-5 — Asian Fusion $$$

☎ 416-979-7172; 100 Simcoe St; mains $24-41; ☽ 11:30am-3pm Mon-Fri, 5:30-10pm Mon-Sat; ◉ St Andrew

Clean Zen lines, outrageous tropical flowers and mid-century modern designs mix harmoniously in this sexy subterranean lounge. The menu offers a downpour of flavors, listing the likes of halibut seared in ginger-saké sauce or Bangkok bouillabaisse along with lemongrass sorbet to refresh your palate between glorious courses.

SEN5ES Map pp234-5 — Eclectic $$$

☎ 416-935-0400; 318 Wellington St W; breakfast & lunch $5-17, dinner $32-45; ☽ 7am-2pm daily, 6-11pm Tue-Sat, lounge 5pm-1am daily; ◻ 504

This truly divine caterer's creation reigns over the ground floor of the SoHo Metropolitan Hotel (p169). In the sun-drenched airy café, breakfast brings an impeccable cappuccino and chocolate croissant, while the sleek modern dining room harbors a chef's table; nocturnal offerings including goat's cheese beef ravioli and seared scallops with citrus salad and curry yoghurt. Alternatively, dine in the lounge to sample from the same amazing menu for under $25 per plate.

QUEEN STREET & DUNDAS SQUARE

There are plenty of cheap eating options around this busy shopping area to help the discerning traveler avoid a mainstream dining disaster.

CAFÉ CREPE Map pp232-3 — Creperie $

☎ 416-260-1611; 246 Queen St W; crepes $4-7; ☽ 9am-10pm Mon-Thu, to midnight Fri & Sat, 10am-10pm Sun; ♿; ◻ 501

Watch the white-clad chefs deftly ladle the crepe mixture onto the hotplates then swirl it into delicious browned discs using a nifty wooden spatula. Sweet and savory fillings taste as good as they smell – try the coconut and banana special ($7). There are booths at the back, or crepe-escape onto the streets.

TERRONI Map pp232-3 — Italian Deli $

☎ 416-955-0258; 106 Victoria St; meals $11-16; ☽ 9am-10pm Mon-Fri, from 10am Sat; ◉ Queen

A traditional southern Italian grocers and deli, Terroni is a winner! Off-duty Toronto chefs shamble through the doors for wood-oven-fired pizzas, wines by the glass and fresh panini, all approaching perfection. Walls are lined with jars of pasta, olives and preserved peppers, fresh-cut flowers sit on the counter, and razzamatazz big-band jazz keeps the mood 'up.' There's another branch in **Queen West** (Map pp240–1; ☎ 416-504-0320; 720 Queen St W; ⓡ 501).

COMMENSAL
Map pp232-3   Vegetarian Buffet $
☎ 416-596-9364; 655 Bay St, entrance off Elm St; lunch $10, dinner $15; ⓨ 11:30am-9:30pm Mon & Tue, to 10pm Wed-Fri, noon-10pm Sat & Sun; ⓞ Dundas
Cafeteria-style Commensal sells 100-plus buffet dishes, including fresh salads, hot main dishes with international flavors and desserts naturally sweetened with maple syrup or fruit nectars. Most dietary restrictions can be accommodated; only a few dishes approach blandness (which the mod-mall interior design approached years ago). Herbal teas, beer and wine also make the grade.

QUEEN MOTHER CAFÉ
Map pp232-3   International $$
☎ 416-598-4719; 208 Queen St W; mains $9-17; ⓨ 11:30am-1am Mon-Sat, to 11pm Sun; ⓞ Osgoode
Another Queen St institution, Queen Mother Café is beloved for its cozy, dark wooden booths and excellent pan-Asian dim sum (not a regal cream tea in sight!). Canadian comfort food is also on the menu, and check out the display of weird old stuff they found in the walls the last time they renovated.

SAFFRON TREE
Map pp232-3   Indian/Take-out $$
☎ 416-850-3179; 91 Gerrard St W; mains $10-17; ⓨ 11am-10.30pm; ⓞ College
Readers rave about Saffron Tree, an unmissable saffron-hued bastion of spicy delight in the dull hospital wastelands north of Dundas St. Service is utterly polite, and classics like butter chicken and lamb *vindaloo* won't let you down. There's a 10% discount if you want to get take-out and impress your hotel's management with curry aromas.

SENATOR RESTAURANT
Map pp232-3   Diner $$
☎ 416-364-7517; 249 Victoria St; mains $8-28; ⓨ 7:30am-3pm Mon-Fri, 8am-3pm Sat & Sun, 5-7:30pm Wed-Sat; ⓞ Dundas
One for architecture buffs, this '30s art deco luncheonette features curved glass windows, a fluted aluminum counter-face, archaic

CANADIAN BEER GUY
Your typical Canadian is an outdoorsy huntin'-and-fishin' type, fond of caps with ear-flaps and guzzling cheap, watery beer from aluminum cans, right? It'd be misleading to *completely* debunk this stereotype, but in Toronto at least, the typical Canadian Beer Guy is about as rare as a grizzly bear on Yonge St. Downtown restaurants attract sophisticated wine buffs who have been quaffing French, Spanish and Italian varietals for decades, and now enjoy multipage wine lists with quality New World selections from South Africa to Chile, California, the Niagara Peninsula and Australia. Sure, the locals love their lager, but they're more likely to order a Belgian wheat beer or a pint of small-batch microbrew from **Steam Whistle Brewing** (p54) or **Amsterdam Brewing Co** (p50) than anything mass-produced. Leave your hunting cap at home – wining, like dining, in Toronto is a truly worldly experience.

coffee urns and original booths – what a time warp! The menu has shifted marginally upmarket, but the service is still very 'diner.'

BARBERIAN'S STEAK HOUSE
Map pp232-3   Steakhouse $$$
☎ 416-597-0335; 7 Elm St; mains $24-54; ⓨ noon-2:30pm Mon-Fri, 5pm-midnight daily; ⓡ Dundas
This classic steakhouse has been here for decades, and is regularly graced by hungry Hollywood carnivores like Sharon Stone and Edward Norton. John Candy was a regular, but let's not get into any morbid speculation… A New York sirloin will set you back $38. The only word to describe the 15,000-bottle wine cellar is astounding.

CHINATOWN & BALDWIN VILLAGE
Chinatown bubbles over with dozens of inexpensive Cantonese, Szechwan, Hunan and Mandarin eateries, with a not-so-new wave of Thai and Vietnamese restaurants crashing the party.

You mightn't hear many people talking about it, but secretive Baldwin Village is a T.O. foodies' favorite – tastes from Europe, the Americas and Asia served up on sunny summer patios along Baldwin St.

FURAMA CAKE & DESSERT GARDEN

Map pp232-3   Chinese Bakery $

☎ 416-504-57099; 248-250 Spadina Ave; items
$1-4; ☽ 10am-11pm; ⓰; ☒ 510

Always bustling, Furama sells lotus seed
cakes, almond cookies and curried buns for
pocket change. Wash down pineapple butter
cake and some silky, melt-in-the-mouth egg
tarts with a butt-kicking Chinese coffee.

DUMPLING HOUSE RESTAURANT

Map pp232-3   Chinese $

☎ 416-596-8898; 328 Spadina Ave; 12 dumplings
$4-6; ☽ 11am-11pm; ☒ 510

You can't go wrong here – order a mass of
pork, chicken, beef, seafood or vegetarian
dumplings (pan-fried or steamed), impale
them on your chopsticks, dunk them in soy
sauce and dispense with them forthwith.

GOLDSTONE NOODLE RESTAURANT

Map pp232-3   Hong Kong/Cantonese $

☎ 416-596-9053; 266 Spadina Ave; mains $5-10;
☽ 8am-2am Sun-Thu, to 4am Fri & Sat; ☒ 505, 510

The chefs at this mirror-walled restaurant
put on a front-window performance, plating
up humongous mounds of twisted noodles
mixed with chunks of glazed duck and
orange-stained squid while other dismem-
bered beasts dangle from hooks. Diners
leave decimated piles of bowls, scoured
clean of contents. This is apocalyptic eating!

BALKAN BISTRO

Map pp232-3   Turkish/Take-out $

☎ 416-913-0729; 126e McCaul St; mains $6-10;
☽ 11:30am-9:30pm Mon-Thu, to 10pm Fri & Sat;
⓰; ☒ 505

A husband-and-wife team run this joint, a
Turkish take-out dressed up with timber
paneling to look like something much more.
The homemade cooking follows suit, elevat-
ing itself past simple kebabs to meaty mains
served with rice, baked potatoes and grilled
veggies. Try the *hunkar begendi* – Ottoman
veal stew on mashed grilled eggplant.

FUJIYAMA

Map pp232-3   Japanese $

☎ 416-596-1913; 49 Baldwin St; mains $7-10;
☽ 11am-11pm Mon-Fri, from 11:30am Sat & Sun;
☒ 505, 506

Enter this low-key Japanese diner through
a traditional timber arch wrapped in flickering fairy lights, then plant yourself at a
blonde-wood timber booth surrounded by
rice-paper lanterns emanating a soft glow.
The scene is set for non-greasy tempura and
moist teriyaki dishes, plus sushi, udon and
soba noodle fare.

PHỞ' HU'NG

Map pp232-3   Vietnamese $

☎ 416-593-4274; 350 Spadina Ave; mains $6-13;
☽ 10am-10pm; ☒ 510

Clipped service and infernally busy tables
are the price you pay for Phở' Hu'ng's awesome Vietnamese soups. A few dishes may
be a touch too authentic for some (what,
don't you like pork intestines and blood?).
There's another branch in **Bloor-Yorkville** (Map
pp238–9; ☎ 416-963-5080; 200 Bloor St W,
2nd fl; ◉ Museum).

SWATOW

Map pp232-3   Chinese/Late Night $

☎ 416-977-0601; 309 Spadina Ave; mains $8-14;
☽ 11am-2am; ☒ 505, 510

An extensive menu covers cuisine from
Swatow (a city now known as Shantou, on
the coast of China's Guangdong province),
nicknamed 'red cooking' for its potent
splashings of fermented rice wine. Cash only;
be prepared to queue.

BRIGHT PEARL

Map pp232-3   Cantonese/Dim Sum $

☽ 416-979-3988; 2nd fl, 346 Spadina Ave; dim
sum from $3, mains $11-16; ☽ 9am-midnight;
⓰; ☒ 510

Walk by the stone lions up to the 2nd floor
of Hsin Kuang shopping centre and discover
this Cantonese-style banquet hall. Dim sum
rules – dozens upon dozens of dishes (dumplings, wantons, satays, pork buns, spring rolls
etc, including vegetarian) are wheeled out
and enthusiastically proffered. The bathrooms are a source of much pride.

JOHN'S ITALIAN CAFÉ

Map pp232-3   Italian $$

☎ 416-537-0598; 27 Baldwin St; mains $10-20;
☽ 11am-11pm Sun-Thu, 11am-1am Fri & Sat;
☒ 505, 506

John's classic joint wouldn't look out of
place in New York's Little Italy, or even New
Jersey. The patio is the perfect summer-
night stage for a bottle of Chianti and a
cornmeal-crust pizza piled high with top-
pings. The coffee's good too. Hard to beat.

TOP FIVE ROMANTIC RESTAURANTS

7 West Café (right)
Harbour Sixty Steakhouse (p93)
Midi (below)
Mildred Pearce (p109)
Pop Bistro (p110)

MATAHARI BAR & GRILL

Map pp232-3   Malaysian $$
☎ 416-596-2832; 39 Baldwin St; mains $13-20;
🕐 11:45am-3pm Tue-Fri, 5-10pm Tue-Sun;
🚇 505, 506

An urbane hideaway with a peace-and-love vibe, Matahari's walls feature 'Good things are being said about you' and 'Wise men learn more from fools than fools from the wise' inscriptions. Sage words to ponder as you wait for your scented prawns in sweet and spicy tamarind ($18), chicken curry or Singaporean stir-fry. Desserts are inspired; so is the list of ice wines and imported beers.

MIDI Map pp232-3   French Bistro $$

☎ 416-977-2929; 168 McCaul St; mains $13-20;
🕐 11:30am-2:30pm Mon-Sat, 5:30-9:30pm Tue-Sat; 🚇 505

Romantic in a restrained, sophisticated, Gallic kind of way, Midi serves trad faves like Alberta lamb shanks, fresh market fish and steamed mussels (done seven different ways) in its crimson-colored room. Couples purr over tables at night; business types discuss tomorrow's takeovers during lunch, which focuses on quiches, salads and terrines.

YONGE STREET STRIP & CHURCH-WELLESLEY VILLAGE

Yonge St pumps day and night, but isn't one of Toronto's main eat streets. There are some tasty and affordable options here though. Further east, restaurants in the Church-Wellesley Village don't scale particularly lofty heights, but there are a few winners here too.

SAIGON SISTER

Map pp238-9   Vietnamese $
☎ 416-967-0808; 774 Yonge St; mains $7-18;
🕐 11am-11pm Mon-Sat, from noon Sun;
🚇 Bloor-Yonge

Hey sista, you sure are lookin' sharp! Head straight for the gorgeous garden patio, or position yourself among potted cacti to dine on soups, salads and stir-fries, memorable fruit drinks, teas and cocktails. A stylish retreat from the subwoofer chaos on Yonge St.

TEMPUS

Map pp238-9   Persian Fusion $$
☎ 416-929-8893; 508 Yonge St; mains $8-13;
🕐 11:30am-10pm Mon-Fri, noon-11pm Sat, 1-10pm Sun; 🚇 Wellesley

'Speak good words, do good things, help one another' – such are the thoughts of the Darvish Muslim ascetics whose cuisine inspires this restaurant. Super-friendly staff dish up heavy-on-the-meat stews and char-broiled kebabs along with dips and cooling yogurt side dishes.

ourpick 7 WEST CAFÉ

Map pp238-9   Eclectic/Late Night $$
☎ 416-928-9041; 7 Charles St W; mains $9-15;
🕐 24hr; 🚇 Bloor-Yonge

Heeeey, now this place is cool! Three floors of moody lighting, textured jade paint, framed life drawings, wooden church pews and jaunty ceiling angles set the scene for a dazzling selection of pizzas, pastas and sandwiches and 24-hour breakfasts. Make like a vampire sipping blood-red wine (by the glass or bottle) as the moon dapples shadows across the street.

WISH Map pp238-9   Eclectic/Late Night $$

☎ 416-935-0240; 3 Charles St E; mains lunch $9-16, dinner $18-30; 🕐 10am-midnight;
🚇 Bloor-Yonge

Billowy white cushions and scruffy grass tufts fringe this hipster restaurant and lounge, which looks like a winter wonderland year-round. Staff are funky, the cocktail list is dangerous, and you can always count on an omelette to help you through your hangover. Some of the more ambitious menu items need work, but the scene is sexy.

ZELDA'S

Map pp238-9   International/Comfort Food $$
☎ 416-922-2526; 542 Church St; mains $10-15;
🕑 11am-1am Mon-Wed, 11am-2am Thu-Sat,
10am-1am Sun; ⊙ Wellesley
Zany Zelda's has a winning combination
of familiar food, crazy cocktails, wailing
'70s disco and a spacious outdoor patio.
An equally zany Church-Wellesley crowd
adores the brash, colorful atmospheria, es-
pecially on drag queen and leather theme
nights.

KATMANDU

Map pp238-9   Nepalese/Indian $$
☎ 416-924-5787; 517 Yonge St; mains $10-17;
🕑 11:30am-10pm Mon-Sat, from 3pm Sun;
⊙ Wellesley
If 13 different types of *naan* and *roti* bread
doesn't spark your interest, you're probably reading the wrong guidebook. Use the
aforementioned breads to mop up your
selection from the huge menu of beef,
goat, lamb, chicken and vegetarian curries.
And check out the amazing clear-day photo
of the Himalayas by the door!

FIRE ON THE EAST SIDE

Map pp238-9   Eclectic $$
☎ 416-960-3473; 6 Gloucester St; mains $10-24;
🕑 noon-1am Mon-Fri, 10am-midnight Sat & Sun;
⊙ Wellesley
A stone's throw from Yonge St, this ultra-
chic neighborhood dining room feels just
like someone's living room. A haywire
fusion kitchen works variations on African,
Caribbean, Acadian French and Cajun
themes, from spicy crab cakes ($12) to
'kitchen sink' omelettes (containing every-
thing but; $12). Desserts are made by
the chef.

ETHIOPIAN HOUSE

Map pp238-9   Ethiopian $$
☎ 416-923-5438; 4 Irwin Ave; mains $12-28;
🕑 noon-1am; ⊙ Wellesley
It's a packed and popular place with
African-inspired murals on the walls, but
there's no silverware in sight as *sherro wot*
(seasoned chickpeas) and *gored-gored*
(spiced beef) are slathered onto moist
injera (bread). Save time for a traditional
coffee-roasting ceremony, when the aroma
of frankincense fills the air.

FOCACCIA RESTAURANT

Map pp238-9   Modern European $$
☎ 416-323-0179; 17 Hayden St; mains $14-28;
🕑 11:30am-2:30pm Mon-Fri, 6-11pm Tue-Sat;
⊙ Wellesley
Focaccia fills a woody room in a cute yel-
low Victorian house just off Yonge St. Oddly
enough there's no focaccia on the compact,
well-considered menu, just contemporary
Euro fare with a fusion twist. Try the grilled
calamari with parsley pesto and tomato jam
($9), followed by bison striploin with merlot
and black grape sauce and yam gratin ($28).

BYZANTIUM Map pp238-9   Fusion $$
☎ 416-922-3859; 499 Church St; mains $15-25;
🕑 11am-3pm Sun, 5pm-1am daily; ⊙ Wellesley
Slick interior design, hip young staff and
lots of laughter – get your doting sugar
daddy/mommy to take you to Byzantium.
Soften them up with a breakfast martini
(gin, Cointreau, marmalade, lemon juice and
sugar syrup), then direct them towards the
signature Caesar Salad or more adventurous
offerings like ostrich medallions with summer ratatouille and roasted sweet potato.

BISTRO 990 Map pp238-9   French $$$
☎ 416-921-9990; 990 Bay St; mains $21-42
🕑 noon-11pm Mon-Fri, 5:30-11pm Sat & Sun;
⊙ Wellesley
Ground zero for Toronto International Film
Festival starlets bunking down at the Sutton Place Hotel, Bistro 990 feels a bit lost
on a blustery reach of Bay St, but continues
to serve fine French standards like duck in
blackberry jus and rabbit fricassee. The wine
selection is excellent, but unless you're Sean
Penn, service can be surly.

BLOOR-YORKVILLE

The fickle Yorkville crowd confuses itself
trying to remember which eatery is 'in' this
week. Eating here is too often about being
seen in the scene rather than great cooking.

WANDA'S PIE IN THE SKY

Map pp238-9   Bakery Café $
☎ 416-925-7437; 7a Yorkville Ave; meals $5-10;
🕑 8am-6pm Mon-Wed, to 7pm Thu & Fri, 9am-
7pm Sat; 🔊 ; ⊙ Bay
Be prepared for flexibility when ordering,
since daily specials advertising a healthy

half-sandwich with soup or salad ($7) sell out faster than you can get in the door. A sugar rush is guaranteed by one of Wanda's fantastical dessert creations, maybe a slice of Ontario sour cherry or Niagara peach pie.

OKONOMI HOUSE

Map pp238-9   Japanese $
☎ 416-925-6176; 23 Charles St W; mains $6-12; ⏰ 11:30am-10pm Mon-Fri, noon-10pm Sat, noon-8pm Sun; ⓜ Bloor-Yonge
Authentic Okonomi House is one of the only places in Toronto, and perhaps North America, dishing up *okonomiyaki*, a savory Japanese cabbage pancake filled with your choice of meat, seafood or vegetables. It's perfect cold-weather comfort food (just ask Toronto's police force).

DUKE OF YORK Map pp238-9   Pub Grub $
☎ 416-964-2441; 39 Prince Arthur Ave; mains $10-13; ⏰ 11am-midnight; ♿ ; ⓜ St George
Admittedly it's a chain, yet the very Brit, student-filled Duke of York pub is the place for traditional ploughman's lunches, bangers and mash, Brick Lane curries, savory pies and, of course, fish and chips (wrapped in pages from a British daily!). Children are welcome upstairs.

INDOCHINE

Map pp238-9   Thai/Vietnamese $$
☎ 416-922-5840; 4 Collier St; mains $10-19; ⏰ 11:30am-3pm & 5-11pm Mon-Sat, 5-10pm Sun; ⓜ Bloor-Yonge
Simple and unpretentious, this discrete timber-slatted food room is a real find in this neck of the woods. Signature dishes include live Vancouver crab sautéed in lemon, garlic and wine, and spicy tamarind crab fried in blackbean sauce. There are plenty of vegetarian, fried rice and stir-fry noodle options too. Finish with a Vietnamese coffee or a disconcerting-looking purple rice desert.

BLOOR STREET DINER

Map pp238-9   Continental/Canadian $$
☎ 416-928-3105; Manulife Centre, 55 Bloor St W; mains $12-19; ⏰ noon-1am; ♿ ; ⓜ Bloor-Yonge
Its humble-sounding name belies just how swanky this place actually is, with its banquettes, starched tablecloths, formal table service by attentive servers and a Parisian-style patio. Steaks and rotisserie fare are as distinguished as the wine list; the buffet brunch ($19) is an exercise in indulgence. Hit the café section out the front for speedy muffins, bagels and take-out sandwiches.

FLOW Map pp238-9   Fusion $$$
☎ 416-925-2431; 133 Yorkville Ave; mains $30-36; ⏰ 5-11pm Mon-Thu, to midnight Fri & Sat; ⓜ Bay
Catering to a 'money is no object' clientele, slung-low Flow flows seamlessly from gulf prawns with summer berry compote to sour cherry-crusted Australian lamb with grilled asparagus, seasonal mushrooms, potato and passionfruit jus. After dark a sexy crowd moves in, transforming the room into a cocktail lounge.

SASSAFRAZ

Map pp238-9   Californian/Continental $$$
☎ 416-964-2222; 100 Cumberland Ave; mains $30-45; ⏰ 11am-2am; ⓜ Bay
With a red-carpet parade of celebs trotting in and out on a regular basis (Jude Law, Matthew McConaughey, Joan Collins and the like), Sassafraz feels more like LA than T.O. Jazz combos serenade weekend brunches, while sassy receptionists distribute the clientele between the sun-drenched sidewalk tables and indoor garden courtyard. The food? Predictably good.

BRUNCH MUNCH

Torontonians are single-minded in their search for the perfect weekend brunch (a combination of breakfast and lunch). Sleep late, then shuffle off for pancakes with fresh Ontario peaches and maple syrup, or maybe eggs Benedict with smoked salmon.

Appealingly urbane, **Byzantium** (opposite) dishes up a weekend brunch worth queuing for. **Latitude** (p105) serves spicy Latin brunches, heavy on hot salsa, eggs, cornmeal and fruity sangria, **Xacutti** (p107) does South Asian fusion and **Bright Pearl** (p100) is the place for Cantonese dim sum. Vegetarians, try **Fressen** (p108).

Hung over? Redeem yourself with comfort food at **Insomnia** (p105), **Mel's Montréal Delicatessen** (p105), **Toast** (p111) or **Edward Levesque's Kitchen** (p111). Head to the café section of the **Bloor Street Diner** (left) for a quick caffeine fix and a gap-filling bagel, or book a table inside for a more demure hangover cure.

BLOOR-YORKVILLE

UNIVERSITY OF TORONTO & THE ANNEX

The Annex bursts with budget Bloor St W eateries, most catering to lean U of T student budgets. West of Honest Ed's, The Annex dissipates into Koreatown – sushi shops and barbecue grills abound.

HODO KWAJA

Map pp242-3   Korean Bakery $

☎ 416-538-1208; 656 Bloor St W; cakes 6 for $1.25; ⛭ ; 🚇 Christie

Most of the space inside this Korean hole-in-the-wall bakery is consumed by an incredible cake-making contraption, imported from Korea at a cost of $30,000. The whirring machine produces bite-size walnut cakes at a rate of 1000 per hour – grab a bagful to round-out your morning coffee experience.

PAPA CEO Map pp242-3   Italian $

☎ 416-961-2222; 654 Spadina Ave; pizza slices $3-4; ⛭ 9am-4am; ⛭ ; 🚇 510

Papa Ceo seems to be winning its age-old pizza war with **Cora Pizza** two doors away. Gourmet slices here are enormous – grab a chunky slab of 'Marlon Brando' (mozzarella, pesto, ground beef, onions and mushrooms) and retreat to the back tables where Italian *Serie A* soccer dances across TV screens beneath air-conditioning vents.

TACOS EL ASADOR

Map pp242-3   Mexican $

☎ 416-538-9747; 690 Bloor St W; mains $4-8; ⛭ noon-9pm; 🚇 Christie

For an authentic taste of old Mexico, tether your horse to a bike rack and sit your saddle-sore behind down in this taco-sized Koreatown canteen. Burritos, enchiladas, nachos, tostadas and guacamole clatter across tiny timber tables beneath Mexican flags. Crane your neck to check the hockey score on the TV and swallow some cold Corona in the same movement.

FUTURE BAKERY & CAFÉ

Map pp242-3   International/Comfort Food $

☎ 416-922-5875; 483 Bloor St W; meals $5-9; ⛭ 8am-2am; ⛭ Bathurst

Future Bakery stays busy selling budget dishes like cheese crepes and homemade borsht with sour cream. Out on the huge street-side patio, lecture-dodgers slap backs and chug pints or push through all-night study sessions with bowls of café au lait and slabs of caramel cheesecake. Twisted '60s psychedelic pop contorts the airwaves.

HARBORD FISH & CHIPS

Map pp242-3   Seafood/Take-out $

☎ 416-925-2225; 147 Harbord St; meals $6-13; ⛭ 11:30am-10pm; ⛭ ; 🚌 94

This graffiti-covered, white-brick fish shack wins big smiles for its generous portions of haddock, halibut and shrimp, all freshly fried. Get yours wrapped up in newspapers, or chow down at outdoor paint-peeling picnic tables while your laundry spins at Coin-O-Rama across the street.

BY THE WAY CAFÉ

Map pp242-3   Mediterranean/Canadian $

☎ 416-967-4295; 400 Bloor St W; mains $8-15; ⛭ 9am-9:30pm Sun-Tue, to 10:30pm Wed, to 11:30pm Thu-Sat; ⛭ Bathurst, Spadina

An Annex fixture, this faded yellow corner bistro has a daily-changing menu of Mediterranean and New World fusion dishes, with plenty of creative choices for vegetarians. Service is A+ and the wine list features Niagara ice varietals and labels from Oregon and Australia. Why do people forsake the cozy booths inside for the crowded patio?

VICTORY CAFÉ Map pp242-3   Pub Grub $

☎ 416-516-5787; 581 Markham St; mains $8-15; ⛭ 4pm-2am Mon-Fri, 10am-2am Sat & Sun; ⛭ Bathurst

Writers, artists, musicians, students and publishers shuffle down Markam St and congregate around the leafy Victory Café patio. There's a truly bohemian vibe here, with Tuesday-night poetry readings and jazz quartets regularly be-bopping it up. The food is pub-style – wings, steaks, curries and burgers – served with a minimum of fuss and washed down with a swathe of beers on tap.

REAL THAILAND Map pp242-3   Thai $

☎ 416-924-7444; 350 Bloor St W; mains $8-16; ⛭ 11:30am-midnight; ⛭ Spadina

Truly authentic Real Thailand must have T.O.'s tiniest patio, but locals still flood through the doors here, looking to sate their chili and coconut-milk addictions. The menu features over 100 items including standards like *tod mun pla* (fish cakes; $9), *tom yum goong* (spicy soup; $9) and *larb* (salads; $8). Lunch specials are monumental.

INSOMNIA Map pp242-3
Comfort Food $

☎ 416-588-3907; 563 Bloor St W; mains $9-16; ☻ 11am-2am; ⊛ Bathurst

Can't sleep? Yawn into this arty café, where DJs take over after 10pm spinning R&B, lounge and rock. The eclectic menu has real staying power: roll up early for weekend brunch, hot cocktails on a cold night ($6.50), lunchtime pizza and pasta, or loosely defined tapas anytime. Nightly drinks specials and wi-fi internet access will help keep you awake.

MEL'S MONTRÉAL DELICATESSEN
Map pp242-3
Canadian/Comfort Food $

☎ 416-966-8881; 440 Bloor St W; mains $9-19; ☻ 24hr; ⅋ ; ⊛ Spadina

You're here for one thing and one thing only: Mel's famous Jumbo Smoked Meat Sandwich ($11). A cardiac arrest on a plate, this 8oz spectacular struggles to contain many layers of Mel's old-fashioned meat, shipped in from Québec twice weekly and cut against the grain to keep the juices in. Along with a pile of corkscrew fries and an 10oz beer, one feed will last you a week.

LATITUDE Map pp242-3
Latin American $$

☎ 416-928-0926; 89 Harbord St; mains $10-20; ☻ 11:30am-3pm daily, 5:30-10pm Mon-Sat; ⬚ 510

A Uruguayan chef takes care with pan–Latin American fare, and although the menu occasionally speaks of Asia, there's always fried yucca or plantains on the side. Looking for a romantic back patio? Head past the intimate wine bar, where the mojitos and margaritas kick like a mule.

SERRA Map pp242-3
Italian $$

☎ 416-922-6999; 378 Bloor St W; mains $12-25; ☻ noon-11pm; ⊛ Spadina

Serra is an unassuming neighborhood joint with funky retro lighting and cute staff, managing to be hip without straying too far from classic Italian stylings (on the walls and on the plates). Try a wood-oven pizza with grilled tiger prawns, scallops, artichoke hearts and ricotta ($14) or a herb-rubbed free-range chicken breast with sweet potato, spinach and mustard jus. *Perfecto*!

PATIO SYMPATICO

If you're not from Canada, you might find Toronto's obsession with patios a little weird. I mean, everybody eats outside, don't they? In Barcelona, maybe, but in T.O., the short, hot summer is followed by month after endless month of leafless trees and sunless freeze. The only people who do anything outside between October and May are hockey players and homeless people. During summer it's a case of culinary *carpe diem* as Torontonians cram onto restaurant patios – pot-plant-strewn timber decks, cordoned-off sidewalk sections and tent-like annex structures – and laugh it up in the sun, quaffing wine and savoring multicultural edibles. Don't ridicule their enthusiasm – if revenge is a dish best served cold, then Toronto's winter is vengeful indeed…

Our top five Toronto patios:

Bar Italia (p106)

Future Bakery & Café (opposite)

John's Italian Café (p100)

Pure Spirits (p96)

Urban (p97)

KENSINGTON MARKET & LITTLE ITALY

Hot, hectic and fragrant, Kensington Market explodes with Italian butchers, West Indian roti shops, Middle Eastern groceries, fruit markets and home-spun bakeries.

Stretching along College St, Little Italy is an eating and meeting hotspot. Many places double up as bars and clubs after dark; most are fully licenced.

GLOBAL CHEESE
Map pp240-1
Fromagerie $

☎ 416-593-9251; 76 Kensington Ave; cheeses from $3 per pound; ☻ 9am-7pm Mon-Fri, 8am-6pm Sat, 9am-5pm Sun; ⅋ ; ⬚ 510

OK, so it's not technically a place where you can sit down and eat, but WOW, have you ever seen such an *amazing* cheese shop? Fevered crowds elbow for a spot near the counter where staff, hidden behind teetering stacks of cheese, distribute slivers of Greek feta, Canadian gouda, Argentine parmesan, Spanish manchego and Swiss ementhal. Taste a few, order a wedge then hit the streets.

AKRAM'S SHOPPE

Map pp240-1   Middle Eastern $

☎ 416-979-3116; 191 Baldwin St; items $3-6;
☻ 10am-6pm Mon-Sat, 11am-4pm Sun; ☒ 510

Walking into spicy-smelling Akram's takes you on a magic-carpet ride through the kitchens of the Middle East – tubs of hummus, fresh-baked pita bread, organic ice-cream, halal meats, pots of nuts, vats of olives and spices, a wall of hookah pipes and freshly made gluten- and wheat-free falafels. Stock up for a picnic.

JUMBO EMPANADAS

Map pp240-1   Chilean/Take-out $

☎ 416-977-0056; 245 Augusta Ave; items $3-6;
☻ 9am-8pm Mon-Sat, 11am-6pm Sun; ☒ 510

Real Chilean empanadas (toasted sandwich-like delights stuffed with beef, chicken, cheese or vegetables) and savory corn pie with beef, olives and eggs always sell out early in the day. Bread and salsas are also homemade.

FULL MOON VEGETARIAN RESTAURANT

Map pp240-1   Chinese Vegetarian $

☎ 416-203-1210; 638 Dundas St W; mains $6-10;
☻ 11am-9:30pm Sun-Thu, to 10:30pm Fri & Sat;
☒ ; ☒ 505

Despite its lonesome location, Full Moon serves a chameleonic array of faux-meat dishes that have seduced Kensington Market's fiscally challenged residents. Cheery chef Ken Quah works wonders with mock beef, chicken and fish dishes. Try the house special: vegetarian fish with black bean sauce ($8.50) and finish off with some sweet sesame paste rice balls (six for $3).

RICE BAR

Map pp240-1   Organic Café $

☎ 416-922-7423; 319 Augusta Ave; mains $6-10;
☻ 11am-10pm Tue-Sun; ☒ 506

Create your own rice bowl at Rice Bar: choose your rice (basmati, jasmine, rice noodles or a daily infused-rice special), add protein (tofu, chicken, beef or shrimp), sauces (everything from coriander to miso BBQ), garnish to taste then hurl your chopsticks into the bowl. It also does salads, sandwiches, organic tea and coffee and a sensational vegan stew.

SUPERMODEL PIZZA

Map pp242-3   Pizza/Take-out $

☎ 416-533-9099; 772 College St; pizzas $6-13;
☻ 11am-midnight; ☒ ; ☒ 506

The motto stutters, 'Our crust is as thin as supermodel' – no prizes for grammar, and we didn't see any bulimic waifs chomping down slices, but we're willing to take the bait for one of their Florentine special pizzas (pesto, spinach, roast peppers and feta).

EL TROMPO Map pp240-1   Mexican $

☎ 416-260-0097; 277 Augusta Ave; mains $6-13;
☻ 11am-8pm Tue-Thu, to 9pm Fri, noon-9pm Sat, noon-6pm Sun; ☒ 506

El Trompo is a rustic, hole-in-the-wall taqueria, specializing in corn quesadillas, guacamole, huitlacoche cheese dishes and, of course, tacos. Heartfelt Spanish renditions of Righteous Brothers classics bounce off the adobe-mottled walls and resonate across the bright sidewalk patio.

BAR ITALIA Map pp242-3   Italian $$

☎ 416-535-3621; 582 College St; mains $10-17;
☻ 11am-1am Mon-Thu, to 2am Fri, 10:30am-2am Sat, 10:30am-1am Sun; ☒ 506

Trendsetters come and go, but Bar Italia remains a place to be seen and to relax. Grab an excellent sandwich or lightly done pasta, with a lemon gelato and a rich coffee afterward – while the entire afternoon or evening away. You might need to pay the mob for a seat on the deep-set street front patio.

PHIL'S ORIGINAL BBQ

Map pp242-3   Southern $$

☎ 416-532-8161; 838 College St; sandwiches $8, mains $13-22; ☻ noon-3pm Mon-Sat, 5-9pm Mon-Thu, to 10pm Fri & Sat; ☒ 506

'Real smoke. Real slow. Real good.' American barbecue-belt immigrants, these folks are passionate about 'cue. Order up a mess of heartbreakingly tender beef brisket and dry-rub smoked meats and smother the lot in homemade sauces. On the down side, service can be a little 'northern' (brrrr…).

65 DEGREES Map pp242-3   Italian $$

☎ 416-588-7377; 584 College St; mains $14-29;
☻ 5pm-midnight; ☒ 506

This relatively new kid on the Little Italy block seems to be making good, serving grilled steaks, lamb, chicken and seafood,

NOCTURNAL NIBBLES

Never fear, Cinderella, there's always good foraging after midnight in Toronto. You can depend on **Greektown** (The Danforth; p109) and **Little Italy** (p105) or stylish restaurants that don't shut their kitchens until midnight or later, and on Spadina Ave in **Chinatown** (p99), neon-lit noodle shops stay open practically all night. Other late-night eateries include **Richtree Market Restaurant** (p94), **Sassafraz** (p103), **Gypsy Co-op** (p108) and **Insomnia** (p105).

When even these trusty standbys shut down, hungry night-owls turn to Toronto's all-night diners, serving meals for $10 or less. A 24-hour weekend opener, retro **Mars Food** (Map pp242–3; ☎ 416-921-6332; Little Italy, 432 College St; mains $5-11; ⏱ 7am-8pm Sun-Thu, 24hr Fri & Sat; 🚋 506, 510) makes famous buttery muffins and waitstaff know regulars by name. Legend has it that the classic diner **Fran's** (Map pp238–9; ☎ 416-923-9867; Yonge Street Strip, 20 College St; mains $8-13; ⏱ 24hr; Ⓜ College) has never closed since it opened its doors in the 1940s. Not far away at the darkly romantic **7 West Café** (p101), lovers canoodle over wineglasses beneath Botticellian drawings. Scoffing 2am sandwiches at **Mel's Montréal Delicatessen** (p105) is an experience to tell your grandkids about.

along with classically hewn pasta and risotto dishes. We can recommend the gnocchi with Alaskan lobster, mixed peppers, baby spinach and cherry tomatoes in a zingy lemon saffron sauce ($16). The interior design is downright sexy.

XACUTTI Map pp242-3   Indian Fusion $$
☎ 416-323-3957; 503 College St; small plates $7-15, large plates $19-27; ⏱ 6:30pm-midnight Tue-Sat, 10:30am-4pm Sun; 🚋 506

It's pronounced 'Sha-koo-tee,' but don't worry too much about that. Focus instead on the gorgeous stained-glass shopfront, beyond which swirls of chocolate brown and jet black come alive with saffron accents – a befitting setting for exotic Indian dishes like Bengal chicken curry with cashew basmati ($24), supplemented by a well-versed wine list. Take-out isn't below them; Sunday brunch is a cool fusion exercise.

LEÃO D'OURO
Map pp242-3   Portuguese $$$
☎ 416-926-9889; 356 College St; mains $18-35; ⏱ noon-11pm Tue-Sun; 🚋 506

This place has been here for 30 years and, except for the odd hockey game on TV, remains unflappably Portuguese – pretty Portuguese staff, 100% Portuguese wine and a superb Portuguese menu. Try the signature Seafood Rice for two with whole grilled fish ($60), or maybe the Santola à Leão – steamed crab with house special dip ($35).

CHIADO Map pp242-3   Portuguese Seafood $$$
☎ 416-538-1910; 864 College St; mains $38-48; ⏱ noon-3pm Mon-Fri, 5-10pm daily; 🚋 506

Classy Chiado sits among laundromats and used-car dealerships at the not-so-classy

western end of Little Italy, but it's well worth suffering the surrounds. Start with the grilled tiger shrimp with piri-piri, roasted jalapeños and banana peppers, then move on to the grilled octopus with roasted sweet-pepper salsa. Service is formal and faultless; framed oils enliven the walls.

QUEEN WEST & WEST QUEEN WEST

Queen West sees Asian, Latin American and European flavors fused together in funky surrounds. New restaurants along King St W, between Spadina Ave and Bathurst St, are also worth a diversion, as are the hip West Queen West eateries (west of Trinity Belwoods Park).

DUFFLET PASTRIES
Map pp240-1   Bakery/Take-out $
☎ 416-504-2870; 787 Queen St W; items $2-23; ⏱ 10am-7pm Mon-Sat, noon-6pm Sun; 🚋 501

Dufflet Rosenberg's desserts grace the end-of-night tables of Toronto's most prestigious restaurants. Maneuver yourself towards the counter at her retail bakery for buttery cookies, rich tarts, layer cakes, pies, flans and sinfully good chocolate cakes.

LE GOURMAND
Map pp240-1   Specialty Café/Take-out $
☎ 416-504-4494; 152 Spadina Ave; meals $5-10; ⏱ 7am-9pm Mon-Fri, 9am-6pm Sat, 9am-4pm Sun; 🚋 510, 501

A nirvana for foodies, Le Gourmand is a classy grocery store stocking Napa Valley

Eating

QUEEN WEST & WEST QUEEN WEST

mustards, rare Mexican chocolates and jars of Italian eggplant pesto. Peruse the deli case and pastry shelves, sip a foamy cappuccino or cool off with a homemade gelato. As for breakfast, can we tempt you with a Portobello mushroom and goats' cheese omelette ($9)?

FRESSEN

Map pp240-1   Eclectic Vegetarian $

☎ 416-504-5127; 478 Queen St W; mains $10-14; ⏰ 5:30-10pm Mon-Fri, 10am-3pm Sat & Sun; 🚋 501

The zenith of vegetarian and vegan dining in Toronto, Fressen has brilliant service and sumptuous brick-and-wood dining room (with gold ceiling!) that make for an enjoyable night out, even for carnivores. A strong and stylish organic menu picks through world cuisines, depending on what's seasonal when you visit. The weekend vegan brunch is a hit.

RED TEA BOX

Map pp240-1   Pan-Asian Café $$

☎ 416-203-8882; 696 Queen St W; sandwiches & salads $7-12, lunch or afternoon tea $25; ⏰ 10am-6pm Mon, Wed & Thu, to 7pm Fri & Sat, noon-5pm Sun; 🚋 501

The jewel-like Red Tea Box has genuine South Asian flair. Handwoven Thai textiles drape the walls and locals queue for their monthly changing bento boxes ($25), a fusion world of taste-bud temptations. Everything's gorgeously presented, and seasonally inspired. Exotic and inviting afternoon teas (p95) are held Monday to Saturday from 2pm, and noon to 4pm Sunday.

IRIE FOOD JOINT

Map pp240-1   Caribbean $$

☎ 416-366-4743; 745 Queen St W; mains $9-16; ⏰ 4pm-midnight Mon, noon-11pm Tue & Wed, noon-midnight Thu-Sun; 🚋 501

A seductive Caribbean dining room with earth-toned chairs and a long bar, Irie adheres to the simple staples of 'Food, music, art, culture.' Mussels are served in ginger-mango-citrus cream sauce, jerk chicken wings with a pot of pepper sauce and fresh seafood main meals are true succulence defined. DJs spin tunes on some nights.

GYPSY CO-OP

Map pp240-1   International/Late Night $$

☎ 416-703-5069; 817 Queen St W; pastas $9-16, mains $14-22; ⏰ 6-10pm Mon-Fri, 11am-2am Sat & Sun; 🚋 501

Trendy Queen West eateries come and go, but this bohemian food room – with its quirky decoupage tabletops, retro lighting and abused floorboards – is an enduring favorite. Contemporary cuisine comes with international twists, like the miso- and hot mustard-glazed BC halibut ($22) and the red snapper fillet with curried Jamaican pumpkin ($23). Upstairs is **Hooch** (p131) lounge.

SWAN Map pp240-1   Eclectic Comfort Food $$

☎ 416-532-0452; 892 Queen St W; mains $10-20; ⏰ noon-10pm Mon-Fri, 10am-10pm Sat & Sun; 🚋 501

Fickle Queen Westers remain smitten with Swan, a swanky, nostalgic diner just off the beaten path by Trinity Bellwoods Park. You'll find upscale comfort food like nothing anyone's family ever cooked; from oyster omelettes to racks of beer-marinated ribs, dishes satisfy both the stomach and the soul.

JULIE'S Map p231   Cuban $$

☎ 416-532-7397; 202 Dovercourt Rd; mains $15-19; ⏰ 5:30-11pm Tue-Sun; 🚋 501

This West Queen West neighborhood secret (not so secret now, eh?) has customers driving from as far away as Buffalo to enjoy trad Cuban dishes like *ropa vieja* (shredded beef in spicy tomato sauce with ripe plantains, white rice and black beans; $17). The restaurant was once a grocery store, and every effort has been made (or rather, not made) to preserve the vibe: original linoleum floors, old store shelves, even the 1960s sign. The front patio is a winner.

RODNEY'S OYSTER HOUSE

Map pp240-1   Seafood $$

☎ 416-364-3790; 469 King St W; mains $15-25; ⏰ 11:30am-1am Mon-Sat; 🚋 504, 510

A classic underground oyster bar run by a PEI oyster boy made good, Rodney's flies in a dozen types of fresh oysters from both Pacific and Atlantic Oceans. Dungeness crabs, lobsters, Fundy scallops and seafood chowders swim their way onto the long daily menu, which ends at a N'awlins-style banana flambé. Well-chosen beer and wine pairings are available.

MILDRED PEARCE

Map p231 — International $$$
☎ 416-588-5695; 99 Sudbury St; mains $20-33; ☺ noon-2pm Mon-Fri, from 11am Sat, 5:30-10:30pm daily; ⓥ 501

In a former book-binding warehouse in an industrial tumbleweed pocket of West Queen West, Mildred Pearce is an unexpected treasure. Shimmering drapes reach floor-to-ceiling, framing full-wall murals of medieval feasting scenes. Super-courteous staff deliver meaty mains like pan-seared veal liver with bacon-roasted fingerling potatoes, rapini, Roquefort and thyme shallot jus ($26). Wine is served in shimmering balloons polished like diamonds. Who's Mildred? She's the fictional character Joan Crawford played in her 1945 Oscar-winning role.

SUSUR

Map pp240-1 — Eclectic Fusion $$$
☎ 416-603-2205; 601 King St W; mains $40-45; ☺ 6-11pm Mon-Sat; ⓥ 504, 511

Order à-la-carte, or let superstar chef Susur Lee take you on a whimsical journey through his elaborate tasting menus (six courses $120; vegetarian $75). Racing from Europe to the New World to Asia and back again, each plate is a magical study in contrasts, complemented by an imaginative wine list. Make sure you don't miss Susur's signature Thai green curry rack of lamb. You will need to book several weeks in advance.

TOP FIVE VEGETARIAN & VEGAN

The **Toronto Vegetarian Association** (☎ 416-544-9800; www.veg.ca) doles out free advice about eating out, cooking classes and September's annual vegetarian food fair.

Our favorites for atmosphere and inventive vegetarian cuisine are as follows:

Susur (above)

Commensal (p99)

Fressen (opposite)

Full Moon Vegetarian Restaurant (p106)

Rice Bar (p106)

EAST TORONTO

Greektown (The Danforth) along Danforth Ave gets thrillingly busy on hot summer nights – casual souvlaki joints and upscale mezes (Greek tapas) restaurants stay open late and the ouzo flows. Traditional bakeries and delis take over during the day. You can also get upmarket pub grub at **Allen's** (p118).

Whether you're bunking down in a B&B or just strolling around, historic Cabbagetown offers a handful of unique places to dine. Further east, epicurean haunts are sprinkled along Queen St E in Leslieville. For a wallet-friendly place with a side order of cultural experience, you can't beat Little India, trailing along Gerrard St E, just west of Coxwell Ave.

BAR-BE-QUE HUT Map pp244-5 — Indian $
☎ 416-466-0411; 1455 Gerrard St E; mains $6-15; ☺ noon-10pm Mon-Fri, from 11am Sat & Sun; ⓥ 506

They could probably change their name now (designed not to threaten virginal North American palates in 1976) but it's so well known it'd be business suicide! The fantastic funk of spices welcomes you at the door, luring you towards succulent North Indian tandoor slabs of chicken, sizzling curry pots or assorted *naan*, *paratha* and *kulcha* breads. Live Bolly-rock on weekends.

RAASHNA

Map pp244-5 — South Indian & Sri Lankan $
☎ 416-929-2099; 307 Wellesley St E; mains $7-12; ☺ 11:30am-11pm; ⓥ 506

Raashna, which means 'tasty' in Sanskrit, fills an out-of-kilter, cinnamon-colored Cabbagetown bungalow with wonderful surprises. Try the South Indian beef devil curry ($7) or Sri Lankan 'String Hopper Kottu' ($8). Service can be reluctant, but the prices are unbeatable – only a dollar or two for appetizers like deep-fried lentil dumplings with coconut chutney.

REAL JERK Map pp244-5 — Caribbean Bar $$
☎ 416-463-6055; 709 Queen St E; mains $5-15; ☺ 11:30am-10pm Mon-Thu, to midnight Fri, 1pm-midnight Sat, 2-10pm Sun; ♿ ; ⓥ 501, 502, 503, 504

You'd have to be a real jerk not to like this sunny Caribbean kitchen, serving classic jerk chicken, oxtail and goat curries, 'rasta pasta' and Red Stripe beer. Inside it feels just like a huge beach bar, with reggae, tropical decor and Jamaican flags hanging everywhere.

LESLIE JONES

Map pp244-5   Contemporary Canadian $$
☎ 416-463-5663; 1182 Queen St E; mains $9-15; ☿ 10am-10pm Tue-Sat, bar to 2am; 🚋 501, 502, 503

If you're not paying attention, you'll walk right past this moody, dim-lit room just east of Jones St in boomtown Leslieville (Leslieville, Jones St, Leslie Jones…oh so pithy). All-day breakfasts draw local arty types, while pasta dishes, meaty mains and sandwiches like jerk pork with mango salsa and chili mayo ($9) are great value.

SIDDHARTHA Map pp244-5   Indian $$
☎ 416-465-4095; 1450 Gerrard St E; mains $9-15; ☿ 11:30am-2:30pm & 4:30-10:30pm; 🚋 506
Siddhartha's special chicken korma (vegetables cooked with Indian spices and garnished with dried fruit; $9) may sound a bit weird, but it's delicious. So are their classic curries. They're also south of Queen West (Map pp240-1; ☎ 416-703-6684; 647a King St W; 🚋 504) – same hours, but you'll pay a few dollars more.

CHAPTER ELEVEN

Map pp244-5   Contemporary Canadian/Late Night $$
☎ 416-926-8811; 557 Parliament St; mains $9-17; ☿ 4:30am-2am Mon-Fri, from 11am Sat & Sun; 🚋 506

Part lounge bar, part restaurant, Cabbagetown's Chapter Eleven derives its name from a US term for bankruptcy. Perhaps they're tempting fate, but if they keep doing what they're doing now, bankruptcy won't ever be a problem. The menu has plenty of appetizers (hummus, deep-fried pepperoni, wings; $4 to $6), or tackle something more substantial like the spinach salad with goat's cheese, grapes, cherry tomatoes, chicken, sliced almonds and balsamic vinegar ($11).

OUZERI Map pp244-5   Greek $$
☎ 416-778-0500; 500a Danforth Ave; mezes $5-10, mains $12-20; ☿ 11:30am-11pm Sun-Thu, 11:30am-midnight Fri & Sat; ◉ Chester
Sensibly priced mezes and sophisticated seafood endear this friendly place to local

families. Roasted eggplant with a Greek salad and a cold beer will set you back around $15. There's live traditional Greek music on some nights (avoid if escalating bouzouki music isn't your thing).

JOY BISTRO

Map pp244-5   Contemporary Canadian $$
☎ 416-465-8855; 884 Queen St E; mains $14-25; ☿ 7am-10pm; 🚋 501, 502, 503
The most recent venture by chef David Chrystian, Joy has a joyous parkside patio or fabulously stripy bench seats inside. Order from a menu emphasizing traditional meat dishes with French overtones (duck confit, Manitoba pork belly, slow-roasted lamb shank, etc). The wine list is impressively global, and the service impeccable. They play Jeff Buckley downstairs; upstairs is a bar called Over Joy (ha-ha).

PAN ON THE DANFORTH

Map pp244-5   Greek $$
☎ 416-466-8158; 516 Danforth Ave; mezes $6-12, mains $15-25; ☿ noon-11pm Sun-Thu, to 2am Fri & Sat; ◉ Chester
Colorful, casual Pan serves unpretentious fare with traditional Greek flavors, like Santorini chicken stuffed with spinach and feta, served with cracked pepper, new potatoes and seared veggies ($18). Finish with a chocolate baklava for dessert.

MYTH Map pp244-5   Greek/Late Night $$
☎ 416-461-8383; 417 Danforth Ave; mezes $6-16, meals $16-29; ☿ noon-midnight Sun-Wed, to 1am Thu, to 2am Fri & Sat; ◉ Chester
Inside a converted movie house, Myth serves the Danforth's chicest mezes beneath bizarre medieval machinations suspended from the ceiling. Small portions of mezes approach mythical prices, but the balsamic-marinated octopus with roasted peppers or Mediterranean stuffed calamari might be the best you'll ever have.

POP BISTRO

Map pp244-5   Contemporary Canadian $$
☎ 416-461-9663; 686 Queen St E; mains $17-20; ☿ 5:30-11pm Tue-Sat, 11am-3pm Sun; 🚋 501, 502, 503
This exquisitely designed, narrow bistro just east of the Don River is a shining light of class on an otherwise uninspiring strip of

TOP FIVE TORONTO COOKBOOKS

- *The ACE Bakery Cookbook* by Linda Haynes and James Chatto (2003) – by a beloved local bakery, supplier to top hotels.
- *The Chef's Table* by Lucy Waverman (2000) – captures the creations of T.O. chefs during the annual **Toronto Taste** (p112).
- *Great Canadian Cuisine* by Anita Stewart (1999) – recipes from Canadian Pacific Railway luxury hotels across Canada, including Toronto's **Fairmont Royal York** (p167).
- *Niagara Flavours: Recipes from Southwest Ontario's Finest Chefs* by Brenda Matthews and Linda Bramble (2003) – a contemporary guide to wine country cooking
- *Wanda's Pie in the Sky* by Wanda Beaver (2002) – almost as good as visiting her eponymous Yorkville **café** (p102)

Queen St E. A simple menu of half a dozen appetizers and as many mains is balanced and well conceived, embracing the likes of beef and chevre salad with pork shallot reduction ($10) and lamb meatloaf with blue cheese and sweet potato ($17). Sunday brunch features eggs done in every way.

TOAST Map pp244-5　　Contemporary Canadian $$
☎ 416-469-8222; 993 Queen St E; mains $16-25;
🕑 11:30am-3pm Tue-Fri, 6-10pm Thu-Sat; 🚋 501, 502, 503
Part the velvet curtains and enter an artsy, oldfangled bistro that's best at weekend brunch, when just $11 buys eggs benedict or French toast stuffed with cranberries and cream cheese. Check out the '50s decor and celebrity-signed toasters (Clive Owen, Colin Farrell)!

EDWARD LEVESQUE'S KITCHEN

Map pp244-5　　Eclectic Canadian $$
☎ 416-465-3600; 1290 Queen St E; breakfast & lunch mains $6-12, dinner mains $16-30; 🕑 11am-3pm Wed-Fri, 6-10pm Tue-Sat, 9am-3pm Sat, 9am-4pm Sun; 🚋 501, 502, 503
Inside the front window of a retro-looking diner, chef Edward's clattering skillet yields nouveau Canadian comfort food with seasonal ingredients, his influences ranging from Asian to Italian. Scallop, leek, lemon and asparagus risotto ($24), or a slab of chocolate 'nemesis' cake with fennel confit ($8) guarantee a satisfaction reaction.

TOWN GRILL

Map pp244-5　　Contemporary Canadian $$$
☎ 416-963-9433; 243 Carlton St; mains $21-29;
🕑 5:30-10pm Tue-Sat; 🚋 506
A posh surprise on a humble Cabbagetown corner, this grill and bistro serves sophis-

ticated contemporary Canadian fare in a simple, elegant room. Locals rave about the chef's wizardry with all things related to fowl. Four-course tasting menus are magical; desserts even better.

THE BEACHES

At its most crowded on summer weekends, Queen St E trawls through The Beaches, offering up a string of gourmet restaurants – some flop, some fly.

KING'S TABLE Map p246　　Seafood $
☎ 416-694-3474; 2248 Queen St E; meals $6-12;
🕑 noon-9pm Tue-Sat, to 8pm Sun; ♿ ; 🚋 501
A fraternal, back-slapping feeling suffuses this storefront, which we'll crown King of The Beaches' fish-and-chip shops. Cheery tables fill up fast as diners demand hearty halibut or salmon grills and basic salads.

ALI'S TANDOORI CURRY HOUSE

Map p246　　Indian/Bangladeshi $
☎ 416-694-3056; 2458 Queen St E; mains $9-13;
🕑 noon-10:30pm Mon-Thu, to 11pm Fri-Sun; 🚋 501
There aren't many tables at Ali's, and the kitchen is pretty much in the middle of the room, but it all adds to the atmosphere. Ali is from Bangladesh, and he uses a lot of Bangladeshi techniques in his cooking. Feel free to specify exactly how hot you want your curry cooked (mild to molten magma), peruse the wine list then kick back into a low-key beachy evening.

NEVADA Map p246　　International $$
☎ 416-691-8462; 1963 Queen St E; mains $8-15;
🕑 11am-11pm; 🚋 501
Painted in warm adobe hues, Nevada has a menu that isn't quite sure where it's from,

wandering the map from Thai chicken salad to Shanghai cashew chicken stir-fry to vegetarian fajitas. Confusing, yes, but impressively versatile. Brunch plates are stacked high with blueberry pancakes or Montréal corned-beef hash.

BEACHER CAFÉ

Map p246   Contemporary Canadian $$
☎ 416-699-3874; 2162 Queen St E; mains $8-17; ⏰ 10am-11pm Mon-Fri, 9am-11pm Sat, 9am-10pm Sun; ⛴ 501

Looking like a seaside cottage from a Virginia Woolf novel, this long-standing café has a narrow but eternally sought-after sidewalk patio. Particularly good are the egg and pancake brunches, while as the afternoon loses momentum Beaches wives discuss their husbands' indiscretions over merlot, jazz and seafood. Local artwork changes monthly.

AKANE-YA

Map p246   Japanese $$
☎ 416-699-0377; 2214 Queen St E; mains $13-26; ⏰ 5-10:30pm; ⛴ 501

You'll swear you can feel the North Pacific breeze when you bite into tender eel sushi and yellowtail sashimi at this modern dining room, filled with black lacquer, mini origami and *shoji* screens. The prices are high, but so is the quality. Try something with *uni* (sea urchin) in it, knocked down with some Asahi or Sapporo.

SPIAGGIA

Map p246   Modern Italian $$
☎ 416-699-4656; 2318 Queen St E; mains $19-23; ⏰ 5-11pm; ⛴ 501

A contemporary Italian bistro lifting the tone of far Queen St E, Spaggio delivers its fare in a homely interior or on the front patio, perfect on a balmy summer eve. Starters include simply prepared mussels and calamari plates and light salads moving on to grilled meat, chicken and fish mains. The wine selection takes some beating.

TORONTO ISLANDS

Aside from fast-food vans dotted around the amusement park, there's only one place to eat on the Islands. So bring a picnic!

TORONTO TASTE

Every year, usually between April and June, Toronto's top chefs and epicurean elite get together to hobnob, drink fine wines and dine at the **Toronto Taste** (☎ 416-408-2594; www.torontotaste.ca). For $225, anyone can sample tasting-sized portions of dishes approaching culinary perfection. It's also a guilt-free feast, since all proceeds benefit the charity Second Harvest, which redistributes excess food from restaurants, hotels and grocery stores to social service agencies and people in need.

Over five dozen restaurants participate in the Taste, with a litany of Toronto chefs like Mark McEwan, Anthony Walsh, Jamie Kennedy and Chris Klugman whipping up delicate and daring concoctions. The yearly shindig is garnished with a wine auction, netting Second Harvest around half a million dollars. Tempted? Buy tickets *waaay* in advance.

RECTORY CAFÉ

Map p247   Canadian/International $
☎ 416-203-2152; Ward's Island, 102 Lakeshore Ave; mains $7-15; ⏰ 11am-5pm Wed-Sun Oct-May, 10am-10pm daily Jun-Sep; ⛴ Ward's Island

Propped up next to the boardwalk on Ward's Island, this cozy art gallery café serves light meals, apple cider and weekend brunch in the garden with views over the seawall to Tommy Thompson Park. Reservations are recommended for brunch and dinner, although you can always stop by for a quick snack and some liquid refreshment. Try the tuna melt ($10).

GREATER TORONTO AREA (GTA)

A clutch of Toronto's finest dining rooms are located around or north of St Claire Ave. If you've got the time, trek out to Corso Italia on St Clair W, west of Dufferin St, for authentic Italian food and espresso. Elsewhere, Portugal Village, west of Ossington Ave on Dundas St W, offers macho espresso bars, bakeries and Portuguese seafood.

VANIPHA LANNA Map p231   Thai/Laotian $$
☎ 416-654-8068; 863 St Clair Ave W; mains $10-15; ⏰ 4-10pm Tue & Sat, noon-10pm Wed-Fri; ⛴ 512

If you're here for dinner, impossible-to-miss Vanipha Lanna will emerge from the gloom like some kind of southeast Asian carwash crossed with a birthday cake. Inside the food ranges from fiery seafood creations to familiar noodles, plus unusual dishes like *khao moak ga* (spiced chicken in banana leaves) and satisfying sampler plates and platters. Fake orchids and portraits of Thai royals adorn the room.

JOV BISTRO Map p231 — Eclectic $$$

☎ 416-322-0530; East York, 1701 Bayview Ave; mains $25-35; ⏰ 5:30-11pm; 🚌 11

Divining its name from the initials of its chef owners, sassy JOV Bistro is a neighborhood space for independent-minded foodies. Dinner and weekend reservations should be made in advance, but the forethought is worth it, especially for witty French reinterpretations of classic seafood dishes. You'd be best served by taking the chefs up on their 'Trust Me' four-course dinner ($70; wine pairings extra).

SCARAMOUCHE

Map p231 — Modern French $$$

☎ 416-961-8011; 1 Benvenuto Pl, off Avenue Rd; mains $25-48; ⏰ 5:30-10pm Mon-Sat; 🚌 512

Scaramouche, Scaramouche, do you do the fandango? Lording over a hilltop south of St Clair Ave, this classy restaurant offers top-notch modern French cuisine with a dash of tasteful invention, and views through tall oaks to the downtown skyline. Porches and Beamers swing into the circular driveway; don't forget your gold credit card. Benvenuto Pl is off Edmund Ave, which runs west off Avenue Rd.

CELESTIN Map p231 — French $$$

☎ 416-544-9035; 623 Mt Pleasant Rd; mains $28-45; ⏰ 6-11pm Tue-Sat; 🚇 St Clair then 🚌 74

Chef Pascal Ribreau's imaginative French cooking triumphs inside a converted 1920s bank, where tantalizing *amuse-bouche*

(amusements for the mouth) precede artful mains of succulent duck confit, pan-seared giant prawns with smoked pepper compote or roasted Québec squab. Celestin's atmosphere induces serenity, with widely spaced tables and superb waitstaff who are on a first-name basis with the wines cellared in the old bank vault.

NORTH 44°

Map p231 — Contemporary Continental $$$

☎ 416-487-4897; 2537 Yonge St; mains $32-45; ⏰ 5-11pm Mon-Sat; 🚌 97

All deluxe mosaics and sculpted metal, Mark McEwan's sleek North 44° is still one of North America's top tables (Toronto sits at a latitude of 44° north, if you were wondering…). Solid main courses, such as a whole seared BC halibut baked in banana leaves with leek hearts, braised onion, coconut and coriander ($41), are paired with selections from a mind-boggling international wine list (17 pages, excluding bibliography). Magnificent.

AUBERGE DU POMMIER

Map p230 — French $$$

☎ 416-222-2220; North York, Yonge Corporate Centre, 4150 Yonge St; lunch $21-28, dinner $34-43; ⏰ 11:30am-2:30pm Mon-Fri, 5-10pm Mon-Sat; 🚇 York Mills then 🚌 97

A culinary college for Toronto's best chefs, graceful Auberge du Pommier is constructed from a pair of 19th-century woodcutters' cottages. Plates of roast lamb loin with olive tapenade and Provençal vegetables ($38), and butter-poached lobster glazed with citrus and tarragon ($40) look like they should be in a gallery (or at least a cookbook). Wine selections focus on French vintages, plus a few Niagara labels. It's a long hike from the city centre north of the intersection of Yonge St and York Mills Rd, opposite William Carson Cres.

Entertainment

Entertainment

There's no drought of good times to be had in Toronto. In fact, it's a very entertaining place, having shaken off its goody-two-shoes reputation to now wallow in as much New World decadence as established high art. Whether you're craving a jazzy quartet, a slick urban bar, an indie film festival or a bag full of laughs at a downtown comedy night, you'll have no trouble finding it here. Alternatively, some classy classical at the Glenn Gould Studio, off-beat Canadian theatre, a punky rock outfit or a sleepy afternoon at a brewpub is sure to satisfy. Coffee culture is thriving, as is dance, spoken word and lesbigay nightlife. Toronto's infamous club scene is incendiary and fast-changing. On top of this, there are free outdoor festivals and concerts going on nearly every weekend, especially in summer.

The city's most encyclopedic entertainment guide is inside the free alternative weekly *Now*, while *Xtra!* and *Eye Weekly* keep a finger on the club, alt-culture and live-music pulse. All three daily newspapers (p203) provide weekly entertainment listings, too. Glossy *Toronto Life* magazine (p203) publishes a monthly 'What's On' guide.

Tickets

For an added booking fee, **Ticketmaster** (☎ 416-870-8000; www.ticketmaster.ca) sells tickets for major concerts, sports games, theatre and performing arts events. Buy tickets either online or at various city outlets, including the **Rogers Centre** (p53), the **Hummingbird Centre for the Performing Arts** (p134) and T.O. Tix (below). The classified sections of newspapers and alternative weeklies also list tickets available for every event in town, from opera to Tragically Hip concerts. Scalpers unashamedly work all major events – for a price, any seat is yours.

For half-price and discounted same-day 'rush' tickets, **T.O. Tix** (Map pp232–3; ☎ 416-536-6468 ext 40; www.totix.ca; Dundas Square, 1 Dundas St E; ☿ noon-6:30pm Tue-Sat; ◉ Dundas) has a booth on Dundas Square. These tickets for theatre, comedy and dance performances, even as far away as Stratford or Niagara-on-the-Lake, are sold in person on a first-come, first-served basis only. You can check what's available first by calling. Rush tickets may also be available at theatre box offices.

WHAT'S FREE?

- Canadian Opera Company (p133) – free lunch-time concerts at the Four Seasons Centre for the Performing Arts.
- Healey's (p126) – free Tuesday open-jam nights and Saturday muso matinees.
- Glenn Gould Studio (p134) – free noon concerts.
- Graffiti's (p126) – free acoustic rock, jazz, spoken word and cabaret in Kensington Market.
- Free Times Café (p127) – as the name infers, free live music most nights.
- National Film Board Mediatheque (p118) – often has free screenings.
- Second City (p133) – free improv comedy sets after the last show ends.
- Hard Rock Café (p119) – buy a beer and watch the Blue Jays or Argonauts for free.
- Toronto Music Garden (p54) – free outdoor concerts during summer.
- University of Toronto Faculty of Music (p134) – free admission to some performance classes and concerts.

CINEMA

Perhaps more than any other pastime, Torontonians cherish going out to the movies (could it possibly have something to so with the weather in Toronto?). If it is first-run releases that you are looking for, the Bloor-Yorkville neighborhood contains cinemas that are often used for film festivals. Arthouse cinemas are scattered throughout the neighborhoods, while IMAX movies play at **Famous Players Paramount** (p118) in the Entertainment District, **Cinesphere** (p52) in Ontario Place and the **Omnimax** (p79) which can be found at the Ontario Science Centre.

Tickets

First-run movie tickets cost $12 to $14 for adults, less for students and seniors. Matinee shows (before 6pm weekdays, earlier on weekends) cost around $9. Tuesday is discount day (aka 'Cheap-ass Tuesday') – expect to pay around $8.

Festivals

It seems there's always a film festival going on in Toronto, whether it's the famous **Toronto International Film Festival** (p27) or special-interest series like the **Hot Docs Canadian International Documentary Film Festival** (☎ 416-203-2155; www.hotdocs.ca) in April, the **Inside Out Toronto Lesbian & Gay Film & Video Festival** (☎ 416-977-6847; www.insideout.on.ca) in May, or the sci-fi and horror **After Dark Film Festival** (p15) in October.

ALLIANCE ATLANTIS CUMBERLAND 4
Map pp238-9

☎ 416-646-0444; www.allianceatlantiscinemas.com; Bloor-Yorkville, 159 Cumberland St; adult/child $12/9; ☻ noon-midnight; Ⓔ Bay

This pint-sized multiplex screens a mix of independent films and hand-picked, left-of-centre Hollywood releases. Moviegoers can swing by the lobby cappuccino bar for some above-par baked goods before the show. There's a similar, slightly more mainstream branch at **The Beaches** (Map p246; ☎ 416-646-0444; 1651 Queen St E; 🚋 501) with parallel hours and prices.

BLOOR CINEMA Map pp242-3

☎ 416-516-2330; www.bloorcinema.com; The Annex, 506 Bloor St W; adult/child $6/4; ☻ noon-midnight; Ⓔ Bathurst

Often voted the city's fave repertory cinema, this art deco theatre with a two-tiered balcony screens a wonderful schedule of new releases, art-house flicks, shorts, documentaries and vintage films. Buy an annual membership card ($3) and pay just $4 per movie.

CINEFORUM Map pp242-3

☎ 416-603-6643; http://thecineforum.tripod.com; Little Italy, 463 Bathurst St; over/under 24 $20/10; ☻ screenings 7pm & 9pm Sat-Thu; 🚋 506, 511

Irascible Torontonian character Reg Hartt has ads wrapped around telephone poles advertising his Cineforum – the front room

of his skuzzy Victorian rowhouse where he showcases classic and avant-garde films. Animation retrospectives are his specialty, as are rare Salvador Dali prints. Come prepared for idiosyncratic lectures designed to expand your consciousness, sometimes delivered right while the movies are playing. Seats 20; bring your own food and drink.

CINEMATHEQUE ONTARIO Map pp232-3

☎ 416-968-3456; www.cinemathequeontario.ca; box office Bloor-Yorkville, 1st fl, Manulife Centre, 55 Bloor St W; nonmember/student $11/6; ☻ box office 10am-6pm Mon-Sat, closed late Aug & Sep; Ⓔ Bloor-Yonge

Popular Cinematheque Ontario screens world cinema, independent films and retrospectives of famous directors, sometimes introduced by film critics and Canadian authors. About 400 films are shown annually at Jackman Hall at the **Art Gallery of Ontario** (p64). Nonmembers can purchase tickets at the Manulife Centre box office 30 minutes before the day's first screening (be sure to show up early, since tickets sell out quickly).

CINEPLEX ODEON VARSITY
Map pp238-9

☎ 416-961-6303; www.cineplex.com; Bloor-Yorkville, 2nd fl, Manulife Centre, 55 Bloor St W; adult/child $12/9; ☻ noon-midnight; Ⓔ Bloor-Yonge

This state-of-the-art multiplex shows a great range of movies, from Hollywood blockbusters to small-budget indie releases. VIP theatres have extra leg room, table service and smaller screens (with good sound). The downtown branch **Cineplex Odeon Carlton** (Map pp238–9; ☎ 416-598-2309; Yonge Street Strip, 18-20 Carlton St; adult/child $10/8; ☻ 12:45pm-midnight; Ⓔ College) attracts a diverse crowd by screening major independent films and some truly bizarre offerings.

DOCKS DRIVE-IN THEATRE Map p231

☎ 416-461-3625; www.thedocks.com; East Toronto, 11 Polson St; adult/child $12/3.50 Fri & Sat; per car $15 Sun; ☻ from 8:30pm Fri-Sun Apr-Oct

What, a drive-in in downtown Toronto? Cool! This waterfront yard has space for 500 cars, and skydeck seats for non-motorists. Double bills feature first-run movies at dusk, and the usual fast food is on hand. The Docks also has a minigolf course and **nightclubs** (p130).

FAMOUS PLAYERS PARAMOUNT

Map pp234-5

☎ 416-368-5600, IMAX ☎ 416-368-6089; www
.famousplayers.com; Entertainment District, 259
Richmond St W; adult/child $12/8.50, IMAX $14/11;
☻ noon-midnight; ⊖ Osgoode

Famous Players' gargantuan multiplex
features new releases and the latest in
IMAX technology, including 3D. It's always
screening a dozen movies or more, with
some off-beat picks found among the bigger mainstream releases. You might think
twice about tackling the improbably long
escalators after a few beers at the bar.

FOX CINEMA Map p246

☎ 416-691-7330; www.festivalcinemas.com; The
Beaches, 2236 Queen St E; adult/concession/child
$9/4.50/4.50; ☻ 7pm-midnight Mon, Tue, Thu &
Fri, from 1:30pm Wed, from 2pm Sun; ☒ 501

Behind a cute little art deco shopfront
among The Beaches cafés is this arty cinema, screening offbeat Hollywood fare
(think Half Nelson, Black Dahlia, An Incon-
venient Truth) and classics by Woody Allen
and David Lynch. 'Movies 4 Moms' sessions
happen on Wednesday afternoons.

NATIONAL FILM BOARD
MEDIATHEQUE Map pp234-5

NFB; ☎ 416-973-3012; www.nfb.ca/mediatheque;
Entertainment District, 150 John St; day pass $2;
☻ 1-7pm Mon & Tue, 10am-7pm Wed, 10am-10pm
Thu-Sat, noon-5pm Sun; ⊖ Osgoode

Aiming to 'reconnect Canadians with their
past, present and future on film,' the NFB
has opened its vast collection of 3200
audiovisual gems to the public. Attend a
low-cost (or sometimes free) film screening
in an intimate, 80-seat cinema, or try one of
the personal touch-screen viewing stations.
Rare DVDs and videotapes are available for
rent or purchase.

ROYAL CINEMA Map pp242-3

☎ 416-516-4845; www.theatred.com; Little Italy,
608 College St; adult/concession/child $10/5/5;
☻ 6:30pm-midnight Mon-Sat, 1:30pm-midnight
Sun; ☒ 506

By the time you read this, the newly renovated Royal – a funky art deco Little Italy
landmark – will have opened its doors and
made a triumphant return to the Toronto

alternative cinema scene. Well, that's what
they have planned… Expect documentaries, second-run and repertory releases –
anything from Monty Python to Hong Kong
punch-'em-up flicks.

DRINKING

Drinking in Toronto is a liberal indulgence.
Unless we've indicated otherwise, the pubs
listed below open at 11am and stay open
until 2am. Bars keep serving until 2am too,
but don't generally open their doors until
around 4pm (perfectly timed for the after-
work rush). Licensed clubs stay open until
4am. And who knows how many illegal
speakeasies there are where you can get a
drink at any tick of the clock?

Strict antismoking bylaws prohibit
nicotine-fixing in virtually any indoor public
place, which means you can enjoy your martini without your favorite shirt smelling like
an ashtray in the morning. The Liquor Control Board of Ontario (LCBO) limits where
and how alcohol can be sold, but its moral
creed is more anachronistic than draconian.
Toronto's main LCBO (Map p231; ☎ 416-922-
0403; www.lcbo.com; Rosedale, 10 Scrivener
Sq; ☻ 10am-10pm Mon-Fri, 9am-10pm Sat,
11am-6pm Sun; ⊖ Summerhill) is in the
former North York train station, built by
the Canada Pacific Railroad in the early 20th
century. It's Canada's largest liquor store,
with a dazzling array of Niagara ice wines
and over 100 vintages for sampling (call for
details; nominal fees apply).

Coffee culture in Toronto dates back to
the '60s, when many a bedraggled Kerouac
wannabe pulled up a pew in a Yorkville coffee shop and pondered the next hitchhike.

PUBS

Considering how Toronto has gradually
distanced itself from its British beginnings,
it's odd that the city has so many out-of-
the-box Brit-pub chains, instead of water-
ing holes with genuine character. They're
still out there though – you just need to
know where to look.

ALLEN'S Map pp244-5

☎ 416-463-3086; Greektown, 143 Danforth Ave;
⊖ Broadview

Saloon-style Allen's has daunting beer,
wine and whiskey lists, with over 200

single-malt scotches and 100% Canadian vino. The vibe strays into Celtic territory a little too much, but at least it's authentic – Irish staff, Irish musicians and Irish cooks who make the best sweet-potato fries you'll ever have in your life.

BRASS TAPS Map pp244-5
☎ 416-966-9440; Cabbagetown, 221 Carlton St; 🚋 506

This atmospheric, split-level pub is the kind of place where you can read a book over a slow pint during the day, then whoop-it-up at night with a crankin' jukebox, pool tables and an eclectic crowd of after-workers, students and locals. They have Creemore Springs on tap, and the food is top-notch – try the 'Brass Taps Deluxe' pizza.

C'EST WHAT? Map pp234-5
☎ 416-867-9499; Old York, 67 Front St E; 🚋 503, 504

Over 30 whiskeys and six dozen Canadian microbrews are on hand at this underground pub near the St Lawrence Market. An in-house brewmaster tightly edits the all-natural, preservative-free beers on tap – drink your way across the nation with confidence. There's live music most nights at the Music Showbar (p126).

CIRO'S Map p231
☎ 416-533-4914; Greater Toronto Area, 1013 Bloor St W; ⊖ Lansdowne

Way out west in the emerging West Bloor Village neighborhood, dodge the dealers and duck into Ciro's for a come-as-you-are beer and a game of pool as old soul crackles on the stereo. The good-looking owners inherited Ciro's from their parents, and they've refused to gentrify it – the crusty old Bukowskis at the bar still feel right at home.

ESPLANADE BIERMARKT Map pp234-5
☎ 416-862-7575; Old York, 58 The Esplanade; ⊖ Union

The BierMarkt bouncers act like they're guarding some kind of mythical realm of ultimate pleasure. Ignore them. What you're here for is a beer menu that chases the finest ales, lagers and pilsners around the planet, from Belgium to South Africa to Trinidad, with more than 150 varieties all

told. Avoid European labels actually brewed in Ontario, which lose flavor in trans-Atlantic translation.

GLADSTONE HOTEL Map p231
☎ 416-531-4635; West Queen West, 1214 Queen St W; 🚋 501

This formerly down-at-heel historic hotel revels in Toronto's avant-garde arts scene. In the Melody Bar there's karaoke from 9pm, Thursday to Saturday, while the Art Bar and Gladstone Ballroom sustain off-beat DJs, poetry slams, jazz, book readings, alt-country and blues. Cover varies, usually $10 or less.

HARDROCK CAFÉ Map pp234-5
☎ 416-341-2388; Harbourfront, Rogers Centre, 1 Blue Jays Way; 🕙 11am-11pm; ⊖ Union, 🚋 509, 510

Yeah, we know, it's a big-ass multinational chain, but you just can't beat this view! Where else can you sit with your pint by a huge plate-glass window and watch the Toronto Argonauts (p142) bump into further success, or the Toronto Blue Jays (p140) fail to live up to expectations. And it's free! The usual collection of John Mellencamp guitars and signed Aerosmith records adorns the walls.

LION ON THE BEACH Map p246
☎ 416-690-1984; The Beaches, 1958 Queen St E; 🚋 501

An expansive pub that spills out onto The Beaches sidewalk (lyin' on the beach – ged-dit?). A respectably long beer list and hearty pub grub (tex-mex, bangers and mash, fried

LORD FIRKIN FOX & THE BISHOP OF ELEPHANT ARMS

What the hell is with all the Irish and English theme pubs in Toronto? Everywhere you look, perfectly decent Canadian bars have sold out to Anglo-Celtic pub chains and subjected themselves to horrible faux-Yorkshire makeovers, complete with plastic bookshelves, irritating twiddle-dee-dee soundtracks and stodgy Brit ales. Something to do with a lack of Canadian national identity? A desire to be perceived as more European than American, perhaps? Either way, we don't approve. Find yourself a good ol' Canuck bar and don't come out until the pub plague has passed.

rainbow trout) keeps everyone occupied. Kids run around between people's legs.

MADISON AVENUE Map pp242-3

☎ 416-927-1722; The Annex, 14-18 Madison Ave; ⑤ Spadina

Consuming three Victorian houses, the Madison is positively elephantine. A 25-to-35 crowd is lured through the doors – billiards, darts, a sports bar, polished brass, antique-looking lamps lighting the curtained upper floors at night, *five* patios and plenty of hot babes. Strictly no rollerblades; hot babes on rollerblades OK.

MILL STREET BREWERY Map pp244-5

☎ 416-681-0338; Old York, bldg 63, Distillery District, 55 Mill St; ⑧ 503, 504

With eight specialty beers brewed on site (and what a site the Distillery District is!) these guys are a leading light in local microbrewing. An arty crowd of locals and tourists quaffs swirling pints of wheat beer, seasonal fruit beers, Cobblestone Stout and the famous Coffee Porter. On a sunny afternoon, the courtyard is the place to be.

PILOT TAVERN Map pp238-9

☎ 416-923-5716; Bloor-Yorkville, 22 Cumberland St; ⑤ Bloor-Yonge

A pumping after-worker, The Pilot got its start during WWII, which explains the

aviation-themed decor and why it calls the patio the Flight Deck – an airborne terrace among the office tower windows. Stop by for live jazz sets on Saturday and Sunday afternoons from 3pm.

REBEL HOUSE Map p231

☎ 416-927-0704; Rosedale, 1068 Yonge St; ⑤ Rosedale

Just north of Yorkville, rough-and-tumble Rebel House has 16 Canadian brews on tap, Ontario wines and well-trained chefs (yes, chefs) in the kitchen. Bend elbows with neighborhood drinkers beneath the ex-rebel dangling from the gallows on the sign.

RED ROOM Map pp240-1

☎ 416-929-9964; Kensington Market, 444 Spadina Ave; ⑧ 506, 510

The Red Room rules. Part pub, part diner, part funky lounge – this arty room is the place to drag your hungover bones for a recuperative pint of microbrew, an all-day breakfast (burgers, curries, pasta) and an earful of Stones, The Who and Led Zepp. Sink into a booth and forget your misdemeanors.

VILLAGE IDIOT Map pp232-3

☎ 416-597-1175; Baldwin Village, 126 McCaul St; ⑧ 505

The Idiot is a cherry-red, black and brass boozer on the southern fringe of Baldwin

---

STRANGE BREW

Anyone who sits down for a beer and tastes the fizzy carbonation of Canada's old-school brews (Molson, Moosehead, Labatt et al) may well ask, 'Is this real beer, or Canada Dry?' Faced with such blandness, Ontario's beer-drinkers take solace in microbrews – small batch brews, usually preservative-free and often with a serious alcoholic punch.

Many city pubs and bars have an excellent selection of microbrews on tap from established Ontarian brewers like Sleeman, Steam Whistle, Amsterdam and Creemore Springs, but aside from these middleweights, you'll find it difficult to buy quality brews to take home. **The Beer Store** (www.thebeerstore.ca) has outlets around Toronto, but it's a private monopoly owned by the major breweries, who limit the number of microbrews sold. The government-run **LCBO** (p118) is the only other place you can buy booze, but it sells more international brands than locals. Many T.O. beer boffins hold out for the **Toronto Festival of Beer** (☎ 416-640-0966; www.beerfestival.ca), sponsored by the Beer Store, which rolls around at Fort York every August. Almost 20,000 fans turn out to sample products from over 30 local microbreweries.

With the market so tied up, microbreweries pull a few tricks to stay in business. One is to tempt the drinking public to on-site retail stores, like the ones at **Steam Whistle Brewing** (p54) and **Amsterdam Brewing Co** (p50), which offer tours and tastings. 'Brewpubs' are another trick, including redoubtable **C'est What?** (p119) and the recently refurbished **Mill Street Brewery** (above), which offers samples of its delicious coffee porter inside a renovated Victorian distillery. It doesn't make its own beer, but **Allen's** (p118) has an encyclopedic list of brews. The **Esplanade BierMarkt** (p119), **Beer Bistro** (p94) and **Smokeless Joe** (p123) deserve honorable mentions.

If you're thinking you have to really know where to look for good beer in Ontario, you're right. Recommended regional brews include Conners Best Bitter, Kawartha Lakes' Raspberry Wheat, Cameron's Cream Ale, the Ste André Vienna Lager and the Headstrong Pale Ale from Big Hole Brewing Co. Watch your back for **Niagara Falls Brewing Co** (p185), the first folks in North America to make Eisbock, a daredevil of a sweet, malty 'ice' beer with a potency of nearly 10%.

Village. Management aims for an Olde English interior, but (thankfully) comes up a bit short, the irrepressible student crowd helping to keep things local. Belgian beers on tap, great pub food and afternoon rays streaming in.

WHEAT SHEAF TAVERN Map pp240-1
☎ 416-504-9912; Queen West, 667 King St W; 🚋 501, 504, 511
At Toronto's longest running pub (since 1849), a host of faithful regulars shuffle and mutter around dartboards, pool tables, a kickin' jukebox and relaxed streetside patio. It's a bit out of the way, but we like it that way. Half-price wings Sunday to Tuesday.

BARS
The T.O. bar scene embraces everything from sticky-carpet Queen West beer holes to slick Little Italy martini bars, downtown money-waster wine rooms and a predictably effervescent smattering of gay and lesbian bars. Thirsty work.

BLACK EAGLE Map pp238-9
☎ 416-413-1219; Church-Wellesley Village, 457 Church St; Ⓦ Wellesley
A charred-out, lawless tomb, Black Eagle lures leather-men, uniform fetishists and denim boys. Hardcore gay porn plays on big screens; the art on the walls is well hung in all senses of the expression. Check your clothes at the door for seriously gritty theme nights (not for the mild-mannered).

CASTRO'S LOUNGE Map p246
☎ 416-699-8272; The Beaches, 2116 Queen St E; 🚋 501
An unexpected attitude-free zone in The Beaches, this renegade bar has 120-plus Canadian microbrews and import beers, vintage movie posters and hardwood tables, around which cluster local literati, conspiracy theorists, political activists and slacker hangers-on. Keep an ear to the ground for beer tastings, spoken word events and live music.

CIAO EDIE Map pp242-3
☎ 416-923-5300; Little Italy, 489 College St; 🚋 506; 511
Edie may have said goodbye, but this subterranean hotspot keeps on truckin'

with '60s mod colors, light-hearted lamps, whimsical decor and retro tunes spinning in the background. Cocktails are deadly; it's gay-friendly too.

CREWS/TANGO/ZONE Map pp238-9
☎ 416-972-1662; Church-Wellesley Village, 508 Church St; Ⓦ Wellesley
This three-pronged joint sees women kicking up the heat at Tango, next door to the men's bar Crews and the cabaret-style Zone. Show up for karaoke nights, drag queen/king shows and DJs spinning their stuff, usually during the weekends.

CRUSH Map pp240-1
☎ 416-977-1234; Queen West, 455 King St W; ◷ 11:30am-10:30pm Mon-Fri, 5pm-10:30pm Sat; 🚋 504, 510
It's easy to develop a crush on Crush, an impressively designed wine bar offering dozens of varietals by the glass. Sommelier Eric Gennaro conducts wine-tasting evenings for everyone from novices to experts, served by some of the friendliest waitstaff in the city.

ourpick CZEHOSKI Map pp240-1
☎ 416-366-6787; Queen West, 678 Queen St W; 🚋 501
Everyone raves about Czehoski, a timber-faced bar that manages to be bohemian, classy and understated all at once. The beer and wine lists are extensive, the bar food first-rate, cocktails potent, service friendly, music 'schmoove' and interior design magazine-worthy. The only thing worth arguing about is how to pronounce the name.

DRAKE HOTEL Map p231
☎ 416-531-5042; West Queen West, 1150 Queen St W; 🚋 501
Despite its shameless social-rung-climbing and increasingly lofty opinion of itself, the iconic Drake Hotel put West Queen West on the map. Accommodation, live music venue, café, restaurant and bar – there's little that isn't on offer, and nothing that's done badly.

FOUNDATION ROOM Map pp234-5
☎ 416-364-8368; Old York, 19 Church St; 🚋 503, 504
A 30-plus crowd of city drifters descends into this plush, Middle Eastern–inspired room near St Lawrence Market – all dark

DRINKING

LLBO VS LCBO

Huh? What's the difference? The **Liquor Licensing Board of Ontario** (LLBO) grants permits to restaurants to serve alcohol – you'll see glaring LLBO signs in the front windows of many city eateries. The **Liquor Control Board of Ontario** (LCBO) is a different kettle of fish (or keg of beer) altogether. It's Ontario's official government liquor store, selling wine, spirits and beer to the thirsty masses. It's similar to the Scandinavian system of regulating alcohol sales, but far less expensive and uptight! The flagship Rosedale **LCBO** (p118) is a booze-hound's paradise.

wooden floors, Moroccan lanterns, mirrored walls and red velvet cushions. DJs play house; bottled beers and martinis seem to be in every hand.

HEMINGWAY'S Map pp238-9

☎ 416-968-2828; Bloor-Yorkville, 142 Cumberland St; ◉ Bay

Equal parts sports pub, singles' bar and jazz venue, Hemingway's is an undeniable Yorkville hot spot. The heated double-deck rooftop patio makes for a vivacious night full of opportunity among an upwardly-mobile crowd of bright young things.

LABYRINTH LOUNGE Map pp242-3

☎ 416-925-7775; The Annex, 298 Brunswick Ave; ◉ Bathurst

Bad-ass rock and 'Shit happens' nights collide with stand-up comedy, jam sessions and guest DJs at this bar out the back of the **Future Bakery & Café** (p104). The student crowd morphs between the two venues with little regard for boundaries, haircuts or study.

LIBRARY BAR Map pp234-5

☎ 416-368-2511; Financial District, Fairmont Royal York Hotel, 100 Front St W; ◉ Union

A clubby atmosphere pervades this opulent room, with rich wood paneling and overstuffed chairs. Debonair barman Mike whips up the best classic martinis in town, although wilder combinations appear on the menu – chocolatini or banana split martini, anyone?

PÄAEEZ Map pp242-3

☎ 416-537-0767; Little Italy, 569 College St; 🚃 506

The Apostrophe Police wouldn't approve of the 'Martini's' on the menu, but don't let a little wayward grammar stop you from slurping them down. Try a 2½oz 'Belvedere Beauty' (vodka, lychee liqueur, passionfruit juice and cinnamon; $11). Tapas helps postpone your alcoholic demise.

REDS Map pp234-5

☎ 416-862-7337; Financial District, First Canadian Place, 77 Adelaide St W; 🕒 11:30am-11pm Mon-Fri, 5:30-10pm Sat; ◉ St Andrew

Reds probably has the best wine list in Toronto (heavy on the reds) but it comes at a cost – prices start at around $12 a glass. Still, if you feel like hobnobbing with the downtown moneymakers in sexy surrounds, Reds is for you.

SLACK'S Map pp238-9

☎ 416-928-2151; Church-Wellesley Village, 562 Church St; ◉ Wellesley

Bridging the divide between gays, lesbians, urban cowboys and straights all searching for a little glitz, quasi-retro Slack's opens its gorgeous French doors and backlit bar to all

A BREW WITH A VIEW

For a free rooftop view of the city, head to **Panorama** (Map pp238–9; ☎ 416-967-0000; Bloor-Yorkville, 51st fl, Manulife Centre, 55 Bloor St W; 🕒 5pm-1am Sun-Wed, to 2am Thu-Sat; ◉ Bay), which has the city's highest licensed patio. It's a bit tricky to find, but it's worth it for the sunset. If you stand up in the Rooftop Lounge at the **Park Hyatt** (p172), you can scan the city over the balcony. There are eye-popping views of Lake Ontario and the Toronto Islands from the bar stools at **Canoe** (p94) restaurant, but they're not as good as those from Horizon's Café at the **CN Tower** (p51), where you can stew over the view with a brew. Next to a Harbourfront film lot, the **Waterside Sports Club** (Map pp244–5; ☎ 416-203-0470; Harbourfront, 225 Queens Quay E; 🕒 11:30am-11pm Mon-Fri, 11am-8pm Sat & Sun; 🚃 75) has unobstructed lakefront views from the patio. Check out movie stars on a break (Meg Tilley, Jeff Bridges, Mark Wahlberg) and sweaty young Torontonians fresh off the nearby racquetball courts.

When all else fails, you can't beat a chilled bottle of wine at a quiet lakeside patch on the **Toronto Islands** (p75).

comers. An eventful monthly calendar features comedy shows, karaoke, drag shows, live music and art installations.

SMOKELESS JOE Map pp234-5
☎ 416-728-4503; Entertainment District, 125 John St; 🚋 501

Buried below street level in Clubland, this narrow where-everybody-knows-your-name bar sells over 250 different types of beer (the menu is a book). Some of the rarest brews aren't sold in stores, so stop by for a pint or two. Or three. It was one of the first places in T.O. to ban smoking. Thanks Joe.

SOCIAL Map p231
☎ 416-532-4474; West Queen West, 1100 Queen St W; 🚋 501

Industrial un-faced brickwork and exposed timber beams clash with zebra-print couches and neon at The Social, an old Mafia joint turned übercool bar. 'I can't believe they're playing that' rock from the '70s and '80s titillates the hipster crowd. DJs sporadically; closed Sunday and Tuesday.

SUPERMARKET Map pp240-1
☎ 416-840-0501; Kensington Market, 268 Augusta Ave; 🚋 506

It looks like it probably once was a supermarket, but they ain't selling groceries any more. Instead, fill your shopping trolley with jazzy hip-hop DJs, themed costume parties (Rocky Horror, Casual Sex, Halloween, etc), occasional live bands and Asian-fusion dinners. Kensington Market at its kookiest.

TRANZAC Map pp242-3
☎ 416-923-8137; The Annex, 292 Brunswick Ave; 🚇 Bathurst

Drop in and say 'G'day' at the Toronto Australia New Zealand Club (Tranzac), where the bar is bolstered by a graffiti wall, theatre space, satellite TV sports and live performances Monday to Thursday (Pay What You Can) – anything from indie rock to bluegrass, poetry readings and book launches.

TURF LOUNGE Map pp234-5
☎ 416-367-2111; Financial District, 330 Bay St; 11:30am-midnight Mon-Fri, noon-7pm Sat; 🚇 King

If horse racing gets you all hot and bothered, this patch of turf is for you. It's a sassy room with a banking chamber vibe and a strict dress code (no runners, shorts or track suits), where the nags gallop around the world's racks on big-screen TVs.

UNDERGROUND GARAGE Map pp234-5
☎ 416-340-0365; Entertainment District, 365 King St W; 🚋 504, 510

Trying valiantly to keep it real in the otherwise skin-deep Entertainment District, this urban rock bar is down a steep staircase lined with Led Zeppelin, Willie Nelson and John Lennon posters. Wailing guitars, cold beer and good times – just as it should be. It doesn't usually get going until 9pm; cover under $5.

WOODY'S/SAILOR Map pp238-9
☎ 416-972-0887; Church-Wellesley Village, 465-467 Church St; 🚇 Wellesley

On any given night, red-hot Woody's sells more beer than any other bar in the country. The city's most popular gay bar complex has a glad-bag of tricks, from drag shows, 'best ass' contests, leather sessions, billiards tables and nightly DJs. Sailor is a slick bar off to one side.

COFFEEHOUSES

Walk straight past Toronto's lousy chain coffee shops and point your caffeine habit towards somewhere more free-thinking. Many restaurants and cafés will also let you linger over a cup of coffee and dessert.

ADDIS ABABA Map p231
☎ 416-538-0059; West Queen West, 1184 Queen St W; 🕐 5pm-midnight; 🚋 501

Coffee Ethiopian style: green coffee beans roasted over a flame in an iron pot, ground and 'steeped' in boiling water in a tall clay pot, then poured into ceramic cups on a tray with smoldering frankincense. Amazing!

TOP FIVE TORONTO COFFEE-HOUSES

Bar Italia (p106)

Dufflet Pastries (p107)

Future Bakery & Café (p104)

Le Gourmand (p107)

Mercatto (p94)

B ESPRESSO BAR Map pp234-5

☎ 416-866-2111; East Toronto, 111 Queen St E;
⏰ 7:30am-5pm Mon-Fri, 10am-3pm Sat; 🚊 501
The coffee creed at funky B is 'Steamy, rich, smooth, strong, fine, bold, delicious.' Hot damn, has coffee ever sounded so sexy? Almost as sexy as the Italian staff with mean caffeine coursing through their veins.

JET FUEL Map pp244-5

☎ 416-968-9982; Cabbagetown, 519 Parliament St; ⏰ 7am-8pm; 🚊 506
So arty and cool, this hangout is for east-end gentrifiers, cyclists and literati who like to jeer at the beautiful people of Yorkville. The best coffee east of Yonge St.

KAFFEEHAUS KONDITOR Map p246

☎ 416-693-7997; The Beaches, 1856 Queen St E;
⏰ 8:30am-6pm Wed-Sat, to 5pm Sun; 🚊 501
Konditor is a traditional, Germanic coffeehouse at the city end of The Beaches strip, serving piping hot coffee and Teutonic staples like goulash, chicken schnitzel and what's allegedly the world's best apple strudel. Who are we to argue?

KALENDAR Map pp242-3

☎ 416-923-4138; Little Italy, 546 College St;
⏰ 11:30am-10pm Mon-Wed, to 11pm Thu, to midnight Fri, 10:30am-midnight Sat, 10:30am-10pm Sun; 🚊 506
As much a bistro as it is a coffeehouse, Kalendar's darkly lit booths fill with cooing couples, so you'll have to scramble for a seat. The kitchen creates delicious pastry-wrapped 'scrolls,' naan pizzas and orange-ginger-carrot soup, plus generous desserts.

LOUIE'S COFFEE STOP Map pp240-1

☎ 416-593-9263; Kensington Market, 235 Augusta Ave; ⏰ 8:30am-6:30pm Mon-Thu, to 7pm Fri, 7:30am-6:30pm Sat; 🚊 501
Standing on a busy corner of Kensington Market since 1965, Louie's coffee shack is a mellow oasis, with vintage jazz and plastic grapevines on the eaves. There's not much room inside, so get your espresso to go.

MOONBEAN COFFEE COMPANY Map pp240-1

☎ 416-595-0327; Kensington Market, 30 St Andrews St; ⏰ 7am-9pm; 🚊 510
'Nothing here is just ordinary,' says the dude behind the counter, and that's true. Serving the best latte west of Yonge St, Moonbean has organic and fair trade coffees, all-day breakfasts for around $6, and 'Bite Me' vegan cookies. Grind your own beans from $10 per pound.

REMARKABLE BEAN Map p246

☎ 416-690-2420; The Beaches, 2242 Queen St E;
⏰ 7am-10pm; 🚊 501
A Beaches favorite serves up shepherd's pie and still-in-the-pan homemade desserts to go with your latte or maté (South American 'tea of life'). Snooty middle-aged guys who've retired too early clog up the window seats.

EIGHT BALL, CORNER POCKET

Billiards, pool and snooker have a devoted following among Torontonians, keen for a few games and a sly beer on the way home or an epic late-night session on the baize.

Academy of Spherical Arts (Map p231; ☎ 416-532-2782; Greater Toronto Area, 38 Hanna Ave, off Atlantic Ave; $15 per hr; ⏰ noon-2am Mon-Fri, 5pm-2am Sat; 🚊 504) Not quite as imposing as it sounds, but some of the antique billiards tables here are hand-carved (one was once owned by the Prince of Wales).

Andy Poolhall (Map pp242-3; ☎ 416-923-5300; Little Italy, 489 College St; $12 per hr; ⏰ 6pm-2am Mon & Sat, from 7pm Sun & Tue-Fri; 🚊 506, 511) A swingin' spot to shoot some stick, with DJs and half-price Mondays.

Charlotte Room (Map pp234-5; ☎ 416-598-2882; Entertainment District, 19 Charlotte St; $12 per hr; ⏰ 3pm-1am Sun-Thu, noon-2am Fri & Sat; 🚊 504, 510) A clubby spot with customized tables, great food, sexy staff and an in-house pro.

Pegasus Bar (Map pp238-9; ☎ 416-927-8832; Church-Wellesley Village, 489b Church St; $8.50 per hr; ⏰ 11am-2am; 🚇 Wellesley) Classic rock and red felt above an adult video store in the Gay Village.

Rivoli Pool Hall (Map pp232-3; ☎ 416-596-1501; Queen Street, 334 Queen St W; $6-8 per hr; ⏰ 2pm-2am; 🚊 501) Upstairs from the Rivoli live music and comedy club (p126).

TANGO PALACE COFFEE COMPANY
Map pp244-5

☎ 416-465-8085; Leslieville, 1156 Queen St E;
☼ 7am-11pm Sun-Thu, 7am-midnight Fri & Sat;
🚋 501, 502, 503

En route to The Beaches, this artsy, stained-glass coffeehouse sits quietly among the Leslieville antiques and design shops. Sip inside among feathery miscellanea on old-fashioned tables and chairs, or linger on the sunny sidewalk over a rich croissant and a dark-roasted brew – ahhh, heaven…

LIVE MUSIC

In the rock department, megatours play the echo-riddled voids of the Rogers Centre (p53), the Air Canada Centre (p50) and the Molson Amphitheatre (p52) at Ontario Place. Major independent rock rooms include Phoenix (p126), the Opera House (p126) and Koolhaus inside Guvernment (p131). Smaller venues for rock, reggae, jazz, blues and alternative sounds crop up all over town.

It's not all loud rock 'n' roll around here – blues, jazz and folk are also going concerns. In The Danforth, Allen's (p118) has fast-paced Celtic jam sessions, usually on Tuesday and Saturday nights, while jazz, blues and folk musos spontaneously shake the rafters at Healey's (p126), the Pilot Tavern (p120), Hemingway's (p122) and Graffiti's (p126). Check out www.jazzintoronto.com for jazz club listings and a full calendar of gigs, concerts and festivals.

Tickets

For touring acts, contact Ticketmaster (p116). For local acts, you can usually buy tickets at the door. Expect to pay anywhere from nothing to a few dollars on weeknights, up to $20 or more for breakthrough weekend acts. Under-19s aren't admitted to bars where alcohol is served, except for all-ages shows.

Festivals

Anyone who doubts that Toronto's live music scene measures up should check out the North by Northeast festival (NXNE; p13) in June. The challenger is the new Virgin Music Festival (p15) – who will win the battle for rock festival glory? Unconcerned, the summertime Downtown Jazz Festival (p13) and Beaches International Jazz Festival (p14) keep fingers snappin'.

ROCK, REGGAE & ALTERNATIVE

Dust off your Iggy Pop T-shirt, don your Eddie Vedder Doc Martens and get rockin' in Toronto's live music rooms. Queen St and Queen West are alt-rock central.

BIG BOP Map pp240-1

☎ 416-504-6699; www.thebigbop.com; Queen West, 651 Queen St W; shows free-$20; ☼ 8pm-2am; 🚋 501

There's always a bellicose crowd of goths, bad-ass metal fiends and hardcore hardheads pacing around outside this venue. Upstairs Holy Joe's is a groovy little room made for acoustic shows, while serious indie bands plug in at the 2nd-floor Reverb. The ground-floor Kathedral stage also has low-cover acts, and a dance floor.

BOVINE SEX CLUB Map pp240-1

☎ 416-504-4239; www.bovinesexclub.com; Queen West, 542 Queen St W; shows free-$10; ☼ 9pm-2am; 🚋 501

Don't worry, this isn't some kind of twisted fetish establishment. BSC is a maverick punk, metal and retro rock room that's been here since the 1991, one of the first venues to latch onto the Queen West arts explosion. A rusty tangle of scrap metal spews down over the front wall to the doorway.

CAMERON HOUSE Map pp240-1

☎ 416-703-0811; www.thecameron.com; Queen West, 408 Queen St W; shows free-$5; ☼ 4pm-2am Mon-Fri, 3pm-2am Sat & Sun; 🚋 501, 510

Singer-songwriters and soul, jazz, classic country and other alt-music performers grace the stage at the Cameron House, a veteran Queen West venue. Artists, musicians, dreamers and slackers crowd out both front and back rooms. Don't miss Sunday evening's Mad Bastard Cabaret ('accordion singing about love, lust and Spain').

EL MOCAMBO LOUNGE Map pp240-1

☎ 416-777-1777; www.elmocambo.ca; Kensington Market, 464 Spadina Ave; shows free-$8; ☼ 9pm-2am; 🚋 510, 506

The derelict palm-tree nightclub sign suggests Miami, but it's all local bands at the internally renovated El Mocambo – alt-rock, hip-hop, reggae jams, funk, jazz and anything else. This is the place where Mick Jagger once writhed as the ex-prime minister's wife danced approvingly on the tabletops.

GRAFFITI'S Map pp240-1

☎ 416-506-6699; www.graffitisbarandgrill.com; Kensington Market, 170 Baldwin St; admission free; 🕙 11am-2pm; 🚊 510

This diverse bohemian bar has credible acoustic rock, roots, blues and jazz acts, as well as open-mic nights and 'cabarets' that could (and usually do) embrace any subject. There's Sleeman Cream Ale on tap, jazzy murals, Persian rugs and beautifully painted marble tabletops.

HEALEY'S Map pp240-1

☎ 416-703-5882; www.jeffhealys.com; Queen West, 178 Bathurst St; shows free-$10; 🕙 8pm-2am Tue-Sat; 🚊 501

The 300-capacity Healey's has an idiosyncratic line-up of rock, blues, soul and roots. Swing by when owner Jeff Healey (p30), a Canadian music icon, audiophile and radio DJ, gets up on the stage with his house band. Tuesday open-jam nights and Saturday muso matinees are free!

HORSESHOE TAVERN Map pp232-3

☎ 416-598-4753; www.horseshoetavern.com; Queen Street, 370 Queen St W; shows free-$20; 🕙 bar noon-2:30am, music room 9pm-2am; 🚊 501, 510

Well past its 50th birthday, the legendary Horseshoe still plays a crucial role in the development of local indie rock. Not so local, The Police played here to an almost empty house on their first North American tour when Sting did an encore in his underwear. Tuesday is usually no-cover music night!

LEE'S PALACE Map pp242-3

☎ 416-532-1598; www.leespalace.com; The Annex, 529 Bloor St W; shows $10-15; 🕙 8pm-12:30am Sun-Thu, 9pm-2am Fri & Sat; 🚇 Bathurst

Legendary Lee's Palace has set the stage over the years for Dinosaur Jr, Smashing Pumpkins and Queens Of The Stoneage. Kurt Cobain started an infamous bottle-throwing incident when Nirvana played here in 1990. With booming acoustics, it's definitely still an ear-throbbing alt-rock venue. Upstairs is the clubby Dance Cave (p130).

MUSIC SHOWBAR Map pp234-5

☎ 416-867-9499; www.cestwhat.com; Old York, 67 Front St E; shows $5-10; 🕙 9:30pm-2am Sat-Wed; 🚊 503, 504

Off to one side at C'est What? (p119), Music Showroom is a small-capacity live venue with a stellar sound system. Expect intimate pop-rock with an edge – Jeff Buckley, The Tea Party and Wilco all played here. Tickets are sold at the door – first come, first served.

OPERA HOUSE Map pp244-5

☎ 416-466-0313; www.theoperahousetoronto.com; East Toronto, 735 Queen St E; shows $15-20; 🕙 varies; 🚊 501, 502, 503

The old Opera House is an early 1900s vaudeville hall. Over the years rockers like The Black Crowes, Rage Against The Machine, Eminem, A Perfect Circle and Beck have all strutted out beneath the proscenium arch.

PHOENIX Map pp244-5

☎ 416-323-1251; www.libertygroup.com; East Toronto, 410 Sherbourne St; shows around $25; 🕙 varies; 🚊 506

The 1000-capacity Phoenix has occupied the former Harmonie Club, a grand ol' room that now sees the harmonious rock of bands like The Tragically Hip. Huge Superman and Wolverine murals might inspire your crowd-surfing efforts. Check the website for upcoming shows.

RIVOLI Map pp232-3

☎ 416-596-1980; www.rivoli.ca; Queen Street, 334 Queen St W; shows $5-10; 🕙 7pm-2am; 🚊 501

The everlovin' Rivoli offers a lot to the city, with nightly live music (rock, indie and solo singer-songwriters), weekly stand-up comedy (p133) and monthly hip-hop nights. CD launches and art shows and Saturday-night DJs complete a very renaissance picture. There's also an upstairs pool hall (p124), and the food is fabulous!

SNEAKY DEE'S Map pp242-3

☎ 416-603-3090; www.sneaky-dees.com; Kensington Market, 431 College St; shows free-$10; 🕙 11am-3am Mon & Tue, to 4am Wed-Fri, 9am-4:30am Sat, 9am-3:30am Sun; 🚊 506, 511

Spangled with graffiti on the prominent Bathurst St/College St corner, Sneaky Dee's

TOP FIVE LIVE MUSIC ROOMS

Cameron House (p125)

El Mocambo Lounge (p125)

Horseshoe Tavern (opposite)

Rex (right)

Silver Dollar Room (right)

isn't so sneaky-looking. The downstairs bar has battered booths with skeletons painted on them; upstairs is a darkened breeding ground for new T.O. rock talent.

JAZZ, BLUES & FOLK

Big band, be-bop, smoky swamp blues and acoustic balladry – Toronto has it all, dotted around the downtown area.

DOMINION ON QUEEN Map pp244-5

☎ 416-368-6893; www.dominiononqueen.com; East Toronto, 500 Queen St E; shows free-$10; ⏰ 11am-1am Mon-Sat, to 11pm Sun; 🚋 501, 502, 503

This jazzy pub has been around a while, earning a rep for sassy vocalists, trios and sextets through to full-blown swing bands. Music starts nightly around 9pm. Beers have a crafty edge, and there's plenty of *vin rouge* to ease you through life and heartbreak in the big city.

FREE TIMES CAFÉ Map pp240-1

☎ 416-967-1078; www.freetimescafé.com; Kensington Market, 320 College St; admission free; ⏰ 11am-1am Mon-Thu, to 2am Fri & Sat; 🚋 506

Maintaining a hippie Jewish vibe, this small back-room venue is the oldest folk club in T.O., with free music most nights. The pints are cheap, the food substantial and James Brown keeps it tight on the stereo. Open-mic nights are usually on Mondays; sign up by 7pm.

GROSSMAN'S TAVERN Map pp232-3

☎ 416-977-7000; www.grossmanstavern.com; Chinatown, 379 Spadina Ave; shows free; ⏰ 11am-2am; 🚋 510

Inside this grubby 1940s tavern near Kensington Market, the emphasis is on singin' the blues, but acoustic rock and folk acts also get a look-in. There's music nightly –

the Sunday-night jam session has been raising the roof for decades. Incidentally, Dan Akroyd worked up his routine for *The Blues Brothers* here.

HUGH'S ROOM Map p231

☎ 416-531-6604; www.hughsroom.com; Greater Toronto Area, 2261 Dundas St W; shows $15-30; 7pm-2am Wed-Sat; 🚇 Dundas West

Hugh's is one of Toronto's only dedicated old-school folk venues for local and touring acts. Mandolin, ballads, floral shirts and sincerity by the truckload. Save a few dollars by booking in advance.

RESERVOIR LOUNGE Map pp234-5

☎ 416-955-0887; www.reservoirlounge.com; Old York, 52 Wellington St E; admission free Mon, $5 Tue-Thu, $7 Fri & Sat; ⏰ 9pm-2am Mon, from 8pm Tue-Sat; 🚋 503

This seductive supper club is jumpin' with swing and boogie-woogie – book ahead. If these bands don't get your feet tapping, you're probably dead. Good Southern soul food is served, and the bartenders are real friendly. You might bump into Prince, Nick Nolte or Tom Jones malingering in a corner.

REX Map pp232-3

☎ 416-598-2475; www.therex.ca; Queen St, 194 Queen St W; shows free-$7; ⏰ 6:30pm-12:30am Mon-Thu, to 1:30am Fri, noon-1:30am Sat, noon-12:30am Sun; 🚋 501

Make a be-bop beeline for The Rex, which, courtesy of a three million dollar makeover, has risen from its pugilistic, blue-collared past to become an outstanding jazz and blues venue. Over a dozen different Dixieland, experimental and other local and international acts play the joint each week. Drinks are cheap, and the cover affordable.

SILVER DOLLAR ROOM Map pp240-1

☎ 416-763-9139; www.silverdollarroom.com; Kensington Market, 486 Spadina Ave; shows $10-18; ⏰ 9pm-3am Mon, 8pm-3am Wed-Sat; 🚋 506, 510

Crankin' electric blues and southern acoustic slide guitar reign supreme at the legendary Silver Dollar. Big-name touring acts from down south (Detroit, New Orleans, Chicago, etc) kick up ticket prices, sometimes above $30 on weekends, but there's no cover for mid-week bluegrass jams and Saturday afternoon shows.

ARTFUL TUNES

An avant-garde venue that defies classification is the **Music Gallery** (Map pp232–3; ☎ 416-204-1080; www.musicgallery.org; Queen St, Church of St George the Martyr, 197 John St; tickets $10-25; ☾ shows from 7pm Thu-Sun; ⓡ 501), which showcases experimental music, including chamber groups, electronica, jazz, acoustic and world beats. Acts with names like the Dirty Projectors and the Singing Saw Shadow Show appear alongside a large helping of improvisation and performance art. Look for free lunchtime concerts and mini-festivals.

TOP O' THE SENATOR Map pp232-3

☎ 416-364-7517; www.thesenator.com/top_o
.html; Dundas Square, 249 Victoria St; admission $7-10; ☾ 8:30pm-1am Tue-Sat, 8pm-1am Sun; ⓞ Dundas

Upstairs in a historic building just east o' the Eaton Centre, the sassy jazz standards drifting from the Senator's stage are seductive and hypnotic. Musicians and bartenders fill patrons' dreams and martini glasses every night except Monday. Serious hepcats like Branford Marsalis play here when they're in town.

THEATRE

Toronto and first-rate theatre (p33) go hand-in-hand. Big-time Broadway musicals have their tryouts, indefinite runs and encore engagements year-round on downtown's Theatre Block and near Dundas Square. Upstart companies favor smaller venues around the Harbourfront and the Distillery District. Check out www.on-stagetoronto.ca or scan newspapers and alternative weeklies for current listings.

Tickets

Tickets for major productions are sold through **TicketKing** (☎ 416-872-1212, 800-461-3333; www.ticketking.com). For half-price tickets, go to **T.O. Tix** (p116) or inquire about 'rush' tickets at theatre box offices. Discounted tickets are normally available for students, seniors and arts workers. Many smaller nonprofit theatres stage at least one **Pay What You Can** (p130) performance per week, often a Sunday matinee.

Festivals

High-flying theatre festivals at **Stratford** (p191) and **Niagara-on-the-Lake** (p193) are a day trip away from Toronto. During summer, the **New World Stage International Performance** (www.harbourfrontcentre.com/nws) series happens at the **Harbourfront Centre** (p52), while the eccentric **Toronto Fringe Festival** (p14) takes place at miscellaneous venues – as a general rule, the sexier the title, the worse the play tends to be. **Native Earth Performing Arts** (☎ 416-531-1402; www.nativeearth.ca) sponsors a festival, held in autumn, that is filled with new Aboriginal plays and dances from both Canada and the USA.

BUDDIES IN BAD TIMES THEATRE
Map pp238-9

☎ 416-975-8555; www.buddiesinbadtimestheatre
.com; Church-Wellesley Village, 12 Alexander St; tickets around $20; ☾ box office noon-8pm Tue-Sat, to 5pm Sun; ⓞ College

Buddies in Bad Times is an innovative venue for Canadian lesbigay and alternative theatre that's been wowing crowds since 1979. Original plays here often weave together Canadian themes, contemporary dance and jazz. It's tiny – only 300 seats for the main stage, and there are even fewer in **Talullah's Cabaret** (admission $2-6; ☾ 10:30pm-3am Fri & Sat), a clubby performance space for comedians, writers and singers. So book early!

CANON THEATRE Map pp232-3

☎ 416-872-1212, 800-461-3333; www.mirvish
.com; Dundas Square, 244 Victoria St; tickets $25-120; ☾ box office 10:30am-6pm Mon, to 8pm Tue-Sat, 11am-3pm Sun; ⓞ Dundas

Another member of the Ed Mirvish theatrical cartel is this 1920s-era Pantages vaudeville hall. A stone's throw from Dundas Square, the Canon is a hot ticket for big musical extravaganzas like *Wicked* and *We Will Rock You*.

CANSTAGE Map pp244-5

Canadian Stage Company; ☎ 416-368-3110; www
.canstage.com; East Toronto, 26 Berkeley St; tickets $20-95; ☾ box office 10am-6pm Mon-Sat; ⓡ 503, 504

Contemporary CanStage produces top-rated Canadian and international plays by the likes of David Mamet and Tony Kushner. Plays are staged at its own 260-seat theatre and the 880-seat St Lawrence Centre for the Arts (right) down on Front St in Old York.

DIESEL PLAYHOUSE Map pp234-5

☎ 416-971-5656; www.dieselplayhouse.com; Theatre Block Park, 56 Blue Jays Way; tickets $10-40; ☺ box office 10am-5pm Mon-Fri, noon-5pm Sat & Sun; ⬚ 503, 504

Pretty much anything can happen on the Diesel's two stages: drama, sketch comedy, cabaret, musicals, live bands, even 'Ultimate Fighting' on the big screen. It's inside the old Second City (p133) building, and they've astutely retained the drinks-and-food table-service policy from the old days.

DREAM IN HIGH PARK Map p231

☎ 416-367-1652 ext 500; www.canstage.com; High Park, 1873 Bloor St W; admission adult/child $15/free; ☺ 8pm Tue-Sun Jul-Sep; ⊙ High Park

Through Toronto's long summer evenings, CanStage's annual presentation of Shakespeare happens under the stars in High Park. Expect *Much Ado About Nothing,* or *The Comedy of Errors* perhaps. Show up early and take a blanket.

ELGIN & WINTER GARDEN THEATRE CENTRE Map pp232-3

☎ 416-872-5555; www.mirvish.com; Dundas Square, 189 Yonge St; tickets $25-100; ☺ box office 11am-5pm Tue-Sat; ⊙ Queen

The restored double-decker Elgin & Winter Garden Theatre Centre (p61) stages high-profile concerts and productions by the likes of Meatloaf, the Canadian Ballet and Opera Atelier. If you're not 100% engrossed in the act, treat your eyes to the architecture.

FACTORY THEATRE Map pp240-1

☎ 416-504-9971; www.factorytheatre.ca; Queen West, 125 Bathurst St; tickets $23-35, previews $12; ☺ box office 1-7pm Tue-Sat, shows 7pm Tue-Sat & 1:30pm Sun; ⬚ 511

Inside an off-the-beaten-path Victorian mansion, this innovative theatre company – the 'home of the Canadian playwright' – has been busy for 35 years. The independent SummerWorks Theatre Festival (☎ 416-410-1048; www.summerworks.ca) stages plays here too, as do performers from the Toronto Fringe Festival (p14). Sunday matinees are Pay What You Can.

LORRAINE KIMSA THEATRE FOR YOUNG PEOPLE Map pp244-5

☎ 416-363-5131; www.lktyp.ca; Old York, 165 Front St E; tickets $15-20; ☺ box office 9am-6pm, shows vary; ⬚ 503, 504

Toronto's oldest nonprofit theatre delivers enlightening children's plays from Canada and around the planet. The theatre's varied program includes storytelling dramas, musical adaptations and comedies. Themes are timely, diverse and multicultural. Some shows are signed for the hearing-impaired.

PRINCESS OF WALES THEATRE

Map pp234-5

☎ 416-872-1212, 800-461-3333; www.mirvish.com; Theatre Block, 300 King St W; tickets $25-100; ☺ Royal Alexandra Theatre box office (below); ⬚ 504

Working in tandem with the Royal Alexandra down the street, the POW is also owned by Ed Mirvish (p33). Book tickets for the splashy Broadway musicals playing here at the Royal Alex box office.

ROYAL ALEXANDRA THEATRE

Map pp234-5

☎ 416-872-1212, 800-461-3333; www.mirvish.com; Theatre Block, 260 King St W; tickets $25-100; ☺ box office 10:30am-6:30pm Mon, to 8:30pm Tue-Sat, 11am-3pm Sun; ⬚ 504

Commonly known as the 'Royal Alex,' it's one of the most impressive theatres in the city. It's amazing to think it almost became a parking lot in 1963! Expect renderings of plays such as Tennessee Williams' *Orpheus Descending,* and mainstream fodder like Joan Collins and Linda Evans starring in *Legends.*

ST LAWRENCE CENTRE FOR THE ARTS Map pp234-5

☎ 416-366-7723; www.stlc.com; Old York, 27 Front St E; ☺ box office 10am-6pm Mon-Sat; ⊙ Union

The 880-seat St Lawrence Centre for the Arts functions as a second, larger venue for CanStage (opposite), and also hosts dance, classical and contemporary music, opera, operetta and musicals.

PAY WHAT YOU CAN

How refreshing! In a spirit of goodwill and artistic open-heartedness, many Toronto events – from classical concerts to gallery openings, rock gigs, spoken-word nights and theatre performances – adopt a 'Pay What You Can' (PWYC) pricing policy. In essence, this means they're free, but artists still appreciate your pocket change.

THEATRE PASSE MURAILLE
Map pp240-1

Theatre Beyond Walls; ☎ 416-504-7529; www .passemuraille.on.ca; Queen West, 16 Ryerson Ave; tickets $20-35, previews $16; ◷ shows from 8pm Tue-Sat; ⓐ 501
Alternative Theatre Beyond Walls is in the old Nasmith's Bakery & Stables buildings. Since the 1960s, its cutting-edge productions have focused on radical new plays with contemporary Canadian themes. Post-performance chats with the cast and producers are usually held on the first Tuesday evening after the show opens. Sunday matinees are Pay What You Can.

YOUNG CENTRE FOR PERFORMING ARTS Map pp244-5

☎ 416-866-8666; www.youngcentre.com; Old York, bldg 49, Distillery District, 55 Mill St; tickets $15-45; ◷ box office 1-8pm Tue-Sat; ⓐ 503, 504
Opening in January 2006, the $14 million Young Centre houses four separate performance spaces, utilized by theatrical tenants including Soul Pepper (www.soulpepper.ca), Moonhorse Dance Theatre (www.danceumbrella .net/clients_moonhorse.htm) and George Brown Theatre Co (www.georgebrown.ca/theatre). There's an onsite bookshop and bar too.

CLUBBING

Whether it's a big-floored, hi-tech dance club or a sweaty underground room, what's in vs what's not in 'Clubland' (p62) changes in the blink of an eye. Cover charges of $5 to $20 apply on weekends (depending on which DJs are playing), although early birds and ladies may get in free some nights. Hats, sportswear, ripped jeans and under-19s are usually not allowed. You can put yourself on the VIP list (no waiting, no cover) at individual club websites or via www.club

crawlers.com, which has event listings and reviews. Toronto's rave scene was once out in the open, until city officials started cracking down. Still, look out for flyers at record shops. Most clubs open their doors around 9pm or 10pm (some don't really get going until even later) and close around 4am.

Club Strips & Neighborhoods

Mainstream dance clubs crowd the Entertainment District, nicknamed 'Clubland', between Queen and King Sts W, mostly along the smaller streets of Duncan, John and Peter. The place is jam-packed on weekends; check out the beautiful people queuing and find a club that suits your taste. A lot of bars in the gay Church-Wellesley Village have DJ nights. Alternative dance clubs lie along Queen West and The Annex. Restaurants, bars and lounges in Little Italy tend to morph into cool groove pits after dark. Midsize independent rock venues like Phoenix (p126) and Koolhaus (opposite) often give their dance floors over to clubbers.

COMFORT ZONE Map pp240-1
☎ 416-763-0909; www.clubcrawlers.com/comfort zone.php; Kensington Market, 480 Spadina Ave; admission $10; ◷ 10pm-6am Thu, midnight-7am Fri, 3am-4pm Sat; 6am Sun-6am Mon; ⓐ 510
Lose track of time in this underground trip-hop club, where 24-hour pilled-up party people come when everywhere else has closed. It's grungy, but dress nice (no ripped stuff). The 24-hour Sunday session is the stuff of legend.

DANCE CAVE Map pp242-3
☎ 416-532-1598; www.leespalace.com; The Annex, 529 Bloor St W; admission free Mon & Thu, $6 Fri & Sat; ◷ 10pm-2am Mon & Thu-Sat; ⓔ Bathurst
Upstairs at Lee's Palace (p126), Dance Cave is thick with U of T young 'uns, dancing up a storm to retro '80s grooves, Brit Pop, garage rock and '60s soul tunes. There's no cover except on weekends.

DOCKS NIGHTCLUBS Map p231
☎ 416-469-5655; www.thedocks.com; East Toronto, 11 Polson St, off Cherry St; admission $10-20; ◷ 10pm-3am Thu-Sun
A lakeshore entertainment complex, the Docks has multiple nightclubs, all with

huge dance floors, and a breezy outdoor patio. It's primed at the height of summer, when 2000 people gyrate through special event nights. Public transport isn't an option – take a cab.

EL CONVENTO RICO Map pp242-3
☎ 416-588-7800; www.elconventorico.com; Little Italy, 750 College St; admission free-$8; 9pm-4am Fri & Sat; 506

Inside a former church beyond some impressive steel gates, this gender-bending Latino dance palace sees as many straight as gay clientele these days, but drag shows still triumphantly storm the stage. Check out the salsa and meringue dance lessons that carve up the floor from 9pm on Fridays.

FEZ BATIK Map pp234-5
☎ 416-204-9660; www.fezlounge.com; Entertainment District, 129 Peter St; admission free-$10; 10pm-4am Fri & Sat; 501

Fez Batik mixes live music and DJs, sometimes scoring a winner. Four floors of lounging, chatting and grooving go along with a full kitchen, Moroccan tea room and gargantuan streetside patio underneath. It's about as laid-back as Clubland gets.

FLY Map pp238-9
☎ 416-410-5426; www.flynightclub.com; Yonge Street Strip, 8 Gloucester St; admission $10-25; 10pm-4am Fri & Sat; Wellesley

Winner of a proud crop of 'Toronto's Best Club' awards, gay-focused Fly is a shirts-off musclefest, flying in the face of conformity with state-of-the-art sound and light and US and international DJs spinning hardhouse, tribal and trance.

GUVERNMENT Map pp234-5
☎ 416-869-0045; www.theguvernment.com; Harbourfront, 132 Queens Quay E; admission $10-15; 10pm-4am Thu-Sat; 6, 75

For diversity of venues, nothing beats the gargantuan Guv. Although critics say it's too mainstream and full of suburbanites, DJs play hip-hop, R&B, progressive house and tribal music to satisfy all kinds of appetites. Rooftop skyline views are as impressive as the Arabian fantasy lounge and art deco bar. Koolhaus is the midsize live venue.

HOOCH Map pp240-1
☎ 416-703-5069; www.gypsyco-op.com; Queen West, 815 Queen St W; 9pm-2am irregular nights; 501

Lounging around upstairs from Gypsy Co-op (p108), Hooch heats up with rare grooves and hipster moves on various nights of the week, often with no cover charge. DJs spin soul, jazz, house, swing and drum 'n' bass, while tarots are read in a darkened corner.

MATADOR Map p231
☎ 416-533-9311; Greater Toronto Area, 466 Dovercourt Rd, west of Ossington Ave; 2am-5:30am Fri & Sat; 506

For more than 40 years there's been after-hours chaos at the Matador's huge dance floor, just west of Little Italy. Shuffle in under the rusty ballroom sign for live bands playing honky-tonk and classic rock. It's alcohol-free, but if you're up this late, chances are you won't need any more.

MOD CLUB Map pp242-3
☎ 416-588-4663; www.themodclub.com; Little Italy, 722 College St; admission $5-25; 9pm-3am Wed-Sun; 506

Celebrating all things post-WWII and UK Mod, this excellent retro club plays electronic, indie and Britpop, with occasional live acts like Paul Weller, The Killers and Muse taking the stage. Up-to-the-nanosecond lighting technology rifles across Yellow Submarine–era murals, giving way to candle-lit chill-out rooms.

REPUBLIK Map pp234-5
☎ 416-598-1632; www.republiknightclub.com; Entertainment District, 261 Richmond St W; admission $5-15; 10pm-4am Wed-Sat; 501, 505

Resident DJs Lil Pete and Dave Campbell spin old-skool, drum 'n' bass, alt-rock and hip-hop at this massive club, divided into three rooms: the main club, the Vision Room and Toronto's largest smoking room. Friday's new rock and alternative nights take a more rockin', less pill-poppin' approach to life.

SONIC Map pp232-3
☎ 416-599-5550; www.sonicnightclub.com; Chinatown, 270 Spadina Ave; admission $30-50; midnight-4am Fri-Sun; 501, 505

NYC club mogul David Morales opened Sonic in 2006 with unprecedented hooplah

GAY & LESBIAN NIGHTLIFE

During **Toronto Pride** (p13), which runs for one week in June, about a million visitors descend on the Church-Wellesley Village. For information on Toronto's gay-friendly neighborhoods, queer happenings and marriage licenses at City Hall, turn to p201. Otherwise the best source for finding out what's on now is the free alternative weekly *Xtra!* (p203). Mainstream venues with queer-friendly vibes include **Allen's** (p118), **Cameron House** (p125) and **Ciao Edie** (p121). If you're lucky, you might be in town for an **It's a Boy's Life** (www.itsaboyslife.com) dance event at Koolhaus at **Guvernment** (p131). Other happening local haunts include:

Black Eagle (p121)

Buddies in Bad Times Theatre (p128)

Crews/Tango/Zone (p121)

El Convento Rico (p131)

Fly (p131)

Pegasus Bar (p124)

Slack's (p122)

Talullah's Cabaret (p128)

Woody's/Sailor (p123)

and hype. Is it worth the astronomical cover charge? Well, if you like your clubs large, loud and gregarious and your clubbers minimally clad, then the answer is yes.

TONIC Map pp234-5

☎ 416-204-9200; www.tonicnightclub.com; Entertainment District, 117 Peter St; admission free-$12; ☿ 10pm-3am Wed-Sat; ▣ 510

Tonic bills itself as 'neutral' and 'abstract,' but the grape-like disco balls above the entry lobby suggest otherwise. 'Uni Night' on Thursday draws a slightly more literate crowd than 'Fashion Friday.' Album launch parties by Diddy and others of his ilk see a steep decline in the skin-to-clothing ratio.

COMEDY & SPOKEN WORD

The alternative weekly *Now* knows what's on in the comedy clubs, and lists book and poetry readings at libraries, universities and bars like **Castro's Lounge** (p121) and **Free Times Café** (p127). Note most clubs and

bars don't admit under-19s. **Insomniac Press** (☎ 416-504-9313; www.insomniacpress .com) tracks the city's reading series and literary events.

BAD DOG THEATRE Map pp244-5

☎ 416-491-3115; www.baddogtheatre.com; Greektown, 138 Danforth Ave; tickets $5-15; ☿ shows 8pm Tue-Sat; ▣ Broadview

Ace improvisers Marcel St Pierre and Kerry Griffin lead the charge into Saturday night 'Improv Unleashed' gag-fests. There's a free drop-in improve workshop at 7pm on Saturday before the show, and an open stage on Wednesday.

BRUNSWICK HOUSE Map pp242-3

☎ 416-964-2242; www.thebrunswickhouse.com; The Annex, 481 Bloor St W; tickets $5; ☿ 8-11pm Wed & Sat; ▣ Spadina

Between student karaoke nights and horse racing, the comedy schedule at the boozy, big-screen Brunswick House includes a version of *Saturday Night Live* by local troupe **The Sketchersons** (www.thesketchersons.com). On Wednesday it's **Late Night Giggin'** (www .latenitegiggin.com) – stand-up, live music and debauchery.

HARBOURFRONT READINGS SERIES
Map pp234-5

☎ 416-973-4000; www.readings.org; Harbourfront, York Quay Centre, 235 Queens Quay W; admission $8; ☿ usually 7:30pm Wed Sep-Jun; ▣ 509, 510

If you want to hear the new voice of Canada's writers, then this is the place. For more than 30 years, literary giants have headlined at Toronto's Harbourfront Centre. You'll find that tickets for Wednesday night readings don't cost much, but you will shell out a lot more for special events and October's **International Festival of Authors** (p15).

LAUGH RESORT Map pp234-5

☎ 416-364-5233; www.laughresort.com; Entertainment District, 370 King St W; tickets $7-15; ☿ shows 8:30pm Wed & Thu, 8:30pm & 10:30pm Fri & Sat; ▣ 504, 510

Squeeze inside the small, split-level Laugh Resort, where Ellen DeGeneres, Ray Romano and Adam Sandler once cracked jokes and served up the big laughs. New talent takes the stage on Wednesday nights, which can be a bit hit-and-miss, but it'll only cost you $7.

RIVOLI Map pp232-3
☎ 416-596-1980; www.rivoli.ca; Queen Street, 334 Queen St W; shows $5-10; ⏱ 8pm Mon & Tue; 🚃 501

Big laughs liven up the Rivoli on Monday nights when Alt.Comedy Lounge (www.altdotcomedylounge.com) hams it up in a cabaret-style setting. On Tuesday nights check out the Sketch Comedy Lounge (www.sketchcomedylounge.com), where local stand-up comedians and international acts perform new material.

SECOND CITY Map pp234-5
☎ 416-343-0011, 800-263-4485; www.secondcity.com; Entertainment District, 51 Mercer St; tickets $20-28; ⏱ box office noon-11pm daily, shows 8pm Tue-Fri & Sun, 8pm & 10:30pm Sat; 🚃 504

Sharing its name with a comedy club in Chicago, the club's moniker dates from the days when each city was perceived to be playing second fiddle, Chicago to New York City, and Toronto to Montréal. But the 300-seat Second City is legendary, and many *Saturday Night Live* comics started here. Improv performances held after the last show ends are free.

YUK YUK'S Map pp234-5
☎ 416-967-6425; www.yukyuks.com; Entertainment District, 224 Richmond St W; cover $10-20; ⏱ from 8pm Tue-Sat; Ⓜ Osgoode

A bit like the brass plucked chicken door handles, acts here are sometimes funny and sometimes just a joke. Canadian and international touring acts appear regularly, with famous faces on some weekends. Jim Carrey cut his comic teeth here. Cover for Tuesday's 'Amateur Night' is just $3.

TOP FIVE QUIRKY NIGHTS ON THE TOWN

Cineforum (p117)

El Convento Rico (p131)

Matador (p131)

Tallulah's Cabaret (p128)

Theatre Passe Muraille (p130)

CLASSICAL MUSIC & OPERA

Toronto's major classical and opera venues include Roy Thomson Hall (p59), which also sells tickets for performances at Massey Hall (p62). Together they present a world of music, from opera tenors to chamber groups, Ravi Shankar and Ladysmith Black Mambazo. Other performances take place at the Hummingbird Centre for the Performing Arts (p134). Construction of downtown's magnificent Four Seasons Centre for the Performing Arts is finally complete – a grand new home for the Canadian Opera Company (below) and the National Ballet of Canada (p135).

Other outfits to listen out for include:

Amici Chamber Ensemble (☎ 416-368-8743; www.amiciensemble.com)

Opera Atelier (☎ 416-703-3767; www.operaatelier.com)

Toronto Chamber Choir (☎ 416-763-1695; www.geosites.com/torontochamberchoir)

Toronto Mendelssohn Choir (☎ 416-598-0422; www.tmchoir.org)

Tickets & Festivals

Buy tickets for major events through Ticketmaster's Artsline (☎ 416-872-1111; www.ticketmaster.ca). During summer, affordable (even free) performances happen at various churches and outdoor venues, as well as during major festivals. Go to www.newmusicconcerts.com for avant-garde performances by Canadian and international composers, including those at the Music Gallery (p128).

CANADIAN OPERA COMPANY
Map pp232-3

☎ 416-363-8231; www.coc.ca; Queen Street, Four Seasons Centre for the Performing Arts, 145 Queen St W; tickets $20-275; ⏱ box office 11am-7pm Mon-Sat, 11am-3pm Sun; Ⓜ Osgoode

Warbling their pipes for over half a century, Canada's national opera company can claim to have invented Surtitles, which projects text translations visible to the audience over a proscenium arch. Advance single tickets sell out quickly; check the website about a month before opening night for details. Free concerts happen at the Richard Bradshaw Amphitheatre year-round, usually Tuesday and Thursday at noon.

CHURCH OF THE HOLY TRINITY
Map pp232-3

☎ 416-598-4521; www.holytrinitytoronto
.org; Dundas Square, 10 Trinity Sq; admission $5;
☽ noon Mon late May-early Sep; ◉ Dundas
Nestled behind Eaton Centre (p153), the
welcoming Church of the Holy Trinity
opens its doors on summer Music Mondays
for wonderful medieval, classical, folk and
modern music performances.

GLENN GOULD STUDIO Map pp234-5
☎ 416-205-5555; www.glenngouldstudio.cbc.ca;
Theatre Block, Canadian Broadcasting Centre, 250
Front St W; tickets $15-40; ☽ box office 2-6:30pm
Mon-Fri, 2-8pm Sat, shows vary; ◉ Union; 🚋 504
Free noontime concerts are given in the
Glenn Gould Studio (named after the famous
pianist; p31), where the soundtrack for *Schin-
dler's List* was recorded. You'll need to purchase advance tickets for highly esteemed
concerts of classical and contemporary music
by soloists, chamber groups, choirs and
sinfonia that play between September and
June.

HARBOURFRONT CENTRE Map pp234-5
☎ 416-973-4000; www.harbourfrontcentre.com;
Harbourfront, York Quay Centre, 235 Queens Quay
W; tickets $10-40; ☽ box office 1-6pm Tue-Sat;
🚋 509, 510
A high bastion of T.O. culture, the vibrant
Harbourfront Centre puts on a variety of
world-class musical performances throughout the year, including Sunday family
shows and free outdoor summer concerts
in the Toronto Music Garden (p54) and on the
Concert Stage.

HUMMINGBIRD CENTRE
FOR THE PERFORMING ARTS
Map pp234-5

☎ 416-393-7469; www.hummingbirdcentre.com;
Old York; 1 Front St E; ☽ box office 10am-5:30pm
Mon-Fri, 10am-1pm Sat; ◉ Union
With an entry awning protruding over
Front St like a Hummingbird beak, this
place is hard to miss. Book through Ticketmaster (p116) or at the box office for shows
like *Annie*, performances by the American
Dance Theatre or maybe the Soweto Gospel Choir. In true North American style,
there's pizza and beer available in the
lobby.

TORONTO CENTRE FOR THE ARTS
Map p230

☎ 416-733-9388; www.tocentre.com; Greater Toronto Area, North York, 5040 Yonge St; tickets from
$10; ☽ box office 11am-6pm Mon-Sat, noon-4pm
Sun; ◉ North York Centre
The 1000-seat George Weston Recital Hall
is home to the Toronto Philharmonia (☎ 416-
499-2204; www.torontophil.on.ca) and the
Amadeus Choir (☎ 416-446-0188; www
.amadeuschoir.com). The 1700-seat Main
Stage Theatre and intimate Studio Theatre
also host ballet and theatre. It's a long way
to the top of Yonge St.

TORONTO SYMPHONY ORCHESTRA
Map pp234-5

☎ 416-593-4828; www.tso.ca; Entertainment
District, Roy Thompson Hall, 60 Simcoe St; tickets
$30-120; ☽ box office 10am-6pm Mon-Fri, noon-
5pm Sat; ◉ St Andrew
A range of classics, Cole Porter–era pops
and new music from around the world are
presented by the TSO at Roy Thomson Hall (p59),
Massey Hall (p62) and the Toronto Centre for the
Arts (above). Consult the website for the
answers to such questions as 'What if I need
to cough?' and 'Should I clap yet?'

TRINITY-ST PAUL'S CENTRE
Map pp242-3

☎ 416-964-6337; The Annex, 427 Bloor St W;
☽ box office 10am-1pm & 2-6pm Mon-Fri;
◉ Spadina
The world-renowned Tafelmusik (www
.tafelmusik.org; tickets $22-77) baroque
orchestra and chamber choir performs most
of the time at atmospheric Trinity-St Paul's
United Church, as does the Toronto Consort
(www.torontoconsort.org; tickets $14-48) for
early medieval and renaissance music. Check
schedules for family matinees, meet-the-
musician nights and the annual sing-along
to Handel's *Messiah* at Massey Hall.

UNIVERSITY OF TORONTO FACULTY
OF MUSIC Map pp238-9

☎ 416-978-3744; www.music.utoronto.ca; box
office: St George campus, Edward Johnson Bldg, 80
Queen's Park; tickets $12-26; ☽ box office 1-7pm
Mon-Fri; ◉ Museum
U of T's scholarly and professional music
faculty presents a series of concerts –

orchestral, chamber, wind ensembles, jazz and new music – at various venues around the university's St George campus. An afternoon of tea and opera at the MacMillan Theatre costs less than $30. Vocal classes and select concerts at Walter Hall are free.

DANCE

Keep an eye out for unique productions by the city's multicultural dance troupes, including Middle Eastern **Arabesque Dance Company** (p199), Chinese-inspired **Xing Dance Theatre** (☎ 416-413-0957; www.xingdancetheatre .com) and Afro-Caribbean **Ballet Creole** (☎ 416-960-0350; www.balletcreole.org).

Festivals

During August the **Toronto International Dance Festival** (p14) happens at the Distillery District. Over half of the performing artists are from Toronto, with others hailing from abroad.

DANCEMAKERS Map pp244-5
☎ 416-367-1800; www.dancemakers.org; Old York, bldg 58, Distillery District, 55 Mill St; tickets $15-40; ⑧ 503, 504
A physically provocative contemporary dance troupe, Dancemakers is emotive, expressionist and minimalist by turns. Their repertoire evolves under the guidance of artistic director and resident choreographer Michael Trent, with passion-driven Canadian themes. They also run dance classes from $8.50 per class.

HARBOURFRONT CENTRE Map pp234-5
☎ 416-973-4000; www.harbourfrontcentre.com; Harbourfront, Premiere Dance Theatre, Queen's Quay Terminal, 3rd fl, 207 Queens Quay W; tickets $10-40; ⑨ box office 1-6pm Tue-Sat; ⑧ 509, 510
A focal point for Canadian dance companies, the Harbourfront Centre also hosts a kaleidoscopic array of international touring troupes, usually performing at the two-tiered **Premiere Dance Theatre** in the Queen's Quay Terminal. Classical Indian dances, traditional folk performances and modern French comedies are among the productions staged here. Dancespeak, a chance to talk with the dancers, usually takes place on the second night of the performance run. Buy tickets at the Harbourfront box office at the York Quay Centre, 235 Queens Quay W.

NATIONAL BALLET OF CANADA
Map pp232-3
☎ 416-345-9595, 866-345-9595; www.national .ballet.ca; Queen Street, Four Seasons Centre for the Performing Arts, 145 Queen St W; tickets $40-170; ⑨ box office 11am-7pm Mon-Sat, 11am-3pm Sun; ⑩ Osgoode
Pirouetting joyfully in its new Four Seasons Centre home, the National Ballet actively commissions new and experimental works by choreographers from across Canada, the USA and around the world. Traditional ballets like *The Nutcracker* also get a run. Ask about Ballet Talk introductory lectures often given one hour before curtain time.

TORONTO DANCE THEATRE
Map pp244-5
☎ 416-967-1365; www.tdt.org; Cabbagetown, 80 Winchester St; tickets $16-40; ⑨ varies; ⑧ 506
Kinetic and poetic, this contemporary dance troupe performs at a restored church in Cabbagetown and the Harbourfront Centre's **Premiere Dance Theatre** (left) during winter and early spring. The annual Four at the Winch event spotlights four works by emerging Canadian choreographers. The **School of Toronto Dance Theatre** also performs in Cabbagetown – opening nights are highly recommended!

Activities

Activities

It takes more than a little slush and a chilly zephyr to keep Torontonians from being active. They propel themselves into all kinds of outdoor activities in all seasons – in summer, cycling, blading and running along lakeshore trails, hiking up the city's ravines and paddling on Lake Ontario; in winter, ice-skating, skiing and snowboarding, or trekking out to the ski resorts around Ontario. Hardcore cyclists skitter across icy February roads; dogged hockey players skate over artificial ice in the July heat.

If you're not feeling so intense, the lakefront beaches and ravine trails will keep you happy, walking or cycling for kilometres. Or head over to the Rogers Centre (p53) or Air Canada Centre (p50) to watch the fortunes of T.O.'s pro sports teams ebb and flow.

Torontonians are quick to adopt the latest fitness and healthy lifestyle crazes. Whatever they're doing in Los Angeles or Vancouver, you're sure to find it here, too. Treat yourself to a Thai massage, twist yourself silly with yoga, indulge in an organic spa or ink yourself in with a new tattoo.

OUTDOOR ACTIVITIES

It's probably stating the obvious, but most organized outdoor activities happen during summer, from late May to early September. Winter sports pick up the slack between November and March. Contact **Toronto Parks & Recreation** (☎ 416-392-1111; www.city .toronto.on.ca/parks) for a seasonal activity Toronto fun guide, or browse its voluminous website for all kinds of activities. Equipment rentals are available at Europe Bound Outfitters (p151), where baby carriers, binoculars, backpacks, trekking poles, ice-climbing gear and snow shoes can be hired for around $10 per day. See also Mountain Equipment Co-op (p151) and Hogtown Extreme Sports (p151).

CYCLING, IN-LINE SKATING & RUNNING

For cyclists, in-line skaters and runners, the Martin Goodman Trail (Map pp234–5) is the place to go. This paved recreational trail stretches from The Beaches through Harbourfront to the Humber River in the west. Along the way at Cherry St, you can connect to the Don Valley mountain bike trails (Map p231). On the Toronto Islands (p75) the south-shore boardwalk and the interconnecting paved paths are car-free zones. You can also cycle or skate around hilly High Park (p77). If you fancy a longer trek, the Martin Goodman Trail is part of the **Lake Ontario Waterfront Trail** (www.water fronttrail.org), stretching 450km from east of Toronto to Niagara-on-the-Lake, where you pick up the paved recreational trail alongside Niagara Parkway (p181).

Recommended maps for cyclists include MapArt's *Toronto with Bicycle Routes* ($3.95) and the *Official Lake Ontario Waterfront Trail Mapbook* ($9.95). A recreational cycling club, the **Toronto Bicycling Network** (☎ 416-760-4191; www.tbn.on.ca) is an excellent informational resource, with organized rides open to nonmembers for a small fee. Check the website or call for in-line skating events.

Rental

Toronto's **Community Bicycling Network** (Map pp240–1; ☎ 416-504-2918; www.com munitybicyclenetwork.org; Queen West, 761 Queen St W; ☺ noon-6pm Mon-Fri; 🚋 501) runs BikeShare (www.bikeshare.org). For adult/student $50/30 per year, members can borrow and return a single-speed yellow bike from any of 16 centrally located hubs for up to three days.

Europe Bound Outfitters (Map pp234–5; ☎ 416-601-1990; 47 Front St; $30 per day; ☺ 10am-7pm Mon-Fri, to 6pm Sat, 11am-5pm Sun; 🚋 503) rents mountain bikes and tandem bikes with helmets. Bicycles and in-line skates can also be rented from the following:

High Park Cycle & Sports (Map p230; ☎ 416-614-6689; Greater Toronto Area, 2878 Dundas St W; bike hire per day $30; ☺ varies; Ⓜ Keele)

Toronto Islands Bicycle Rental (Map p247; ☎ 416-203-0009; Toronto Islands, near Centre Island; bicycles/tandems per hr $6/13, 2/4-seat quadricycles per hr $16/28; ⏰ 11am-5pm daily Jun-Aug, Sat & Sun only May & Sep; 🚢 Centre Island)

Wheel Excitement (Map pp234–5; ☎ 416-260-9000; www.wheelexcitement.ca; Harbourfront, 249 Queens Quay W; bicycles & in-line skates per hr/day $12/27; ⏰ 10am-6pm Mon-Fri year round, 10am-7pm Sat & Sun late Apr-Oct; 🚋 509, 510)

GOLF

Work the kink out of your swing at the golf courses around the Niagara region, including Legends Golf Course (p185) at Niagara Falls. The Docks (p117) has a driving range, and there's also a Frisbee (disc) golf course on Ward's Island (p77). Other options include:

BEACH FAIRWAY GOLF COURSE
Map p231

☎ 416-686-4101; Greater Toronto Area, 411 Victoria Park Ave; golf balls per bucket $7-13; ⏰ 8am-dusk mid-Mar–early Nov; ◉ Victoria Park
Five minutes walk from the subway, this 300-yard fairway has 33 adjustable tees, seven target greens, an artificial putting green, two bunkers and an 18-hole mini-golf course – as close as you can get to playing golf in Toronto without actually playing!

GLEN ABBEY GOLF CLUB Map p180

☎ 905-844-1811, 800-288-0388; www.glenabbey.com; 1333 Dorval Dr, Oakville; 18 holes $92-235; ⏰ 7am-dusk Apr-Oct, 10am-4pm Nov-Mar
Golfers will know Glen Abbey, the first course designed solely by Jack Nicklaus. It's where the pros play during the Bell Canadian Open. The club is a 40-minute drive west of downtown via the QEW, past Hwy 407 in the suburb of Oakville.

WOODEN STICKS Map p180

☎ 905-852-4379; www.woodensticks.com; 40 Elgin Park Dr, Uxbridge; 18 holes incl cart hire $175-220; ⏰ 7am-7pm May-Oct
The 12 tribute holes at Wooden Sticks are inspired by famous holes on the PGA tour, from Scotland to Florida. Take Hwy 401 east, the 404 north then exit at Bloomington Rd. Drive east to Goodwood and then Uxbridge.

HIKING

Feel like stretching your legs? Take one of our walking tours (p82), or delve into Toronto's city parks, nature reserves or ravines. Alternatively, hook up with one of the following groups for hardy day hikes:

Hike Ontario (☎ 416-426-7362; www.hikeontario.com)

Toronto Bicycling Network (below)

Toronto Bruce Trail Club (☎ 416-763-9061; www.torontobrucetrailclub.org)

Toronto Parks & Recreation (opposite) oversee the city's self-guided Discovery Walks. These are structured, creatively-mapped walks through areas including the Don Valley Hills & Dales, Uptown Toronto, Downtown Toronto, Eastern Ravines & Beaches, Western Ravines & Beaches, Humber River, Old Mill & Marshes and Central Ravines, Belt Line & Gardens. Part of the Central Ravines walk is included in our Green Ravine Scenes walk (p85). Pick up free Discovery Walks maps from City Hall (p60), or download them from the Parks & Recreation website.

ICE-SKATING, SKIING & SNOWBOARDING

There are cool places to ice-skate downtown, including Nathan Phillips Square (Map pp232–3) and the Harbourfront Centre (p52) behind the York Quay Centre. These rinks are open daily from 10am to 10pm, mid-November to March. Entry is free; skate rental is $7. Call Toronto Parks & Recreation (opposite) for information on other rinks, including at Kew Gardens (Map p246) and Trinity Bellwoods Park (Map pp240–1). If it's *really* cold, you can skate on Grenadier Pond (p231).

In winter, the **North York Ski Centre** (Map p230; ☎ 416-395-7931; Greater Toronto Area, Earl Bales Park, 4169 Bathurst St; day pass $25; ⏰ 1-9:30pm Mon, 10am-9:30pm Tue-Fri, 9am-8pm Sat, 9am-6pm Sun; ◉ Sheppard-Yonge then 🚌 84) and **Centennial Park Snow Centre** (Map p230; ☎ 416-394-8754; Greater Toronto Area, Centennial Park, 256 Centennial Park Rd; day pass adult/student/child $25/20/20; ⏰ 10am-9:30pm Mon-Fri, 9am-9pm Sat, 9am-6pm Sun; ◉ Royal York then 🚌 48) offer skiing and snowboarding.

For more downhill skiing and snowboarding opportunities, see p194.

SWIMMING & WATERSPORTS

Torontonians don't like swimming in Lake Ontario, despite the presence of a dozen city beaches tended by lifeguards from July to August. Water quality can be lousy, especially after rain, so check with Toronto's **Beach Water Quality Hotline** (☎ 416-392-7161; www.city.toronto.on.ca/beach) first.

Dive into Toronto's Olympic-sized outdoor swimming pools, open dawn-to-dusk during summer:

Christie Pitts Park Pool (Map pp242–3; ☎ 416-392-0745; The Annex, 750 Bloor St W; adult/child $2.50/free; Ⓜ Christie)

DD Summerville Pool (Map p246; ☎ 416-392-0740; The Beaches, Woodbine Park, 1675 Lake Shore Blvd E; adult/child $4/2; Ⓡ 501)

High Park Municipal Pool (Map p231; ☎ 416-392-0695; 1873 Bloor St W; adult/child $2.50/free; Ⓜ High Park)

Sunnyside Gus Ryder Pool (Map p231; ☎ 416-392-1111; Greater Toronto Area, 1755 Lake Shore Blvd W, adult/child $2.50/free; Ⓜ Keele then Ⓜ 80)

Rentals & Lessons

Harbourfront Canoe & Kayak Centre (Map pp234–5; ☎ 416-203-2277, 800-960-8886; www.paddletoronto .com; Harbourfront, 283A Queen's Quay W; canoes per hr/day $20/40, kayaks $20/50, tandem kayaks $30/65; Ⓒ office 9am-6pm; Ⓡ 509, 510) Paddle around their pond or out to the Toronto Islands. Private and group lessons, plus evening and weekend paddles and an on-site sailing school.

Queens Quay Sailing & Powerboating (Map pp234–5; ☎ 416-203-3000; www.qqy.ca; 275 Queens Quay W; sailboats per 3hr from $99, power boats per hr from $60; Ⓒ 9am-9pm daily May-Sep, 10am-6pm Mon-Fri Oct-Apr) Rents sailboats and power boats, and gives lessons.

TOP FIVE TORONTO SPORTING ENDEAVORS

- Cycling around the **Toronto Islands** (p75) – life seems better on two wheels.
- Hiking through **Toronto's ravines** (p139) – a leafy retreat from the city heat.
- Ice-skating at **Nathan Phillips Square** (Map pp232–3) in the shadows of sexy City Hall.
- Swimming at the **Sunnyside Gus Ryder Pool** (above) – all that remains of a huge amusement park, demolished to make way for the Gardiner Expwy.
- Trying to score a ticket to a **Leafs game** (p142) without remortgaging your house.

Toronto Windsurfing Club (Map p231; ☎ 416-461-7078; www.torontowindsurfingclub.com; Greater Toronto Area, 2 Regatta Rd; rental per hour $80; Ⓒ varies; Ⓜ Union then Ⓜ 172) Windsurfing rental and lessons at Cherry Beach. Get off the bus at Commissioners St and walk 10 minutes south.

TENNIS

Toronto's **Municipal tennis courts** (☎ 416-392-1111) are open April to October. Other courts include those at High Park (p77), Hanlan's Point (p76) on Toronto Islands and Trinity Bellwoods Park (Map pp240–1). They're usually available for free on a first-come-first-served basis, with an hour or half-hour time limit. Permits are necessary during peak summer times.

At The Beaches, **Kew Gardens Tennis Club** (Map p246; ☎ 416-699-1635; www.kewgardens tennis.ca; The Beaches, Kew Gardens, 77 Kew Beach Ave; day pass $10; Ⓒ 9am-4pm Mon-Fri, 6-9pm Sun; Ⓡ 501) has 10 outdoor courts and runs private lessons for $50 per hour (less for groups).

WATCHING SPORTS

Torontonians love watching sport. There's professional baseball and football through the summer; ice hockey, basketball and lacrosse through the winter.

Tickets & Reservations

Ticket prices for major sporting events go through the roof. **Ticketmaster** (☎ 416-872-5000; www.ticketmaster.ca) sells advance tickets, as do the box offices at the Air Canada Centre (p50) and Rogers Centre (p53). Ticket scalping is illegal, but that doesn't seem to stop anybody from doing it. Scalpers often hang around Union Station.

BASEBALL
TORONTO BLUE JAYS

☎ 416-341-1000; www.bluejays.com; Rogers Centre, 1 Blue Jays Way; tickets from $9; Ⓒ regular season Apr-Sep

Toronto's sporadically successful Major League Baseball team plays at the **Rogers Centre** (p53). Buy tickets with a credit card by phone, online or through **Ticketmaster** (p116) for a fee. You can buy tickets for cash at the Rogers Centre box office near

LOCAL VOICES: NICK BENTLEY

Aside from a couple of trips to Europe and the Pacific, **Nick Bentley**, 25, has lived in Toronto his entire life. A dedicated Toronto Blue Jays fan and bottomless well of statistics and historical player info, he recently curtailed his baseball enthusiasms to pursue full-time law studies. He usually has his head buried in a textbook, but glances up occasionally to check the score.

Toronto is utterly sports mad – are the Blue Jays, Maple Leafs or Raptors liable to win anything soon?
Well, Chicago Cubs' baseball fans have been waiting since 1908 for their team to win a championship again! The Blue Jays won back-to-back World Series in 1992 and '93, but the mighty (and wealthy) New York Yankees have been keeping them out of first place lately. The Jays' new owners have loosened the purse strings a bit though, which should mean we'll be nipping at the Yankees' heels again soon. The Leafs haven't won the Stanley Cup since 1967, but they're one of the most profitable teams in the NHL. Hockey-mad Torontonians accept nothing less than a competitive team. The Raptors have sagged since Vince Carter left town, but they're rebuilding at the moment and adding a lot of international players – the team's almost as ethnically diverse as Toronto!

Where's your favorite place for a beer?
I like Kalendar (p124) on College St in Little Italy. It's a hip little French-style bar with intimate tables, worn wooden floors, exposed brick walls, the sound of the espresso machine…Perfect for a date or a conversation, and the patio is great for people-watching. It has an old-world, European feel, but the streetcars give it a Toronto twist and they have these great crepe-like 'scroll' creations – really tasty.

Where do you take friends who've never been to Toronto before?
The Distillery District (p56). It's an old cobble-stoned quarter of restored historic factories, full of art galleries and restaurants and there's a new theatre there too. It's like a window into Toronto's past when we made bootleg liquor to sell to the US during Prohibition.

What makes you laugh about Toronto?
The fact that we live beside one of the largest freshwater lakes in the world, but most Torontonians never so much as dip their toes into Lake Ontario. Instead, they pack into cars and head two hours north to Cottage Country – the weekend traffic jams are pretty nasty. The city's really cleaned up the waterfront recently – they say the water at Toronto's beaches is cleaner than what you'll find off some Australian cities.

What do you miss most about Toronto when you're away?
The greenery – it really humanizes the neighborhoods. You can jog, rollerblade or cycle continuously for dozens of kilometres through the ravines and parks.

What key controversial issue faces Toronto today, and what are your thoughts on it?
The need to upgrade the city's infrastructure – housing, new parks, and public transit – to accommodate the increasing population. The GTA is on pace to become the third biggest municipality in North America – around 75,000 immigrants and refugees roll into town every year. You have to wonder how the city will increase downtown population density without compromising the neighborhood flavors which make Toronto so unique. I think more high-rise buildings are unavoidable.

Gate 9. The cheapest seats are way up above the field. Instead, try for seats along the lower level baselines (from $32) where you have a better chance of catching a fly-ball (or wearing one in the side of the head). The Jays haven't won a championship since 1993, but who knows, this could be their year.

BASKETBALL
TORONTO RAPTORS

☎ 416-815-5500; www.raptors.com; Harbourfront, Air Canada Centre, 40 Bay St; tickets from $12.50; ☉ regular season Oct-Apr; ⊙ Union
The 'Raps' have been around since 1995, competing in the American National

Basketball Association (NBA). Before Vince Carter left town (see p18), they made the payoffs a few times, but were eliminated without causing much of a flap. They slam-dunk at the **Air Canada Centre** (p50). Single game tickets, which can cost hundreds of dollars, are sold through **Ticketmaster** (p116).

FOOTBALL
TORONTO ARGONAUTS
☎ 416-341-2700; www.argonauts.on.ca; Rogers Centre, 1 Blue Jays Way; tickets from $20; ☾ regular season Jun-Oct; ◉ Union

The Toronto Argonauts of the fast-paced professional Canadian Football League (CFL) crack helmets at the **Rogers Centre** (p53). They haven't won the Grey Cup since 2004, but over the past century the Argonauts have brought home more championships than any other Canadian team (15, two ahead of Edmonton). Bring a jacket as the game may be hot, but the open-roof Rogers Centre cools off at night.

HOCKEY
TORONTO MAPLE LEAFS
☎ 416-815-5500; www.mapleleafs.com; Harbourfront, Air Canada Centre, 40 Bay St; tickets from $24; ☾ regular season Oct-Apr; ◉ Union

The 13-time Stanley Cup winning Maple Leafs slap the puck around the **Air Canada Centre** (p50) in the National Hockey League (NHL). Every game sells out in advance, but a limited number of same-day tickets go on sale through **Ticketmaster** (p116) at 10am and at the Air Canada Centre ticket wicket from 5pm. You can also buy tickets via the website from season ticket holders who aren't attending – expect to pay around $80 and up. Coach Paul Maurice's post-match dissertations are as entertaining as the games.

HORSERACING
WOODBINE RACETRACK Map p230
☎ 888-675-7223; www.woodbineentertainment com; Greater Toronto Area, Rexdale, 555 Rexdale Blvd; admission free, minimum bet $2; ☾ races 7:30pm Mon, Tue & Thu-Sat, 1pm Fri-Sun Apr-Dec; ◉ Woodbine

Secretariat's last race was run at Woodbine Racetrack, where the action revolves around thoroughbreds and standardbreds (harness racing). Look out for the statue of Canada's famous racehorse Northern Dancer.

The racetrack is northwest of downtown Toronto off Hwy 427, near Hwy 27. Take the subway to Woodbine, then the shuttle bus picking punters up before post time (usually noon or 6:45pm) and returning them 20 minutes after the last race.

LACROSSE
TORONTO ROCK
☎ 416-596-3075; www.torontorock.com; Harbourfront, Air Canada Centre, 40 Bay St; tickets from $23; ☾ regular season Jan-April; ◉ Union

Lacrosse may not immediately spring to mind when someone mentions Canadian sports, but the 13-team **National Lacrosse League** (www.nll.com) has been building momentum for two decades. The Rock are red hot, having won the championship five times in nine years. Games at the **Air Canada Centre** (p50); tickets through **Ticketmaster** (p116).

HEALTH, FITNESS & WELLBEING

A plethora of gyms, yoga and Pilates studios guarantees you'll be able to work out, no matter how cruel the weather is outside. Most large hotels have a fitness centre and swimming pool; sometimes facilities are available to non-guests for a fee.

GYMS & HEALTH CLUBS

Private gyms usually charge $15 to $20 for a day pass; ask about weekly or monthly membership deals. Community Recreation Centres (CRCs) charge around $10 per day; some offer pay-as-you-go fitness classes. Contact Toronto Parks & Recreation (p138) for locations, including the following, both of which have swimming pools:

St Lawrence CRC (Map pp244–5; ☎ 416-392-1347; www.slcrc.ca; Old York, 230 The Esplanade; adult/child $2.50/free; ☾ public swimming 6:30-8:30am Mon, Tue, Thu & Fri, 11:30am-1:30pm Mon-Fri, 5-7pm Mon, Wed & Fri; 🚋 503, 504)

The Beaches CRC (Map p246; ☎ 416-392-0740; fax 416-392-0324; The Beaches, 6 Williamson Rd; adult/child $2.50/free; ☾ public swimming 8:30-9:30am Mon-Fri, 3:30-4:30pm Sat & Sun; 🚋 501)

DIESEL FITNESS Map pp234-5

☎ 416-595-9900; www.dieselfitness.ca; Entertainment District, 99 Spadina Ave; day pass $20; ☯ 6am-11pm Mon-Thu, 6am-9pm Fri, 8am-8pm Sat & Sun; ☲ 504, 510

Around the corner from the Theatre Block, this gym's in-house DJ booth and 'fuel bar' (juice, espresso and high-speed internet) are staffed by friendly pros. Often voted Toronto's best gym, there's yoga, spin, Pilates, capoeira, urban funk and Kick-Cardio Combat classes on offer. Massage and spa services are available too.

EPIC FITNESS Map pp238-9

☎ 416-960-1705; Yonge Street Strip, 9 St Joseph St; per month $42; ☯ 6am-midnight Mon-Thu, to 11pm Fri, 7:30am-8pm Sat, 7:30am-7pm Sun; ☺ Wellesley

A boutique gym with a resident DJ, Epic's impressive three-story loft is perfect for yoga, Pilates, spin, cardio and weight training. It's a dumbell's throw from the Church-Wellesley Village, so expect a lot of moustaches and waxed chests.

METRO TORONTO YMCA Map pp238-9

☎ 416-975-9622; www.ymcatoronto.org; Yonge Street Strip, 20 Grosvenor St; day pass adult/child $14/7; ☯ 6am-11pm Mon-Fri, 7am-8pm Sat & Sun; ☺ College

The nonprofit YMCA's enormous downtown complex houses two full-sized gyms, racquetball courts, indoor and outdoor tracks and a 25m pool. Fitness classes (over 130 per week) are led by volunteers. International YMCA members are eligible for guest privileges. For non-members, your first visit is free with appropriate photo ID!

MILES NADAL JEWISH COMMUNITY CENTRE Map pp242-3

☎ 416-927-6211; www.milesnadaljcc.ca; The Annex, 750 Spadina Ave; day pass adult/child $15/10; ☯ 5:30am-10pm Mon-Thu, to 7pm Fri, 7am-7pm Sat & Sun; ☺ Spadina

Next to the U of T campus, this snazzy community institution is open to all. Facilities include a gigantic gym, swimming pool, fitness classrooms, an on-site coffee shop and juice bar. They also run classes in everything from Ski Conditioning to Feldenkrais and tai chi. Some facilities require that you be accompanied by a member – call in advance.

UNIVERSITY OF TORONTO ATHLETIC CENTRE Map pp238-9

☎ 416-978-3437; www.ac-fpeh.com; University of Toronto, 55 Harbord St; day pass $15; ☯ 7am-11pm Mon-Fri, 10am-5pm Sat & Sun; ☲ 510

On the St George campus, this high-quality athletic centre has affordable day passes and monthly memberships for just $69. Its two buildings hold two pools (50m and 25m), squash courts, an indoor track, sports halls, cardio/weight rooms and a dance studio.

YOGA & PILATES

Mainstream and alternative yoga studios are scattered around the city, many also offering Pilates classes. See also Diesel Fitness (p143).

Prices & Schedules

A casual visit yoga class will cost between $15 to $18, but sometimes your first class

---

EXERCISING THE SOUL

Yoga and other Asian traditions have often been divorced from their spiritual roots in North America, but Toronto still has a few spots to quell your inner demons. When you feel like the urban jungle is closing in, **Zen Buddhist Temple** (Map pp240-1; ☎ 416-658-0137; www.zenbuddhisttemple.org; Kensington Market, 297 College St; admission free; ☯ 10am-6pm Mon-Fri, noon-4pm Sat, 9:30am-5:30pm Sun; ☲ 506, 510), founded by the Buddhist Society for Compassionate Wisdom, offers beginners' meditation retreats, relaxation workshops and free Sunday morning and afternoon Zen practice sessions (9:30am and 4pm). Open your heart to the dharma at **Tengye Ling Tibetan Buddhist Temple** (Map pp242-3; ☎ 416-966-4656; www.tengyeling.ca; The Annex, 11 Madison Ave; admission free; ☯ discourse 7:30pm Tue; ☺ Spadina), where English-language discourses are followed by breathing and walking meditation. Otherwise, pull up a pew (literally) in **St James Cathedral** (p57), **Church of the Holy Trinity** (p60) or **St Andrew's Presbyterian Church** (p59) and find your inner peace (you know you left it lying around here somewhere…).

costs from $5 to $10, or is free. A one-week introductory pass can cost just $25. 'Community' classes, which are usually taught at off-peak times by instructors in training, are often half-price. Some places charge a nominal fee for mat rental. Schedules vary, but you will find that most are open daily.

DOWNWARD DOG YOGA CENTRE
Map pp240-1

☎ 416-703-8805; www.downwarddog.com; Queen West, 735 Queen St W; casual class adult/student $16/12; ☽ 8am-9pm; ☒ 501

In yoga-happy Queen West, this studio focuses on Ashtanga yoga, emphasizing forceful flow series. Check the website for special events like improvisational 'yoga jams,' musical performances and wellness workshops.

ELISSA GALLANDER YOGA STUDIO
Map pp244-5

☎ 416-463-4094; www.elissayoga.com; Greektown, Big Carrot, Suite 211, 348 Danforth Ave; introductory/casual class $10/18; ◉ Chester

The objective here is, 'Using gravity and the natural wave-like movement of the breath to lengthen the spine and establish alignment and balance.' Now everyone could use a little of that!

SIVANANDA YOGA VEDANTA
CENTRE Map pp242-3

☎ 416-966-9642; www.sivananda.org/toronto; The Annex, 77 Harbord St; casual class $14; ☽ 9am-9pm Mon-Fri, to 5pm Sat, 4-7pm Sun; ☒ 510

A blink of a third eye from University of Toronto, Sivananda hosts free 90-minute introductory yoga classes on Sunday afternoons, usually at 4pm. Otherwise, check the website or give them a call for class schedules.

TWIST YOGA STUDIO Map pp242-3

☎ 416-972-1551; www.twistyoga.net; The Annex, 2nd fl, 322 Bloor St W; casual class $15; ☽ 7am-10pm; ◉ Spadina

Twist yourself into all manner of unusual shapes at this friendly Annex studio, which runs Ashtanga and Hatha classes, plus pre- and post-natal sessions and 'Mom & Baby' classes. Check the website for an up-to-date schedule.

YOGA SANCTUARY Map pp238-9

☎ 416-928-3236; www.theyogasanctuary.net; Yonge Street Strip, 2 College St; first/casual class $10/17; ☽ 10am-11:30pm Mon, Tue, Thu & Sat, 7:30am-9:30pm Wed & Fri, 8am-10pm Sun; ◉ College

Yoga classes happen inside a lovely 19th-century redbrick and sandstone ballroom, used for painting by the Group of Seven (p35) once upon a time. Ashtanga is the focus; Hatha, pre- and post-natal exercises, and Pilates classes are also on the menu.

ROCK CLIMBING
Chalk-up your fingertips, don your nifty rubber shoes and up you go.

JOE ROCKHEAD'S CLIMBING GYM
Map p231

☎ 416-538-7670; www.joerockheads.com; Greater Toronto Area, 29 Fraser Ave; day pass $15, shoes or harness rental $5; ☽ noon-11pm Mon-Fri, 10am-7pm Sat & Sun; ☒ 509, 511

Across the road from a delicious-smelling bread factory north of Exhibition Place, this well-regarded gym (owned by Canadian climbing champ Bob Bergman) has 80 climbing routes and two dedicated bouldering areas. They're open 'til 9pm on weekends from November to April.

TORONTO CLIMBING ACADEMY
Map pp244-5

☎ 416-406-5900; www.climbingacademy.com; East Toronto, 100A Broadview Ave; admission adult /child/student $14/9/12, shoes or harness rental $5; ☽ noon-11pm Mon-Fri, 10am-10pm Sat & Sun; ☒ 501, 502, 503, 504

Across the Don River in a tall, hangar-like space, the Toronto Climbing Academy has 50 different indoor routes over multidimensional terrain. If you've never climbed before, call and book yourself a lesson with a gravity-defying expert in a safe environment.

MASSAGE, SPAS & SALONS
If you're sapped by the summer heat or freeze-dried by the winter wind, Toronto offers plenty of places to revive your body, skin and hair. Check the alternative weeklies (p203) for salon and spa coupons, special promotions and new openings.

Most day spas offer registered massage therapy (RMT), facials, manicures and pedicures, waxing and tanning services. Both men and women are welcome, unless otherwise stated. Expect to pay upwards of $80 for an hour-long massage, and at least $50 for a 'quickie' facial. A basic haircut and style usually costs around $50 and up. Many of the spas listed here also offer hair care. Try to make appointments 24 hours ahead.

For a more permanent reminder for your time in T.O., duck into one of the city's many tattoo parlors (which usually double as piercing studios) and get a picture of the Leafs' Mats Sundin tattooed on your buttock.

BODY CLINIC Map pp238-9

☎ 416-324-8999; www.bodyclinic.ca; Bloor-Yorkville, Ste 2011, 11 Yorkville Ave; 🕑 9am-9pm Mon-Fri, 10am-8pm Sat, to 5pm Sun; 🚇 Bloor-Yonge

An upscale holistic wellness centre, the Body Clinic is famed for its healing hot stone massage (30-minute session $60). Acupuncture, naturopathic medicine, reflexology, reiki and 'computer-neck' massage fall into line with its motto of 'urban body healing.'

COUPE BIZZARRE Map pp240-1

☎ 416-504-0783; www.coupebizzarre.com; Queen West, 704 & 710 Queen St W; 🕑 noon-8pm Mon-Fri, 10am-6pm Sat, noon-6pm Sun; 🚋 501

Cutting-edge Coupe Bizzarre, a radical import from Montréal, is the DJ's choice. If you're open to a brave new look, volunteer to be a model and get a free haircut (coloring surcharge $20). It stocks Black & White pomade, the same stuff that Elvis used.

ELIZABETH MILAN PREMIER DAY SPA
Map pp234-5

☎ 416-350-7500; www.elizabethmilanspa.com; Financial District, Fairmont Royal York, 100 Front St W; 🕑 9am-7pm Mon-Wed, 8:30am-8pm Thu & Fri, 8:30am-7pm Sat, 10am-5pm Sun; 🚇 Union

This professional day spa offers services for men, women, couples and even teens. Its determined owner has searched the world for exotic beauty regimens, and also created some of her own, such as the 90-minute Chocolate Body Indulgence featuring a fondue body wrap ($175). Hotel chefs prepare spa lunches upon request.

ELMWOOD SPA Map pp232-3

☎ 416-977-6751, 877-284-6348; www.elmwoodspa.com; Dundas Square, 18 Elm St; 🕑 9am-9pm Mon-Fri, 9am-8pm Sat, 10:30am-6:30pm Sun; 🚇 Dundas

Sitting pretty for more than two decades, this award-winning spa for men and women is a luxurious escape. Treat yourself to a deluxe facial with a three-course lunch in your bathrobe for $160, or select from 10 different types of 75-minute massage (from $130). Champagne manicures are *de rigueur*. A one-time pass to the swimming pool, whirlpool, steam room and sauna costs $20.

HOUSE OF LORDS Map pp238-9

☎ 416-962-1111; www.houseoflordshair.com; Yonge Street Strip, 639 Yonge St; 🕑 8:30am-8pm Mon-Sat, 11am-6pm Sun; 🚇 Bloor-Yonge

The receptionist here doubles as a DJ, interrupting raging house to announce, 'I need a color and cut in five minutes – who's up?' to the multitudinous staff. They've treated the tresses of David Bowie and Alice Cooper over the years, and it retains a punkish attitude. Walk-ins are accepted; basic guys/gals cuts from $14/20.

SALON JIE Map pp238-9

☎ 416-926-0026; www.salonjie.com; Bloor-Yorkville, 38 Avenue Rd; 🕑 9am-6pm Mon-Wed, 10am-7pm Thu, 9am-7pm Fri, 9am-5pm Sat, 11am-4pm Sun; 🚇 Bay

When we asked these guys which subway station their customers use, they looked shocked and said, 'No one who comes here *ever* takes the subway!'. This is no ordinary hair salon. Don't be surprised if some limo-riding fashion model, A-list celeb or real-life princess is being coiffed by master stylist Jie Matar in the next chair.

SHIATSU SCHOOL OF CANADA
Map pp242-3

☎ 416-323-1818; www.shiatsucanada.com; Little Italy, 547 College St; 🕑 9am-8pm Mon-Fri, 9:30am-4:30pm Sat; 🚋 506

At the professional school's student clinic, your 75-minute shiatsu treatment costs $55. Ten-minute shiatsu tune-ups cost just $10. Acupuncture is also available. Reflexology and bruise-making cupping treatments are also available. Workshops are open to the public.

STILLWATER Map pp238-9

☎ 416-926-2389; www.stillwaterspa.com; Bloor-Yorkville, Park Hyatt, 4 Avenue Rd; ⏰ 9am-10pm Mon-Fri, 8am-10pm Sat, 10am-5:30pm Sun; ◉ Museum

The Park Hyatt hotel's serene spa has made a splash with its full range of modern aesthetic services and specialty treatments, including blackberry hand massages, seaweed wraps and underwater aquatherapy. Spa lunches are taken in the tea lounge.

SUDI'S THE SPA Map pp238-9

☎ 416-922-0813; www.sudis.com; Bloor-Yorkville, Suite 271, Hazelton Lanes Shopping Centre, 87 Avenue Rd; ⏰ 9am-8pm Mon-Fri, to 6pm Sat, 10am-5pm Sun; ◉ Bay

Run by an Iranian immigrant who built her ritzy Yorkville business from the ground up, Sudi's 'cosmopolitan exotica' shines through in aromatherapy body massage, Persian body scrubs and eyebrow threading. His-and-hers three-hour spa packages start at $200; full-body laser hair removal (except your head) costs $7000.

SUTHERLAND-CHAN CLINIC Map p231

☎ 416-924-1107 ext 10; www.sutherland-chan .com; The Annex, 330 Dupont St; ⏰ by appointment Mon-Fri; ◉ Dupont

Students of Swedish massage will apply their healing hands by appointment only (one-hour session including physical assessment and massage $35). Specialty clinics are offered for pregnant women, seniors,

---

TOP FIVE BODY-BEAUTIFUL TORONTO

Diesel Fitness (p143)

House Of Lords (p145)

New Tribe (below)

Stillwater (left)

Yoga Sanctuary (p144)

---

sports players, the disabled and dancers at off-site locations around the city.

PIERCINGS & TATTOOS

You'd run out of body parts before running through all of Toronto's tattoo and piercing shops. A few favorites include the following:

New Tribe (Map pp232-3; ☎ 416-977-2786; www .newtribe.ca; Queen Street, 2nd fl, 232 Queen St W; ⏰ 11am-8pm Mon-Thu, 11am-10pm Fri & Sat, noon-6pm Sun; 🚋 501) Top tatts, plus standard and custom body jewelry.

Tat-a-Rama (Map p246; ☎ 416-693-2331; www.tat-a -rama.com; The Beaches, 2219 Queen St E; ⏰ noon-7pm Mon-Wed & Sat, to 8pm Thu & Fri, to 6pm Sun; 🚋 501) Piercing and custom tattoos, with portfolios available online.

Way Cool Tattoos (Map pp240-1; ☎ 416-603-0145; www.waycool-queen.com; Queen West, 675 Queen St W; ⏰ noon-midnight Mon-Sat, noon-8pm Sun; 🚋 501, 511) A biker-style shop (in the best possible way) that also does piercing.

Shopping ∎

Shopping

There's no denying it – Toronto is a city of shopaholics. In addition to the array of retail giants – many of which are not present in any other Canadian city – every main street, hip suburb and ethnic neighborhood of T.O. has its own treasure trove of independent shops and edgy boutiques. Armed with time and patience, fashionistas will uncover some extremely well-kept secrets, while more leisurely shoppers will enjoy the colorful and sometimes highly unusual shops in each of Toronto's districts. Vintage clothing, locally made artisan crafts, bookstores and a heaving local and international designer scene are all to be found amidst the vibrant cultural landscape, which has shoppers flocking from all corners of the country. And with tax refunds and attractive exchange rates for US and European visitors, Toronto is a retail haven for international travelers.

Shopping Strips

Queen St W, east of Spadina Ave as far as the colossal Eaton Centre mall, was once known as 'the' shopping mecca. These days, the urban streetwear shops that remain punctuate a shiny parade of big-name retailers. Further west, around Trinity Bellwoods Park (or West Queen West as it's locally known), you'll find an enticing mixture of vintage, designer and specialty record shops as well as boutiques crammed with delights of a most unusual variety.

Bloor-Yorkville has long been known as the city's swankiest shopping district, a far cry from its early days in the '60s as the hippies' Flower Power quarter. Bloor's Vogue-worthy designer shops and sparkling jewelers complement the antique, fine-art and specialty shops sprinkled around Yorkville's narrow streets and along Yonge St in affluent Rosedale. If dealing with huffy salesclerks isn't your ideal way to spend a day – or your pocketbook simply isn't up to the task – it's still a great place for window-shopping and day-dreaming.

Chinatown, known mainly for its colorful markets and restaurants, sits just south of Kensington Market, Toronto's own vintage village, where bargains can sometimes still be found among the racks of leather jackets and boho-chic microshops. In Little Italy imported Italian fashions mix with the most up-and-coming in Canadian chíc.

A landmark for students and followers of counter culture in all varieties, The Annex, just west of the University of Toronto's St George campus, is home to a mixed bag of specialty book stores, hip-yet-affordable local designs, and multilevel shops to please the most dedicated of film and pop culturites. Honest Ed's (p157), a bargain bazaar as old as time itself, is a must-see if only for the kitsch factor, and Markham Village provides a calming antidote of crafts, alt.culture locales and more niche bookstores.

TAX REFUNDS

Visitors are eligible for refunds of the 6% federal Goods and Services Tax (GST) paid on nonconsumable goods and short-term accommodation, provided they spend at least $200 and that each eligible receipt totals over $50 before taxes. All original receipts (credit-card slips are not sufficient) must be stamped by customs before leaving the country, whether at the airport (*before* you check in!) or a land-border crossing, where you'll need to make your goods available for inspection.

Drivers can obtain instant cash refunds for claims of less than $500 at participating land border duty-free shops, including those at Sarnia, Windsor, Niagara Falls and Queenston. Otherwise mail your stamped receipts within one year of the purchase date, along with boarding passes and a completed GST rebate booklet available at tourist offices or directly from the federal **Visitor Rebate Program** (☎ 902-432-5608, 800-668-4748; www.cra.gc.ca/visitors). Allow four to six weeks for processing.

Don't be misled by private companies that distribute 'official tax refund' booklets at visitor centres and duty-free stores. These companies offer to obtain your refund for you and then take up to 20% (minimum $10) for their services. But it's usually just as fast and easy to do it yourself.

A true testament to Canadian climes, Torontonians and visitors can shop whatever the weather in the underground PATH network (p215), a 27km underground maze lined with everyday and discount shops of all varieties. Along the scenic Harbourfront, true blue Canadiana can be bought at the artisan shops and also, in a sense, at the outdoor shops for campers, trekkers and climbers on King St west of the Theatre Block. Along the Yonge Street Strip and the Church-Wellesley Village is a mix of music, lesbigay-friendly and random specialized shops – everything from rare Disney stereographs to full-body leather.

The Design Strip, which runs along King St W between Jarvis and Parliament Sts, is the go-to place for Canadian and international design, while the Distillery District draws in the crowds with a multitude of art galleries, craft studios and design shops, all housed inside factories from the Victorian era. Leslieville, along Queen St E, takes shoppers back in time with its enticing antique, retro design and furnishing shops, and Greektown along Danforth Ave mixes health food stores with souvlaki and hip housewares. You'll find some hidden gems north of downtown, at the intersection of Yonge and Eglinton – nicknamed 'young and eligible' after its residents of the same description.

Opening Hours

Typical retail shopping hours are 10am until 6pm Monday to Saturday, noon to 5pm Sunday. But this varies depending on the season, the neighborhood and the amount of foot traffic. Prime shopping areas and malls may stay open until 9pm, especially from Thursday onward. Some shops are closed Sunday, a tradition held over from the days of 'Toronto the Good,' when Eaton's department store drew its curtains to discourage 'sinful' window-shopping. Where no opening hours appear with the following reviews, assume that the usual hours described here apply.

HARBOURFRONT

During weekends in summer, the Harbourfront Centre (p52) sponsors an outdoor International Marketplace with vendors selling crafts, jewelry and home decor from the Americas, Africa and Asia.

ARCTIC NUNAVUT

Map pp234-5   Art & Crafts

☎ 416-203-7889, 800-509-9151; www.ndcorp.nu.ca; ground fl, Queen's Quay Terminal, 207 Queens Quay W; ⏰ 10am-6pm; ◉ 509, 510
Inuit handicrafts inlcuding carved *Inuksuk* figurines, and Taloyoak dolls as well as Arctic-related books, music and DVDs are all sold at Arctic Nunavut. Every penny of the proceeds go towards the Nunavut Development Corporation, which supports artisans from Canada's Aboriginal-run territory. There's another store in Terminal 3 at Pearson International Airport (☎ 416-776-5100).

BOUNTY Map pp234-5   Art & Crafts

☎ 416-973-4000; www.harbourfront.on.ca; 235 Queens Quay W; ⏰ 11am-6pm Tue-Sun; ◉ 509, 510
This contemporary, not-for-profit craft shop can be found inside York Quay Terminal, just west of the Queen's Quay Terminal.

CLOTHING SIZES

Measurements approximate only, try before you buy

Women's Clothing

Aus/UK	8	10	12	14	16	18
Europe	36	38	40	42	44	46
Japan	5	7	9	11	13	15
USA	6	8	10	12	14	16

Women's Shoes

Aus/USA	5	6	7	8	9	10
Europe	35	36	37	38	39	40
France only	35	36	38	39	40	42
Japan	22	23	24	25	26	27
UK	3½	4½	5½	6½	7½	8½

Men's Clothing

Aus	92	96	100	104	108	112
Europe	46	48	50	52	54	56
Japan	S		M	M		L
UK/USA	35	36	37	38	39	40

Men's Shirts (Collar Sizes)

Aus/Japan	38	39	40	41	42	43
Europe	38	39	40	41	42	43
UK/USA	15	15½	16	16½	17	17½

Men's Shoes

Aus/UK	7	8	9	10	11	12
Europe	41	42	43	44½	46	47
Japan	26	27	27½	28	29	30
USA	7½	8½	9½	10½	11½	12½

Among its wares are creative cards and beautiful dyed scarves, and all proceeds from sales go towards programming at the Harbourfront. Artisans in the adjacent **Craft Studio** (☎ 416-973-4963; ⏰ 10am-6pm Tue-Sun) blow hot glass, mould clay, weave textiles, design jewelry and teach classes.

THE CANADIAN NATURALIST

Map pp234-5   Art & Crafts

☎ 416-203-0365; ground fl, Queen's Quay Terminal, 207 Queens Quay W; ⏰ 10am-6pm; 🚋 509, 510
Some questionable souvenirs – like native figurines and crystal CN Towers – along with high-quality tees, sweats, pewter, an array of Canadian art and maple syrupy edibles are available at this shop.

TILLEY ENDURABLES

Map pp234-5   Outdoors Equipment

☎ 416-203-0463, 800-363-8737; www.tilley.com; ground fl, Queen's Quay Terminal, 207 Queens Quay W; ⏰ 10am-6pm; 🚋 509, 510
Known the world over, this Canadian company produces some of the finest, toughest threads imaginable. All Tilley's signature hats, which have been worn by everyone from famous explorers to royalty, as well as many of their clothing lines, are guaranteed for life.

FINANCIAL DISTRICT

The heart of Toronto's business sector, most shops here are gift and souvenir-oriented.

BAY OF SPIRITS GALLERY

Map pp234-5   Art & Crafts

☎ 416-971-5190; 156 Front St W; ⏰ 10am-6pm Mon-Sat, 11am-5pm Sun; Ⓤ Union
The works of Norval Morrisseau – the first native artist to solo exhibit at the National Gallery of Canada – are proudly displayed in this atmospheric space, which carries native art from across Canada. Look for the Pacific West Coast totem polls (from miniature to 14 feet tall), Inuit carvings and *inuksuit*.

GAME TREK Map pp234-5   Toys & Collectibles

☎ 416-597-0149; arcade level, Fairmont Royal York, 100 Front St W; ⏰ 9am-9pm Mon-Fri, to 8pm Sat, 10am-7pm Sun; Ⓤ Union
A classic toy shopping experience is to be had amongst the dart sets, elaborate chess-

boards and model cars at Game Trek. You can even bring home a little piece of the city with an edition of Toronto Monopoly.

OLD YORK

Stroll through Toronto's only historical district and its most popular market, and get in touch with the latest emerging artists and craftspeople.

DISTILLERY DISTRICT

Map pp244-5   Art & Crafts

☎ 416-364-1177; www.thedistillerydistrict.com; 55 Mill St; ⏰ daily; 🚋 503, 504
This restored Victorian-era factory complex provides a refreshingly unusual backdrop for shopping. In building 32, **Auto Grotto Automobilia** (Map pp244–5; ☎ 416-304-0005; ⏰ 11am-6pm Sun-Wed, 11am-7pm Thu-Sat) displays model cars, art deco racing posters, vintage memorabilia and just about anything to please an auto enthusiast. **Pikto** (☎ 416-203-3443; ⏰ 9am-7pm Mon-Fri, 10am-7pm Sat, noon-6pm Sun) is a unique professional photo lab and bookstore, with a great gallery. Art lovers will be in heaven in the multitude of galleries spread throughout the buildings, and you'll find clay artists, glass-bead and jewelry designers, and furniture makers in the **Case Goods Building** (Map pp244–5) further south.

ST LAWRENCE SUNDAY ANTIQUE

MARKET Map pp234-5   Antiques & Collectibles

☎ 416-392-7120; www.stlawrencemarket.com; 92 Front St E; ⏰ 5am-5pm Sun; 🚋 504
Show up early to the North Market, which every Sunday is overrun by salt-of-the-earth antique dealers with mixed bags of treasures and flea-market kitsch. Across the street is the regular ol' **St Lawrence Market** (p57).

THEATRE BLOCK & ENTERTAINMENT DISTRICT

Though stage lovers might get their fix in this neighborhood, it's also the place to shop for anything related to the great outdoors.

EUROPE BOUND OUTFITTERS

Map pp234-5   Outdoors Equipment

☎ 416-205-9992; www.europebound.com; 383 King St W; ☺ 10am-8pm Mon-Wed, to 9pm Thu & Fri, 9am-6:30pm Sat, 11am-5:30pm Sun; ⓡ 504

Maps, guidebooks, trekking equipment, and even durable baby strollers are on the market here for rough and tumble travelers of all sizes. If you're seeking brand-name gear such as Columbia and North Face, this is your place.

HOGTOWN EXTREME SPORTS

Map pp234-5   Outdoors Equipment

☎ 416-598-4192; www.hogtownextreme.com; 401 King St W; ☺ 11am-8pm Mon-Fri, 10am-6pm Sat, 11am-5pm Sun; ⓡ 504

Diehard extreme sports addicts might want to stop here to marvel at the selection of skate and snowboarding gear, clothing and accessories, as well as bikes of every variety. Bike and snowboard tune-ups are also done on location.

MOUNTAIN EQUIPMENT CO-OP

Map pp234-5   Outdoors Equipment

☎ 416-340-2667, 888-847-0770; www.mec.ca; 400 King St W; ☺ 10am-7pm Mon-Wed, to 9pm Thu & Fri, 9am-6pm Sat, 11am-5pm Sun; ⓡ 504

A church of sorts for journeyers and lovers of the great outdoors, MEC requires a membership for purchase – it will only set you back $5 and lasts a lifetime, supporting the co-op's not-for-profit status and equitable-sourcing policies. Mountain Equipment also runs workshops, has equipment rentals and offers repair services .

TORONTO ANTIQUE CENTRE

Map pp234-5   Antiques & Collectibles

☎ 416-345-9941; 276 King St W; ☺ 10am-6pm Tue-Sun; ⓡ 504

A stroll through the well laid out Antique Centre is a welcome respite from the busy streets – and from your run-of-the-mill junk shops and overpriced antique dealers. From low-end collectibles to high-end valuables, connoisseurs have been known to locate some very undervalued treasures from other parts of the world amid the stalls, booths and showcases of this treasure trove. If you have the time, this place is well worth a visit.

QUEEN STREET & DUNDAS SQUARE

Once Toronto's edgiest shopping district, Queen Street's indie appeal has moved further west, and has seen an influx of chain stores instead. Some oldies and goodies have remained, however, and it's an excellent place to find a used record – try **Second Vinyl** (Map pp232–3; ☎ 416-977-3737; 2 McCaul St; ☺ 11am-7pm Mon-Fri, 11am-6pm Sat; ⓡ 501).

BLACK MARKET MEGAWAREHOUSE

Map pp232-3   Vintage

☎ 416-591-7945; 319 Queen St W; ☺ 11am-7pm Mon-Fri, 10am-7pm Sat, 11am-6pm Sun; ⓡ 501

Like the name implies, this megabasement is an outlet crammed with less high-end vintage and older printed tees, passed down from its older sister across the street.

BLACK MARKET VINTAGE CLOTHING

Map pp232-3   Vintage

☎ 416-591-7945; 319 Queen St W; ☺ 11am-7pm Mon-Fri, 10am-7pm Sat, 11am-6pm Sun; ⓡ 501

A new paint job and new walls have given the Black Market a facelift, but this Queen Street landmark's still got the same soul. Follow the psychedelic stairway to a mecca for screened T's and retro gear.

BOOMER Map pp232-3   Men's Fashion

☎ 416-598-0013; 309 Queen St W; ☺ 10:30am-7pm Mon-Fri, 10:30am-6pm Sat, 1-5pm Sun; ⓡ 501

Edgy menswear of a more forward than traditional variety line the racks of this exclusive boutique, where cooler-than-thou salespeople gladly guide dedicated followers of fashion through a sleek selection of suits, sports jackets, coats and denim.

CHANGE ROOM

Map pp232-3   Fashion

☎ 416-977-0088; 425 Queen St W; ☺ 10am-7pm Mon-Thu, 11am-8pm Fri & Sat, noon-6pm Sun (later in summer); ⓡ 501

Young urbanites can shop at this modish stop – the sister store to Show Room (see p 000) – for searing hot labels and a renowned selection of Ben Sherman dress shirts.

LOCAL VOICES: LARA CERONI

Lara Ceroni, 29, grew up west of Toronto in Burlington, Ontario. She started her art history degree at the University of Western Ontario in London, Ontario, and finished it in London, England! Post-UK, Lara moved to Toronto and landed a job with fashion mag *Elle Canada*. Now, as *Elle's* Online Editor and a four-year Toronto veteran, she's the perfect person to deliver the low-down on Toronto's fashion scene.

Toronto Fashion Week was last week – how did it go?
Toronto Fashion Week isn't like New York Fashion Week or Paris Fashion Week, but we don't need it to be. I think we stand on our own. There's an abundance of fashion design talent in Canada – remarkable designers with incredible vision and beautiful collections, but they're still very humble, hard-working, sweet and modest, and that was really evident. There was a lot of love in the room!

From an outsider's perspective, Torontonians look pretty 'snappy.' Do you think so?
I do. We're very conscious of how we look and how we present ourselves. Toronto is a stylish, very trend-based city – you see a lot of Paris Hilton look-a-likes – but we're not very European. If you go to Montréal, you feel like you're walking through Paris or London – it's all very beautiful, luxe and lovely – but Toronto is a street-driven, 'downtown' city like New York, and our clothing reflects that. It's edgy, urban, and a little bit aggressive, with avant-garde, eccentric looks. We're not into froufrou, fluffy European fashion.

Where are the places to shop for international designers?
For big labels, Bloor and Yonge is where it's at – all the celebrities shop there. There's a new Gucci boutique there, a new Prada. During the Toronto International Film Festival, you'll always see fans milling around Corbo,, because inevitably someone famous will show up! For Chanel, YSL, Gucci, everybody and their mother goes to Marc Laurent.

How about local designers?
There's a community of local designers around West Queen West who sell vintage, reworked, one-of-a-kind fashions. Boutique Letrou has really modern Canadian design. **TNT Woman** (p156) has Pink Tartan, a really popular Canadian label. I always tell people to go to Fresh Collective (p158) – kitschy, handmade, reworked pieces that no one else will have. **Preloved** (Map pp240–1; ☎ 416-504-8704; 613 Queen St W; 11am-7pm Mon & Tue, 11am-8pm Wed-Fri, 11am-7pm Sat, noon-6pm Sun; 🚋 501) too, also on Queen.

And vintage gear?
Kensington Market! Courage My Love (p158) has vintage from the '30s to the '70s, and beads from Tibet, leather goods from Indonesia. There's incense wafting through the air and there are all these drawers – it's a treasure trove! Also Brava in West Queen West – high-end, specialized vintage from the 1900s.

It's so humid here in summer and so freezing in winter – do Torontonians need enormous wardrobes to cope?
No, it's all about layering! That's the Toronto mantra – it's all about layers. We have the hottest 100°F weather here, and you wear slip dresses, tanks, shorts, T-shirts and linen to combat the heat. Then in winter when it's ridiculously cold you just take everything in your closet, throw it all on together and wrap yourself up in a humongous parka – and it works!

What are the essential Toronto wardrobe items?
Jeans. Denim is huge. Two years ago everybody had designer jeans – the whole celebrity jean obsession infiltrated Toronto. But now just really good-looking jeans, and boots.

Cowboy boots?
NOOOOO! Not here, that's Calgary! No, for women, a tall, solid, good-lookin' pair of black boots.

Do you own a toque?
Yes I do! I have a lot of them! That's a Canadian style statement for sure.

Do they have ear flaps?
NO! That's so cliché Canadian. No, just a regular toque hat – an absolute winter necessity. We've evolved this very practical hat into something very stylish – I have 10 or 15 of them!

C-SQUARED Map pp232-3 — Shoes

☎ 416-595-5606; 365 Queen St W; ⏰ 10am-9pm Mon-Fri, to 8pm Sat, 11am-6pm Sun; 🚋 501

Urbanites need shoes meant for walking – style is a plus, but comfort is essential. C-Squared provides both as HQ for imported famed European brands including Camper, Papillon, Birkenstock, Bench and Firetrap.

EATON CENTRE

Map pp232-3 — Shopping Mall

☎ 416-598-8560; 220 Yonge St; ⏰ 10am-9pm Mon-Fri, 9:30am-7pm Sat, noon-6pm Sun; Ⓜ Queen, Dundas

You can find it all at this immense, landmark mall, named after the historic Eaton's department store that was once housed here. Canadian and international chain and department stores, as well as movie theatres, gift shops, fashion and fast food are all inside.

EKO Map pp232-3 — Jewelry

☎ 416-593-0776; 288 Queen St W; ⏰ 11am-7pm Mon-Wed, to 8pm Thu & Fri, 10am-7pm Sat, noon-6pm Sun; 🚋 501

It may appear empty from the outside, but hidden in the sunken window boxes that line the walls of Eko you'll find a mesmerizing collection of jewels – ranging from ethnic-inspired necklaces to contemporary rings.

FRIENDLY STRANGER

Map pp232-3 — Specialty Shop

☎ 416-591-1570; 241 Queen St W; ⏰ 11am-8pm Mon-Sat, noon-6pm Sun; 🚋 501

Need a baking pan for your pot-leaf-shaped cookies? The Friendly Stranger – where customers and salesclerks alike all seem equally amicable – carries a wide array of pot paraphernalia as well as hemp clothes and accessories. Leaflets stating the facts on illegal substances line the front wall.

JOHN FLUEVOG Map pp232-3 — Shoes

☎ 416-581-1420; www.fluevog.com; 242 Queen St W; ⏰ 11am-7pm Mon-Wed, 11am-8pm Thu & Fri, 11am-7pm Sat, noon-6pm Sun; 🚋 501

Legendary Vancouver-based designer John Fluevog has always marched to the beat of his own drum, and this local favorite now carries bags and a line of hemp Veggie Vogs in addition to the famed granny platform boots and classic footwear. Reheeling and resoling is also done at this shop which

was once a diner – check out some of the original fittings.

MENDOCINO Map pp232-3 — Fashion

☎ 416-593-1011; 294 Queen St W; ⏰ 11am-7pm Mon-Thu, to 8pm Fri, 10am-7pm Sat, noon-6pm Sun; 🚋 501

For catwalk fashion before it hits the sidewalks run to Mendocino, which prides itself on bringing European trends and high-end brand names to Canada's fashionistas first.

MUCHSTORE Map pp232-3 — Fashion

☎ 416-591-7400; www.muchstore.ca; 277 Queen St W; ⏰ 10am-7pm Mon-Wed, to 9pm Thu & Fri, to 6pm Sat, noon-5pm Sun; 🚋 501

Music lovers should head here for fashions showcased on Much Music, Canada's music TV station, as well as pop star-designed labels by names like Kelly Osbourne and Simple Plan, and MuchMusic memorabilia.

PAGES BOOKS & MAGAZINES

Map pp232-3 — Books & Magazines

☎ 416-598-1447; www.pagesbooks.ca; 256 Queen St W; ⏰ 9:30am-10pm Mon-Fri, 10am-10pm Sat, 11am-8pm Sun; 🚋 501

Open your mind at one of Toronto's oldest independent bookstores, which stocks an excellent selection of contemporary literature and books addressing cultural theory and social issues, as well as indie mags and 'zines. Pages also produces the excellent 'This is Not a Reading Series'.

SHOW ROOM Map pp232-3 — Fashion

☎ 416-977-3888; www.theshow-room.com; 278B Queen St W; ⏰ 10am-8pm Mon-Thu, 11am-9pm Fri, noon-7pm Sat & Sun; 🚋 501

Five thousand pairs of jeans are housed on both levels of this lofty space, many of which can be seen on the finely toned rears of LA and European hipsters. Show Room's fitting rooms are bar none and pretty much any cut or size of denim is on site.

SILVER SNAIL COMIC SHOP

Map pp232-3 — Toys & Collectibles

☎ 416-593-0889; 367 Queen St W; ⏰ 10am-6pm Mon & Tue, to 8pm Wed-Fri, to 7pm Sat, noon-6pm Sun; 🚋 501

Silver Snail is home to action-figure versions of every conceivable hero and villain, from cult classics to big name box-office hits, as well as classic, rare and of-the-moment comic books.

STEVE'S MUSIC

Map pp232-3   Musical Instruments

☎ 416-593-8888; 415 Queen St W; ☽ 9:30am-6pm Mon-Wed, 9:30am-9pm Thu & Fri, 10am-5:30pm Sat, 11am-5pm Sun; 🚋 501

The mothership for musicians amateur and pro (Colin James stops in all the time), Steve's has been dealing in instruments of every variety, as well as DJ gear and pro recording equipment, for 30 years. The abundance of knowledgeable and extremely helpful staff is always on the ready to answer questions and provide impromptu jam sessions.

YONGE STREET STRIP & CHURCH-WELLESLEY VILLAGE

Mainly gay-friendly shops are to be found around Church and Wellesley, with some odds and ends, like Fastball Sportscards (below).

FASTBALL SPORTSCARDS

Map pp238-9   Toys & Collectibles

☎ 416-323-0403; 624 Yonge St; ☽ 11am-7pm Mon-Wed, to 7:30pm Thu & Fri, 11am-6pm Sat, noon-4pm Sun; ⓦ Wellesley

If it's signed Maple Leaf hockey jerseys, original Walt Disney art and stereographs, sci-fi collectibles, rare 20th-century sports cards or autographed photos you're after, this is your place. Make sure to talk shop with the friendly owner.

TOP FIVE FEMME-FRIENDLY SHOPS

Come As You Are (p159)

Good for Her (p157)

Lilith (p160)

Secrets From Your Sister (p157)

Toronto Women's Bookstore (p156)

GLAD DAY Map pp238-9   Books & Magazines

☎ 416-961-4161, 877-783-3725; 598A Yonge St; ☽ 10am-6:30pm Mon-Wed, to 9pm Thu & Fri, to 7pm Sat, noon-6pm Sun; ⓦ Wellesley

As Canada's oldest queer bookstore, Glad Day's been importing lesbigay material since 1970. Central to Toronto's colorful gay village, they are now proud to stock over 11,000 book, DVD and periodical titles.

NORTHBOUND LEATHER

Map pp238-9   Specialty Fashion, Sex & Fetish, Home Decor

☎ 416-972-1037; www.northboundleather.com; 586 Yonge St; ☽ 11am-7pm Mon-Wed, 10am-9pm Thu & Fri, 10am-6pm Sat, noon-5pm Sun; ⓦ Wellesley

Don't let the wholesome name fool you. Though Northbound does deal in standard coats and jackets, the specialty here is fetish wear and fantasy fashion for men and women. If you just can't get enough, the showroom on the 2nd floor carries home decor items such as ottomans and floor coverings.

PROPAGANDA Map pp238-9   Fashion

☎ 416-961-0555; 686 Yonge St; ☽ 11am-7pm Mon-Sat, 1-5pm Sun (later in summer); ⓦ Wellesley

Tongue-in-cheek meets street chic at Propaganda, promoters of local and Canadian designers. Check out the handmade jewelry, bag and clothing creations, often emblazoned with mischievous slogans.

SAM THE RECORD MAN

Map pp232-3   Music

☎ 416-646-2781; www.samtherecordman.com; 347 Yonge St; ☽ 11am-7pm Mon-Sat, 1-5pm Sun (later in summer); ⓦ Wellesley

Seeking the latest in drum 'n' bass? Some retro Maritime folk music? With a little patience, everyone from opera devotees to easy listeners will find what they need at this multilevel landmark amongst Canadian record stores.

THIS AIN'T THE ROSEDALE LIBRARY

Map pp238-9   Books

☎ 416-929-9912; 483 Church St; ☽ 10am-10pm Mon-Thu, to 11pm Fri & Sat, 1-9pm Sun; ⓦ Wellesley

What the mainstream considers offbeat, they consider mainstream at this lesbigay community institution, which means modern first editions, novels, nonfiction titles, children's books and heaps of magazines.

BLOOR-YORKVILLE

The upper crust of Toronto's districts, luxury – at a price – can be found at Bloor-Yorkville, dubbed Toronto's 'Mink Mile.' Worth exploring, as some of Toronto's most unique and specialized shops can be found in this area's nooks and crannies. Canadian retail institutions, like **The Bay** (Map pp234–5; ☎ 416-972-3333; 44 Bloor St E; 10am-8pm Mon-Wed, 10am-9pm Thu & Fri, 8am-7pm Sat, noon-6pm Sun; ⊕ Bloor-Yonge) department store and **Roots Athletics** (Map pp238–9; ☎ 416-323-3289; 100 Bloor St W; 10am-9pm Mon-Sat, 10am-7pm Sun; ⊕ Bay) are also here, as well as a huge **H&M** (Map pp238–9; ☎ 416-920-4029; 13-15 Bloor St W; 10am-7pm Mon-Wed, 10am-9pm Thu & Fri, noon-6pm Sun; ⊕ Bloor-Yonge).

BATA SHOE MUSEUM GIFT SHOP

Map pp238-9   Gifts
☎ 416-920-2665; 327 Bloor St W; ⏰ 10am-5pm Tue, Wed, Fri & Sat, to 8pm Thu, noon-5pm Sun & Mon, closed Mon Sep-May; ⊕ Museum
Gift up for every shoe-lover you know at this cute sideline to one of Toronto's most fascinating museums, with shoe occasion cards, calendars and books about shoes, shoe posters and even shoe-motif scarves.

THE COOKBOOK STORE

Map pp238-9   Books & Magazines
☎ 416-920-2665; 850 Yonge St; ⏰ 9:30am-7pm Mon-Wed, to 8pm Thu & Fri, 11am-7pm Sat, noon-6pm Sun; ⊕ Museum
You won't see a selection of Canadian-authored cookbooks like this elsewhere, and will probably find yourself among chefs who peruse them on their lunch breaks, along with European cookbooks and magazines from the UK and Australia.

DIVINE DECADENCE ORIGINALS

Map pp238-9   Vintage
☎ 416-324-9759; 136 Cumberland St; ⏰ varies, anytime by appointment; ⊕ Bay
Never has vintage shopping been so lavish – or so pricey. Akin to stepping into a fairy godmother's walk-in closet – and then

some – Divine is filled with gowns befitting Cinderellas and Prince Charmings from every era, all with serious money to spend.

GUILD SHOP Map pp238-9   Art & Crafts
☎ 416-921-1721; www.craft.on.ca; 118 Cumberland St; ⏰ 10am-6pm Mon-Wed, to 7pm Thu, 6pm Fri & Sat, noon-5pm Sun; ⊕ Bay
The Guild Shop offers a peaceful break from the froufrou vibes of Yorkville, with unique glasswares, prints and carvings both modern and traditional. The shop is run by the Ontario Crafts Council, which has been promoting artisans for over 70 years.

KIDDING AWOUND

Map pp238-9   Toys & Collectibles
☎ 416-926-8996; 91 Cumberland St; ⏰ 10:30am-6pm Mon-Sat, noon-5pm Sun; ⊕ Bay
A colorfully jumbled mess of fun awaits kids of all ages at Kidding Awound, including yo-yos, vintage collectibles, board games and retro novelty items.

MY PET BOUTIQUE Map pp238-9   Petshop
☎ 416-368-6896; 94 Cumberland St; ⏰ 10am-6pm Mon-Wed, to 7pm Thu & Fri, to 6pm Sat, noon-5pm Sun; ⊕ Bay
If your cat needs a hat, this upscale boutique's your best bet. Doggie carrier bags, pet greeting cards, and even kitty caviar are sold here, plus a wide range of pet cosmetics.

THEATREBOOKS Map pp238-9   Books
☎ 416-922-7175; www.theatrebooks.com; 11 St Thomas St; ⏰ 10am-7pm Mon-Fri, to 6pm Sat, noon-5pm Sun; ⊕ Bay
Get thee to Theatrebooks for books on film, opera, dance and all aspects of theatre, as well as original scripts, the latest screenwriting software, DVDs and videos. Launches, readings, lectures and workshops are held on site, and all stock is available to order.

THOMAS HINDS TOBACCONIST

Map pp238-9   Specialty
☎ 416-927-7703; 800-637-5750; www.thomas hinds.ca; 8 Cumberland St; ⏰ 9am-7pm Mon-Tue, to 9pm Wed-Fri, to 6pm Sat, noon-5pm Sun; ⊕ Bloor-Yonge
There's a wide selection of tobacco products and pipe tobaccos here, but the Cuban cigars and Cubita coffee (which has

A BIBLIOPHILE'S TREASURE TROVE

Torontonians are an awfully literate bunch. In addition to the bookstores we reviewed, here are a few you might not want to miss:

Balfour Books (Map pp242–3; ☎ 416-531-9911; Little Italy, 601 College St; ⏲ noon-11pm; ☒ 506) Thousands of titles are packed into this old-world bookstore in Little Italy.

Ballenford Books on Architecture (Map pp242–3; ☎ 416-588-0800; Markham Village, 600 Markham St; ⏲ noon-5pm Sun & Mon, 10am-6pm Tue & Wed, 10am-7pm Thu, 10am-6pm Sat; ☒ Bathurst, ☒ 510, 511) One-stop shopping for lovers of books and architecture.

Dragon Lady Comics & Paper Nostalgia (Map pp242–3; ☎ 416-536-7460; Little Italy, 609 College St; ⏲ noon-8pm; ☒ 506) This unusual spot vends classic comics, collectibles and vintage mags.

Indigo (Map pp238–9; ☎ 416-925-3536; Bloor-Yorkville, 55 Bloor St W; ⏲ 9am-10pm Sun-Wed, to 11pm Thu-Sat; ☒ Bloor-Yonge) This megagiant chain carries pretty much every subject under the sun – and what they don't have, they'll order.

Librarie Champlain (Map pp244–5; ☎ 416-364-4345; East Toronto, 468 Queen St E; ⏲ 9am-6pm Mon-Thu, to 8pm Fri, to 5pm Sat; ☒ 501) It's the largest French-language bookstore in Toronto, selling magazines, language-learning materials, videos and Montréal Jazz Festival recordings.

Sleuth of Baker Street (Map p231; ☎ 416-483-3111; Greater Toronto Area, 1600 Bayview Ave, south of Eglinton Ave; ⏲ 10am-6pm Tue-Sat, noon-4pm Sun; ☒ 11) Mystery, thriller, out-of-print and first edition books are all here – as well as a good dose of Sherlockiana.

Toronto Women's Bookstore (Map pp242–3; ☎ 416-922-8744, 1-800-861-8233; 73 Harbord St; ⏲ 10:30am-6pm Mon-Wed & Sat, 10:30am-8pm Thu & Fri, noon-5pm Sun; ☒ Spadina)

---

connoisseurs flocking) are the hot items, especially for American aficionados.

TNT WOMAN Map pp238-9 Fashion
☎ 416-975-1810; 55 Avenue Rd; ⏲ 10am-6pm Mon-Wed, to 7pm Thu, to 6pm Fri & Sat, noon-5pm Sun; ☒ Bloor-Yonge

Fashionistas will think they've died and gone to heaven among the rows of high-end designer labels. You're more likely to spot a celebrity here than jeans for under $400.

UNIVERSITY OF TORONTO & THE ANNEX

A grab bag of shops and restaurants is to be had in this stately neighborhood, renowned as one of the friendliest in the city.

A DIFFERENT BOOKLIST
Map pp242-3 Books
☎ 416-538-0889; www.adifferentbooklist.com; 746 Bathurst St; ⏲ 10am-6pm Mon-Wed & Sat, to 7pm Thu & Fri, closed Sun; ☒ Bathurst, ☒ 510, 511

Caribbean and African literature lines the shelves of this cheerful bookstore, as

well as a line of dual-language books for children (in English and Urdu/Portuguese/Swahili/Serbian, and many others). Course textbooks are available too.

BEGUILING
Map pp242-3 Books & Magazines
☎ 416-533-9168; 601 Markham St; ⏲ 11am-7pm Mon-Thu & Sat, to 9pm Fri, noon-6pm Sun; ☒ Bathurst

Lovers of pop culture, indie comic books, 'zines and limited edition artworks and posters had best slot in some serious time on both floors of this shop. For upcoming events, check the associated website (www.torontocomics.com).

CLAY DESIGN
Map pp242-3 Art & Crafts
☎ 416-964-3330; www.claydesign.ca; 170 Harbord St; ⏲ 11am-6pm Tue-Fri, 10am-6pm Sat, noon-5pm Sun; ☒ Spadina

This pottery studio is one of Harbord Street's handful of eclectic shops, and features a host of earthenware treasures, from vases to plates to teapots. Classes are taught here and the shop also hosts pottery parties.

DAVID MIRVISH BOOKS

Map pp242-3   Books

☎ 416-531-9975; www.dmbooks.com; 596 Markham St; 🕙 10am-7pm Mon-Fri, 11am-6pm Sat & Sun; ⊕ Bathurst

The only bookstore specializing in new art books in the country, this former gallery is a calm, spacious atmosphere for browsing through books on architecture, photography, cooking, design, graphic arts, film and more. Those in the know come just to view the renowned Frank Stella painting, which adorns the back wall.

GOOD FOR HER

Map pp242-3   Sex & Fetish

☎ 416-588-0900, 877-588-0900; www.goodforher .com; 175 Harbord St; 🕙 11am-7pm Mon-Thu, to 8pm Fri, to 6pm Sat, noon-5pm Sun, women & transgender patrons only 11am-2pm Thu, noon-5pm Sun; 🚌 94

This friendly, cozy shop celebrates women's sexuality and prides itself as a great environment to peruse an impressive array of high quality sex products. The staff are helpful, the reading chairs are comfortable, and you'll find everything from movies and books to erotic art and massage oils. Check the website for frequent sex-positive workshops.

HONEST ED'S

Map pp242-3   Department Store

☎ 416-537-1574; 581 Bloor St W; 🕙 10am-9pm Mon-Fri, to 6pm Sat, 11am-6pm Sun; ⊕ Bathurst

Through the doors of Honest Ed's lies a little taste of back in the day – not to mention a good bargain or two. A Toronto institution, Ed's is the place to hit for tacky souvenirs and tackier home décor, as well as drugstore items, packaged food, movies and DVDs – often at discount prices. The walls are covered with memorabilia posters of plays, circuses and musicals from every era, and glamorous black and white photos of the Mirvish brothers in their younger days.

LITTLE CHLOE'S CHIC BOUTIQUE

Map pp242-3   Petshop

☎ 416-923-7297; 128 Harbord St; 🕙 11am-7pm Sun-Sat; 🚌 93

Marilyn Monroe would surely approve of this boudoir-style shop…even though it caters to four-legged beauties only. Look forward to being greeted at the door by Johnny Cash (a schnauzer-bichon mix). Inside, leopard print and feather boas abound, as well as humane muzzles, natural foods and treats, dog sweaters, denim jackets and T-shirts worthy of Hollywood celebs.

OUTER LAYER Map pp242-3   Giftware

☎ 416-324-8333; 430 Bloor St W; 🕙 10am-8pm Mon-Wed, to 9pm Thu-Fri, to 7pm Sat, noon-6pm Sun; ⊕ Spadina

Hipster gift shops aren't hard to find in the big city, but Outer Layer stands out from the sea with an extensive selection of imported soaps and bath products in addition to the usual unusual cards, stationary and gift wrap.

PARENTBOOKS Map pp242-3   Books

☎ 416-537-8334; 201 Harbord St; 🕙 10:30am-6pm Mon-Sat; 🚋 511

With reading material on everything from autism to sexuality, this is the place for parents and parents-to-be to find resources and information in a welcoming atmosphere. There are also books and language CDs for kids themselves.

SECRETS FROM YOUR SISTER

Map pp242-3   Lingerie

☎ 416-538-1234; 476 Bloor St W; 🕙 11am-7pm Mon-Fri, 10am-6pm Sat, noon-6pm Sun; ⊕ Spadina

Any woman will agree: there's something to be said for the right bra. While most department stores carry a limited range of bra sizes, Secrets from Your Sister carries size 28 through 44, and cup sizes AA to JJ. The friendly staff are trained to fit customers – and the bright colors and fun prints are a far cry from the drab neutral tones usually available in 'unusual' sizes.

SEEKERS BOOKS

Map pp242-3   Books

☎ 416-925-1982; 509 Bloor St W; 🕙 noon-midnight Sun-Sat; 🚋 511

With a fair-trade shop in the back selling food, T-shirts, and books and DVDs on global issues, this subterranean independent bookstore is one-stop-shopping for the social-justice and politically minded in a relaxed atmosphere. New and used books on every subject are also available.

SUSPECT VIDEO & CULTURE
Map pp242-3   Specialty
☎ 416-588-6674; www.suspectvideo.com; 605 Markham St; ☽ noon-11pm Sun-Sat; ⓐ Bathurst
A local favorite, Suspect specializes in rare and foreign videos and DVDs, from cult horror to kung-fu. Graphic novels and horror mags also stock the shelves, and there's more to be found at the store on **Queen St West** (Map pp240–1; ☎ 416-504-7135; 619 Queen St W; noon-11pm Mon-Sat, 1-10pm Sun; ⓡ 501).

TROVE Map pp242-3   Fashion
☎ 416-516-1258; 793 Bathurst St; ☽ 11am-7pm Mon-Fri, 10am-6pm Sat, noon-5pm Sun; ⓐ Bathurst
Those who won't suffer to be 'beautiful' will find an oasis from pinching skyscraper heels at Trove. This mother-daughter owned boutique prides itself on a large selection of fashion-forward but comfortable shoes, as well as vintage sunglasses, Canadian-designed jewelry, and leather and vegetarian handbags.

KENSINGTON MARKET & LITTLE ITALY
Long known as the stomping grounds for T.O.'s boho chic, Kensington Market is the city's vintage wonderland. Both it and Little Italy are home to great indie boutiques and locally-designed duds.

BUNGALOW Map pp240-1   Vintage
☎ 416-598-0204; 273 Augusta Ave; ☽ 11am-6:30pm Mon-Fri, to 6pm Sat, 1-5pm Sun; ⓡ 505, 510
Vintage-loving guys and gals can search this spacious shop for used clothes and furniture, as well as freshly-made designs. The uncrowded, well-organized racks are a nice change from many of Kensington's cramped digs, and there's a good selection of vintage boots.

COURAGE MY LOVE
Map pp240-1   Vintage
☎ 416-979-1992; 14 Kensington Ave; ☽ 11:30am-6pm Mon-Fri, 11am-6pm Sat, 1:30-5pm Sun; ⓡ 505, 510
'Peace on Earth' reads the sign above the door of this Kensington landmark and local favorite, which wheels and deals in vintage garb. Check out the incredible collection of buttons, the 1950s menus, as well a constant stream of new handmade pieces.

C-PUB Map pp240-1   Fashion
☎ 416-913-2021; 24 Kensington Ave; ☽ noon-6:30pm Mon-Thu, 11:30am-7pm Fri & Sat, noon-6pm Sun; ⓡ 510
Search through the new imports from Hong Kong and Japan here and you might stumble across a pair of jeans or a handbag you'd find on Queen West with a far smaller price tag. Though prices are low, watch for quality – some bargains are too good to be true.

EXILE Map pp240-1   Fashion
☎ 416-596-0827; 20 Kensington Ave; ☽ 10am-7pm Mon-Sat, to 6pm Sun; ⓡ 505, 510
Exile's endless maze of vintage gear is much older than it looks…but after you get lost amid the disco balls and yellow walls holding leather jackets, cowboy boots, furs and costume rentals, you might start to forget what year you're in, too.

FRESH BAKED GOODS
Map pp240-1   Fashion
☎ 416-966-0123; 274 Augusta Ave; ☽ 11am-7pm Mon-Sat, noon-5pm Sun; ⓡ 506
A true taste of Toronto style is to be had at this miniboutique – sister to **Fresh Collective** (☎ 416-594-1313; 692 Queen St W; 11am-7pm Mon-Sat, noon-6pm Sun; ⓡ 501) – which rents out space to local designers. Check it out for beaded jewelry and funky knitwear by Laura-Jean the Knitting Queen.

TOP FIVE VINTAGE SHOPS

Cabaret (opposite) An elegant step back in time.

Chatelet (opposite) Shabby chic plus La Vie en Rose.

Courage My Love (right) For original and costume-worthy pieces.

Divine Decadence Originals (p155) Shop happily ever after in this fairytale boutique.

Red Indian Art Deco (p161) Connect with your inner Easy Rider.

SOUNDSCAPES Map pp242-3 · Music
☎ 416-537-1620; 572 College St; ⌚ 10am-11pm Sun-Thu, to midnight Fri & Sat; 🚋 506
If you're struck with the need for bluegrass or spoken word in the wee hours, head here. Good prices, lots of local and rare finds and concert tickets are specialties. You'll also find listening booths, books, mags and DVDs on music, and friendly staff.

THINGS JAPANESE Map pp242-3 · Giftware
☎ 416-967-9797; 378 College St; ⌚ 11am-7pm Mon-Sat, noon-6pm Sun; 🚋 506
A Zen garden-like tranquility welcomes visitors to peruse through beautiful tea sets and canisters, calligraphy tools, origami kits and kimonos. Sushiphiles will get their fill of elegant serving plates and chopsticks. Unusual incense brands and scents are also available.

TOUCHED BY AN ANGEL
Map pp242-3 · Fashion
☎ 416-929-5293; 424 College St; ⌚ 11am-5:30pm Mon-Sat; 🚋 506
This shop's array of colors and textures of yarn is so fantastic, you'll want to take up knitting (if you haven't already). Refreshingly affordable hats, handbags, scarves, footwear and jewelry await you as well, mostly designed by the owner.

QUEEN WEST & WEST QUEEN WEST
Any shopper will find their fix in this enticing mix of imported shoes, divine antiques, and fresh fashion for men and women that line this überhip street.

ANNIE THOMPSON STUDIO
Map pp240-1 · Fashion
☎ 416-703-3843; 674 Queen St W; ⌚ 11am-6pm Tue-Sat, 1-5pm Sun; 🚋 501
Internationally known designer Annie Thompson's motto, 'Personality is a terrible thing to waste,' is obvious by the artistic and unique designs of the clothing, handbags and backpacks in this Queen West staple. Canadian-designed jewelry is available here too.

TOP FIVE LOCAL FASHION DESIGNERS' SHOPS

Annie Thompson Studio (left)

Common Cloth (Map p231; ☎ 416-203-7710; 1233 Queen St W; ⌚ 11am-7pm Tue-Sat, noon-5pm Sun, Mon by appointment only; 🚋 501)

Fresh Collective (opposite)

Girl Friday (p160)

Response (p161)

CABARET Map pp240-1 · Vintage
☎ 416-504-7126; 672 Queen St W; ⌚ 11am-6pm Mon-Sat, to 7pm Thu & Fri, 1-5pm Sun; 🚋 501
Retrophiles should be sure not to miss this exquisite shop, which features an impressive selection of vintage wear. A fanfare of lace, brocade, tulle and top hats is organized by color, and, given the mint condition of each piece, up for grabs at very reasonable prices.

CAPRI BOUTIQUE Map pp240-1 · Shoes
☎ 416-364-2762; 695 Queen St W; ⌚ 11am-7pm Mon-Thu & Sat, to 8pm Fri, noon-6pm Sun; 🚋 501
High-end imported footwear is the specialty here, where sleek shelves are lined with shoes that come straight from the runways of Milan. Solid service that follows up with customers has created a cult following of shoe addicts.

CHATELET Map pp240-1 · Home Decor
☎ 416-603-2278; www.chatelethome.com; 717 Queen St W; ⌚ 11am-6pm Mon-Sat, noon-5pm Sun; 🚋 501
Shabby chic is redefined in this pink and white paradise of style from the 1700s. A mix of antique and new, silk cushions and chandeliers, Chatelet is French country life through rose-colored glasses.

COME AS YOU ARE
Map pp240-1 · Sex & Fetish
☎ 416-504-7934, 877-858-3160; www.comeas youare.com; 701 Queen St W; ⌚ 11am-7pm Mon-Wed, to 9pm Thu & Fri, to 6pm Sat, noon-5pm Sun; 🚋 501
Catering to both sexes and every variety of orientation, Canada's pioneering co-op sex shop sells sex-positive books, DVDs,

magazines and toys, as well as erotic art and cards. Browse in comfort or visit the website for news on the latest workshops, including tantra and erotic photography.

COSMOS RECORDS Map pp240-1   Music
☎ 416-603-0254; 607A Queen St W; ☉ noon-7pm Mon-Wed, to 8pm Thu-Sat, 1-6pm Sun; ⊞ 501
If your soul aches for funk and rare groove, this shop's got it – on vinyl, and in pristine condition. Jazz, Latin and African beats are also on the menu.

FLEURTJE Map pp240-1   Fashion
☎ 416-410-4948; 917 Queen St W; ☉ noon-6pm Mon-Wed, to 7pm Thu & Fri, 11am-6pm Sat, noon-5pm; ⊞ 501
Expect the unexpected at Fleurtje – including funky kids clothes and made-to-order vegetarian bags designed by the owner. True to its motto ('Come in and see what Canadians can do'), all featured designers are from Toronto, Montréal and the Maritimes.

F/X Map pp240-1   Fashion
☎ 416-504-0888; 515 Queen St W; ☉ 11am-7pm Mon-Wed, to 8pm Thu & Fri, to 7pm Sat, noon-6pm Sun; ⊞ 501
The tornado of girliness that hits you upon entering F/X makes it worth just a visit, even if tutus, Hello Kitty paraphernalia, colored wigs and rhinestone jewelry aren't your scene. The store carries its own line of nail polish in every shade of the rainbow, and, on the 2nd floor, gowns to befit every manner of princess.

GET OUTSIDE Map pp232-3   Fashion
☎ 416-593-5598; 437 Queen St W; ☉ 10:30am-8:30pm Mon-Fri, 10am-8:30pm Sat, 11:30am-7:30pm Sun; ⊞ 501
Another Toronto institution for comfortable yet stylish footwear, this haven of sneakers, skate shoes and flip-flops has been satisfying urban walkers for over 10 years.

GIRL FRIDAY Map pp240-1   Fashion
☎ 416-364-2511; 740 Queen St W; ☉ noon-7pm Mon-Fri, 11am-7pm Sat, noon-5pm Sun; ⊞ 501
Proof that office clothes don't need to be boring lives in this small but delightful boutique, where pretty yet edgy pieces are stylish enough to last. Formal dresses and

jeans are up for grabs too, at both this and the College St location.

GRREAT STUFF Map pp240-1   Fashion
☎ 416-536-6770; 870 Queen St W; ☉ 11am-7pm Tue & Wed, 11am-8pm Thu, 11am-7pm Fri, 10am-6pm Sat, noon-5pm Sun; ⊞ 501
Although at first glance it may seem a melee of vintage finds, everything is brand spanking new in this men's clothing shop, which specializes in one-of-a-kind designer samples as well as chic European lines.

HEEL BOY Map pp240-1   Shoes
☎ 416-362-4335; 682 Queen St W; ☉ 10am-7pm Mon-Wed, to 9pm Thu & Fri, to 7pm Sat, noon-6pm Sun; ⊞ 501
Slightly more upscale than average, Heel Boy's beautifully-crafted leather bags compliment an impressive range of classically stylish shoes for she and he.

JAPANESE PAPER PLACE
Map pp240-1   Giftware
☎ 416-703-0089; www.japanesepaperplace.com; 887 Queen St W; ☉ 10am-6pm Mon-Wed & Sat, to 8pm Thu & Fri; ⊞ 501
Lanterns, beautiful stationery, and ornately decorated paper in thousands of varieties adorn the shelves of the Japanese Paper Place, where workshops and events are often held. Prices are high, but so is quality – many sheets are made by hand and one-of-a-kind.

KIEHL'S Map pp232-3   Beauty
☎ 416-977-3588; www.kiehls.com; 407 Queen St W; ☉ 10am-8pm Mon-Fri, to 7pm Sat, noon-6pm Sun; ⊞ 501
If it's reminiscent of an old apothecary, that's probably because Kiehl's originated in 1851 and has stayed the same in many ways. The label's famed no-frills bottles of face, hair and body potions are legendary amongst beauty connoisseurs – and justifiably so.

LILITH Map pp240-1   Fashion
☎ 416-504-5353; 541 Queen St W; ☉ 11am-6pm Mon, to 7pm Tue & Wed, to 8pm Thu–Sat, noon-6pm Sun; ⊞ 501
Touting 'sustainable clothing to empower women,' this Queen West boutique carries clothes all made in-store and sized to fit all

body types, as well as kids' clothes made from scrap fabric, and a maternity line.

MAGIC PONY Map pp240-1 Specialty
☎ 416-861-1684; www.magic-pony.com; 694 Queen St W; ⊙ 11am-6pm Mon-Sat, noon-6 Sun; 🚊 501

Described as a 'concept shop' by its owners, Magic Pony, which originated as a website, deals in Japanese books, figures, designer toys and T-shirts you have to see to believe. The ever-changing gallery at the back features ultramodern graphic design and illustration exhibits.

POLKA DOT KIDS Map pp240-1 Kids
☎ 416-306-2279; 917 Queen St W; ⊙ noon-6pm Mon-Fri, 11am-6:30pm Sat & Sun; 🚊 501

For a breath of fresh air and an answer to Nintendo overload, browse through cheery Polka Dot for a refreshing array of old-fashioned, all-natural wooden toys, knitted and linen booties, and patterned lunch boxes that hearken back to simpler times.

RED INDIAN ART DECO
Map pp240-1 Antiques
☎ 416-504-7706; 536 Queen St W; ⊙ 10am-5pm Tue-Sat; 🚊 501

This vintage treasure trove of household goods might be more at home in Queen West's Leslieville, but an antique alarm clock or a melamine diner-style kitchen table are a refreshing diversion from clothing, shoes and jewels.

RESPONSE
Map pp240-1 Fashion
☎ 416-366-5394; 690 Queen St W; ⊙ 11am-6pm Tue & Wed, to 7pm Thu & Fri, to 6pm Sat, noon-5pm Sun, by chance Mon; 🚊 501

Let party frocks, mohair beaded shawls, sparkling jewelry and velvet shoes nourish your inner diva at this boutique, where most pieces are designed by the owner. Check out the jewelry imported from Brazil.

TIMMIE DOG OUTFITTERS
Map pp240-1 Pets
☎ 416-203-6789; 867 Queen St W; ⊙ 10am-8pm Mon-Sat, noon-5pm Sun; 🚊 501

Fastidious pooches and fussy cats will do well at Timmie, where top-notch toys, treats and accessories are displayed in a manner befitting of any LA boutique. Things you never knew your pet always wanted include aesthetically pleasing scratching posts, wall-mounted dog bowls and, if the season is right, doggie Halloween costumes.

THE TIN TAJ
Map pp240-1 Giftware
☎ 416-703-7515; 913 Queen St W; ⊙ noon-6pm Tue-Fri, noon-4pm Sat; 🚊 501

Every square inch of wall and ceiling in this colorful shop seems to be home to some whimsical tin delight. Wares come from all over the world but this is definitely a place for unique Canadian memorabilia, reasonable prices and lots of fun.

GOING GREEN

Though it's Canada's largest city, Torontonians are renowned for being environmentally conscious. A variety of fringe shops and bookstores caters to sustainable living, organic lifestyle products and fair trade. Our picks are:

Another Story Bookshop (Map pp244-5; ☎ 416-462-1104; Greektown, 164 Danforth Ave; ⊙ 11am-7pm Mon-Fri, 10am-6pm Sat, noon-6pm Sun; ⊕ Broadview) Books about diversity, equity and social justice. Has a children's section.

Big Carrot (Map pp244-5; ☎ 416-466-2129; Greektown, 348 Danforth Ave; ⊙ noon-8pm Mon-Fri, to 7pm Sat, to 6pm Sun; ⊕ Broadview) Water purifiers and sprout growers are available at this healthy superstore, which offers refills for water dispenser bottles.

Grassroots (p162)

Mountain Equipment Co-op (p151)

Seekers Books (Map pp242-3; ☎ 416-925-1982; The Annex, 509 Bloor St W; ⊙ 'til midnight; ⊕ Bathurst) Enlightenment may come tumbling down from the shelves of used academic and popular titles.

Toronto Hemp Company (Map pp238-9; ☎ 416-920-1980; www.torontohemp.com; 665 Yonge St;) Cannabis culture resource centre and shop that sells high quality hemp and related products.

EAST TORONTO

On 'The Danforth,' as it's known to locals, you can browse everything from colorful imported clothing to hip homewares and upscale bridal boutiques.

EL PIPIL Map pp244-5   Fashion

☎ 416-465-9625; 267 Danforth Ave; ☼ 10am-7pm Mon-Fri, to 6pm Sat, noon-5pm Sun; ◉ Broadview
Home adornments, boutique fashions and Canadian-designed accessories are the special at this charming shop, all at enticing prices.

GRASSROOTS Map pp244-5   Specialty

☎ 416-466-2841, 888-633-5833; Carrot Common, 327 Danforth Ave; ☼ 10am-7pm Mon-Fri, to 6pm Sat, noon-6pm Sun; ◉ Chester
If you're searching for some one-stop shopping for all things earth-friendly, look no further. Grassroots carries environmentally sound household items galore – even hemp coffee filters and organic bed linen are available here. It's also a used battery drop-off depot. And there's another branch in the Annex (Map pp242–3; ☎ 416-944-1993; 408 Bloor St W; 10am-8pm Mon-Fri, 10am-7pm Sat, noon-6pm Sun; ◉ Spadina).

LA DI DA Map pp244-5   Fashion & Beauty

☎ 416-849-5388; 128 Danforth Ave; ☼ 11am-7pm Tue-Fri, to 7pm Sat, noon-6pm Sun; ◉ Broadview
There's a spa and nail bar at the back of this divalicious boutique, specializing in hard to find skincare products, silver jewelry and gorgeous, affordable women's clothing.

THE BEACHES

The Beaches' cheerful shopping strip is a great escape from the hustle and bustle of the city.

ARTS ON QUEEN

Map p246   Art & Crafts

☎ 416-699-6127; 2198 Queen St E; ☼ 11am-7pm Mon-Fri, 9am-7pm Sat, 11am-7pm Sun; ⓡ 501
It'll be hard to leave this cruisy store and gallery empty-handed. One-of-a-kind pottery, glassworks, photography and modern, fun art pieces are mostly made by Ontario-based artists, many who live in the Beaches area.

BOA Map p246   Fashion

☎ 416-694-6867; 2116B Queen St E; ☼ 11am-7pm Mon-Fri, 10am-6pm Sat, 11am-6pm Sun; ⓡ 501
Boa's hip yet classy designs and bright, vibrant fabrics stand out in the Toronto crowd – perhaps because most of the clothes are imports from LA. There's another store on Yonge St (Map p230; ☎ 416-895-9372; 3217 Yonge St).

FROOSH Map p246   Beauty

☎ 416-686-3967; 2230 Queen St E; ☼ 11am-7pm Mon-Sat, noon-5pm Sun; ⓡ 501
Handmade bath products are all made in-house at Froosh, and the space in the back holds workshops for making more, from soap to body butter. The store also carries soaps for babies and pets, and some vegan products.

KIDS AT HOME

Map pp244-5   Kids, Home Decor

☎ 416-698-9726; 2086 Queen St E; ☼ 10am-6pm Mon-Thu, to 9pm Fri, to 6pm Sat, 11am-5pm Sun; ⓡ 501
A store sure to please style-savvy moms and dads, this shop carries kid-friendly art, as well as small-sized beds and linen. Be sure to look up at the chandeliers and around at the enticing quilts and wall hangings.

A CITY GONE TO THE DOGS

Toronto's posh pooch culture has seen the birth of specialty pet shops in almost every district. By this we don't mean exotic animals for sale, but rather boutiques catering to animals every needs…think designer food bowls, organic pet birthday cakes, high-end fur shampoos and, of course, a range of outfits. Whether you're an animal-lover, a pet owner or simply up for some fun, hit **Little Chloe's Chic Boutique** (p157), Yorkville's **My Pet Boutique** (p155), or **Timmie Dog Outfitters** (p161) on Queen West. **Bark & Fitz** branches at **The Beaches** (Map p246; ☎ 416-699-1313; 2116 Queen St E 2570); **Yonge St Strip** (Map p231; ☎ 416-483-4431; 2570 Yonge St); **Bloor-Yorkville** (Map p231; ☎ 416-916-6207; 1959 Bloor St W) – will meet Bowser's every need, and **Urban Dog** (☎ 416-361-1037; 37 Parliament St), near the Distillery District, offers doggie daycare, boarding, a spa and a walking service, as well as high quality foods, velour beds and pooch perfume.

THE NAKED SHEEP

Map pp244-5   Art & Crafts

☎ 416-691-6320; 2144 Queen St E; ⊙ 11am-7pm Tue-Thu, to 6pm Fri, 10am-6pm Sat, noon-5pm Sun; ⛟ 501

Stitch 'n' Bitchers and knitting grannies alike will find yarn, knitting and crochet accessories and other crafty things at this bright, friendly store. Classes are taught here almost every night and all are welcome to make use of the couches to hang out, sit and knit!

GREATER TORONTO AREA

Fabulous finds don't always come easy. Venture beyond the beaten path and discover some of Toronto's hidden gems.

BOJ DÉCOR Map p231   Home Decor

☎ 416-545-0088; 685 Mt. Pleasant Rd; ⊙ 11am-6pm Mon-Sat; ⊕ Eglinton

If there were such a thing, Boj would be reminiscent of a Parisian boudoir that's traveled through time. With antique European furniture mixed with a seemingly random collection of quirky odds and ends (like a chandelier made of antlers), Boj seems it would be more at home in a trendier location…but that's part of its charm.

HOLT RENFREW LAST CALL

Map p230   Fashion

☎ 905-886-7444; 1 Bass Pro Mills Dr; ⊙ 10am-9pm Mon-Sat, 11am-7pm Sun

A discount haven for budget-savvy fashionistas, Last Call carries last year's fashions from Bloor-Yorkville's exclusive **Holt Renfrew** (Map pp238–9; ☎ 416-922-2333; 50 Bloor St W; ⊙ 10am-6pm Mon-Wed, 10am-8pm Thu & Fri, 10am-6pm Sat, noon-6pm Sun; ⊕ Bloor-Yonge) at up to 60% off. There are monthly promotions, too.

MADE YOU LOOK

Map p231   Jewelry

☎ 416-463-2136; 1338 Queen St W; ⊙ 10am-6pm Mon-Wed, to 9pm Thu & Fri, to 6pm Sat, noon-5pm Sun; ⛟ 501

A vibrant marketplace for local jewelers, trinkets and treasures in dozens of styles – including glass beads, contemporary metals, and delicate gold – are displayed here. Many more can be viewed in each designer's look book, and custom work is available.

Sleeping ■

Sleeping

Hold onto your wallets, this is gonna get ugly...Unless you're going to five Maple Leafs games a week, finding good-value accommodations in Toronto will be the most expensive part of your trip. From Victoria Day through to Labour Day – and beyond that for as long as the summer weather holds – decent places to stay will be full, night after night, and you're likely to have to spend a small fortune to rest your weary head. Even less-desirable hotels and B&Bs display 'No Vacancy' signs on Friday and Saturday nights. Rooms are booked out months in advance during Caribana, Toronto Pride or the Toronto International Film Festival (see p201 for a list of major holidays and events). Our advice: except for during the deep-freeze winter months, book as far in advance as humanly possible.

Hotel rates vacillate wildly from day to day, many places charging double or triple the off-peak rates in summer and on major holidays. Some hostels, guesthouses and B&Bs may not charge tax, but hotels certainly will. Always ask if parking, local phone calls and high-speed internet access are included, as well as inquiring about discounts for students, seniors, CAA/AAA members and long-term stays. Many hotels offer internet booking discounts and package deals via their own websites. Play your cards right at smaller hotels, B&Bs and guesthouses, and you may able to negotiate a tasty deal during slow periods.

Cheap sleeps in Toronto are thin on the ground. There are some great youth hostels and guesthouses out there though, offering dormitory beds from $22 to $30, and private rooms (often with bathroom) for under $80. Internet access, luggage storage, common kitchens, shared bathroom and laundry facilities, and weekly discounts are usually thrown into the mix. Beware that some hostels may unfairly pull the rug out from under you by reneging on bookings or stuffing corridors with extra bunks at busy times. Many hostels, guesthouses and B&Bs don't have air-conditioning, which can present unsavory issues during the city's sweltering summer.

In the midrange department, Toronto's excellent crop of B&Bs are the best bet. Cheaper chain hotels like Howard Johnson and Days Inn are solid options, if thin on character. They often have 'doubles' (which may mean two beds, not just double occupancy) starting near $100, as do Toronto's older independent hotels. Most midrange and top-end downtown hotels are practically interchangeable, as the Hilton and Westin proved when they simply swapped their respective establishments in the late '80s.

Craving something with a little character? Downtown also offers historic hotels, boutique digs and lakefront properties. At luxury hotels, you'll pay upwards of $180 for fully-equipped, spacious accommodations. These top-end establishments all have swimming pools, fitness rooms, valet parking, bars and restaurants, as well as concierges desperate to satisfy your every whim. Luxury B&Bs serving full, hot breakfasts can charge over $120 per night for rooms and suites outfitted with all the amenities, including bathroom, telephone and cable TV. Zzzzzzz...

PRICE GUIDE

The dollar-sign symbols in reviews in this chapter represent the price of a standard double room before taxes.

$$$	over $160 per night
$$	$80-160 per night
$	under $80 per night

BLUE JAY DOUBLE PLAY

The **Renaissance Toronto** (opposite) at the Rogers Centre became fabulously notorious when, during one of the first Blue Jays baseball games, a couple in one of the upper-field side rooms – either forgetfully or gregariously – became involved in some sporting activity of their own with the lights on, much to the crowd's amusement. Such a scoring performance was later repeated at another game. After that, the hotel insisted on guests signing waivers that stipulated there would be no more such free double plays.

HARBOURFRONT

There are a handful of upmarket, big-name options not far from the lake – water views!

WESTIN HARBOUR CASTLE

Map pp234-5   Hotel $$$

☎ 416-869-1600, 800-937-8461; www.westin.com; 1 Harbour Sq; d from $190; P $17-30; 🖳 🖳 ♿ ⛹ 🛗 509, 510

If this were a hamburger, it'd be with 'the works' – restaurants, shops, gym, conference centre, pool, disabled-access suites etc. Staff are surprisingly chipper for such a big hotel. Maybe the lobby keeps them amused, with enough marble to rival any Hollywood mansion. Tasty lake views.

RADISSON PLAZA HOTEL ADMIRAL

Map pp234-5   Hotel $$$

☎ 416-203-3333, 800-333-3333; www.radisson.com; 249 Queens Quay W; d from $200; P $18; 🖳 🖳 🛗 509, 510

The oft-forgotten Radisson has a quasi-nautical theme, situated right on the lakeshore. Free wi-fi in every room and outdoor pool are bonuses. Internet specials sometimes include deals with full breakfast and free in-room movies. The muzac in the corridors is almost cheesy enough to be cool.

RENAISSANCE TORONTO

Map pp234-5   Hotel $$$

☎ 416-341-7100, 800-468-3571; www.renaissancehotels.com; 1 Blue Jays Way; d/ste from $290/325; P $20-25; 🖳 🖳 ♿ ⛹ 🚇 Union

Seventy of the more expensive rooms here overlook the Rogers Centre playing field – if you book one, be prepared for floodlights and hollering sports fans! If you'd rather use your room for sleeping, the restaurant and bar also overlook the field. Enclosed walkways extend to Union Station.

FINANCIAL DISTRICT

The Financial District cashes in with some decent and stylish sleeping options.

HOTEL VICTORIA Map pp234-5   Hotel $$

☎ 416-363-1666, 800-363-8228; www.hotelvictoria-toronto.com; 56 Yonge St; d $105-150; 🖳 🚇 King

One of Toronto's best small downtown hotels is the early 20th-century Hotel Victoria.

Refurbished throughout, it still maintains a few old-fashioned features, including a mighty fine lobby and a warm welcome at the 24-hour reception desk. Rates include complimentary continental breakfast and health club privileges.

STRATHCONA Map pp234-5   Hotel $$

☎ 416-363-3321, 800-268-8304; www.thestrathconahotel.com; 60 York St; d from $115; 🖳 ⛹ 🚇 St Andrew

'Think of us as a launch pad' is the marketing angle at this unpretentious, familiar hotel. The usual amenities (including Web TV) mightn't make you launch into the stratosphere, but for the downtown area it's reasonably priced. Stop by the tour desk en route to the pub downstairs.

FAIRMONT ROYAL YORK

Map pp234-5   Historic Hotel $$$

☎ 416-368-2511, 800-441-1414; www.fairmont.com/royalyork; 100 Front St W; d from $190; P $14-33; 🖳 🖳 ♿ ⛹ 🚇 Union

Since 1929 the eminent Royal York has accommodated everyone from Tina Turner to Henry Kissinger. Built opposite Union Station by the Canadian Pacific Railway, its mock-chateau design adds character to Toronto's modern skyline. The rooms exude richness and style and carry rates that rise depending upon the seasonal demand. Epic (p95) and the Library Bar (p122) are both worth a second look.

HILTON TORONTO

Map pp234-5   Hotel $$$

☎ 416-869-3456, 800-445-8667; www.hilton.com; 145 Richmond St W; d/ste from $190/210; P $27; 🖳 🖳 ♿ ⛹ 🚇 Osgoode

A surprisingly sleek high-rise, where even the standard rooms have Web TV, high-speed internet access and an on-demand CD library. For cityscape views, book one of the 32nd-floor suites. Be sure to ask about B&B rates, weekend romance packages and family-sized summer deals.

CAMBRIDGE SUITES HOTEL

Map pp234-5   Hotel/Extended Stay $$$

☎ 416-368-1990, 800-463-1990; www.cambridgesuitestoronto.com; 15 Richmond St E; ste $220-500; P $16; 🖳 ♿ ⛹ 🚇 Queen

A polished executive hotel offering two-room cityscape suites with in-room DVDs and free high-speed internet access. Guests enjoy a deluxe breakfast buffet, full-service business centre and penthouse fitness room with city skyline views. Happy travellers make plans for the day in the lobby, perhaps discussing a return in January when rates sink to as low as $150.

OLD YORK

Old York accommodations range from sublime luxury down to the local HI youth hostel.

HOSTELLING INTERNATIONAL
TORONTO Map pp234-5   Hostel $
☎ 416-971-4440, 877-848-8737; www.hostelling toronto.ca; 76 Church St; dm/d $27/65; 🖵 🕿 🛜 504
This award-winning hostel gets votes for renovations that include a rooftop deck, airconditioning and electronic key locks. Beds in quad rooms may not cost any more than those in larger dormitories, so ask when making reservations. Pub crawls and quiz and casino nights keep things entertaining.

COSMOPOLITAN
Map pp234-5   Boutique Hotel $$$
☎ 416-350-2000, 800-958-3488; www.cosmotoron to.com; 8 Colborne St; ste from $228; 🅿 $29; 🖵 ♿ 🌐 King
A swanky international crew of business bods and celebs traverses the corridors of the Cosmo, Toronto's newest boutique bolt-hole. Suites have lake views, showers as big as bedrooms and sexy interior design. Staff are serene and courteous, directing you to the Asian fusion restaurant, 24-hour gym and full-service spa. Absolute opulence.

LE ROYAL MERIDIEN KING EDWARD
Map pp234-5   Historic Hotel $$$
☎ 416-863-9700, 800-559-3821; www.toronto.le meridien.com; 37 King St E; d from $275; 🅿 $28; 🖵 ♿ 🛁 🌐 King
The glorious 'King Eddy' is Toronto's oldest hotel, named for King Edward VII, who gave it the royal seal of approval over a century ago. The lobby is a showpiece of baroque plasterwork, marble and etched glass – 100% class, a measure sometimes lacking in the oblique front-of-house staff.

THE BEST HOTELS FOR...
- A taste of history – time warp at the **Fairmont Royal York** (p167).
- A drink – the **Drake Hotel** (p175), a boozy beacon in West Queen West.
- Celeb-spotting – rock stars and screen idols hideout at the **Sutton Place Hotel** (p172).
- Watching the game – watch a Blue Jays or Argonauts sporting renaissance at the **Renaissance Toronto** (p167).
- Kids – splash down the indoor waterslide at the **Delta Chelsea Toronto Downtown** (opposite).
- Pets – pooches and purrers are welcome at **Banting House Inn** (p176).
- Peace and quiet – **Accommodating The Soul B&B** (p177) at the low-key Beaches.
- A naughty weekend – heart-shaped, plumb-red Jacuzzis and fluffy pillows at the **Comfort Suites City Centre** (p176).
- Guest services and amenities – the **Grand Hotel & Suites** (p170) leaves others in its wake.
- Backpackers – **Canadiana Backpackers Inn** (below) is a world-wide melting pot.

THEATRE BLOCK & ENTERTAINMENT DISTRICT

These abutting districts offer slick, urbane hotels and Toronto's favorite youth hostel.

CANADIANA BACKPACKERS INN
Map pp234-5   Hostel $
☎ 416-598-9090, 877-215-1225; www.canadiana lodging.com; 42 Widmer St; dm $25-30, s/d $65/75; 🅿 $15; 🖵 🛜 504
Toronto's largest hostel is a sure-fire winner, occupying a run of appealing Victorian townhouses in the Entertainment District. A long list of plusses includes free wi-fi internet, a movie theatre, BBQ nights, free pancake breakfasts, gas cooking, laundry facilities and a crop of immaculate new private rooms. You'll find it hard to feel homesick here.

HOLIDAY INN ON KING
Map pp234-5   Hotel $$$
☎ 416-599-4000; www.hiok.com; 370 King St W; d from $160; 🅿 $18; 🖵 🕿 ♿ 🛁 🛜 504
Book yourself in for a Theatre Block holiday in this conspicuous white hotel that

seems to have been airlifted straight off Waikiki Beach. Standard rooms open out to lake or city views, while the seasonal rooftop pool gazes onto the CN Tower. Children under age 12 stay and eat free; internet deals can be a steal. Service is stern but efficient.

HÔTEL LE GERMAIN
Map pp234-5   Boutique Hotel $$$
☎ 416-345-9500, 866-345-9501; www.germainto ronto.com; 30 Mercer St; d $240-500, ste $475-900; Ⓟ $28; 🖳 ♿ 🔥 504

Hip and harmonious, seven-story Le Germain resides in a quiet Entertainment District side street. Clean lines, soothing spaces and Zen-inspired materials deliver the promised 'ocean of well-being.' Guests are pampered with Aveda bath amenities, in-room Bose stereos, wi-fi internet access, a rooftop terrace and cathedral-ceilinged lobby library.

SOHO METROPOLITAN HOTEL
Map pp234-5   Boutique Hotel $$$
☎ 416-599-8800, 800-668-6600; www.metropolitan .com/soho; 318 Wellington St W; d from $275; Ⓟ $25-30; 🖳 🔥 ♿ 🔥 504

A snazzy boutique hotel in the heart of downtown, the SoHo Met effects flawless service. Exquisite amenities include Italian linen, marble bathrooms, king-sized beds, remote-controlled lighting, wi-fi internet access, a helpful *Clefs d'Or* concierge and a health club spa. Don't miss epicurean Sen5es (p98).

QUEEN STREET & DUNDAS SQUARE

It's not the happening-est of areas to stay, but who needs action when you're trying to sleep?

RESIDENCE COLLEGE HOTEL
Map pp234-5   University Housing $
☎ 416-351-1010; residencecollegehotel@uhn.on .ca; 90 Gerard St W; s & d without bathroom from $50; 🔥 🔵 College

Unlike most college accommodations, this one's open to the public year round, so you can follow the college kids around and crash their parties. It's an unremarkable building in an unremarkable location,

and the rooms are definitely nothing flash, but this is a really solid option if all you are looking for is a cheap, safe room for the night.

DAYS INN TORONTO DOWNTOWN
Map pp232-3   Hotel$$
☎ 416-977-6655, 800-329-7466; www.daysinn .com; 30 Carlton St; d $80-160; Ⓟ $18; 🖳 🔥 🔥; 🔵 College

You always know what you're going to get at the Days Inn – affordable, no-frills accommodations, and in this case, a central location. Reception at times seems dramatically undermanned, but staff are bubbly with their apologies. Ride the weary elevators to the upper floors for the best views.

HOUSE ON MCGILL Map pp232-3   B&B $$
☎ 416-351-1503; www.mcgillbb.ca; 110 McGill St; s/d from $60/90; 🔵 College

Six color-coded guest rooms occupy this three-story 1890s townhouse, which, despite the odd 1980s glass brick, has managed to retain its historic charms (narrow-gauge floorboards, timber dados, etc). The streets around here can be a bit iffy after dark, but there's good security. Grab a handful of jellybeans from the jar in the hall on your way out.

LES AMIS B&B Map pp232-3   B&B $$
☎ 416-591-0635; www.bbtoronto.com; 31 Granby St; s/d/tr from $85/100/130; 🔵 College

Run by a multilingual Parisian couple, this cheery nonsmoking B&B offers full, gourmet vegetarian (or vegan) breakfasts. Cozy rooms have futon beds and that's-just-how-I-would-have-done-it appeal; bathrooms are shared. The only drawback is a slightly sketchy location, despite being just steps from the Eaton Centre. G&L travelers are welcome.

DELTA CHELSEA TORONTO DOWNTOWN Map pp232-3   Hotel $$
☎ 416-595-1975, 800-268-1133; www.deltahotels .com; 33 Gerrard St W; d/ste from $100/250; Ⓟ $23-29; 🖳 🔥 ♿ 🔥 🔵 College

Who says one hotel can't be all things to all people? With nearly 1600 rooms, Toronto's largest and arguably best-value hotel throngs with tourists, business travelers and families. If you're traveling with kids,

BOOKING B&BS

Despite recent occupancy-related bylaws which put the clamp on some of the larger B&Bs around town, Toronto's B&Bs are still great places to stay. Be forewarned that some B&Bs require a two-night minimum stay, especially on weekends. A great place to start looking online is www.bbcanada.com, which has nearly 100 listings in the city.

B&B reservations agencies check, list and book rooms in the participating members' homes. When you indicate your preferences, all attempts will be made to find a particularly suitable host. If you're in town and want to check last-minute availability, it may be able to help during normal business hours. If you're planning on staying for more than a few days, these agencies also rent out suites and apartments on a weekly or monthly basis, which can work out to be a very good deal. It's almost always better value than staying at hotels.

Reliable agencies include the following:

Bed & Breakfast Homes of Toronto (☎ 416-363-6362; www.bbcanada.com/associations/toronto2) Handles residential area B&Bs, anything from modest family homes to deluxe suites.

Downtown Toronto Association of Bed and Breakfast Guest Houses (☎ 416-410-3938; www.bnbinfo.com) Rooms in various neighborhoods, mostly in renovated Victorian houses.

Toronto Bed & Breakfast Reservation Service (☎ 705-738-9449, 877-922-6522; www.torontobandb.com) The oldest association in town has about a dozen members in central Toronto.

---

you'll appreciate the apartment-style family suites and indoor waterslide. Prices vary wildly with season, day of the week and occupancy rates.

GRAND HOTEL & SUITES

Map pp232-3   Hotel/Extended Stay $$$

☎ 416-863-9000, 877-324-7263; www.grandhotel toronto.com; 225 Jarvis St; d/ste from $150/200; Ⓟ $16; 🖳 📷 ♿ 🚼 Ⓜ Dundas

This glass-fronted turret proffers perks that put other hotels to shame, including shuttle services, partly compensating for a slightly unsavory location. All of the rooms have free wi-fi internet access, two TV/ DVDs, dual phone lines, CD players, kitchenette and marble bathrooms. There's also a complimentary breakfast buffet and a 450 sq meter fitness club, indoor pool and spa. Nice one!

SHERATON CENTRE TORONTO

Map pp232-3   Hotel $$$

☎ 416-361-1000; www.sheraton.com /centretoronto; 123 Queen St W; d from $150; Ⓟ $33; 🖳 📷 ♿ 🚼 Ⓜ Osgoode, Queen

Thoughtful perks like the guaranteed fast-response concierge distinguish this downtown high-rise from its competitors. There's an Olympic-sized pool, Jacuzzi suites available and self-service check-in/out terminals in the impressive chrome-coated lobby. Ask about discounted theatre and festival packages.

CHINATOWN & BALDWIN VILLAGE

Most folks come here to eat, not to sleep. Why not break with tradition?

BALDWIN VILLAGE INN

Map pp232-3   B&B $$

☎ 416-591-5359; www.baldwininn.com; 9 Baldwin St; d without bathroom $85-105; 🖳 📷 505, 506

Squished between a Kowloon dim sum restaurant and an art gallery, this new B&B neatly plugs a gap in the market with quality B&B accommodations right on Baldwin St. Waste your time on the high-speed wi-fi internet, or lounge about in the courtyard.

YONGE STREET STRIP & CHURCH-WELLESLEY VILLAGE

There are a couple of mainstream hotels and plenty of fly-by-night and better-established B&Bs in the gay Church-Wellesley neighborhood, some only accepting male guests.

CROMWELL APARTMENTS

Map pp238-9   Serviced Apartments/Extended Stay $$

☎ 416-962-5670; www.cromwell.sites.toronto.com; 55 Isabella St; studio $90-105, 1-bed apt $100-140, 2-bed apt $240; Ⓟ free; 🖳 Ⓜ Wellesley

This balconied high-rise is party central for gay lads from around the planet. The decor is ho-hum and the finishes are all a bit scuffed, but even the studios have a kitchen. Wi-fi internet access costs a one-time $20 fee. Minimum rental is three days, but they're flexible in the off season.

VICTORIA'S MANSION GUESTHOUSE

Map pp238-9   B&B $$

☎ 416-921-4625; www.victoriasmansion.com; 68 Gloucester St; s $79-96, d $105-120, studio $145-160; P $10; 🖵 ⊖ Wellesley
Festooned with international flags, gay-friendly Victoria's Mansion accommodates mid-range travelers for short and long-term stays in a renovated 1880s redbrick heritage building. Studios have kitchenettes; management can be a little stand-offish.

GLOUCESTER SQUARE INNS OF TORONTO

Map pp238-9   B&B $$

☎ 416-966-0013; www.gloucestersquare.com; 512 Jarvis St, 514 Jarvis St & 10 Cawthra Sq; d $110-180, ste $200-550; P free; 🖵 ⊖ Wellesley
Gloucester Square has thirty gorgeous rooms in three historic buildings (one designed by famous architect EJ Lennox), where guests enjoy unabashed opulence. Ceiling fans revolve above Persian rugs, McCausland stained glass and Chinese urns. The breakfast buffet runs until 1pm; ask about spa packages. Samantha Fox bounced around on the four-poster bed in the attic suite.

COMFORT HOTEL Map pp238-9   Hotel $$

☎ 416-924-1222, 800-424-6423; www.choicehotels.ca/cn228; 15 Charles St E; d from $125; P $10; 🖵 ♿ ⊖ Bloor-Yonge

The embodiment of nameless, faceless hotel anonymity, this is the place to stay if you're on the run from the law – stable, risk-free accommodations where you won't arouse much suspicion (least of all from the receptionists). Renegades under 18 stay free!

BEARFOOT INN Map pp238-9   B&B $$

☎ 416-922-1658, 888-871-2327; www.bearfootinn.com; 30a Dundonald St; d $125-175; 🖵 ⊖ Wellesley
Go barefoot at Bearfoot (or altogether nude), an immaculately maintained gay B&B not far from the Church St beat. Plush bathrobes, wi-fi internet, a sauna and a small gym add to the appeal. Winter hibernation specials discount what are already good value rooms.

COURTYARD MARRIOTT

Map pp238-9   Hotel $$

☎ 416-924-0611, 800-874-5075; www.courtyardtoronto.com; 475 Yonge St; d from $150; P $20; 🖵 ⌨ ♿ 🏊 ⊖ College
Renovated to within an inch of its identity in 2000, this towering hotel offers amicable service, a walk-to-everything location and all the usual mod-cons, including a gym, hot-tub and pool. Some of the beds are a little hammock-shaped, but the high-falutin' suits who stay here don't seem to mind.

BLOOR-YORKVILLE

Rack rates here at times exceed what you'd pay at top-notch downtown hotels. More affordable rooms are few and far between.

TOP 10 PERKS AT TORONTO ACCOMMODATIONS

- A bar crawling distance from your dorm at **Global Village Backpackers** (p175).
- A sensational gourmet vegetarian breakfast at **Les Amis B&B** (p169).
- Shooting pool at the pub next door to **Madison Manor** (p173).
- Bunking down where the Beatles, Teddy Roosevelt and the Duke of Windsor slept sweetly at **Le Royal Meridien King Edward** (p168).
- Luxury suites with 24-hour butler service at the **Windsor Arms** (p172).
- Sleeping with the ghost of 'Papa' Hemingway at **Clarion Hotel & Suites** (p176).
- The complimentary cappuccino bar at **Hôtel Le Germain** (p169).
- The excellent onsite spa **Stillwater** (p146) at the **Park Hyatt** (p172).
- Unwinding on the Toronto Islands at **Barb's Island Loft** (p177).
- Watching the lake change moods from high in the **Westin Harbour Castle** (p167).

LOWTHER HOUSE Map pp238-9 B&B $$

☎ 416-323-1589, 800-265-4158; www.lowther house.ca; 72 Lowther Ave; d $70-160; P free; ⊖ St George

Equidistant from Yorkville, several museums and the University of Toronto's St George campus, this restored century-old Victorian mansion charms guests with its gardens and common-area fireplace. Suites will spoil you with a marble double Jacuzzi bathroom or a sun room. *Parlez-vous Français? Pas de problèm mes amis.*

HOWARD JOHNSON INN

Map pp238-9 Hotel $$

☎ 416-964-1220, 877-967-5845; www.hojo.com; 89 Avenue Rd; d from $120; P $15; 🖳 🚡 ⊖ Bay

To say HoJos is nothing flash could be the understatement of the decade, but it's the cheapest accommodation you'll find in ritzy Yorkville. Rates for standard-issue rooms, with down-to-earth wood and brick decor, include continental breakfast. Kids stay free!

HOLIDAY INN TORONTO MIDTOWN

Map pp238-9 Hotel $$

☎ 416-968-0010; www.holiday-inn.com/toronto midtown; 280 Bloor St W; d from $150; P $15; 🖳 ⊖ St George

The familiar green banners outside this high-rise, brown brick monolith do little to improve the look of the place, but inside the rooms are better than your average chain hotel. The location is also prime, near U of T and the big T.O. museums.

SUTTON PLACE HOTEL

Map pp238-9 Luxury Hotel $$$

☎ 416-924-9221, 866-378-8866; www.suttonplace .com; 955 Bay St; d/ste from $160/280; P $25-33; 🖳 🖭 🚳 🚡 ⊖ Wellesley

Toronto International Film Festival starlets dash in and out of this luxurious hotel with over-the-top European-stylings. It's as ugly as sin from the outside, but inside are carefully placed antiques, tapestries, gilded mirrors and chandeliers. Classical music wafts through the corridors; service is outstanding.

INTERCONTINENTAL TORONTO YORKVILLE Map pp238-9 Luxury Hotel $$$

☎ 416-960-5200, 800-267-0010; www.toronto.inter continental.com; 220 Bloor St W; d from $225; P $30; 🖳 🖭 🚳 🚡 ⊖ St George

Opposite the Royal Conservatory of Music is the seductive InterContinental. Nothing is lacking here, personalized attention from the multilingual staff complimenting round-the-clock business services, high-speed wi-fi internet, an indoor pool and sauna.

PARK HYATT Map pp238-9 Luxury Hotel $$$

☎ 416-925-1234, 800-233-1234; www.parkhyatt toronto.com; 4 Avenue Rd; d from $250; P $32; 🖳 🚳 🚡 ⊖ Museum

Ooh-la-la! The sophisticated Park Hyatt has an impressive circular drive with fountains and a rooftop skyline lounge. Add the award-winning Stillwater (p146) spa into the mix and you've made an already excellent hotel even better. Some rooms have king beds, marble bathrooms and calming colors. Check the website for weekend packages.

WINDSOR ARMS

Map pp238-9 Historic Hotel $$$

☎ 416-971-9666; www.windsorarmshotel.com; 18 St Thomas St; ste from $300; P $25; 🖳 ⊖ Bay

The Windsor Arms is an exquisite piece of Toronto history, no matter whether you're staying the night or just dropping in for afternoon tea (p95). It's a 1927 neo-gothic mansion boasting a grand entryway, stained-glass windows, polished service and its own coat-of-arms. The muted, distinguished atmosphere makes you want to whisper.

UNIVERSITY OF TORONTO & THE ANNEX

The quiet residential streets around The Annex offer some of the best-value (and best quality) B&Bs in Toronto. During summer the U of T campus offers student housing to tourists.

U OF T STUDENT HOUSING SERVICE

Map pp238-9 University Housing/Extended Stay $

☎ 416-978-8045; www.housing.utoronto.ca; 214 College St; s & d without bathroom from $45, per month from $350; 🚋 506

This university service rents rooms by the day, week or month from early May through to late August. Of the many student dormitories, the Innis Residence (Map pp238-9; ☎ 416-978-2512; www.utoronto.ca/innis/residence; 11 St George St; P $6; ⊖ St George) is handily placed. Rates sometimes include breakfast and maid service.

VICTORIA UNIVERSITY

Map pp238-9   University Housing/Extended Stay $

☎ 416-585-4522; www.vicu.utoronto.ca; 140 Charles St W; s/tw without bathroom $50/71; ⊖ Museum

Set in beautiful grounds, Victoria University opens its doors from early May until late August. Full complimentary breakfast is served in the old-world dining hall; local phone calls are free. One night's advance deposit required. Ask about monthly deals and reduced rates for students and seniors.

CAMPUS CO-OPERATIVE RESIDENCE INC

Map pp238-9   University Housing/Extended Stay $

CCRI; ☎ 416-979-2161; www.campus-coop.org; 395 Huron St; s & d per month $380-600, plus membership fee $25; ⊖ Spadina

Campus Co-operative Residence Inc (CCRI), an independent housing cooperative, owns dozens of semidetached Victorian houses, ranging from bookish brownstones to frat-slob animal houses. Rates for furnished single rooms (there are only a few doubles available) vary depending on room size, but all have shared kitchen and bathroom facilities. There's a one-month minimum stay and if you need parking, get a reserved spot in writing. Pets are allowed.

GLOBAL GUESTHOUSE

Map pp242-3   Guesthouse $

☎ 416-923-4004; singer@inforamp.net; 9 Spadina Rd; s without/with bathroom $58/68, d $68/78; ⊖ Spadina

Mildly chaotic, well-worn and lovable, this old-fashioned redbrick Victorian with beautiful carved gables sits just north of Bloor St, pretty much on top of Spadina subway station. There's a shared kitchen and spacious rooms featuring cable TV, hippie wall hangings, woody floors and murals. It fills up quickly, so book well in advance. Good security; free local calls.

HAVINN Map p231   Guesthouse $

☎ 416-922-5220, 888-922-5220; www.havinn.com; 118 Spadina Rd; s/d without bathroom $54/69; ℗ free; ▯ ⊖ Dupont

Havinn is something of a haven on busy Spadina Rd, with six tidy rooms and immaculate

shared bathrooms revolving around a communal kitchen. Breakfast includes croissants, bagels, yogurt, fruit and fresh muffins. The vibe is low-key and cheery – hard to beat!

CASTLEGATE INN

Map p231   B&B/Extended Stay $$

☎ 416-323-1657; www.castlegateinn.com; 219 Spadina Rd; s & d $60-100, weekly rates from $315; ℗ free; ▯ ♿ ⊖ Dupont

One of the best budget-to-midrange bargains in Toronto, this casual B&B is owned by avid travelers who also know how to run a business. Their three houses (37 rooms) are all within striking distance of U of T and Yorkville. Continental breakfast included.

ANNEX GUEST HOUSE

Map pp242-3   Guesthouse $$

☎ 416-922-1934; www.annexguesthouse.com; 83 Spadina Rd; d from $90; ℗ free; ▯ ⊖ Spadina

Engaging the principles of 'vastu,' an Indian architectural science promoting tranquility through natural materials and asymmetrical layouts (similar to feng shui), this place opened in 2004 and has some gorgeous rooms. Wooden floors, handmade bedspreads and crafted copper bowls highlight the spaces, which are amazingly peaceful given busy Spadina Rd is right outside.

CASA LOMA INN

Map pp242-3   Guesthouse $$

☎ 416-924-4540; www.casalomainn.com; 21 Walmer Rd; s/d from $85/95; ℗ $10-15; ▯ ⊖ Spadina

When it's all lit up at night, this breathtaking turn-of-the-20th-century inn seems like a pint-sized version of its namesake (p68). Each of 26 nonsmoking rooms has a TV, fridge, microwave, air-conditioning and immaculate bathroom. No breakfast, but Bloor St is three minutes' walk away.

MADISON MANOR Map pp242-3   B&B $$

☎ 416-922-5579, 877-561-7048; www.madisona venuepub.com; 20 Madison Ave; d $100-180; ℗ $10-15; ⊖ Spadina

Guests at this boutique B&B with natty white woodwork enjoy daytime billiard parlor privileges at the nearby Madison Avenue (p120). All rooms have a bathroom, air-con and internet access; a few have fireplaces or balconies, too. Continental breakfast included; kids excluded.

FEATHERS B&B Map p231   B&B $$

☎ 416-534-1923; www.bbcanada.com/1115
.html; 132 Wells St, off Bathurst St; s without
bathroom from $75, d with/without bathroom
from $105/95, studio apt per week $665; P free;
🚇 511

Lilting classical music sets the scene at this
snug, artistic B&B, full of spooky antique
Japanese dolls and dusty Indonesian puppets doing their best to stop themselves
writhing into motion. Healthy breakfasts
include locally baked bread, yogurt, fruit
salad, tea and coffee (not included in studio
apartment rates).

FRENCH CONNECTION Map p231   B&B $$

☎ 416-537-7741, 800-313-3993; www.thefrench
connection.com; 102 Burnside Dr, off Bathurst St;
s/d from $110/140; P free; 🖥 ⊙ St Clair West
French Connection's stand-out features
include an open fireplace, grand piano and
gourmet French-inspired breakfasts. Elegant,
cottage-inspired suites have king-sized beds,
one with a private terrace and whirlpool tub.
Simpler single and double rooms, without
bathrooms, have extra-long natural-fiber
beds for long nights of Gallic dreaming.

COACH HOUSE

Map p231   Guesthouse/Extended Stay $$
☎ 416-899-0306; www.thecoachhouse.ca; 117
Walmer Rd; ste $150-175, weekly rates $850-950;
P free; 🖥 ⊙ Spadina
Smug in its ivy-clad affluence, this 1902
house offers a one-bedroom coach house
with a loft bedroom decorated in French
country style, or an apartment-style suite
with kitchenette. Both accommodations
have cable TV/DVD, air-conditioning and
high-speed internet access. Breakfast provi-
sions are provided in a cute welcome basket.

TOP FIVE SLEEPS WEST OF YONGE STREET

- Best luxury hotel – **SoHo Metropolitan Hotel** (p169)
- Best backpackers – **Canadiana Backpackers Inn** (p168)
- Best historic hotel – **Windsor Arms** (p172)
- Best B&B – **French Connection** (above)
- Best midrange penny-pincher – **Castlegate Inn** (p173)

TERRACE HOUSE BED & BREAKFAST

Map p231   B&B $$
☎ 416-535-1493; www.bbinfocanada.com/terrace
house; 52 Austin Tce; d $150-225; P free; ⊙ St
Clair West

Travelers recommend this historic 1913
home a short walk west of Casa Loma,
which boasts North African rugs, cast-iron
bed-heads, a library and full, hot gourmet
breakfasts (quiche and strawberry-and-
ricotta pancakes!). Some rooms come
without a bathroom. Austin Tce runs east
of Bathurst St.

KENSINGTON MARKET & LITTLE ITALY

Little Italy's side streets contain some classy
B&Bs. There are a few basic hostels around
Kensington Market, but they're mainly for
down-on-their-luck strugglers rather than
travelers.

LAKEVIEW VICTORIAN

Map pp240-1   Apartment/Extended Stay $$
☎ 416-821-6316; 42 Lakeview Ave; www.lakeview
victorianbb.com; d 3-nights/week/month from
$375/750/2400; P free; 🖥 🚇 505, 506
Tall, pale and vaguely gothic-looking (a bit
like Richard E Grant), this 1880s Victorian
home just west of Little Italy contains a
snug, one-bed apartment with full kitchen,
bathroom and sunroom. There may have
been a lake view from here sometime dur-
ing the last Ice Age, but it seems to have
receded.

PALMERSTON INN BED & BREAKFAST

Map pp242-3   B&B $$
☎ 416-920-7842; www.palmerstoninn.com; 322
Palmerston Blvd; s/d from $100/130; P free;
🖥 🚇 506
This classy 1906 Georgian mansion has an
outdoor deck, library and a mile-a-minute
hostess. All rooms have wi-fi internet access, fluffy bathrobes, slippers and fresh
flowers. The single rooms are especially
appealing, with accents like stained glass,
skylights and antique beds. Cheaper
rooms have shared bathrooms; full hot
breakfast and afternoon sherry round-out
the deal.

POSH DIGS

Map pp242-3   Self-contained Apartments $$
☎ 416-964-6390; www.poshdigs.ca; 414 Markham
St; apt $140-155; **P** free; 🖳 🚇 506
Comfortably ensconced in their new
location around the corner from the old
one, Posh Digs continues to offer spiffy,
air-conditioned accommodations in its
pied-de-terre apartment (sleeps two)
and excellent attic loft (sleeps four). The
friendly Scots who run the joint can be
coerced into giving you winter discounts.
No kids under 10.

QUEEN WEST & WEST QUEEN WEST

There are a handful of good options way
out west.

GLOBAL VILLAGE BACKPACKERS

Map pp234-5   Hostel $
☎ 416-703-8540, 888-844-7875; www.globalback
packers.com; 460 King St W; dm $27-29, d from
$73; 🖳 🚇 504, 511
This kaleidoscopically colored independent
hostel was once the Spadina Hotel, where
Jack Nicholson, the Rolling Stones and
Leonard Cohen dreamed dreams of fame
and glory. The vibe is relaxed but not lax,
with good security and helpful staff. There's
a party-centric bar, outdoor patio and
regular Niagara trips, too.

BEACONSFIELD Map p231   B&B $$
☎ 416-535-3338; www.bbcanada.com/771.html;
38 Beaconsfield Ave, east of Dufferin St; d without bathroom $95, 1-/2-bedroom ste $150/170;
P free; 🧑‍🦽 🚇 501
Good-time Beaconsfield is a Victorian boutique B&B owned by an artist-actor couple
who have filled the house with murals and
distractions. Eclectic suites have a bathroom and either one or two bedrooms.
Full breakfasts are served at tables of toys
(Rubik's Cubes, Russian dolls) for kids big
and small.

DRAKE HOTEL Map p231   Boutique Hotel $$$
☎ 416-531-5042; www.thedrakehotel.ca; 1150
Queen St W; d $179-289; 🖳 🚇 501
Revamped to the tune of a cool $5 million,
this century-old hotel beckons to bohe-

mians, artists and indie musicians (with a
little cash). Artful rooms come with vintage
furnishings, throw rugs, flat-screen TVs and
wi-fi internet access. There's a café, restaurant, **bar** (p121) and live music room onsite
to keep you entertained.

EAST TORONTO

Many of Toronto's best B&Bs inhabit architectural gems around East Toronto. In
historic Cabbagetown, most places are gay-
friendly.

NEILL-WYCIK COLLEGE HOTEL

Map pp232-3   University Housing/Extended Stay $
☎ 416-977-2320; www.neill-wycik.com; 96 Gerrard St E; s/d/tr/f $45/65/70/85; **P** $10; 🚇 College
Pronounced 'Wizz-ick', this budget trav-
eler's favorite operates from early May to
late August. Private bedrooms with tele-
phones are inside apartment-style suites
that share a kitchen/lounge and bathroom. There are laundry facilities, lockers,
TV lounges, a student-run cafeteria for
breakfast and incredible views from the
rooftop sundeck. No air-con = hot August
nights.

ALLENBY Map p231   B&B $
☎ 416-461-7095; www.theallenby.com; 351
Wolverleigh Blvd; s/d without bathroom from
$50/65; **P** free; 🖳 🚇 Woodbine
In the suburban eastern verges of Greektown is spotless Allenby, possibly the
cheapest B&B in Toronto! There are two
bedrooms (perfect for two couples traveling together), sharing a bathroom, a local
telephone (free) and satellite TV. Rates
include continental breakfast; ask about
off-season discounts.

1871 HISTORIC HOUSE B&B

Map pp244-5   B&B $$
☎ 416-923-6950; www.1871bnb.com; 65 Huntley
St; s/d without bathroom from $70/80; **P** free;
🖳 🚇 Sherbourne
What other property can claim both
Buffalo Bill Cody and John Lennon as
one-time guests? In this historic Victorian
home, which displays its art and antiques
in sunny common areas, all rooms share
bathroom facilities, but the coach house
suite has its own Jacuzzi. Hot breakfast
included.

AINSLEY HOUSE Map pp244-5   B&B $$
☎ 416-972-0533, 888-423-3337; www.ainsley house.com; 19 Elm Ave; d without/with bathroom from $70/80; Ⓟ free; Ⓢ Sherbourne
Great value for ritzy Rosedale, these colorful rooms occupy part of a restored ivy-covered mansion on peaceful, leafy Elm St (about as far from a nightmare as you can get). Cooked breakfast includes homemade muffins.

HOMEWOOD INN Map pp244-5   B&B $$
☎ 416-920-7944; www.homewoodinn.com; 65 Homewood Ave; s/d without bathroom from $65/75, with bathroom from $95/115; Ⓟ free; 506
If you can endure some erratic interior design decisions, this place is great value, and genuinely sociable. Guests chat and giggle over breakfast in the tiled dining room. All rooms have a TV and a small fridge; the best rooms are upstairs in the attic.

AMSTERDAM Map pp244-5   Guesthouse $$
☎ 416-921-9797; www.amsterdamguesthouse.com; 209 Carlton St; s/d without bathroom from $65/85; 506
Spangled with UK, US, Canadian and Dutch flags above a grand front porch, Amsterdam is a polished Victorian house that's far from stuffy, with bird's-eye downtown views from the back balcony. The occasional shirtless stoner wanders through the lobby, trying to recall which of the simple, clean and comfy rooms (with air-con and cable TV) is theirs.

BANTING HOUSE INN
Map pp244-5   B&B $$
☎ 416-924-1458, 800-832-8856; www.banting house.com; 73 Homewood Ave; d $85-110; Ⓟ free; 506
Maple syrup breakfast smells accompany an old-time jazz soundtrack at Banting House, a substantial redbrick B&B not far from Church St. Rooms are decked-out in a rich palette of reds and blonde woods, and there's a lovely courtyard at the back with an enormous oak tree. It's pet-friendly, too. Cheaper rooms have shared bathrooms.

CLARION HOTEL & SUITES
Map pp244-5   Historic Hotel $$
☎ 416-921-3142, 800-387-4788; www.choice hotels.ca/cn534; 592 Sherbourne St; d/ste from $85/200; Ⓟ $13; Ⓢ Sherbourne

During the 1920s Ernest Hemingway stayed in this Victorian mansion while he worked as a reporter for the *Toronto Star*. The modern extension out the back is far from spectacular, but contains some family-sized suites.

COMFORT SUITES CITY CENTRE
Map pp244-5   Hotel $$
☎ 416-362-7700, 877-316-9951; www.comfort sutiestoronto.com; 200 Dundas St E; d/ste from $90/100; Ⓟ $16-19; 505
Friendly staff, great facilities and 'Romance Suites' with cherry-red, heart-shaped Jacuzzis go some way towards taking your mind off the dodgy location. The streets east of here are worth avoiding at any time of day, but that won't bother you if you're holed up here with your husband's best friend/boss' wife for the weekend.

TORONTO TOWNHOUSE B&B
Map pp244-5   B&B $$
☎ 416-323-8898, 877 500 0466; www.torontotown house.com; 213 Carlton St; d $100-170; 506
Quaint without being twee, the six rooms inside this typically noble row-house are beautifully restored, basking in the fact that they've survived the cull of Cabbagetown B&Bs that's happened over the past few years. Breakfast includes homemade cereal, baked goodies, hot pancakes and omelettes. Ask about long-term rates at their Riverdale property.

PIMBLETT'S DOWNTOWN
TORONTO B&B Map pp244-5   B&B $$
☎ 416-921-6898; www.pimblett.ca; 242 Gerrard St E; s/d from $85/105; 506
Run by a quirky English gent/John Cleese wannabe who used to work at London's

---

TOP FIVE SLEEPS EAST OF YONGE STREET
- Best historic hotel – **Clarion Hotel & Suites** (left)
- Best boutique hotel – **Cosmopolitan** (p168)
- Best French-speaking B&B – **Au Petit Paris** (opposite)
- Best quirky B&B – **Pimblett's Downtown Toronto B&B** (above)
- Best penny-pincher – **Neill-Wycik College Hotel** (p175)

Mayfair Hotel, Pimblett Downtown's 10 rooms have names such as the Prince Charles Bedroom and Queen Elizabeth's Bedroom, enabling you to 'sleep with the entire Royal Family.' Expect lashings of Monty Python-esque humor to be served up with the wonderful full English breakfasts.

MULBERRY TREE Map pp244-5   B&B $$
☎ 416-960-5249; www.bbtoronto.com/mulberry tree; 122 Isabella St; s/d with bathroom from $95/120; Ⓟ $5; Ⓢ Sherbourne
Mulberry Tree's colorful rooms bloom with warm berry tones, patchwork quilts, artworks, antiques and woody furnishings. Host Paul cooks up a hot breakfast every morning, starring perhaps a quiche, omelettes or crepes with organic tea and coffee. French and German echo through the halls.

ourpick AU PETIT PARIS
Map pp244-5   B&B $$
☎ 416-928-1348; www.bbtoronto.com/aupetit paris; 3 Selby St; s/d from $100/130; Ⓢ Sherbourne
Hardwood floors mix with modern decor inside this exquisite 'bay-and-gable' Victorian home. The pick of the four en suite rooms are the Nomad's Suite, with a skylight and travel photographs on the walls, and the Artist's Suite, with garden views and an extra-large bathtub. The roof patio is a winner.

THE BEACHES

There aren't many places to stay around The Beaches – the locals don't want their 'hood turning into a resort!

ACCOMMODATING THE SOUL
Map p246   B&B $$
☎ 416-686-0619; www.bbcanada.com/atsoul; 114 Waverley Rd; d $120-145; Ⓟ free; 🚋 501
An early 20th-century home boasting antiques and fabulous gardens, these soulful accommodations will delight travelers searching for some tranquility. One room has an en suite, the other two share a bathroom. Full, hot breakfasts are served regardless of which room you're in! Best of all it is just a short stroll from the lakefront.

TORONTO ISLANDS
Perhaps it's a good thing, but you'll only find a handful of places to stay on the Islands; these two are the pick of the bunch.

SMILEY'S B&B Map p247   B&B $
☎ 416-203-8599; www.erelda.ca; Algonquin Island, 4 Dacotah Ave; s or d without bathroom $70, studio apt per night/week $160/800; 🖳 🚶 Ward's Island
Spend the night in 'Belvedere' – a sunny B&B room with shared bathroom and dining with the hosts – or the studio apartment with its own kitchen and bathroom.

BARB'S ISLAND LOFT
Map p247   Self-contained Apartment $$
☎ 416-203-0866; Ward's Island, 9 3rd St; apt $125, per week $600; 🚶 Ward's Island
Shop for groceries before you jump on the ferry then disappear here for a week, cooking your own meals, reading, going for long walks and generally chilling out – ain't life grand? The apartment sleeps three. Try Barb's rhubarb jam and eggplant chutney!

GREATER TORONTO AREA (GTA)
If you don't mind spending a little while on public transport, it's worth seeking out some travelers' favorites in the GTA, particularly around High Park.

CANDY HAVEN TOURIST HOME
Map p231   Guesthouse $
☎ 416-532-0651; 1233 King St W, west of Dufferin St; s & d without bathroom $50; 🚋 504
Woah, what a classic! Run by a charmingly derelict old couple, this rickety, one-of-a-kind guesthouse has been around for decades, so it's truly old-fashioned. The five basic rooms share a bathroom and there's no breakfast, but at these 1970s prices, you won't hear anyone complaining.

GRAYONA TOURIST HOME
Map p231   Guesthouse $$
☎ 416-535-5443; 1546 King St W, east of Roncesvalles Ave; s/d without bathroom from $60/80, f from $110; Ⓟ free; 🚋 504
Grayona has been here for years, but a recent paint job has kept it looking fresh.

AIRPORT ALTERNATIVES

With 24-hour **Airport Express** (p211) bus services to downtown, most travelers won't need to stay near the airport. But if you get caught in blizzard, here are a few quality options with free shuttles to and from the airport:

Delta Toronto Airport West (Map p230; ☎ 905-624-1144, 800-737-3211; www.deltahotels.com; 5444 Dixie Rd; d from $130; P $8; 🖳 🖳 🏊) Spacious rooms, fitness centre and heated indoor pool. Kids under 18 stay free.

Sheraton Gateway (Map p230; ☎ 905-672-7000, 866-716-8101; www.sheraton.com; d Mon-Fri from $250, Sat & Sun from $160; P often free; 🖳 🖳 🏊) Attached to Pearson International Airport's Terminal 3, the Sheraton offers free newspapers, 24-hour gym and indoor pool. Rooms are soundproof.

Wyndham Bristol Place (Map p230; ☎ 416-675-9444, 877-999-3223; www.wyndham.com; 950 Dixon Rd; d Mon-Fri from $200, Sat & Sun from $105; P $14; 🖳 🏊 🖳) The posh Wyndham has spacey rooms with Gordon Gecko-style business chairs. Kids stay free.

The affable Australian owner will show you to your room (your choice of six), with various bathroom and bed configurations to suit you or your brood. Front rooms have lake views over the Gardiner Expwy; $5 surcharge for single-night stays.

INVERNESS Map p230   B&B $$
☎ 416-769-2028; www.bbcanada.com/2918.html; 287 Humberside Ave, off High Park Ave, north of Bloor St W; d $80-95; P free; 🚇 High Park
Possessing a more rural than urban atmosphere, this warm, woody 1920s Arts-and-Crafts styled home is rich on the eyes, filled with antiques, Persian rugs and hardwood furnishings. Some rooms have bathrooms; some don't. Organic breakfasts and a sunny side patio are bonuses.

VANDERKOOY BED & BREAKFAST
Map p231   B&B $$
☎ 416-925-8765; www.bbcanada.com/1107.html; 53 Walker Ave, west of Yonge St; s/d from $65/90; P free; 🚇 Summerhill
Artwork and stained glass dapple the surfaces of this well-located, Tudor-style house just off Yonge St in Rosedale, which has a communal fireplace area beyond the curlicued entry. The two rooms are bright and cheery; one shares a bathroom with

the rest of the house. Breakfast is served overlooking the garden.

BONNEVUE MANOR Map p231   B&B $$
☎ 416-536-1455; www.bonnevuemanor.com; 33 Beaty Ave, west of Jameson Ave; d $100-170; P free; 🚍 🚍 501, 504, 508
Often voted one of the city's best B&Bs, this gay-owned B&B is inside a restored 1890s redbrick mansion with divine handcrafted architectural details. Six guest rooms exhibit warm-colored interiors, and all have bathrooms. Enjoy your cooked breakfast out on the grapevine-covered deck.

TOADHALL BED & BREAKFAST
Map p230   B&B $$
☎ 905-773-4028; www.225toadhall.ca; Richmond Hill, 225 Lakeland Cres; s/d/tr $95/125/175; P free; 🚍
It's worth trekking north of downtown Toronto to stay in this solar-powered home on picturesque Lake Wilcox, with swimming, canoeing and windsurfing right outside the door. There's no air-conditioning, but you can count on cool lake breezes. Salubrious gourmet breakfasts emphasize organic fare (vegetarian options by request). Check the website for driving directions.

Excursions

Excursions

'Yours to Discover' is one of Ontario's slogans, and while Toronto is best known for its metropolitan delights, the surrounding areas are a playground of distractions to suit all tastes. Despite the funhouse feel and overpriced amusements, Niagara Falls is still well worth a visit, and sprinkled with some hidden gems worth every penny. Niagara's wine region takes lovers of the grape on a breathtaking and often decadent tour of colors and tastes, while ski bunnies and snowboarders can get their fix at the peak of Blue Mountain. Quaint, historical villages dot the countryside, each with their fair share of art galleries, theatre and dining ranging from haute cuisine to mom's home cooking. Peak summer season runs from Victoria Day in late May to Labour Day in early September. Opening hours are reduced off-season.

WINING, DINING & WATERFALLS

For the ultimate southern Ontario experience, start the day early and head straight out to the wine country (p186), stopping off along the way to sample the region's famed ice wines (p190) and unusual vintages. Have lunch at one of the vineyards, then get back on the road and make your way to Niagara Falls. Park your car and explore the attractions on foot – the Maid of the Mist (below) is a must, and there are hundreds of distractions, from posh to kitsch. If you can spend the night, escape the crowds in one of the charming B&Bs or splash out on a high-rise room with a view of the falls, and then do more wine-touring the following day.

THE GREAT OUTDOORS

Green is good for the soul, and getting out of town is a huge draw for visitors to the big city. Biking along the Niagara Parkway (below) or through the leafy wine country (p186), hiking through the Avon River or the Shakespearean Gardens in Stratford (p190) or whooshing down the slopes at the Horseshoe Resort and Blue Mountain (p194) are great ways to commute for less than two hours to commune with nature.

ART & THEATRE

The Stratford Festival (p191) and Niagara-on-the-Lake's Shaw Festival (p193) put Ontario on the world's theatre map. Both events continue to gain in stature every year, so although same-day rush tickets are sold, advance planning and accommodation booking are highly recommended. Stratford (p190) boasts numerous art galleries, and the McMichael Canadian Art Collection (p189) in Kleinburg should not be missed.

NIAGARA FALLS

The word Niagara means 'thunder of waters,' and no amount of postcards or brochure photos can prepare you for the sensory experience of looking out onto the torrents of water that spray out over this legendary tourist destination. Known as a honeymoon capital, (the falls are said to emit an ionic force that serves as a natural aphrodisiac), the falls, and their burgeoning theme-park-like attractions, pull in between 12 and 14 million visitors annually – from many different walks of life.

The Christmas tree effect of the rainbow of lights that change color, and fireworks on the weekends, illuminate the Niagara experience in the summer, but even in the winter – when some of the falling water freezes solid and ice juts out over the flow – the majesty of the falls draw an impressive crowd. From the end of November until mid-January, the annual Winter Festival of Lights features concerts, fireworks and nighttime parades.

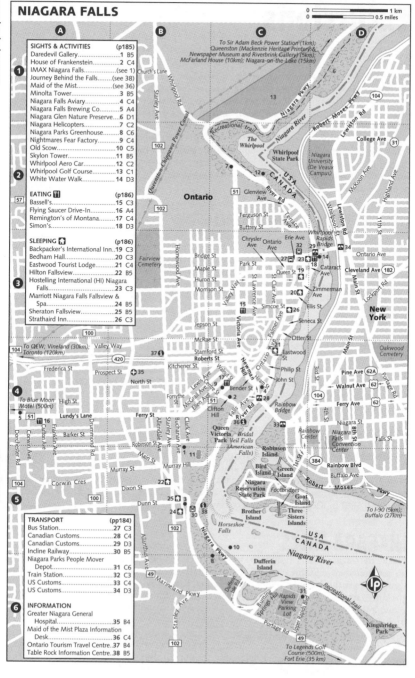

NIAGARA FALLS

0 — 1 km
0 — 0.5 miles

SIGHTS & ACTIVITIES (p185)
Daredevil Gallery..........................1 B5
House of Frankenstein.................2 C4
IMAX Niagara Falls...............(see 1)
Journey Behind the Falls.......(see 38)
Maid of the Mist....................(see 36)
Minolta Tower.............................3 B5
Niagara Falls Aviary.....................4 C4
Niagara Falls Brewing Co............5 A4
Niagara Glen Nature Preserve.....6 D1
Niagara Helicopters.....................7 C2
Niagara Parks Greenhouse...........8 C6
Nightmares Fear Factory..............9 C4
Old Scow..................................10 C5
Skylon Tower.............................11 B5
Whirlpool Aero Car....................12 C2
Whirlpool Golf Course................13 C1
White Water Walk.....................14 D3

EATING 🍴 (p186)
Bassell's....................................15 C3
Flying Saucer Drive-In...............16 A4
Remington's of Montana...........17 C4
Simon's....................................18 D3

SLEEPING 🛏 (p186)
Backpacker's International Inn...19 C3
Bedham Hall..............................20 C3
Eastwood Tourist Lodge............21 C4
Hilton Fallsview........................22 B5
Hostelling International (HI) Niagara
  Falls......................................23 C3
Marriott Niagara Falls Fallsview &
  Spa.......................................24 B5
Sheraton Fallsview....................25 B5
Strathaird Inn...........................26 C3

TRANSPORT (pp184)
Bus Station...............................27 C3
Canadian Customs.....................28 C4
Canadian Customs.....................29 D3
Incline Railway..........................30 B5
Niagara Parks People Mover
  Depot....................................31 C6
Train Station.............................32 C3
US Customs...............................33 C4
US Customs...............................34 D3

INFORMATION
Greater Niagara General
  Hospital..................................35 B4
Maid of the Mist Plaza Information
  Desk......................................36 C4
Ontario Tourism Travel Centre...37 B4
Table Rock Information Centre...38 B5

To Sir Adam Beck Power Station (1km);
Queenston (Mackenzie Heritage Printery &
Newspaper Museum and Riverbrink Gallery) (5km);
McFarland House (10km); Niagara-on-the-Lake (15km)

Church's Lane
Stanley Ave
Whirlpool Rd
Queenston-Chippawa Power Canal
Recreational Trail
Niagara Pkwy
Niagara River
Robert Moses Pkwy
Lewiston Rd
104
College Ave 31
The Whirlpool
Whirlpool State Park
Niagara University (De Veaux Campus)
Mckoon Ave
Highland Ave
USA / CANADA
102
Ontario
51 Glenview Ave
102
Ferguson St
Buttrey St
Whirlpool Rapids Bridge
34
Ontario Ave
Cleveland Ave 182
New York
Main St
Lockport Rd
Oakwood Cemetery
Pine Ave 62A
Walnut Ave 62
Ferry Ave 62
Niagara St
Rainbow Blvd 384
Buffalo Ave
To I-90 (5km); Buffalo (27km)
Robert Moses Pkwy
Recreational Trail
Kingsbridge Park

Fairview Cemetery
Homewood Ave
Bridge St
Maple St
Huron St
Morrison St
Valley Way
Jepson St
McRae St
Stamford St
Roberts St
Kitchener St
North St
Forsythe St
Clifton Hill
Queen Victoria Park
Bird Island
Green Island
Niagara Reservation State Park
Horseshoe Falls
Dufferin Island
Niagara River

Frederica St
Prospect St
420
Valley Way
To QEW; Vineland (30km);
Toronto (120km)
104
100
37
35
Lewis Ave
Walnut Ave
McGrail Ave
Ellen Ave
51
Bender St
2
28
Buchanan Ave
Ontario Ave
Clark Ave
Allendale Ave
Stanley Ave
Robinson St
Main St
Murray St
Murray Hill
Dixon St
Dunn St
102
Marineland Pkwy
Stanley Ave
49
100

To Blue Moon Motel (500m)
High St
5 51 16
Lundy's Lane
Corwin Ave
Carlton Ave
Franklin Ave
Drummond Rd
Barker St
Ferry St
Robinson St
Corwin Cres
104
Dorchester Rd
Dunn St

Glenview Ave
Chrysler Ave
Ontario Ave
Erie Ave
32
29
27 23 14
18
Queen St 19
Cataract Ave
20
Zimmerman Ave
Ellis St
26
Seneca St
Otter St
Eastwood St
Philip St
John St
3rd St
Rainbow Bridge
4th St
33
Rainbow Center
Niagara Falls Convention Center

Robinson Island
American Falls
Bridal Veil Falls
Footbridges
Goat Island
Three Sisters Islands
Brother Island
USA / CANADA
10
8
Burning Springs Hill
Rapids View Parking Lot
31
Portage Rd
49
To Legends Golf Course (500m);
Fort Erie (35km)

To Legends Golf Course (500m); Fort Erie (35km)

182

There are actually two parts to the town of Niagara Falls. 'Old downtown' is where the locals go about their daily lives. It's quiet, but a good place to find a decent B&B or hostel. Enterprising visitors will find a few well-kept secrets worth checking out, and the train and bus stations are in this area – around Bridge St, near the corner of Erie Ave. About 3km south, along River Rd (the **Niagara Parkway**), is the sideshow of overpriced attractions and touristy kitsch that surrounds the falls themselves.

The **American** and **Bridal Veil Falls**, which are on the American side, are overpowered by the grand **Horseshoe Falls** on the Canadian side, which tumble down through clouds of mist into the appropriately named Maid of the Mist pool. First launched in 1846, a **Maid of the Mist** boat tour, which is the longest-running tourist attraction in North America, is one great way to be a part of the action – Marilyn Munroe did it when shooting the 1953 film *Niagara*. Another is to don a plastic poncho and venture through tunnels cut in the rock 100 feet down the side of the cliff, on the **Journey Behind the Falls walk**, which runs year round and affords the full spray experience, after a wait in line. About half a kilometer south of the Horseshoe Falls, you'll see the **Old Scow**, a steel barge which lodged itself on the rocks in 1918 and hasn't budged since. Across the parkway, the **Niagara Parks Greenhouse** allows visitors free year-round admission to floral displays that are home to tropical birds.

Up the incline railway is Clifton Hill, Niagara Falls' famed strip of amusement-park delights, and the street is worth a walk if for no other reason than to be bombarded by the flashing and dinging sights and sounds. Give all mazes and wax museums a miss, but the **House of Frankenstein** is a great stop for some not-so-cheap thrills, as is the **Nightmares Fear Factory**. The **Minolta** and **Skylon Towers** offer observation decks to take in the falls from on high, while the **IMAX theatre** takes viewers on a virtual journey through the history and mythology surrounding the falls.

Up at the town's north end, near the Whirlpool Rapids Bridge, the **Whirlpool Aero Car** takes visitors over the turbulent rapids, or you can take the **White Water Walk** for an equally vertigo-inducing experience. For a taste of what the area once was, the **Niagara Glen Nature Preserve** offers 4km of immense boulders, a mammoth pothole, the leaning rock and the Devil's arch, ending in a gorge. The waterfalls were actually situated here thousands of years ago, and the Niagara Parks Commission offers daily guided nature walks in the summer. Make sure to bring your own water.

You can watch dozens of breeds flutter over exotic flora at the **Butterfly Conservatory**, and explore more species native to Ontario outdoors at the Butterfly Garden. Next door, the **Botanical Gardens & School of Horticulture** provides 100 acres of every variety of garden. Further north, past the **Sir Adam Beck Power Station** and the ghastly floral clock (a 40-foot timepiece on a bed of flowers which changes twice a season), is **Queenston Heights**, the location of a British victory during the war of 1812 when the USA attempted to establish a foothold on the Canadian side. On the site, also known as 'the birthplace of Canada,' a **monument dedicated to Major General Sir Isaac Brock** proudly gives visitors a 50m climb to an impressive view. **Queenston** itself is home to the historic **Mackenzie Heritage Printery & Newspaper Museum**, former residence of Sir William Lyon MacKenzie and birthplace of his politically rebellious newspaper, the *Colonial Advocate*. Nearby is the **Laura Secord Homestead**, where, during the war of 1812, one of Canada's best-known heroines started her 32km journey to warn the British soldiers of an impending attack by the Americans, even though she was an American citizen by birth. The home was reconstructed in 1971 but features authentic period furnishings.

A bit further north is the **McFarland House**, a historic 19th-century home which was used as a hospital by British and American soldiers.

Operating hours for individual attractions vary, so check ahead with the Niagara Parks Commission, which runs helpful but busy information desks at the **Table Rock Information Centre**, located next to the Horseshoe Falls, and at the **Maid of the Mist Plaza**.

TRANSPORTATION

Distance from Toronto Niagara Falls 125km.

Direction Southeast.

Travel time Two hours.

Car Follow the Queen Elizabeth Way (QEW) westbound from Toronto past St Catharines. Exit at Hwy 420 eastbound toward the Rainbow Bridge.

Parking There is limited metered parking around town, but plentiful pay parking lots (from $5 per 30 minutes, or $13 per day). The huge Rapids View parking lot is a little over 3km south of the falls off River Rd.

Bus station (☎ 905-357-2133; 4445 Erie Ave) This is in the old downtown area, away from the falls. Greyhound buses depart frequently for Toronto ($24, 1½ to two hours) and twice or three times daily for Buffalo, New York ($9, one to 1½ hours).

Niagara Airbus (☎ 905-374-8111, 800-268-8111; www.niagaraairbus.com) Offers airport transfers from Toronto's Pearson International Airport.

Niagara Parks People Mover (www.niagaraparks.com/planavisit/peoplemover.php; day pass adult/child $7.50/4.50; ☒ vary Apr-Oct) Rely on the Niagara Parks Commission's economical and efficient bus system. The depot is in the huge Rapids View parking lot. Day passes can be purchased at most stops. Shuttles follow a 15km path from the Rapids View parking lot north past the Horseshoe Falls, Rainbow and Whirlpool Bridges, Whirlpool Aero Car and during peak season, to Queenston village.

Niagara Transit (☎ 905-356-1179; www.niagaratransit.com; shuttle rides adult/child $3.50/1, all-day pass $6,10 tickets $22/19.50; ☒ mid-May–Nov, departures every 30min 9am-1:30am peak season) Niagara Transit provides a shuttle bus service around town. One route, the Red Line, goes around Clifton Hill and other falls attractions, then up Lundy's Lane to the motels and back. The Blue Line runs from the downtown bus and train stations to the falls area attractions, by Table Rock and down the Niagara Parkway to the Rapids View parking lot, then loops back around up Portage Rd and Stanley Ave. The Green Line goes from the Rainbow Bridge north to the Whirlpool Aero Car, then back down River Rd past the B&Bs to Clifton Hill. Out of season, Niagara Transit's regular city buses (adult/child $2.25/1) must be used.

Train VIA Rail runs daily trains from Toronto ($34, two hours), once in the morning and another in the late afternoon or early evening. Some Amtrak routes to/from the USA stop at Niagara Falls. The train station is opposite the bus station.

JoJo Tours (☎ 416-201-6465, 888-202-3513; http://pages.interlog.com/~jojotour/niagaraTours.html; day trips $48) Friendly JoJo Tours offers day trips to the region which include a stop at a winery and Niagara-on-the-Lake.

Moose Travel (☎ 888-816-6673; www.moosenetwork.com; tours $55) Moose Travel runs tours to the falls from Toronto between May and October.

Information

Accessible Niagara (www.accessibleniagara.com) This website provides advice for the mobility-impaired.

Discover Niagara (www.discoverniagara.com) This website offers travel deals and an events calendar.

Greater Niagara General Hospital (Map p182; ☎ 905-378-4647; 5546 Portage Rd) Has a 24-hour emergency room.

Info Niagara (www.infoniagara.com) This privately run website has helpful links.

Niagara Falls After Hours Walk-In Clinic (☎ 905-374-3344; 6453 Morrison St; ☒ 9am-9pm Mon-Fri, 9am-3pm Sat & Sun) For nonemergencies only.

Niagara Falls & Great Gorge Adventure Pass (adult/child $41/26) This pass provides discounts to the Maid of the Mist, Journey Behind the Falls, White Water Walk and the Butterfly Conservatory as well as all-day bus and incline railway travel.

Niagara Parks Commission (☎ 905-371-0254, 877-642-7275; www.niagaraparks.com; ☒ 9am-11pm summer, 9am-4pm rest of year) Runs information desks (open daily) at Maid of the Mist Plaza and Table Rock Information Centre.

Ontario Tourism Travel Centre (☎ 905-358-3221; 5355 Stanley Ave; ☒ 8:30am -5pm, later in summer) On the western outskirts of town. Check the free tourist booklets containing maps and discount coupons for attractions and rides.

Sights & Activities

Botanical Gardens (☎ 905-356-8554; 2565 Niagara Parkway; admission free; ☼ dawn-dusk)

Butterfly Conservatory (☎ 905-358-0025; 2405 Niagara Parkway; adult/child 6-12 $11/6.50; ☼ 9am-5:50pm, later in summer)

Daredevil Gallery (Map p182; ☎ 905-374-4629, 905-358-3611, 6170 Fallsview Blvd; admission free; ☼ 10am-4pm)

The House of Frankenstein (Map p182; ☎ 905-357-9660; 4967 Clifton Hill; adult/child/student $9.95/6.95/7.95; ☼ 10am-11pm Sun-Thu, 10am-1:30am Fri & Sat)

IMAX Niagara Falls (Map p182; ☎ 905-374-4629; www .imaxniagara.com; 6170 Fallsview Blvd; adult/senior/child $12/8.50/6.50)

Incline Railway (Map p182; rides $2; ☼ 9am-midnight Apr–mid-Oct) Weather permitting, it runs from near the Minolta tower down the hill to the Table Rock complex by the falls area, and offers a spectacular view.

Journey Behind the Falls (Map p182; ☎ 905-354-1551; 6650 Niagara Parkway; adult/child $11/6.50; ☼ 10am-5pm)

Laura Secord Homestead (☎ 905-262-4851; 29 Queenston St, Queenston; adult/child $4/3.50; ☼ 9:30am-3:30pm Mon-Fri, 11am-5pm May–mid-Oct)

Legends Golf Course (Map p182; ☎ 905-295-9595, 866-465-3642; www.niagaraparksgolf.com; 9561 Niagara Parkway; green fees $50-125 incl cart rental, golf club rental $15; ☼ Apr-Oct)

Mackenzie Heritage Printery & Newspaper Museum (Map p182; ☎ 905-262-5676; www.mackenzieprintery .ca; 1 Queenston St, Queenston; adult/child $6/free; ☼ hrs vary)

Maid of the Mist (Map p182; ☎ 905-358-5781; www .maidofthemist.com; Maid of the Mist Plaza, 5920 Niagara Parkway; adult/child $14/8.60; ☼ every 15min, weather permitting 9:45am-4:45pm Mon-Fri, 9:45am- 5:45pm Sat & Sun Apr-late Oct, 9:45am-7:15pm summer)

McFarland House (Map p182; ☎ 905-371-0919; 15927 Niagara Parkway; adult/child $4/3.50; ☼ 11am-4pm late May-late Jun, 11am-5pm late Jun-early Sep)

Minolta Tower (Map p182; ☎ 905-356-1501, 800-461-2492; www.niagaratower.com; 6732 Fallsview Blvd; adult/child $4.50/2.50; ☼ 7am-11pm)

Niagara Falls Aviary (Map p182; ☼ 905-356-8888, 866-994-0090; www.niagarafallsaviary.com; 5651 River Rd; adult/child/senior $15/10/14; ☼ 9am-9pm summer, 10am-5pm rest of year)

Niagara Falls Brewing Co (Map p182; ☎ 905-374-1166, 800-267-3392; 6863 Lundy's Lane; tours free, reservations required)

Niagara Helicopters (Map p182; ☎ 905-357-5672; www .niagarahelicopters.com; 3731 Victoria Ave; 10-minute flights adult/child $110/65; ☼ 9am-sunset, weather permitting; individual reservations noon-1pm in winter)

Nightmares Fear Factory (Map p182; ☎ 905-357-367-3327; www.nightmaresfearfactory.com; 5631 Victoria Ave; adult/child $13/9; ☼ 11am-2am)

Riverbrink Gallery (Map p182; ☎ 905-262-4510; www .riverbrink.org; 116 Queenston St, Queenston; adult/child/ senior $5/free/4; ☼ 9am-5pm)

Sir Adam Beck Power Station (Map p182; Niagara Parkway, at the Queenston-Lewiston Bridge; adult/child $8.50/5; ☼ 45min tours 11am-5pm Mon-Fri, 10am-5pm Sat & Sun late Mar-Nov) Free parking and shuttle from the floral clock.

Skylon Tower (Map p182; ☎ 905-356-2651; www.skylon .com; 5200 Robinson St; adult/senior/child $11/6.45/10; ☼ 8am-midnight summer, 11am-9pm rest of year) Its revolving restaurant is more expensive than the Minolta Tower's, but the early-bird dinner special saves you some cash ($35 minimum food charge per person, including elevator ride). Seatings at 4:30pm and 5pm; reservations required.

Whirlpool Aero Car (Map p182; ☎ 888-255-1321; 3850 Niagara Parkway; adult/child $11/6.50; ☼ 9am-5pm Apr-Oct)

White Water Walk (Map p182; 4330 Niagara Parkway; adult/child $8.50/5; ☼ 9am-5pm Apr-Oct)

DAREDEVILS

Surprisingly, more than a few people who have gone over Niagara Falls, suicides aside, have lived to tell about it.

The first successful leap was in 1901, by a schoolteacher named Annie Taylor, who did it in a skirt, no less. This promoted a rash of barrel stunters that continued into the 1920s, including Bobby Leach, who survived the flight but met his untimely death after slipping on an orange peel and developing complications due to gangrene!

In 1984 Karl Soucek revived the tradition with a bright red barrel at the Horseshoe Falls. He made it, but only to die just six months later in another barrel stunt at the Houston Astrodome.

A US citizen who tried to jet ski over the falls in 1995 might have made it – if his rocket-propelled parachute had opened. Another American, Kit Carson, became the first person in recorded history to survive a trip over the falls unaided during 2003. After being charged by the Canadian government with illegally performing a stunt, he joined the circus.

But there's no need to go to such extremes yourself when **IMAX Niagara Falls** (p182) allows everyone to try the plunge – virtually, that is.

Eating

Basell's (Map p182; ☎ 905-356-7501; 4880 Victoria Ave; meals $4-20; ✆ 6am-9pm) Go hungry to Basell's, where the rule of thumb is that grilled cheese is the only meal served at a normal size. Breakfast is served all day (but is 20% extra after 3pm).

Flying Saucer Drive-In (Map p182; ☎ 905-356-4553; 6768 Lundy's Lane; meals $4-16; ✆ 6am-3am Mon-Thu, 6am-4am Fri & Sat) For more kitsch and cheap eats, don't miss this classic diner on the Lundy's Lane motel strip, serving 99¢ breakfast specials until noon.

Remington's of Montana (Map p182; ☎ 905-356-4410; 5657 Victoria Ave; mains $15-40; ✆ 4-10pm Sun-Thu, 4-10:30pm Fri, 4-11pm Sat) This steak and seafood restaurant stands out from the crowd of the tourist area's unalluring eateries.

Simon's (Map p182; ☎ 905-356-5310; 4116 Bridge St; meals $2-15; ✆ 5:30am-7pm Mon-Sat, to 2pm Sun) Having been in the family for 124 years, the knick-knacks and artifacts that stuff every nook and cranny of this museum-like diner are of themselves worth a visit. The food and service at Simon's are great too, and you can gawk at old images of the Falls or read the guestbook while you wait.

THE BIG CHILL

Believe it or not, there was a winter not so long ago when Niagara Falls froze over. On February 24th, 1888, a local newspaper reported that people tobogganed on the ice. On February 4th, 1912, the ice bridge which held awestruck visitors broke, and three lives were lost. The only time the flow of the falls is known to have stopped completely was on March 29th, 1848. Folks celebrated by walking out onto the riverbed and retrieving artifacts.

Sleeping

Backpacker's International Inn (Map p182; ☎ 905-357-4266, 800-891-7022; 4219 Huron St, cnr Zimmerman Ave; dm/d from $22/64) Shabby chic charm lurks in every corner of this family-owned hostel. The house was built in 1896 and is chock full of antiques. There's a midnight curfew, and a continental breakfast is included in the rate.

Bedham Hall (Map p182; ☎ 905-374-8515, 877-374-8515; www.bedhamhall.com; 4835 River Rd; d $90-150) With champagne on check-in, a breakfast menu and fireplaces and Jacuzzis in every room, this is a truly romantic B&B.

Blue Moon Motel (Map p182; ☎ 905-356-0652, 877-789-8700; bluemoonniagara.com; 8445 Lundy's Lane; d/ste from $40/75) Lundy's Lane is famous for its hundreds of motels touting Jacuzzi suites and waterbeds. The friendly staff go the extra mile at this family-run establishment.

Eastwood Tourist Lodge (Map p182; ☎ 905-354-8686; www.theeastwood.com; 5359 River Rd; d $115-150, ste $150-175) A great view, free wireless and friendly owners who speak German and Spanish make this a popular spot.

Hilton Fallsview (Map p182; ☎ 905-354-7887, 800-445-8667; www.niagarafalls.hilton.com; 6361 Fallsview Blvd; d/ste from $99/599) Has a glassed-in pool facing the lobby and views of the falls from the 15th floor up.

Hostelling International Niagara Falls (Map p182; HI; 905-357-0770, 888-749-0058; 4549 Cataract Ave; dm/d from $23/$53) Movie nights and weekly drumming jams jazz up this clean, well-kept, recently renovated hostel.

Marriott Niagara Falls Fallsview & Spa (Map p182; 905-357-7300; 888-501-8916; 6740 Fallsview Blvd; d from $199) You can't sleep much closer to the Falls – this high-rise has all the fixings and is just 100 yards away from the action.

Sheraton Fallsview (Map p182; ☎ 905-374-1077; 877-353-2557; 6755 Fallsview Blvd; d/ste from $129/$199)

Strathaird Inn (Map p182; ☎ 905-358-3421; 4372 Simcoe St; d $65-105) British breakfast is proudly served at this well-kept, Scots-owned inn. Closed January to March.

NIAGARA PENINSULA WINE COUNTRY

You might be surprised to find vineyards in the Great White North. But, situated on the 43rd parallel (similar in latitude to California and south of Bordeaux, France), with a climate similar to some of the famed wine-producing regions of the world (Burgundy, the Loire Valley, Oregon and New Zealand), and drawing from mineral-rich soils, the Niagara Peninsula continues to grow in stature and produce increasingly respected vintages.

It wasn't until the '90s that the region's often splendid ice wines gained worldwide attention. Late-harvest Rieslings have further cemented the area's reputation as a producer of some of North America's top dessert wines. Not surprisingly, the best wines tend to be made from cool-climate grapes, including Cabernet Franc, Gamay, Gewürztraminer and Chardonnay as well as the occasional oddball like Zweigelt and Savagnin.

Wineries are popping up at a steady rate all over the region, numbering over 50 at the time of writing. All use the Vintner's Quality Alliance (VQA) designation, and so, armed with but a wine-route map and guide booklet (available free from most wineries), you can

NEW VINTAGES

The dawn of a new era in winemaking is upon us – one involving sustainable harvesting and fermenting methods, ingredients far surpassing the simple grape, and (gasp!) wine-tasting, minus pretension.

Sunnybrook Farm Estate Winery (p189) makes wines using apricots, pears and even chocolate, and **Flat Rock Cellars** (p189) prides itself on a philosophy of fun when it comes to wine-tasting. Flat Rock and **Stratus Wineries** (p189) both employ a 'gravity-flow' method, where grapes are sorted and crushed on an upper floor, and then the juice is drained down, first to fermenters and then to barrels.

explore them at your leisure. Most are open until 5pm but close earlier in the winter, and tastings are usually free or at a nominal cost if ice wines and rare vintages are involved. Some wineries offer free tours, even without advance reservations.

Driving Tour

The best way to enjoy all that the Niagara Peninsula has to offer is to make your own tour, stopping at the wineries and farm stands that catch your fancy, and ending at Niagara-on-the-Lake. Coming from Toronto, get off the Queen Elizabeth Way (QEW) after about an hour at Exit 78/Fifty Rd, then follow signs to **Puddicombe Farms 1**, where you can pick your own raspberries and cherries in July, or apples in September/October. Puddicombe makes great fruit wines, and has a café which serves light lunches and afternoon tea.

Back on the expressway, the first winery is **Kittling Ridge Estates Wine & Spirits 2**, well known for its award-winning ice wines and late harvest wines. Continuing on Hwy 81, take a right on Mountainview Rd and stop in to take in the sights and tastes at the scenic **Angels Gate Winery 3** and sample some classic reds at **Thirty Bench Wines 4**. Back on the main road (which will become King St), **Thomas and Vaughan Estate Winery 5** is small but produces impressive whites and reds. Pass Martin Rd, hang a left on Victoria St and a quick right onto North Service Rd and head to the **Olde Fashioned Family Eatery and Bar 6** for lunch, and then take in the Toronto skyline from across Lake Ontario at **Kacaba Vineyards 7**. Take a quick right down 7th Ave until you get to hip **Flat Rock Cellars 8** for a glass of 'Sweet Revenge' or 'Rusty Shed.' Tours are given on request. A little bit further east on the main road, hang a right on 5th St and another right onto Pelham Rd and make your way down to **Henry of Pelham Family Estates 9**. This family-run estate's wines have received rave reviews and are some of Canada's best. The Coach House Café and Cheese Shoppe serve up culinary accompaniments.

A short way down, Fifth St becomes Effingham St, home to **White Meadows Farms 10**, an old-fashioned sugar shack open year round and offering tours displaying ancient to modern ways of making maple syrup. Maple sugar in all shapes and forms as well as ice-wine tea are available at the gift shop.

Back on Pelham road going east, it'll take about 20 minutes to reach the large and bustling **Château des Charmes 11**, built to look like a French manse. The vintages here may be

TRANSPORTATION

Distance from Toronto Vineland 90km.

Direction Southwest.

Travel time One to 1½ hours.

Car Take the Queen Elizabeth Way (QEW) westbound past Hamilton. The official Wine Route is signposted at various exits off the QEW, on rural highways and along backcountry roads.

Crush on Niagara (☎ 905-562-3373, 866-408-9463; www.crushtours.com; day tours $69-99) Crush on Niagara offers guided small-group van tours departing from various pick-up points in the Niagara region.

Niagara Airbus (☎ 905-374-8111, 800-268-8111; www.niagaraairbus.com; tours from Toronto $106-150, from Niagara Falls $57-95, from Niagara-on-the-Lake $40) Niagara Airbus stops at well-known wineries; some itineraries include vineyard tours, lunches and shopping in Niagara-on-the-Lake.

Niagara Wine Tours (☎ 905-468-1300, 800-680-7006; www.niagaraworldwinetours.com; 92 Picton St, Niagara-on-the-Lake; tours $65-120; ☯ bike tours May-Oct, van tours year-round) Niagara Wine Tours offers cycle trips around the Niagara Peninsula, with tastings at local wineries and a private vineyard lunch. It also runs van tours of the Niagara-on-the-Lake wine region ($65 to $120).

worth a try if you don't have to queue behind (tour) busloads of visitors. A better bet might be to take a left on Highway 100, also known as Four Mile Creek Rd, and stop at **Hillebrand Estates Winery 12**, proprietors of a unique sparkling wine cellar. Wine-making seminars are offered here, as well as a library for sampling older vintages. Enjoy lunch at its restaurant featuring fresh local produce. Continuing on Four Mike Creek Rd, a quick left on Lake Shore Blvd will take you to **Strewn Winery 13**, where special ice wine tours are given with reservations and 'culinary vacations' give hands-on experience to aspiring chefs. East on Lake Shore Blvd will take you to **Sunnybrook Farm Estate 14**. Peach, pear, plum and chocolate are on the list of ingredients at this winery, and fruit iced wines and fruit maple syrups sweeten the deal.

At Niagara-on-the-Lake, a quick but worthwhile detour down Regional Rd 55/Niagara Stone Rd includes **Jackson Triggs 15**. The sleek, modern building is next to an amphitheatre that treats crowds to concerts throughout the summer, and can be explored via a guided tour, for $5. **Stratus 16**, further down the road, is the first winery in the world to receive LEED certification, which means the harvesting and wine-making is completely ecofriendly. Onsite seminars are offered in the contemporary tasting lounge, and staff are happy to spend one-on-one time with visitors. **Pillitteri Estates 17** stays true to its Sicilian roots with award-winning whites and reds.

Driving back through Niagara-on-the-Lake will take you to the Niagara Parkway, which leads down to **Reif Estate 18**, one of the area's older wineries. Last on our tour, but one of the best-known wineries in Canada, is **Inniskillin 19**, which has distinguished itself in the art of ice wine-making.

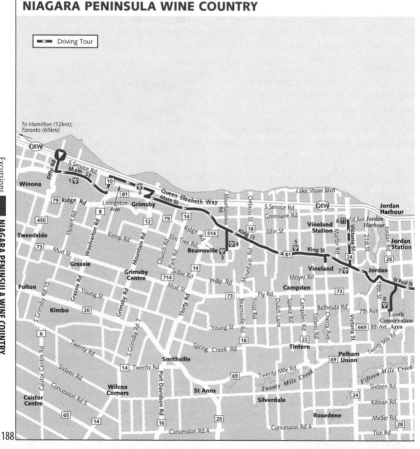

NIAGARA PENINSULA WINE COUNTRY

Sights & Activities

Opening hours will be shorter during winter.

Angels Gate (☎ 905-563-3942; www.angels
gatewinery.com; 4260 Mountainview Rd, Beamsville;
🕐 10am-5pm Mon-Sat, 11am-5pm Sun, tours by
appointment)

Château des Charmes (☎ 905-262-4219; www
.chateaudescharmes.com; 1025 York Rd, Niagara-on-the-
Lake; 🕐 10am-6pm, tours 11am & 3pm)

Flat Rock (☎ 905-562-8994; www.flatrockcellars.com; 2727
7th Ave; 🕐 10am-6pm Mon-Sat, 11am-6pm Sun)

Henry of Pelham Family Estate (☎ 905-684-8423;
www.henryofpelham.com; 1469 Pelham Rd, St Catharines;
🕐 10am-6pm, tours 1:30pm summer)

Hillebrand Estates (☎ 905-468-3201, 800-582-8412;
www.hillebrand.com; 1249 Niagara Stone Rd, Niagara-on-
the-Lake; 🕐 10am-9pm, tours hourly)

DETOUR: KLEINBURG

If it weren't for the **McMichael Canadian Art
Collection** (Map p180; ☎ 905-893-1121, 888-213-
1121; www.mcmichael.com; 10365 Islington Ave,
Kleinburg; adult/child under 5/student/senior/fam-
ily $15/free/12/12/30; 🕐 10am-4pm; **P** $5),
Kleinburg, a rather posh retreat just one hour north
of Toronto off Hwy 27, would be worth a miss. This
gallery's handcrafted wooden buildings (which
include, moved from its original location, painter
Tom Thomson's cabin) are set amid 100 acres of
conservation trails, and olds works by Canada's
best-known landscape painters. The **Group of Seven**
(p35), as well as First Nations, Inuit, and other
acclaimed Canadian artists. Visiting might be best in
the afternoon, as school groups tend to overrun the
gallery on weekday mornings.

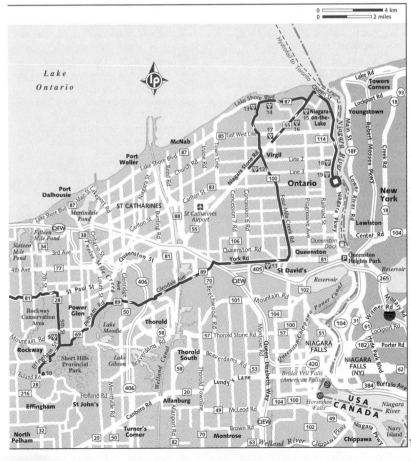

LIQUID GOLD

In 1794, Franconia, Germany, experienced a cold flash that froze vineyards prior to harvest. Desperate winemakers tried to press juice from frozen grapes and voila – the birth of ice-wine.

Winters in the Niagara region might be less harsh than those in Germany, but the area's climatic conditions produce grapes with a higher sugar level.

Although ice wine may have been discovered by accident, great care is taken in the growing and protection of the frozen grapes prior to harvest. The grapes left on the vines after the regular harvest season is finished are covered with netting to protect them from birds. Providing they aren't destroyed from storms or mold, the grapes grow sweeter and more concentrated until they are harvested, which occurs after three days of consistent temperatures of 8°C.

The fragile, icy grapes are then harvested by hand before dawn so the sun doesn't melt the ice and dilute the grape juice. The grapes are then pressed and aged in barrels for up to a year. After decanting, sweet, succulent ice wines are the perfect match for dessert, with a taste of apples or exotic fruits.

It takes 10 times the usual number of grapes to yield a bottle of ice wine, and this, combined with labor-intensive production methods and a high risk of crop failure, are what makes for a pretty pricey result – usually well above $40 per bottle.

Inniskillin Wines (☎ 905-468-3554, 888-466-4754; www.inniskillin.com; Line 3, cnr Niagara Parkway, Niagara-on-the-Lake; ☺ 11am-5:30pm, tours 10:30am & 2:30pm)

Jackson-Triggs (☎ 905-468-4637, 888-589-4637; www.jacksontriggswinery.com; 2145 Regional Rd 55; ☺ 10:30am-6:30pm, tours 10:30am-5pm)

Kacaba Vineyards (☎ 905-562-5625; www.kacaba.com; 3550 King St; ☺ 10am-6pm)

Kittling Ridge Estates Wines & Spirits (☎ 905-945-9225; www.kittlingridge.com; 297 South Service Rd, Grimsby; ☺ 10am-6pm Mon-Sat, 11am-5pm Sun, tours 2pm daily, 11:30am weekends Jun-Sep)

Pillitteri Estates (☎ 905-468-7738; www.pillatteri.com; 1696 Niagara Stone Rd, Niagara-on-the-Lake; ☺ 10am-8pm, tours 12 & 2pm)

Puddicombe Farms (☎ 905-643-1015; www.puddicombefarms.com; 1468 Hwy 8; ☺ 9am-5pm, Wed-Sun Apr-Jun & Nov-Dec)

Reif Estate Winery (☎ 905-468-7738; www.reifwinery.com; 15608 Niagara Parkway, Niagara-on-the-Lake; ☺ 10am-6pm, tours 11:30am & 1:30pm May-Sep)

Stratus (☎ 905-468-1806; www.stratuswines.com; 2059 Niagara Stone Rd, Niagara-on-the-Lake; ☺ 11am-5pm)

Strewn Winery (☎ 905-468-1229; www.strewnwinery.com; 1339 Lake Shore Blvd, Niagara-on-the-Lake; ☺ 10am-6pm, tours 1pm)

Sunnybrook Farm Estate Winery (☎ 905-468-1122; www.sunnybrookfarmwinery.com; 1425 Lake Shore Blvd, Niagara-on-the-Lake; ☺ 10am-6pm)

Thirty Bench Wines (☎ 905-563-1698; www.thirtybench.com; 4281 Mountainview Rd, Beamsville; ☺ 10am-6pm)

Thomas and Vaughan Estate Winery (☎ 905-563-7737; www.thomasandvaughan.com; 4245 King St, Beamsville; ☺ 11am-5:00pm, tours by reservation)

White Meadows Farm (☎ 905-682-0642; www.whitemeadowsfarms.com; 2519 Effingham St; ☺ 10am-5pm Mon-Sat, 11-5pm Sun)

Eating

Henry of Pelham Estates, Puddicombe Farms and **Hillebrand** (see Sights & Activities) have good restaurants.

Olde Fashioned Family Eatery and Bar (☎ 905-562-7669; 3301 North Service Rd, Niagara-on-the-Lake; meals $4-10; ☺ 8am-8pm Sun-Thu, 8am-11pm Fri & Sat). Signs warn customers that this isn't fast food; homemade sandwiches and burgers this tasty take time to make.

STRATFORD

It would have been just one of many slow-paced, southern Ontario towns, which are home to some stunning historical buildings and enchanting nature. But Stratford welcomes a deluge of visitors each year, due to its world-famous Shakespearean festival. Since its inception over 50 years ago, the town has grown in stature, and offers an increased level of tourist activities, attractions and distractions with the passing of each season.

The festival began humbly in a tent at Queen's Park, beside the Avon River. Sir Alec Guinness, who played Richard III on opening night, was the first in a steady stream of well-respected actors to perform on a **Stratford Festival** stage. Now, theatre goers can enjoy a number of other interesting programs, including costume warehouse tours, open discussions with actors, backstage tours, concerts, lectures and dramatic readings by actors. Some of these are free, others charge a nominal fee and require reservations in advance.

The festival season runs from April through 'til November. There are four theatres, all within walking distance of each other and of the town's centre, which stage classic and contemporary dramatic and musical performances, operas and, of course, the main attraction – plays by the bard himself. Main stage productions take place at the modern Elizabethan-style **Festival Theatre**. The **Avon Theatre** on Downie St is the secondary venue, and seats just over 1000. Attached to it is the **Studio Theatre**, an intimate setting which seats 260. The **Tom Patterson Theatre** located on Lakeside Dr has just under 500 seats.

But theatre isn't the only way to enjoy Stratford. The town is enticingly charming, with its stately homes and inns, many of which are heritage sites. You can sit by the Avon River and feed the ducks and swans who swim peacefully along the water, or even hire a boat and join them. The city's gardens are award winning, and can be explored solo or with a garden tour. The **Discovery Centre**, which is a beautifully preserved former teachers' college, houses the **Stratford-Perth Museum**, which shows early 20th-century Canadiana and hosts historical and cultural exhibits. Next to it, **Queen's Park** takes wanderers along footpaths leading from the Festival Theatre and along the river, past the Orr Dam and a stone bridge dating from 1855, to the beautiful **English flower garden**. Near Confederation Park you will come across **Gallery Stratford**, which exhibits portraits of theatre actors, archival photographs and the like.

Some city-centre shops and restaurants are overly quaint, but strolling the streets and gazing upon some of the architecture is still highly recommended. Queen's Park and the Festival Theatre are just north of Ontario St, which has a number of good eateries. From the park, Lakeside Dr takes you back into town and to the **Perth County Courthouse** at York and Ontario Sts. On Downie St, at the corner of Wellington, is **City Hall**, which was built in the Queen Anne Revival style.

TRANSPORTATION

Distance from Toronto Stratford 145km.

Direction Southwest.

Travel time Two to three hours.

Car Take the Queen Elizabeth Way (QEW) west to Hwy 427, driving north to Hwy 401. Take Hwy 401 west to exit 278 (Kitchener), then follow Hwys 7/8 west to Stratford, past Shakespeare village.

Parking A free visitors' day pass for parking in specified lots is available from Tourism Stratford (above).

Bus For select summer weekend matinees, direct buses depart from the York Mill/Yonge subway station at 10am, returning from Stratford at 7pm ($45 round trip); contact the Festival Theatre box office to check schedules and make reservations. Greyhound buses from Toronto ($37, minimum three hours) require a transfer in Kitchener.

Train VIA Rail operates two daily trains from Toronto ($33, two hours). Some Amtrak trains to/from the USA also stop here. Stratford's train and bus station is at 101 Shakespeare St, off Downie St, eight blocks from the town centre.

Information

Tourism Stratford (☎ 519-271-5140, 800-561-7926; www.city.stratford.on.ca; 47 Downie St; ⏰ 8:30am-4:30pm Mon-Fri) Contact Tourism Stratford for a full calendar of arts, cultural and historical events.

Sights & Activities

Boat tours & rentals (☎ 519-271-7739 peak season, 519-271-8681 off season; tours adult/child/student/senior $7/3/4.50/6; ⏰ 10am-6pm) Glide for 30 minutes past swans, grand gardens and theatres. Tours depart from the boathouse on York St. Canoes, kayaks and paddleboats can also be rented ($10 to $20 per hour).

Festival Tours (☎ 519-273-1652; adult/child/concession $13/7/12; ⏰ 10:30am, 12:30pm & 2pm Tue-Sun Jun-Sep, 10:30am Wed May & Oct) Narrated double-decker bus tours depart from York Lane, near the information centre.

Gallery Indigena (☎ 519-271-7881; www.galleryindigena.com; 69 Ontario St; ⏰ noon-4pm Sun & Mon, 10am-5:30pm Tue-Sat)

Gallery Stratford (☎ 519-271-5271; www.gallerystratford.on.ca; 54 Romeo St N; adult/concession $5/4; ⏰ 10am-5pm Tue-Sun summer, closed Dec)

Stone Maiden Inn (☎ 519-271-7129; www.stonemaideninn.com; 123 Church St; bicycles per hr/day $8/25, deposit $200)

Excursions

STRATFORD

Stratford Festival & Festival Theatre Box Office (☎ 519-273-1600, 800-567-1600; www.stratford-festival.on.ca; Festival Theatre, Queen's Park, 55 Queen St; tickets $26-108) Call or go online to request the annual Stratford Festival Visitors' Guide. Tickets go on sale to the general public in early January, and although it's best to call and reserve in advance, they are generally still available on show dates. Spring previews and fall end-of-season shows are discounted up to 50%. Students and seniors also qualify for reduced rates at some shows. A limited number of same-day rush tickets are available at half-price from the festival box office, two hours before the performance, in person or over the phone. Sales of these tickets are limited to four per patron and excludes A+ seating, and rush tickets aren't available for concession shows.

Stratford Garden Festival (www.stratfordgardenfestival .com)

Stratford-Perth Museum (☎ 519-271-5311; www .stratfordperthmuseum.ca; Discovery Centre, 270 Water St; admission by donation; ◷ 10am-5pm Tue-Sat, noon-5pm Sun-Mon, 10am-4pm Tue-Sat Sep-Apr)

Stratford Summer Music (www.stratfordsummermusic.ca)

Tours Free history walks leave the boat house at 9:30am Saturday from May until October and also on Tuesday to Saturday during July and August.

Eating

Church Restaurant (☎ 519-273-3424; 70 Brunswick St, cnr Waterloo St; lunch $8-25, dinner $15-45, prix-fixe dinners from $70; ◷ 11:30am-1:30pm & 5-8:30pm Tue-Sun, Belfry Bar 9pm-midnight Fri & Sat, closed Jan-Mar) A grande old dame of Stratford's culinary scene, the restaurant is set inside the old Christ Church (1874), with organ and altar still intact. Reservations are essential.

Down the Street Bar & Cafe (☎ 519-273-5886; 30 Ontario St; lunch $10-11, dinner mains $17-23; ◷ lunch 11am-3:30pm, dinner 5pm-9:30pm, to midnight during theatre season, bar to 2am) With whiffs of Parisian cafés, this place offers pre-theatre dining, microbrews and wines by the glass.

Old Prune (☎ 519-271-5052; www.oldprune.on.ca; 151 Albert St; lunch $8.50-20, prix-fixe dinner $65, cooking class $45; ◷ lunch 11:30am-1:30pm Wed-Sun, dinner 5-9pm Tue-Sat, 5-7pm Sun) From November until March, the famous Stratford Chef's School trains at this Edwardian house. Expect fresh, often organic and contemporary food with a hint of Québécois culture. Make reservations.

Pazzo Pizzeria (☎ 519-273-6666; 70 Ontario St; meals $8-28; ◷ 11:30am-1am Tue-Sun) Critics rave about the pizza served here. Upstairs, the ristorante has an excellent wine list.

Veg Out (☎ 519-271-9202; 24 Erie St; meals $6-8; ◷ 11:30am-7pm Tue-Thu, 11:30am-8pm Fri & Sat) Fresh juices, smoothies, and amazing meatless dishes are cheerfully served at this vegan restaurant.

York St Kitchen (☎ 519-273-7041; 41 York St; breakfast & lunch $5-8, dinner $10-15; ◷ 8am-8pm) Excellent sandwiches and home-style cooking are dished out at this jazzy little café, covered in inspiring artwork.

Sleeping

Annex Inn (☎ 519-271-1121, 800-361-5322; 38 Albert St; d $125-250) Some rooms have gas fireplaces and whirlpool tubs. The same folks run Bentley's, below.

Bentley's Inn (☎ 519-271-1121, 800-361-5322; www .bentleys-annex.com; 99 Ontario St; ste $95-195) Newly renovated and spacious bi-level suites have skylights.

Olde English Parlour Historic Inn & Suites (☎ 519-271-2772, 877-728-4036; www.oldeenglishparlour.com; 101 Wellington St; d $95-170, r $69-89, ste $139) Some elegant rooms in this 1870s building have Jacuzzis and fireplaces.

Queen's Inn (☎ 519-271-1400, 800-461-6450; www .queensinnstratford.ca; 161 Ontario St; d/ste from $70-99) Near Waterloo St, it's the oldest lodging house in town.

Stratford Festival Visitor Accommodation Bureau (☎ 519-273-1600, 800-567-1600; www.stratfordfestival.ca; d from $50) Offers mainly B&Bs or residents' homes. Also try the Tourism Stratford website for accommodations.

DETOUR: ELORA

It was the early 1800s when the promise of new land and religious freedom drew Mennonites to the region of Kitchener-Waterloo. Today, the rural areas around the twin cities are still populated by many Old Order Mennonite families, who practise the religion, customs and lifestyles of their 19th-century ancestors, without the use of modern technology.

The St Jacobs Farmers Market, about 1½ hours northwest of Toronto, is a perfect way to experience a little bit of history, as you wander amid the stalls and silos vending home-grown produce, baked goods and preserves as well as crafts, quilts and wooden furniture, some made by Mennonites.

You'll see horse-drawn buggies on the small highways to **Elora** (Map p180; www.elora.info.) Located on Hwy 7, this miniscule village teems with beauty and history. The **Elora Mill** (☎ 519-846-9118; 77 Mill St; 11:30am-8:30pm Mon-Fri, 11:30am-midnight Sat & Sun) draws city-dwellers and travelers with charming accommodations, fine dining and a view of the Elora Gorge and the Tooth of Time, the village's landmark. There's a multitude of walking trails, and the streets are lined with 19th-century architecture and shopping to satisfy every taste, including **Sweet Trash Vintage Clothier** (☎ 519-846-0333; 69 Metcalfe St), a treasure chest of frocks and fancies dating from the '30s onwards.

NIAGARA-ON-THE-LAKE

In 1896, writer William Kirby wrote that 'Niagara is as near Heaven as any town whatever.' It seems many tourists agree. Today, Niagara, which was originally a First Nations village, is considered one of the best-preserved 19th-century towns in North America. But tour buses put a damper on most of the old-world charm that remains. If it weren't for the acclaimed Shaw Festival, Niagara-on-the-Lake wouldn't be worth more than the briefest of stops.

Queen St is the main street in the town and is laden with shops and tea rooms. **Ten Thousand Villages**, off the beaten path on Victoria St, deals in fair-trade wares and handicrafts. The people at wonderful **Greaves Jams & Marmalades** are fourth-generation jam-makers. Further east is the Victorian-era **Niagara Apothecary**, now a museum enticingly filled with remedies and jars. And **The Silver Screen** makes for a amusing foray of old movie soundtracks, classic Hollywood memorabilia and old-school ceramic Disney figurines. Special town events, mostly taking place in fair summer weather, include a variety of festivals, a tour of historic homes, outdoors musical concerts and art fairs. Candlelit Christmas strolls, parades and caroling light up the streets in December.

The **Shaw Festival**, which is the only festival in the world devoted to producing the plays of George Bernard Shaw (1856–1950) and his contemporaries, takes place between April and November at the **Festival Theatre**, the historic **Court House Theatre**, and the **Royal George**, which was built as a vaudeville house to entertain the troops in WWI. Seminars, musical readings, special events and informal Q&A conversations with cast members are held throughout the festival season.

South of Simcoe Park, the **Niagara Historical Museum**, Ontario's oldest museum, has an impressive collection ranging from First Nations artifacts to furniture, textiles and Canadiana dating from the War of 1812 and the early settlement of Ontario. Past the Festival Theatre, at the southeastern edge of town, restored **Fort George** was a key battle site in the War of 1812, and holds ghost tours, skills demonstrations and battle reenactments throughout the spring and summer. History buffs will also want to explore the village of **Queenston** (p181) along the Niagara Parkway. **Sentineal Carriages** gives private, guided horse-and-buggy tours of the old town.

TRANSPORTATION

Distance from Toronto Niagara-on-the-Lake 130km.

Direction Southeast.

Travel time Two hours.

Car Take the Queen Elizabeth Way (QEW) westbound past St Catharines to Exit 38/Niagara Stone Rd (Hwy 55), which follows onto Mississauga St intersecting Queen St downtown.

Parking Read the on-street parking signs carefully to avoid being fined. Metered spaces cost $2 or less per hour.

Bus & Taxi First go to Niagara Falls by bus or train, then transfer to a Niagara-on-the-Lake shuttle bus. Taxis from Niagara Falls (☎ 905-357-4000) cost around $38 each way.

Niagara-on-the-Lake shuttle bus (☎ 905-358-3232; one way/round-trip from Niagara Falls $10/18).

Information

Niagara-on-the-Lake Chamber of Commerce (☎ 905-468-1950; www.niagaraonthelake.com; 26 Queen St, cnr King St; ☷ 10am-5pm mid-Oct–Apr, 10am-7:30pm May–mid-Oct) This drop-in point is a helpful visitor information centre that is located two blocks northwest of Simcoe Park.

Sights & Activities

Fort George (☎ 905-468-4257; www.niagara.com /~parkscan; 26 Queens Pde, off Niagara Parkway; adult/ child/senior $11/5.50/9.25; ☷ 10am-5pm May-Nov)

Ghost Tours (☎ 905-468-6621; www.friendsoffortgeorge .ca/ghost.htm; adult/child $10/5; ☷ 8:30pm Sun May-Jun; 8:30pm Mon, Wed-Fri & Sun Jul-Aug, 7:30pm Sun Sep)

Greaves Jams & Marmalades (☎ 905-468-7831; 55 Queen St, cnr Regent St; ☷ 9:30am-6pm Sun-Thu, 9:30am-6:30pm Fri & Sat)

Niagara Apothecary (☎ 905-468-3845; www.niaga raapothecary.ca; 5 Queen St; admission by donation; ☷ noon-6pm mid-May–early Sep)

Niagara Historical Society Museum (☎ 905-468-3912; www.niagarahistorical.museum; 43 Castlereagh St, cnr Davy St; adult/child/student/senior $5/1/2/3; ☷ 10am-5:30pm, 1-5pm Nov-Apr)

Shaw Festival & Festival Theatre Box Office (☎ 905-468-2172, 800-511-7429; www.shawfest.com; 10 Queens Pde; tickets $25-86; ⏰ 9am-5pm Mon-Sat Jan-Apr, 9am-8pm Apr-Nov) Request a complete Shaw Festival guidebook before tickets go on sale in January. Students can book half-price balcony seats for any performance in the Festival Theatre; students and seniors may also attend specially priced matinees.

Zoom Leisure (☎ 905-468-2366; 866-811-6993; 2017 Niagara Stone Rd (Hwy 55), corner East West Line; 1hr/half-/full-day $12/20/30; ⏰ Apr-Oct) Price for bike rental includes a helmet, lock and map. Call in advance for bicycle rentals outside of the regular season.

Eating

Buttery (☎ 905-468-2564; www.thebutteryrestaurant.com; 19 Queen St; meals from $19, feast $55; ⏰ 11am-11pm) This pub-style place puts on a thoroughly kitschy Henry VIII–style dinner theatre feast.

Churchill Lounge (Prince of Wales Hotel; dinner around $20) Casual pub fare with flare.

Escabeche Dining Room (Prince of Wales Hotel; dinner $28-44; ⏰ breakfast, lunch & dinner) Contemporary fine dining with a French twist.

Irish Tea Room (☎ 905-468-4832; 75 Queen St; mains around $10; desserts from $3; ⏰ 9:30am-8pm summer, 9:30am-6pm winter) From a 'proper cup of tea' to a steak & Guinness pie to barm brack, this tea room serves more than a little taste of Ireland.

Niagara Home Bakery (☎ 905-468-3431; 66 Queen St; pastries from $2; ⏰ 9am-6pm Mon-Sat, 9am-5pm Sun) For Cornish pasties, Scotch meat pie and fresh berry pies cooked in an original stone brick oven, stop here.

Sleeping

Niagara-on-the-Lake Reservation Service (☎ 905-468-4263; www.niagaraonthelake.com; d from $60) The chamber of commerce offers a reservations service for most of the town's 200 lovely B&Bs, inns, hotels and cottages, at a cost of $3.50. However, you will find that accommodations are generally quite expensive as well as often being booked out. A two-night minimum stay is often required on weekends.

Prince of Wales Hotel (☎ 905-468-3246, 888-669-5566; www.vintage-hotels.com; 6 Picton St, cnr King St; d $150-300, ste $350-550) This elegant Victorian hotel is opposite Simcoe Park and features some great spots for fine dining and high tea.

Queen's Landing (☎ 905-468-2195, 888-669-5566; www.vintage-hotels.com; 155 Byron St; d/ste from $150/350) A waterfront patio, two restaurants and an indoor saltwater pool are some of the features of this modern hotel.

SKIING & SNOWBOARDING AREAS

Although Toronto is not Whistler by any stretch of the imagination, you can still find some fresh powder slopes within easy driving distance of the city. Depending on the weather, the ski season runs from early December to the middle of March. The nearest place to strap on a snowboard or skis is at **Horseshoe Resort**, which has cross-country trails, a tubing park and seven lifts leading to dozens of runs for skiers and snowboarders. Handily, it also has a hotel, spa, several eateries and a fireside lounge, all surrounded by wilderness just over an hour's drive from Toronto. If the weather is good, consider driving on to **Blue Mountain**, Ontario's largest mountain resort and run by Intrawest. Outside of Collingwood, the resort's 25 acres of fun feature 13 lifts (four of them are high-speed), three terrain parks, multiple pipes and half-pipes and more than 30 assorted ski trails rated from beginner to double-black diamond.

Day or night, the surrounding village is full of shops, restaurants and entertainment. If you're not up for a long drive, turn to p139 for family skiing centres and ice skating within the city limits.

Sights & Activities

Blue Mountain (Map p180; ☎ 416-869-3799, 705-445-0231; www.bluemountain.ca; Blue Mountain Rd, off Hwy 26, Craigleith; lift tickets $34-52, ski & gear rentals $17-44, tube park ride $3.50) Daily lessons available, childcare available.

Horseshoe Resort (Map p180; ☎ 416-283-2988, 800-461-5627; www.horseshoeresort.com; Horseshoe Valley Rd, Barrie; lift pass $25-43, cross-country trail pass $8-17, ski & gear rentals $7-35, tube park ride $3) Supervised kids' programs, daily lessons and discounts for online bookings.

Eating

Kaytoo Restaurant & Bar (☎ 705-445-4100; 176 Jozo Weider Blvd, Collingwood; mains $8-42; ⏰ 11am-2am) A little more cosmopolitan than your average ski-hill fare, even a true Canadian thanksgiving turkey dinner is on the menu here, all with a great lakeside view.

Oliver & Bonacini Café Grill (☎ 705-444-8680; 220 Mountain Dr, Collingwood; breakfast $7-17, lunch $11-19, dinner $12-34; ☺ 7am-10pm, brunch 11am-3pm Sun) One of five upscale restaurants under the same ownership, this is fine alpine dining at its best. An excellent brunch is served on Sundays.

Windy O'Neill's (☎ 705-446-9989; 170 Jozo Weider Blvd, Collingwood; mains from $10; ☺ 11am-last call) Unlike most of its kind, this pub is owned and run by genuine Irish folk. Check out the small, intimate bar downstairs that features live music at weekends.

Sleeping

Blue Mountain (☎ 705-445-0231, 877-445-0231; www .bluemountain.ca; from $140) The resort has a range of accommodations, starting at the Blue Mountain Inn, which is the original and oldest hotel on the premises, up to rental chalets large enough to house families. Rates will vary depending on the season.

Directory ■

Directory

ACCOMMODATIONS

Peak summer season runs from Victoria Day (late May) until Labour Day (early September) during which rates jump as much as 50%. During big-ticket events (p12) like the Toronto International Film Festival and Caribana, you'll have trouble finding any type of accommodations, and if you do, rates can swell to double or triple the norm. See p166 for price ranges, special deals, advice on making reservations and B&B booking services.

Accommodations listings in this book are arranged under neighborhood in budget order. Count on adding room taxes of about 12% to our quoted rates (although visitors may be eligible for a 7% federal GST refund; see p148). Places that offer free parking are marked with a ⓟ. If there's a cost involved, the amount is listed after the icon.

BUSINESS

Despite cries of 'Buy Canadian!,' foreign companies can generally make a buck or two in Toronto. As Canada's convention and trade show epicentre, Toronto hosts over 100 events annually at the Metro Toronto Convention Centre and Exhibition Place. Tourism Toronto (p206) readily assists business travelers and offers corporate incentives.

Hours

Normal business hours are 9am to 5pm weekdays. Some postal outlets may stay open later and on weekends. Banks usually keep shorter hours, but close later on Friday; certain branches are open Saturday morning.

Typical retail shopping hours are 10am to 6pm Monday to Saturday, noon to 5pm on Sunday (although some shops are closed on Sunday). Shopping malls often stay open later, particularly on Thursday night.

Restaurants are usually open for lunch on weekdays from 11:30am until 2:30pm and serve dinner from 5pm until 9:30pm daily, later on weekends. If they take a day off, it's Monday. Breakfast venues are on the increase; weekend brunch is the flavor of the month (if not the decade).

Bars usually open late afternoon (around 4pm), but some unlock their doors around noon. Clubs usually open in the evening around 9pm, but most don't start pumping before 11pm. Bars serve liquor until 2am; dance clubs often stay open until 4am.

Pharmacies, 24-hour supermarkets or convenience stores are a dime-a-dozen. Tourist attractions generally keep longer hours during summer; some close during winter.

Services

Check out the Tourism Toronto (p206) website for business services, including translation, secretarial and equipment rental. Kinko's (p201) offers an impressive range of services, from internet to color printing and Fed Ex drop-offs. Mail Boxes Etc (p204) offers UPS courier services.

CHILDREN

Children and Toronto skip merrily hand-in-hand. In traditional ethnic neighborhoods like Little Italy or Greektown, they'll be fussed over, cheek-pinched and cuddled. Kids receive TTC public transport discounts (see p215), and there's rarely an extra charge for kids staying with parents at motels and hotels. Some B&Bs refuse children under a certain age; others brazenly charge full price for tots. The Delta Chelsea Toronto Downtown (p169) provides a supervised play centre, kids' swim club and affordable babysitting services. Car-hire companies rent car seats, which are legally required for young children. See p61 for a list of attractions that kids might enjoy. For more general information on enjoying travel with kids, check out Lonely Planet's *Travel with Children*.

Kid-friendly venues in this book are indicated with a ⑤.

Baby-sitting

Always ask for a licensed and bonded babysitting service. Typical rates are around $15 per hour plus transportation fee, usually with a three to four hour minimum. Reputable agencies include:

Christopher Robin (☎ 416-483-4744; http://christopher robin.homestead.com)

Improv Care (☎ 416-243-3285; www.improvcare.ca)

CLIMATE

Unless you're well prepared, winter in Toronto can make you wish you'd never been born. January freezes over, with maximum temperatures never topping zeros. The wind-chill factor – lashings from Lake Ontario – can make things feel a whole lot colder. North-south downtown streets become frigid wind tunnels, sending people scurrying like rats into the underground PATH network. In July temperatures can hit the mid-80s for weeks at a time, claustrophobic humidity sapping the very life from your bones…But rug-up or show some skin and you'll be fine!

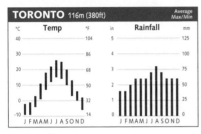

TORONTO 116m (380ft) — Average Max/Min

COURSES

With top-rated universities and multicultural resources galore, Toronto is an excellent place to study something new. Call or check websites for schedules.

Arts & Crafts

Find your inner artisan at the following:

Clay Design (p156)

Craft Studios (Map pp234–5; ☎ 416-973-4000; www .harbourfrontcentre.com; Harbourfront, York Quay Centre, 235 Queens Quay W; 🚇 509, 510) Workshops in glass blowing, textile art, ceramics and jewelry.

Gardiner Museum of Ceramic Art (p66) Wheel-throwing and hand-building ceramic instruction, plus lectures and family days.

Japanese Paper Place (p160)

Textile Museum of Canada (p62) Fabric printing, felt making, needlecraft and beadwork workshops, lectures and discussions.

Toronto's First Post Office (p57) Old York history and traditional quill-and-ink letter writing classes.

Cooking

You'll also find a culinary school in Stratford (p192), a great day-trip from Toronto.

Big Carrot (p93) Vegetarian, vegan, gluten-free and low-cholesterol cooking classes.

Calphalon Culinary Centre (Map pp240–1; ☎ 416-847-2212, 877-946-2665; www.calphalonculinarycentre.com; Queen West, 425 King St W; 🚇 504, 510) Executive Chef Susie Reading (see Local Voices p97) runs internationally-flavored demonstration and hands-on classes to inspire your domestic efforts. Friday night are couples classes.

Dish Cooking Studio (Map p231; ☎ 416-920-5559; www.dishcookingstudio.com; Greater Toronto Area, 390 Dupont St; 🚇 Dupont) Cooking classes with celebrity chefs including 'Trish the Dish' Magwood.

Great Cooks on Eight (Map pp232–3; ☎ 416-861-4333; www.greatcooks.ca; Financial District, 8th fl, Simpson Tower, 401 Bay St; 🚇 Queen) Downtown lunch and evening classes with top local chefs.

Dance

Cut the rug at:

Arabesque Academy (Map pp238–9; ☎ 416-920-5593; www.arabesquedance.ca; Yonge Street Strip, Ste 107, 1 Gloucester St; 🚇 Wellesley) Free introductory bellydancing class.

Dancemakers (p135)

Dancing on King (☎ 416-469-3184; www.dancingon king.com) Hip-hop, tango, tap, swing, ballroom and Latin at various venues; classes from $12.

Toronto Dance Classes (www.torontodanceclasses.com) Online resource for T.O. dance lessons.

Toronto Swing Dance Society (Map p231; ☎ 416-638-8737; www.dancing.org/tsds; Bloor Village, Lithuanian House, 1573 Bloor Street W; 🚇 Dundas West) Drop-in classes $15.

TOSalsa! (www.tosalsa.com) Online salsa listings.

Language

Toronto delivers a world of language learning opportunities. *Comprenez-vous?*

Alliance Française (Map pp242–3; ☎ 416-922-2014; www.alliance-francaise.ca; The Annex, 24 Spadina Rd; 🕙 8am-9pm Mon-Thu, to 3:30pm Fri & Sat; 🚇 Spadina) French.

Berlitz (Map pp238–9; ☎ 416-924-7773; www.berlitz .ca; Bloor-Yorkville, 94 Cumberland St; 🚇 Bay) French, German, Italian, Portuguese and Spanish.

GEOS (Map pp234–5; ☎ 416-599-2120; www.geos toronto.com; Financial District, 59 Adelaide St E; 🚇 Queen) French and Japanese.

Goethe-Institut Gallery (p59) German.

Italian Cultural Institute (Map pp238–9; ☎ 416-921-3802; www.iicto-ca.org; The Annex, 496 Huron St; 9am-1pm & 2-5pm Mon-Fri; Spadina) Italian.

Spanish Centre (Map pp238–9; ☎ 416-925-4652; www.spanishcentre.com; Yonge Street Strip, 46 Hayden St; 10am-9pm Mon-Thu, to 8pm Fri, to 4pm Sat; Bloor-Yonge) Spanish.

CUSTOMS

Adults who are aged 19 and older are allowed to bring in 1.5L of wine or 1.14L of liquor (or a case of beer), 200 cigarettes, 50 cigars and 200g of tobacco. Dispose of perishable items (fruit, vegetables, plants etc) before crossing the border. Mace, pepper spray and many firearms are also prohibited. For the latest regulation information, contact the **Canada Customs & Revenue Agency** (☎ 204-983-3500, 800-461-9999; www.ccra-adrc.gc.ca).

ELECTRICITY

Canada, like the USA and Mexico, operates on 110V, 60-cycle electric power. Gadgets built for higher voltage and cycles (such as 220/240V, 50-cycle European appliances) will function rather pathetically. North American electrical goods have plugs with two (flat) or three (two flat, one round) pins. Overseas visitors should get hold of an adapter for their hair dryers and laptops.

EMBASSIES & CONSULATES

Most countries maintain embassies in Ottawa. Most Toronto consulates are only open during weekday mornings, although some reopen after lunch until 4pm – call before you visit.

Australia (Map pp238–9; ☎ 416-323-1155; www.ahc-ottawa.org; Bloor-Yorkville, Ste 1100, South Tower, 175 Bloor St E; Bloor-Yonge)

Cuba (Map p230; ☎ 416-234-8181; www.embacuba canada.net; Greater Toronto Area, Kipling Sq, 5353 Dundas St W; Kipling)

Denmark (Map pp238–9; ☎ 416-962-5661; www .eksporttilcanada.um.dk/da; Bloor-Yorkville, Ste 2120, 2 Bloor St W; Bloor-Yonge)

France (Map pp238–9; ☎ 416-847-1900; www.consulf rance-toronto.org; Bloor-Yorkville, Ste 2220, 2 Bloor St E; Bloor-Yonge)

Germany (Map pp238–9; ☎ 416-925-2813; www .germanconsulatetoronto.ca; Bloor-Yorkville, 77 Bloor St W; Bay)

Italy (Map pp232–3; ☎ 416-977-1566; www.constoronto .esteri.it; Queen Street, 136 Beverley St; 501)

Japan (Map pp234–5; ☎ 416-363-7038; www.japancg -toronto.org; Financial District, Ste 3300, Royal Trust Tower, 77 King St W; St Andrew)

Mexico (Map pp234–5; ☎ 416-368-2875; Financial District, Ste 4440, 199 Bay St; Union)

Netherlands (Map pp232–3; ☎ 416-598-2520; www .dutchconsulate.toronto.on.ca; Queen Street & Dundas Square, Ste 2106, Eaton Centre, 1 Dundas St W; Dundas)

New Zealand (Map p231; ☎ 416-947-9696; fax 416-947-9696; Greater Toronto Area, 225 MacPherson Ave; Dupont)

Portugal (Map pp232–3; ☎ 416-217-0966; fax 416-217-0973; Queen Street & Dundas Square, Ste 1400, 438 University Ave; St Patrick)

Spain (Map pp234–5; ☎ 416-977-1661; Financial District, Ste 2401, Simcoe Place, 200 Front St W; Union)

Sweden (Map pp238–9; ☎ 416-963-8768; www .swedenabroad.com; Bloor-Yorkville, Ste 2109, 2 Bloor St W; Bloor-Yonge)

Switzerland (Map pp234–5; ☎ 416-593-5371; Theatre Block, Ste 601, 154 University Ave; St Andrew)

UK (Map pp238–9; ☎ 416-593-1290; www.britishhigh commission.gov.uk; Yonge Street Strip, Ste 2800, 777 Bay St; College)

USA (Map pp232–3; ☎ 416-595-1700; http://toronto .usconsulate.gov; Queen Street & Dundas Square, 360 University Ave; St Patrick)

EMERGENCY

Police, fire & ambulance (☎ 911)

Police, non-emergency (☎ 416-808-2222, TDD 416-467-0493)

SOS Femmes (☎ 416-759-0138, ☎ 800-287-8603)

Toronto Rape Crisis Centre (☎ 416-597-8808, TTY 416-597-1214)

SOS Femmes is primarily a French-speaking crisis line. The Toronto Rape Crisis Centre accepts collect calls; some counselors speak French and Spanish. Both organizations are underfunded and understaffed – keep trying if you get a busy signal. Counselors can make referrals to hospital sexual assault care centres. See Medical Services (p202) for hospital emergency rooms and clinics.

GAY & LESBIAN TRAVELERS

Toronto's gay community centres around Church St – called Church-Wellesley Village or simply the 'Gay Village.' Men's bars and clubs outnumber lesbian venues, but Toronto sustains drag kings as well as queens, plus women-only bathhouse nights. Queer readings series happen too. Other lesbigay-friendly neighborhoods include The Annex, Kensington Market, Queen West and Cabbagetown.

In 2003 Toronto became famous for being the first city in North America to legalize same-sex marriage. Apply to **City Hall** (Map pp232–3; ☎ 416-392-7036; www .toronto.ca/registry-services; Queen Street, 100 Queen St W; license $110; ⏱ 8:30am-4:15pm Mon-Fri; ⊕ Queen). The weeklong Pride Toronto (p13) celebrations attract one million folks annually.

Helpful resources include the following:

519 Community Centre (Map pp238–9; ☎ 416-392-6874; www.the519.org; Church-Wellesley Village, 519 Church St; ⏱ 9am-10pm Mon-Fri, to 5pm Sat, 10am-5pm Sun; ⊕ Wellesley)

Canadian Lesbian & Gay Archives (pp238–9; ☎ 416-777-2755; www.clga.ca; Church-Wellesley Village, 202 Wellesley Street E; ⏱ 7:30-10pm Tue-Thu, closed Aug; ⊕ Wellesley)

Fab Style (p203)

Toronto Pronto (www.gaytorontotourism.com)

Glad Day (p154)

Lesbian & Gay Immigration Task Force (☎ 416-392-6874; www.legit.ca)

This Ain't the Rosedale Library (p154)

Xtra! (p203)

HOLIDAYS

During national public holidays, all banks, schools and government offices (including post offices) are closed; transportation, museums and other services adopt a Sunday schedule. Holidays falling on a weekend are usually observed the following Monday. The following public holidays are observed in Ontario:

New Year's Day January 1

Good Friday March/April

Easter Monday March/April

Victoria Day Monday preceding May 24

Canada Day July 1

Civic Holiday (Simcoe Day) 1st Monday in August

Labour Day 1st Monday in September

Thanksgiving 2nd Monday in October

Remembrance Day November 11

Christmas Day December 25

Boxing Day December 26

INTERNET ACCESS

Many accommodations have data ports, some with high-speed internet access. Deluxe hotels usually have business centres with computers, photocopiers, fax and internet services.

Toronto's cheapest internet cafés congregate along the Yonge Street Strip; Bloor St W in The Annex and Koreatown; and Chinatown's Spadina Ave. Rates start at $2 per hour, with multihour deals available. **Grey Region Comics** (Map pp238–9; ☎ 416-975-1718; www.planethobby.net; Yonge Street Strip, 550 Yonge St; ⏱ 9am-midnight; ⊕ Wellesley) has comic-colorful access (not much grey in the region).

Kinko's (☎ 800-254-6567; www.kinkos .ca) offers internet access for 20¢ to 30¢ per minute. Branches open 24-hours include **Queen Street & Dundas Square** (Map pp232–3; ☎ 416-979-8447; 505 University Ave; ⊕ St Patrick) and **The Annex** (Map pp242–3; ☎ 416-928-0110; 459 Bloor St W; ⊕ Spadina).

Major internet service providers (ISPs), have dial-up numbers across Canada for laptop-wielding travelers, including:

AOL (☎ 416-916-0050, 888-265-4357; www.aol.ca)

CompuServe (☎ 888-353-8990; www.compuserve.com)

Earthlink (☎ 800-327-8454; www.earthlink.net)

Wi-fi Access

Increasingly, B&Bs, pubs and cafés are offering free wi-fi internet access; check www .wirelesstoronto.ca, www.wi-fihotspotlist .com or www.wififreespot.com/can.html for locations.

LEGAL MATTERS

The Canadian federal government permits marijuana use for medicinal purposes, but official prescription cannabis is strictly regulated. It's illegal to drink alcohol anywhere other than a residence or licensed premises – other public spaces are off limits.

Biblical retribution awaits those caught driving under the influence (DUI) of alcohol or any illegal substance (eg marijuana). The blood-alcohol limit for driving is 0.08%, which, depending on your metabolism, is around two beers-worth. Penalties include throwing you in jail overnight, followed by a court appearance, heavy fine and/or further incarceration.

If you are arrested, you have the right to remain silent. However, never walk away from law enforcement personnel without permission. After being arrested you have the right to an interpreter and one phone call. For low-cost legal advice, contact **Legal Aid Ontario** (Map pp232–3; ☎ 416-979-1446, 800-668-8258; www.legalaid.on.ca; Queen Street & Dundas Square, Ste 204, 375 University Ave; ⏰ 8am-3:30pm Mon-Fri; ◉ St Patrick).

MAPS

The detailed neighborhood maps in this guide will certainly be enough for most Toronto visits. The Ontario Travel Information Centre (p206) provides free provincial maps for excursions. **MapArt** (www.mapart.com) publishes an excellent series of affordable maps covering central Toronto, the Greater Toronto Area (GTA) and southwest Ontario, sold at bookstores and newsstands. For specialist activity maps, drop by Mountain Equipment Co-op (p151) or Europe Bound Outfitters (p151).

MEDICAL SERVICES

There are no reciprocal healthcare arrangements between Canada and other countries. Non-Canadians must usually pay cash up front for treatment, which is expensive (the standard hospital bed rate for nonresidents is around $2500 per day). Don't forget to take out travel medical insurance! Expect to wait at emergency rooms if your case isn't deemed urgent.

Clinics

Convenient clinics include:

Women's College Hospital (Map pp238–9; ☎ 416-323-6400; www.womenscollegehospital.ca; Yonge Street Strip, 76 Grenville St; ⏰ 24hr; ◉ College) Non-emergency women's and family health.

Dental Emergency Clinic (Map p231; ☎ 416-485-7121; www.dentalemergency.com; Greater Toronto Area, 1650 Yonge St; ⏰ 8am-midnight; ◉ St Clair)

Hassle-Free Clinic (Map pp232–3; ☎ women 416-922-0566, men 416-922-0603; www.hasslefreeclinic.org; Queen Street & Dundas Square, 2nd fl, 66 Gerrard St E; ⏰ women 10am-3pm Mon, Wed & Fri, 4-8pm Tue & Thu; men 4-8pm Mon & Wed, 10am-3pm Tue & Thu, 4-7pm Fri, 10am-2pm Sat; ◉ College) STD/HIV testing and reproductive health.

Emergency Rooms

Toronto's major 24-hour hospitals cluster around University Ave in the Queen Street & Dundas Square area (◉ Queens Park), including the following:

Hospital for Sick Children (Map pp232–3; ☎ 416-813-1500; www.sick kids.on.ca; 170 Elizabeth St, emergency on Gerrard St W)

Mount Sinai Hospital (Map pp232–3; ☎ 416-596-4800, emergency 416-586-5054; www.mtsinai.on.ca; 600 University Ave)

Toronto General Hospital (Map pp232–3; ☎ 416-340-3111, emergency 416-340-3946; www.uhn.ca; 200 Elizabeth St)

METRIC SYSTEM

Canada officially changed over from imperial measurement to the metric system in the mid-1970s, but the systems coexist in everyday life. For example, all speed-limit signs are in kilometres per hour and gasoline is sold by the litre, but produce is often sold by the pound. Use the chart inside the front cover to ease your brain between the two systems.

MONEY

All prices quoted in this book are in Canadian dollars ($) and do not include taxes, unless otherwise noted. Most Canadians don't carry large amounts of cash for everyday use, relying on their credit cards, ATMs and direct debit cards. Unlike the USA, personal checks are rarely accepted. See the inside front cover for exchange rates.

ATMs

Interbank ATM exchange rates usually beat traveler's checks or exchanging foreign currency. Canadian ATM fees are low ($1.50 to $2 per transaction), but your home bank may charge another fee on top of that.

Currency

Paper bills come in $5 (blue), $10 (purple), $20 (green) and $50 (red) denominations. Coins include the penny (1¢), nickel (5¢), dime (10¢), quarter (25¢), 'loonie' ($1) and 'toonie' ($2). The 11-sided, gold 'loonie' features the common loon (a North American water bird), aka the 'Canuck Duck.'

Credit Cards

Visa, MasterCard, American Express and JCB cards are widely accepted in Canada. Credit cards can get you cash advances at bank ATMs, generally for a 3% surcharge. Beware: many US-based credit cards now convert foreign charges using highly unfavorable exchange rates and fees.

Changing Money

Always change your money at a recognized bank or financial institution. Some hotels, souvenir shops and tourist offices exchange money, but their rates won't put a smile on your dial. See the inside front cover for exchange rates.

American Express (☎ 905-474-0870, 800-869-3016; www.americanexpress.com/canada) branches in Toronto only function as travel agencies and don't handle financial transactions. Instead, tackle the banks, or try **Money Mart** (Map pp238–9; ☎ 416-920-4146; www.moneymart.ca; Yonge Street Strip, 617 Yonge St; ◷ 24hr; ⓞ Wellesley).

Affiliated with Marlin Travel (www.marlintravel.ca), **Thomas Cook** (www.thomascook.ca) branches include the following:

Bloor-Yorkville (Map pp238–9; ☎ 416-975-9940, 800-267-8891; 1168 Bay St; ◷ 9am-5:30pm Mon-Fri; ⓞ Bloor-Yonge)

Financial District (Map pp234–5; ☎ 416-366-1961; 10 King St E; ◷ 9am-5pm Mon-Fri; ⓞ King)

Branches of **Travelex** (www.travelex.com /ca) can found at these major locations:

Financial District (Map pp234–5; ☎ 416-304-6130; First Canadian Place, 100 King St W; ◷ 8am-5pm Mon-Fri)

Pearson International Airport Terminal 3 Arrivals (Map p230; ☎ 905-673-7042; ◷ 8:30am-midnight)

Pearson International Airport Terminal 3 Departures (Map p230; ☎ 905-673-7461; ◷ 3:30am-10pm)

Traveler's Cheques

American Express, Thomas Cook, Travelex and Visa traveler's checks in Canadian dollars are accepted as cash at many hotels, restaurants and stores. The exchange rate savings you might make with foreign currency traveler's checks (even US$) rarely compensate for the hassle of having to exchange them at banks or other financial institutions.

NEWSPAPERS & MAGAZINES

Most 'daily' newspapers aren't published on Sunday; the hefty weekend edition appears on Saturday instead.

CityBites (www.citybites.ca) Toronto's free bimonthly food and drink guide.

Eye Weekly (www.eye.net) Free alternative street-press, with an arts and entertainment bent.

Fab Style (www.fabstylequarterly.com) Free glossy G&L quarterly.

Globe & Mail (www.globeandmail.ca) The elder statesman of national daily newspapers.

L'Express (www.lexpress.to) French-language weekly newspaper, published on Tuesdays.

Maclean's (www.macleans.ca) National weekly Canadian news and culture magazine.

Metro (www.metronews.ca) Free daily rag with bite-sized news, sports and entertainment (often left on subway seats).

National Post (www.nationalpost.com) It's Canada's answer to the USA's *Wall Street Journal*.

Now (www.nowtoronto.com) Outstanding alternative weekly (good for events and concerts) free every Thursday.

Toronto Life (www.torontolife.com) Toronto's upscale lifestyle, dining, arts and entertainment monthly mag.

Toronto Star (www.thestar.com) The largest paper in Canada; a comprehensive daily newspaper leaning to the left-of-centre.

Toronto Sun (www.torontosun.com) Sensational tabloid with predictably good sports coverage.

Where Toronto (www.where.ca/toronto) The most informative of the free glossy tourist magazines.

Wholenote (www.thewholenote.com) Free monthly jazz, classical and choral music mag.

Xtra! (www.xtra.ca) Free biweekly alternative G&L street-press.

PASSPORTS

Visitors from almost all countries need a passport. For US citizens, a driver's license is often sufficient to prove residency when entering via land border crossings. However, a birth certificate or certificate of citizenship or naturalization may be required before admission is granted. Permanent residents of the US who aren't citizens should carry their green card.

PHARMACIES

The **Shoppers Drug Mart** (www.shoppersdrug mart.ca) chain has dozens of branches including the following:

Queen Street & Dundas Square (Map pp232–3; ☎ 416-979-2424; 700 Bay St; 🕒 24hr; 🚇 College)

The Annex (Map pp242–3; ☎ 416-961-2121; 360A Bloor St W; 🕒 8am-midnight Mon-Sat, from 10am Sun; 🚇 Spadina)

Yonge Street Strip (Map pp238–9; ☎ 416-920-0098; 728 Yonge St; 🕒 8am-midnight Mon-Fri, from 9am Sat, from 10am Sun; 🚇 Bloor-Yonge)

POST

Canada Post/Postes Canada (☎ 866-607-6301; www.canadapost.ca) may not be remarkably quick, but it's reliable. Standard postcards or 1st-class air-mail letters (up to 30g) cost 51¢ to Canadian destinations, 89¢ to the US, and $1.49 to anywhere else. Toronto no longer has a main post office, but branch post offices and outlets in drugstores are dotted throughout the city.

Poste restante mail should be addressed as follows:

FAMILY NAME, First Name
c/o POSTE RESTANTE
31 Adelaide St E
Toronto, ON M5C 2J0
Canada

Poste restante will be held for 15 days before being returned. Mail can be collected from the **Adelaide St Post Office** (Map pp244–5; ☎ 800-267-1177; Financial District, 31 Adelaide St E; 🕒 8am-5:45pm Mon-Fri; 🚇 Queen); there may be a small charge for the service. Any packages sent to you in Canada will be ruthlessly inspected by the customs officials, who will then assess duties.

Hotel concessions, newsstands and tourist shops also sell stamps, but usually for more than face value. Convenient shipping outlets include **Mail Boxes Etc** (Map pp234–5; ☎ 416-367-9171; www.mbe.ca; Theatre Block, 157 Adelaide St W; 🕒 8:30am-7pm Mon-Fri, 10am-5pm Sat; 🚇 St Andrew).

RADIO

Tune your Toronto ear into the following:

CBC1 (99.1FM; www.cbc.ca) Music, arts and news; 'Definitely Not the Opera,' a Canadian pop culture show, airs on Saturday afternoons.

CBC2 (94.1FM; www.cbc.ca) Classical music and jazz, with 'Saturday Afternoon at the Opera' and nightly 10pm 'After Hours' jazz.

CFRB (1010AM; www.cfrb.com) News-talk radio, featuring the John Moore Show (p19).

CHIN (100.7FM; www.chinradio.com) Multicultural, multilingual programming.

CILQ (107FM; www.q107.com) Classic rock broadcast from Dundas Square.

CIUT (89.5FM; www.ciut.fm) Music and spoken-word from the U of T campus.

CJRT (91.1FM; www.jazz.fm) Nothin' but jazz.

Edge (102.1FM; www.edge102.com) Toronto's premier new-rock station.

Radio Canada (860AM; www.radio-canada.ca) National public broadcasting in French.

SAFETY

Women walking alone after dark east of Yonge St from the Gardiner Expwy north to Carlton St might be mistaken for prostitutes by lecherous curb-crawlers. The southern section of Jarvis St, between Carlton and Queen Sts, especially around Allan Gardens and George St, should be avoided by everyone at night (it's not so great during the day either).

Many social service agencies have recently closed, creating a tide of homeless (often mentally ill) people begging on the streets. This is a real problem for Toronto, but remember that homeless people are more likely to be assaulted or harassed than doing so to you.

Violent crime rates are allegedly falling, but there's at least one gun-related incident in Toronto every day (usually in the outer suburbs). Property theft is increasing slightly. Biker gangs cause occasional problems – give them a wide berth on the highway.

SENIOR TRAVELERS

People over the age of 65 (sometimes 50) typically qualify for the same concession discounts as students. Any photo ID is usually sufficient proof of age. The **Canadian Association of Retired Persons** (CARP; ☎ 416-363-8748, 800-363-9736; www.carp.ca; 1-yr membership $20) has excellent on-line resources; also refer to www.fifty-plus .net.

Elderhostel (☎ 800-454-5768; www.elder hostel.org) specializes in inexpensive, educational packages for people 55 years or older. Accommodations are in university dorms and the programs are so popular that a lottery is often required to select participants. **Routes to Learning Canada** (☎ 613-530-2222, 866-745-1690; www.routestolearning .ca) coordinates Elderhostel programs in Ontario.

TAX & REFUNDS

The Federal Goods and Services Tax (GST), aka the 'Gouge & Screw' or 'Grab & Steal' tax, adds 7% to nearly every product, service or transaction, on top of which usually follows an 8% Ontario retail sales tax. Visitors are eligible for refunds on GST paid for short-term accommodations and non-consumable goods, although the refund process can be a drag (p148).

TELEPHONE

Local calls cost 25¢ from public pay phones, which are either coin- or card-operated; some accept credit cards or have data ports for laptop internet connections.

Dial all 10 phone number digits, including the three-digit area code and seven-digit number, even for local calls. Downtown phone numbers take the 416 (and sometimes 647) area code; GTA telephone numbers adopt the 905 area code.

Always dial '1' before toll-free (800, 888, 877 etc) and domestic long-distance numbers. Some toll-free numbers work anywhere in North America, others only within Canada. International rates apply for calls to the US, even though the dialing code (+1) is the same as for Canadian long-distance calls.

Phonecards

Sold at convenience stores, prepaid phonecards offer superior rates to the country's Bell networks. Phonecards advertising the cheapest rates may charge hefty connection fees, especially via toll-free payphone access numbers. Avoid these surcharges by depositing 25¢ then dialing the local access number.

Cell Phones

North America uses various cell phone systems and most are incompatible with the GSM 900/1800 standard used in Europe, Asia, Africa and Australia. Check with your cellular service provider about using your phone in Canada. Calls may be routed internationally, so beware of roaming surcharges.

USEFUL NUMBERS

- International dialing ☎ 011 + country code
- International operator ☎ 00
- Local directory assistance ☎ 411
- Local operator ☎ 0

Faxes

To send faxes, try Kinko's (p201) or Mail Boxes Etc (opposite). It's $1 to $2 per page for local faxes and $5 for international ones.

TIME

Toronto is in the Eastern time zone (EST/EDT), the same as New York City. During Daylight Saving Time (from the first Sunday in April to the last Saturday in October), the clock moves ahead one hour. During the rest of the year, at noon in Toronto it's

Time	Location
9am	Vancouver
11am	Chicago
1pm	Halifax
5pm	London
6pm	Paris
3am (next day)	Sydney
5am (next day)	Auckland

TIPPING

Tip restaurant servers 15% (equal to the total tax amount on your bill), and up to 20% for excellent service. If the restaurant automatically adds a 'service charge' (usually for groups of six or more), do not double tip. Bartenders get at least $1 per drink, 15% when buying a round. Tip taxi drivers about 10% of the fare, rounding up to the nearest dollar. Skycaps, bellhops and cloak-room attendants get around $2 per item; housekeepers are tipped $2 to $5 per night.

TOURIST INFORMATION

Tourism Toronto (☎ 416-203-2600, 800-499-2514; www.torontotourism.com) telephone agents are available year-round from 8:30am to 5:30pm weekdays. After hours, use their automated touch-tone information menu.

Toronto's **Ontario Travel Information Centre** (Map pp232–3; ☎ 800-668-2746, French ☎ 800-268-3736; www.ontariotravel.net; Dundas Square, 20 Dundas St W; ☺ 10am-7pm Mon-Fri, to 6pm Sat, noon-5pm Sun; ⓓ Dundas) has knowledgeable, multilingual staff and overflowing racks of brochures. They're open 'til 9pm Monday to Friday during summer.

Other Ontario Travel Information Centres are located at US–Canada border crossings, providing information and currency-exchange services. They're open from 8:30am until at least 6pm daily during summer, closing earlier in the off-season:

Niagara Falls (Map p182; ☎ 905-358-3221; 5355 Stanley Ave) West on Hwy 420 from the Rainbow Bridge.

Sarnia (☎ 519-344-7403; 1415 Venetian Blvd) At the Bluewater Bridge.

Windsor (☎ 519-973-1310; 1235 Huron Church Rd) East of the Ambassador Bridge.

TRAVELERS WITH DISABILITIES

Guide dogs may legally be brought into restaurants, hotels and other businesses. Many public service phone numbers and some payphones are adapted for the hearing-impaired. Larger private and chain hotels have suites for disabled guests. About 90% of curbs are dropped and most public buildings are wheelchair accessible. Wheelchair-accessible venues in this book are indicated with a ⓑ.

Only some subway stations and city buses are wheelchair-equipped – look for specially marked stops displaying the blue wheelchair icon. The **TTC** (p214) also runs separate Community Routes that are fully accessible. Their **Wheel-Trans** (☎ 416-393-

4111, reservations ☎ 416-393-4222, TTY ☎ 416-393-4555; www.toronto.ca/ttc /special.htm) service offers door-to-door transport at the cost of a regular bus ticket or subway token. VIA Rail and long-distance bus companies can accommodate wheelchairs if given sufficient advance notice.

Many car-rental agencies provide hand-controlled vehicles or vans with wheelchair lifts for no extra charge (reservations required). Locally, contact **Kino Mobility Inc** (☎ 416-635-5873, 888-495-4455; www.ki nomobility.com). To use disabled parking spaces apply in advance for an Accessible Parking Permit from the **Ontario Ministry of Transportation** (☎ 416-235-2999, 800-387-3445; www.mto.gov.on.ca).

Other helpful resources:

Access Toronto (☎ 416-338-0338, TTY 416-338-0889; www.toronto.ca/accesstoronto)

Beyond Ability International (☎ 416-410-3748; www .beyond-ability.com)

Findhelp Information Services (☎ 211, TTY 416-392-3778; www.211toronto.ca) Multilingual 24-hour help line.

Mobility International USA (☎ TTY 541-343-1284; www.miusa.org)

Society for Accessible Travel & Hospitality (SATH; ☎ 212-447-7284; www.sath.org)

VISAS

Short-term visitors from nearly all Western countries, except parts of Eastern Europe, normally don't require visas. Visa requirements change frequently, so check with the **Canadian Immigration Centre** (www.cic.gc.ca) or the Canadian embassy or consulate in your home country to see if you're exempt.

A passport and/or visa does not guarantee entry. Proof of sufficient funds or possibly a return ticket out of the country may be required. Visitors with medical conditions might be refused entry if they're deemed liable to place a financial burden on Canadian health and social services (ie they admit to needing treatment during their stay in Canada).

If you are refused entry but have a visa, you have the right of appeal at the port of entry. If you're arriving by land, the best course is simply to try again later (after a shift change) or at a different border crossing.

To/from the USA

Visitors to Canada who also plan to spend time in the USA should know that admission requirements are subject to rapid change. Under the US visa waiver program, US visas are not currently required for citizens of the EU, Australia and New Zealand for visits up to 90 days. Check with **US Customs & Border Protection** (www.cbp.gov) for the latest eligibility requirements. Even visitors who don't need a visa pay a US$6 entry fee at land border crossings. Be sure to check that your entry permit to Canada includes multiple entries, too.

WOMEN TRAVELERS

Compared with major US cities, Toronto sets high standards for women's safety. Busy main-street foot traffic continues past midnight, but there are still some neighborhoods to avoid (p204). The TTC makes excellent provisions for women riding public transport after dark (p214). Social service organizations for women run from the 519 Community Centre (p201); see Emergency (p200) for other helpful resources, including sexual assault crisis lines. It is illegal to carry pepper spray or mace in Canada.

WORK

Canadian work permits are difficult to obtain because employment opportunities go first to Canadians. In most cases, you'll need to take a validated job offer from a specific employer to a Canadian consulate or embassy abroad.

Each year, the Canadian **Working Holiday Program** offers a limited number of one-year visas to Australians (A$165) and New Zealanders (NZ$180) between the ages of 18 and 30. Competition is stiff – apply early. Application forms are available through Sydney's **Canadian Consulate General** (☎ 02-9364-3082; www.whpcanada.org.au; L5, 111 Harrington St, Sydney) or New Zealand's **Canadian High Commission** (☎ 04-473-9577; www.dfait-maeci.gc.ca/asia/whp; PO Box 8047, Wellington).

Student Work Abroad Program (SWAP) facilitates additional working holidays for students and those under 30 (sometimes 35). Participants come from nearly 20 countries, including Australia, France, Germany, Mexico, New Zealand, the UK and the USA. Ask **SWAP Canada** (www.swap.ca) or Travel CUTS (p214) about which student travel agency to contact in your own country for further details.

Transportation

Transportation

Flights, tours and rail tickets can be booked online at www.lonelyplanet.com/travel_services.

AIR

Airlines

Major airlines serving Toronto's airports include the following:

Aeroflot (☎ 416-642-1653, 877-209-1935; www.aeroflotcanada.com)

Aeromexico (☎ 905-891-0093; www.aeromexico.com)

Air Canada (☎ 888-247-2262; www.aircanada.ca)

Air France (☎ 800-667-2747; www.airfrance.com)

Air New Zealand (☎ 800-663-5494; www.airnewzealand.com)

Air Transat (☎ 866-847-1112; www.airtransat.com)

Alaska Airlines (☎ 800-252-7522; www.alaskaair.com)

Alitalia (☎ 905-673-2442, 800-268-9277; www.alitalia.com)

All Nippon Airways (☎ 800-235-9262; www.fly-ana.com)

America West Airlines (☎ 800-428-4322; www.americawest.com)

American Airlines (☎ 800-433-7300; www.aa.com)

British Airways (☎ 800-247-9297; www.britishairways.com)

CanJet Airlines (☎ 800-809-7777; www.canjet.com)

Cathay Pacific (☎ 800-268-6868; www.cathaypacific.com)

Continental Airlines (☎ 800-523-3273; www.continental.com)

Cubana Airlines (☎ 416-967-2822, 866-428-2262; www.cubana.cu)

Czech Airlines (☎ 416-363-3174, 800-641-0641; www.csa.cz)

Delta Air Lines (☎ 800-221-1212; www.delta.com)

El Al Israel (☎ 416-967-4222, 800-361-6174; www.elal.co.il)

Finnair (☎ 416-222-0740, 800-461-8651; www.finnair.com)

Japan Airlines (☎ 800-525-3663; www.jal.co.jp/en/)

Korean Air (☎ 800-438-5000; www.koreanair.com)

Lufthansa (☎ 800-563-5954; www.lufthansa.com)

Mexicana Airlines (☎ 800-531-7921; www.mexicana.com.mx)

Northwest Airlines/KLM (☎ 800-225-2525; www.nwa.com)

Olympic Airlines (☎ 416-964-2720; www.olympicairlines.com)

CLIMATE CHANGE & TRAVEL

Climate change is a serious threat to the ecosystems that humans rely upon, and air travel is the fastest-growing contributor to the problem. Lonely Planet regards travel, overall, as a global benefit, but believes we all have a responsibility to limit our personal impact on global warming.

Flying & Climate Change

Pretty much every form of motor transport generates CO_2 (the main cause of human-induced climate change) but planes are far and away the worst offenders, not just because of the sheer distances they allow us to travel, but because they release greenhouse gases high into the atmosphere. The statistics are frightening: two people taking a return flight between Europe and the US will contribute as much to climate change as an average household's gas and electricity consumption over a whole year.

Carbon Offset Schemes

Climatecare.org and other websites use 'carbon calculators' that allow travellers to offset the greenhouse gases they are responsible for with contributions to energy-saving projects and other climate-friendly initiatives in the developing world – including projects in India, Honduras, Kazakhstan and Uganda.

Lonely Planet, together with Rough Guides and other concerned partners in the travel industry, supports the carbon offset scheme run by climatecare.org. Lonely Planet offsets all of its staff and author travel.

For more information check out our website: www.lonelyplanet.com.

Qantas (☎ 800-227-4500; www.qantas.com.au)

Scandinavian Airlines (☎ 800-221-2350; www .scandinavian.net)

Singapore Airlines (☎ 800-663-3046; www.singa poreair.com)

Thai Airways International (☎ 800-426-5204; www .thaiair.com)

United Airlines (☎ 800-864-8331; www.united.com)

US Airways (☎ 800-428-4322; www.usairways.com)

WestJet (☎ 877-937-8538; 800-538-5696; www.westjet .com)

ZOOM Airlines (☎ 613-235-9666, 866-359-9666; www .flyzoom.com)

Airports

Tickets for flights departing Canada, whether purchased in Canada or abroad, usually include departure taxes ($20 from Toronto).

Most Canadian airlines and major international carriers arrive at Canada's busiest airport, **Lester B Pearson International Airport** (YYZ; Map p230; ☎ 866-207-1690, Terminals 1 & 2 ☎ 416-247-7678, Terminal 3 ☎ 416-776-5100; www.gtaa.com), a 27km drive northwest of downtown Toronto (Lester B, a former Canadian Prime Minister, also won the Nobel Peace Prize). Terminal assignments are subject to change, so call ahead or check airport entrance signs carefully. The Greater Toronto Airports Authority (GTAA) recently opened a new multibillion-dollar terminal that will eventually replace Terminals 1 and 2. Except for Air Canada's Star Alliance partners, most international carriers operate from Terminal 3. All terminals have food courts, duty-free stores, medical emergency clinics, baggage storage facilities, lost and found offices, ATMs, currency-exchange booths and information desks. Interterminal courtesy shuttle buses for transit passengers run frequently.

There are **Travelers' Aid Society** (Terminal 1 ☎ 905-676-2868, Terminal 3 ☎ 416-776-5890; www.travellersaid.com; ☾ 10am-9pm) help desks in the arrivals concourses of Terminals 1 and 3.

On the Toronto Islands, small **Toronto City Centre Airport** (TCCA; Map p247; ☎ 416-203-6942; www.torontoport.com/airport. asp) is home to regional airlines, helicopter companies and private flyers. **Air Canada Jazz** (☎ 888-247-2262; www.flyjazz.ca) flights

from Ottawa land at TCCA rather than Pearson – it's quicker because you're already downtown, and you get a good look at the city too!

Getting into Town

Airport Express (☎ 905-564-3232, 800-387-6787; www.torontoairportexpress.com) operates an express bus connecting Pearson International with the Metro Toronto Coach Terminal (p212) and major downtown hotels, including the Westin Harbour Castle, Fairmont Royal York and the Delta Chelsea Toronto Downtown. Buses depart every 20 to 30 minutes from 5am to 1am. Allow 1½ hours to get to/from the airport. A one-way/round-trip ticket costs $16.50/28.50 (cash, credit card or US dollars). Students and seniors receive $2 off one-way fares; kids under 11 travel free. Buses leave Terminals 1/2/3 from curbside locations B3/17/25.

If you're not buried under heavy luggage, the cheapest way to Pearson is via the TTC bus and subway (p214). From the airport, the 192 Airport Rocket bus departs from ground level of Terminal 1 and arrivals levels of Terminals 2 & 3, every 20 minutes from 5:30am to 2am. It's a 20-minute ride to Kipling Station ($2.75, exact change only), where you transfer free onto the Bloor-Danforth subway line using your bus ticket. Allow an hour for the full trip downtown. The 300A Bloor-Danforth night bus runs every 15 minutes from 2am to 5am ($2.75, exact change only). The 300A departs the same locations as the 192; it's a 45-minute run from Pearson to Yonge and Bloor.

A taxi from Pearson into the city takes around 45 minutes, depending on traffic. The GTAA regulates fares by drop-off zone ($46 to downtown Toronto). A metered taxi from central Toronto to Pearson costs around $50.

If you're driving yourself to/from the airport, avoid Hwy 401 during the am/pm rush hours; instead, take the Gardiner Expwy west from Spadina Ave then head north on Hwy 427. Parking at the Terminal 1, 2 and 3 garages costs $3 per half hour, $24 per day. Long-term parking at off-site lots costs around $13 per day or $50 per week, with free terminal shuttles available. For airport car rental information, see p212.

From the Toronto City Centre Airport, **ferries** (Map p247; ☎ 416-203-6945) chug

Transportation

AIR

over to the foot of Bathurst St every 15 minutes from 7am until 10pm. At just 121m, it's allegedly the world's shortest scheduled ferry route! It's free from the mainland to the airport, but costs $5.50 in the other direction. From Bathurst St it's a short walk to Lake Shore Blvd W and the 509 Harbourfront or 510 Spadina streetcars.

BICYCLE, IN-LINE SKATES & PEDICAB

Toronto has 50km of on-street bicycle lanes and over 40km of marked routes for bicycles. In-line skaters can cruise along sidewalks, but it's illegal for cyclists to do so. The free *Toronto Cycling Map* is distributed by the **Toronto Cycling Committee** (☎ 416-392-9253; www.city.toronto.on.ca/cycling). You can download the map online, pick up a copy at **City Hall** (p60; ☎ 416-393-7650) or at the Toronto Reference Library (p67). See p138 for more cycling/skating details, including equipment rental.

Bicycles are permitted on TTC buses, streetcars and subways, except during weekday morning (6:30am to 9:30am) and afternoon (3:30pm to 6:30pm) rush hours, and other times when vehicles become heavily crowded. Bicycles are allowed on some, but not all, Toronto Islands ferries, with additional restrictions during peak periods. Check details at the ticket booths.

Deluxe pedicab rickshaws pedaled by impressively fit, young Torontonians can be hired around downtown during summer. Negotiate fares for longer trips with the driver before clambering aboard. Tip generously.

BUS

Long-distance buses are cheaper than trains, but not as fast or comfortable. Bus lines covering Ontario, the rest of Canada and US destinations lurch out of the **Metro Toronto Coach Terminal** (Map pp232–3; ☎ 416-393-7911; fax 416-979-8772; Dundas Square, 610 Bay St; Ⓜ Dundas; Ⓨ 5:30am-midnight), which has coin lockers and a **Travelers' Aid Society** (☎ 416-596-8647; www.travellersaid.com; Ⓨ 9:30am-5:30pm) help desk, providing accommodation bookings, maps and brochures.

Greyhound (☎ 800-661-8747; www.greyhound.ca) covers much of southwestern Ontario, including the Niagara region and Stratford. Discounts on standard one-way adult fares are given to ISIC cardholders, seniors, children and pairs traveling together. Walk-up rates are the most expensive; purchase tickets at least a week in advance for better fares (advance tickets don't guarantee a seat – you still have to line up!). When making reservations, always ask for the direct or express bus.

Walk-up rates for long-distance routes from Toronto (add $3 for Friday, Saturday and Sunday travel) include the following:

Destination	Cost	Duration
Buffalo	$24	3hr
Chicago	$91	11½-15hr
Detroit	$69	5½-6hr
Montréal	$94	8-9½hr
New York	$99	10-13hr
Niagara Falls	$22	2hr
Vancouver	$370	65-70hr

Coach Canada (☎ 800-461-7661; www.coachcanada.com) offers comparable fares to Niagara Falls, Montréal, Buffalo and New York.

CAR

Unless you're masochistic, we only recommend renting a car for excursions outside Toronto. Driving in the city is a headache: expressways are congested, construction never ends, parking is expensive and parking inspectors are hounds from hell.

Rental

Rates go up and down like the stock market, so it's worth phoning around or scouring the internet for the best deals. Booking ahead will get you a better rate; the airport tends to be cheaper than downtown. Typically, a small car costs $35 to $45 per day, or $250 to $300 per week. But after adding insurance, taxes, excess kilometers and any other fees, you could be handed a fairly hefty bill. Discounted weekend rates (under $100) may include 'extra days,' for example from noon Thursday until noon Monday.

Major international car-rental agencies have reservation desks at Pearson airport, as well as several city-wide offices:

Budget (☎ 800-314-5885, 800-268-9000; www.budget
.com)

Di$count Car & Truck Rental (☎ 877-742-8787; www
.discountcar.com)

National Car Rental (☎ 800-227-7368; www.nation
alcar.ca)

New Frontier Rent-A-Car (Map p230; ☎ 416-675-2000,
800-567-2837; www.newfrontiercar.com; 5875 Airport Rd,
Mississauga; free airport shuttle)

Thrifty Car Rental (☎ 800-847-4389; www.thrifty.com)

Smaller independent agencies offer lower
rates, but may have fewer (and perhaps
older) cars available. Try the following:

Wheels 4 Rent (Map pp240–1; ☎ 416-585-7782; www
.wheels4rent.ca; Kensington Market, 77 Nassau St; ⓡ 510)

Zipcar (Map pp232–3; ☎ 416-977-9008; www.zipcar
.com; Queen West, Ste 205, 147 Spadina Ave; ⓡ 501,
510) Cost-effective and ecoaware city car-sharing.

Driving

In Ontario, petrol (gasoline) averages 80¢
per litre, which is around US$2.60 per US
gallon. Strapping on seat belts is compulsory throughout Canada. You can turn
right on a red light after first having made
a full stop; flashing green lights at intersec-
tions signal protected left turns. All vehicles
must stop for streetcars, behind the rear
doors, while the streetcar is collecting or
ejecting passengers. Drivers must also stop
for pedestrians at crosswalks whenever the
overhead crossing signals are flashing.

With a few exceptions, you can legally
drive in Canada with a valid driver's license
from your home country. If your license
isn't written in English (or French), you may
require an International Driving Permit.
Short-term US visitors can bring in their
own vehicles without special permits, provided they have insurance. If you've rented
a car in the USA and are driving it into
Canada, bring a copy of the rental agreement to avoid border crossing hassles.

On weekends and holidays, especially
during summer, major land border crossings with the USA jam-up quickly. You can
check border wait times online at www.
cbsa-asfc.gc.ca/general/times/menu-e.html
before leaving. Smaller, secondary US–
Canada border crossings aren't usually so
busy; sometimes they're so quiet that the
customs officials have nothing better to do
than tear your luggage apart.

Parking

Private parking lots in Toronto are expensive – usually $3 to $4 per half hour, with an
average daily maximum of $12 or more (or
a flat rate of around $6 after 6pm). Cheap-
est are the municipal lots run by the Toronto Parking Authority (☎ 416-393-7275; www
.greenp.com), which are scattered around
T.O. (look for the green signs). They cost
the same as metered street parking (if you
can find any) – usually $3 per hour. Some
metered spaces have a central payment
kiosk where you purchase your time using
cash or credit card then display the receipt
on your dashboard. Utterly unjustly, it's illegal to park next to a broken meter. Residential streets have only severely restricted
on-street parking. Tow trucks are merciless,
and getting your vehicle back will cost a
shiny pile of 'loonies.'

In this book, Ⓟ is used for accommodations with free parking; if on-site parking
is available for a fee, this amount follows
the icon. Otherwise, ask about pay parking
options nearby.

FERRY

From April to September, Toronto Islands Ferries (Map pp234–5; ☎ 416-392-8193; www
.city.toronto.on.ca/parks/island/ferry.htm)
run every 15 to 30 minutes from 8am to
11pm, taking about 15 minutes to cross
Toronto Inner Harbour. A return ticket
costs adult/child/concession $6/2.50/3.50.
Queues can be ridiculously long on weekends and holidays, so show up early. From
October to March, ferry services are slashed
to a minimum (roughly hourly), only serv-
icing Ward's Island, plus a couple per day
to Hanlan's Point if you're lucky. The Toronto Islands Ferry Terminal is at the foot
of Bay St, off Queens Quay, just west of the
Westin Harbour Castle.

The high-speed international ferry between Toronto and Rochester, New York,
ceased operating in January 2006 after losing $10 million in 10 months, but may one
day be resuscitated.

TAXI

Metered fares start at $3; plus $1.50 for each
additional kilometre, depending on traffic.
Taxi drivers will usually take you where you
want to go without ripping you off – hail

Transportation FERRY

one on the street and watch them brake, U-turn or swerve majestically across several lanes to pick you up. Taxi stands reside outside of hotels, museums, shopping malls and entertainment venues.

Taxi companies include the following:

Crown Taxi (☎ 416-292-1212, 877-750-7878; www .crowntaxi.com)

Diamond Taxicab (☎ 416-366-6868; www.diamondtaxi .ca)

Royal Taxi (☎ 416-777-9222; www.royaltaxi.ca) Also has wheelchair-accessible taxis.

TRAIN

Canadians feel a special attachment to the 'ribbons of steel' from coast to coast, although they don't take the train very often. Union Station (Map pp234–5) is Toronto's main rail hub, with currency exchange and **Travelers' Aid Society** (☎ 416-366 7788; www.travellersaid .com; ☯ 9:30am-9:30pm) help desks on the upper and lower concourses (for accommodations bookings, maps and brochures).

VIA Rail (☎ 416-366-8411, 888-842-7245; www.viarail.ca) services are excellent along the so-called 'Québec-Windsor Corridor,' the heavily trafficked thoroughfare between Québec City and Windsor, Ontario (just across the US–Canada border from Detroit, Michigan). Fares vary wildly, but are significantly cheaper if tickets are purchased at least one week in advance. VIA Rail's Corridor Pass (adult/concession $265/239) is good for 10 days. Below are some typical one-way economy-class fares from Toronto:

Destination	Cost	Duration
Montréal	$92	5hr
Niagara Falls	$22	2hr
Ottawa	$85	4hr
Vancouver	$450	75hr

America's **Amtrak** (☎ 800-872-7245; www .amtrak.com) has an information desk inside Union Station and runs several routes between the USA and Canada. Here's a handful of typical fares:

Destination	Cost	Duration
Boston-Toronto	US$105	18hr
Chicago-Toronto	US$98	15hr
NYC-Toronto	US$82	14hr
NYC-Montréal	US$61	10hr

International passengers are responsible for securing documentation (passports and visas) prior to on-board customs and immigration procedures.

The **GO Train** (☎ 416-869-3200, 888-438-6646; www.gotransit.com) commuter network, run by GO Transit, serves the outer suburbs of Toronto. Service is fast and steady throughout the day, but unless you're staying in the 'burbs, you probably won't make much use of it. A typical fare to Scarborough or Mississauga would be around $3.80.

TRAVEL AGENTS

Travel CUTS (☎ 888-359-2887; www.travel cuts.com) is a reputable budget, youth and student travel agency with branches at **Union Station** (Map pp234–5; ☎ 416-365-0545; upper concourse, 65 Front St W; ☯ 10am-6pm Mon-Fri; ⊙ Union), **King St W** (Map pp234–5; ☎ 416-977-1221; 408 King St W; ☯ 10am-6pm Mon-Fri, 11am-4pm Sat; ⊠ 504, 510), and **College St** (Map pp238–9; ☎ 416-979-2406; 187 College St; ☯ 9:30am-5pm Mon, Thu & Fri, 9am-7pm Wed, 10am-4pm Sat; ⊠ 506).

Weekendtrips.com (☎ 416-599-8747; www .weekendtrips.com) is a travel company serving up sweet deals on weekend getaways to Ottawa, Montréal and other Canadian cities, plus day trips to the Niagara Peninsula and other provincial destinations.

TTC SUBWAY, STREETCAR & BUS

The **Toronto Transit Commission** (TTC; ☎ 416-393-4636; www.city.toronto.on.ca/ttc) operates an efficient subway, streetcar and bus system throughout the city. A helpful *TTC Ride Guide* is available from subway station attendants. More detailed (and very complicated) route maps are posted at streetcar shelters, major bus stops and inside subway cars.

Subway lines operate from approximately 6am (9am on Sunday) until 1:30am daily, with trains every five minutes. The main lines are the crosstown Bloor–Danforth line, and the U-shaped Yonge–University–Spadina line which bends through Union Station. Stations have Designated Waiting Areas (DWAs) monitored by security cameras and equipped with a bench, pay phone and intercom link to the station manager. They're located where the subway guard's car stops along the platform. Subway stations in this book are indicated with a ⊖.

Streetcars are slower than the subway, but you'll see more and they stop every block or two. Streetcars operate from 5am until 1:30am on weekdays with reduced weekend services. Route numbers and destinations are displayed on both front and rear cars. The main east–west routes are along St Clair Ave (512), College St (506), Dundas St (505), Queen St (501 and 502), and King St (503 and 504). North–south streetcars grind along Bathurst St (511) and Spadina Ave (510). The 511 turns west at the lakefront towards the Canadian National Exhibition (CNE) grounds; the 510 turns east towards Union Station. The 509 Harbourfront streetcar trundles west from Union Station along Lake Shore Blvd. Streetcar lines in this book are indicated with a ⊠ icon.

Visitors won't find much use for TTC buses, which are slow and get held up in traffic. Women traveling alone between 9pm and 5am can request stops anywhere along regular bus routes; notify the driver in advance and exit via the front doors. Bus stops with blue-banded poles are part of the limited Blue Night Network which operates basic city routes between 1:30am and 5am daily, running every 30 minutes. Bus routes in this book are indicated with a 🚌.

For more far-flung travel, the TTC system connects with GO Transit's **GO Bus** (☎ 416-869-3200, 888-438-6646; www .gotransit.com) routes in surrounding suburbs like Richmond Hill, Brampton and Hamilton.

Fares & Passes

The regular adult TTC fare is $2.75 (student/senior $1.85, child 70¢). You can transfer to any other TTC bus, subway or streetcar for free using your paper streetcar/ bus ticket or transfer ticket from automated dispensers near subway exits. Exact change is required for streetcars and buses; subway attendants are more forgiving. Ten subway tokens cost $21 (student/senior $14, child $4.70), available from subway stations or stores displaying the TTC ticket agent sign. Day Passes cost $8.50, and can be used by individuals, couples, or two adults and up to four kids traveling together. They're valid for unlimited rides from the start of service until 5:30am the following morning. Weekly Metropasses cost $30 (student/ senior $23.75), and run from Monday to Sunday.

WALKING

Central Toronto is very pedestrian friendly, with leafy residential neighborhoods and compact retail strips. In winter, astute Torontonins forego icy sidewalks and sunless days and burrow into the downtown **PATH** (www.city.toronto.on.ca/path) network – 27km of underground tunnels linking shopping malls, offices and subway stations. If you get lost (we challenge you not to!), look for directions posted on overhead signs and wall maps. With some luck and cunning, you'll eventually surface at Union Station, Eaton Centre or wherever else you meant to go. Then again, you may end up in some anonymous, obscure office building and never be heard from again…

Limerick
County Library

Behind the Scenes

THE LONELY PLANET STORY

The story begins with a classic travel adventure: Tony and Maureen Wheeler's 1972 journey across Europe and Asia to Australia. There was no useful information about the overland trail then, so Tony and Maureen published the first Lonely Planet guidebook to meet a growing need.

From a kitchen table, Lonely Planet has grown to become the largest independent travel publisher in the world, with offices in Melbourne (Australia), Oakland (USA) and London (UK). Today Lonely Planet guidebooks cover the globe. There is an ever-growing list of books and information in a variety of media. Some things haven't changed. The main aim is still to make it possible for adventurous travellers to get out there – to explore and better understand the world.

At Lonely Planet we believe travellers can make a positive contribution to the countries they visit – if they respect their host communities and spend their money wisely. Every year 5% of company profit is donated to charities around the world.

THIS BOOK

This guidebook was commissioned in Lonely Planet's Oakland office, and produced by the following:

Commissioning Editor Emily K Wolman, Jennye Garibaldi

Coordinating Editor Alison Ridgway

Coordinating Cartographers Owen Eszeki, Andrew Smith

Coordinating Layout Designer Pablo Gastar

Managing Editor Geoff Howard

Managing Cartographer Alison Lyall, David Connolly

Assisting Editors Kate James, Donna Wheeler

Assisting Cartographer Hunor Csutoros

Assisting Layout Designers Jacqui Saunders

Cover Designer Pepi Bluck

Project Manager Glenn van der Knijff

Thanks to Sin Choo, Sally Darmody, Ryan Evans, Brooke Lyons, Kate McDonald, Wayne Murphy, Raphael Richards, Cara Smith and Celia Wood

Cover photographs Silhouette of the interior of BCE Place, David W Hamilton/Getty Images (top); Little Sotto Voce Bar, Massimo Borchi/Atlantide (bottom)

Internal photographs by Lonely Planet Images and Corey Wise except the following: p2 Rubens Abboud/Alamy; p7 (#2) Eoin Clarke; p8 Val Duncan/Kenebec Images/Alamy; p4 (#4) Cheryl Forbes; p19 Matthew Plexman; p32, p97, p141, p152 Charles Rawlings-Way; p3, p7 (#1) Glenn van der Knijff; p4 (#2) Raine Vara/Alamy; p7 (#4) Tony Wheeler; p7 (#3) Janusz Wrobel/Alamy.

All images are copyright of the photographer unless otherwise indicated. Many of the images in this guide are available for licensing from Lonely Planet Images: www.lonelyplanetimages.com.

THANKS

CHARLES RAWLINGS-WAY

Thanks to the following folks for their input, generosity, friendship and distraction during the creation of this book: Nick Gallus and Anamitra Deb for the big-screen accommodations and the conversational crew of International Bright Young Things; Bob, Anne, Nick and Chris Bentley (and Sunil) for the warm welcome and hot dinners; Heather Lash, Lara Ceroni, Noel DiTosto and Susie Reading for the inner-city low-down; and Natalie Karneef, Emily Wolman and the in-house LP staff for slap-shooting this puck of a book into the back of the net.

Above all, thank you Meg for sticking around while I do what I love, hemispheres away.

NATALIE KARNEEF

Thanks to mom and dad who taught me to love travel, Phoof for believing in me, and Tony for supporting me, being my navigator and my all-time favorite travel buddy. Thanks to Tegan for sharing the good news, and Chris for showing me around The Hill. Thanks to Jeannine for the tips, Steph and Rita for their T.O. hospitality, and Harold and Marg Erb for their armchair tour-guiding and wonderful, inspiring stories. And thanks to Emily Wolman and Charles Rawlings-Way for their patience and positivity!

OUR READERS

Many thanks to the travelers who used the last edition and wrote to us with helpful hints, useful advice and interesting anecdotes:

Robert Barron, Alice Barton, Nicolena Cassidy-Wright, Joan Chipps, Sebastian Cook, Gina Facchini, Lesley Fraser, Derek Fung, Alexander Gillett, John Grant, Lindsey Kirschner, Luis Henrique Kubota, Luís Kubota, Mary Langridge, Patricia Leah, Angel Ling, Vicky Luker, Scott Macdonald, Gloria Marsh, Blair Martin, Dore Meyers, Carolyn Mill, Elisabeth Mok, Eve Montgomery, Francis Moore, Kate Needham, Vern Nicholson, Clifford Power, Sara Quirk, Sarah Rimmington, Emma Roberts, Rohan Samahon, Elizabeth Schmidt, Hilary Shaw, Luis Ducla Soares, Karl Steinhoff, Jan Thomas, Frederika Tournicourt, Ilse van den Bosch, Johnathan Wells

ACKNOWLEDGMENTS

Many thanks to the following for the use of their content:

Subway and RT Route Map © 2007 Toronto Transit Commission

SEND US YOUR FEEDBACK

We love to hear from travelers – your comments keep us on our toes and help make our books better. Our well-traveled team reads every word on what you loved or loathed about this book. Although we cannot reply individually to postal submissions, we always guarantee that your feedback goes straight to the appropriate authors, in time for the next edition. Each person who sends us information is thanked in the next edition – and the most useful submissions are rewarded with a free book.

To send us your updates – and find out about Lonely Planet events, newsletters and travel news – visit our award-winning website: www.lonelyplanet.com/contact.

Note: We may edit, reproduce and incorporate your comments in Lonely Planet products such as guidebooks, websites and digital products, so let us know if you don't want your comments reproduced or your name acknowledged. For a copy of our privacy policy visit www.lonelyplanet.com/privacy.

Notes

Index

See also separate indexes for Eating (p225), Entertainment (p226), Shopping (p227) and Sleeping (p227).

000 map pages
000 photographs

Index

Index

000 map pages
000 photographs

Index

SHOPPING

SLEEPING

Index

000 map pages
000 photographs

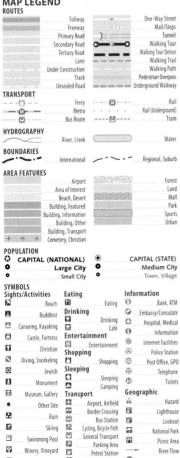

MAP LEGEND

ROUTES

Tollway	One-Way Street
Freeway	Mall/Steps
Primary Road	Tunnel
Secondary Road	Walking Tour
Tertiary Road	Walking Tour Detour
Lane	Walking Trail
Under Construction	Walking Path
Track	Pedestrian Overpass
Unsealed Road	Underground Walkway

TRANSPORT

Ferry	Rail
Metro	Rail (Underground)
Bus Route	Tram

HYDROGRAPHY

River, Creek	Water

BOUNDARIES

International	Regional, Suburb

AREA FEATURES

Airport	Forest
Area of Interest	Land
Beach, Desert	Mall
Building, Featured	Park
Building, Information	Sports
Building, Other	Urban
Building, Transport	
Cemetery, Christian	

POPULATION

◎ CAPITAL (NATIONAL)	◉ CAPITAL (STATE)
● Large City	● Medium City
● Small City	● Town, Village

SYMBOLS

Sights/Activities	Eating	Information
Beach	Eating	Bank, ATM
Buddhist	**Drinking**	Embassy/Consulate
Canoeing, Kayaking	Drinking	Hospital, Medical
Castle, Fortress	Café	Information
Christian	**Entertainment**	Internet Facilities
Diving, Snorkeling	Entertainment	Police Station
Jewish	**Shopping**	Post Office, GPO
Monument	Shopping	Telephone
Museum, Gallery	**Sleeping**	Toilets
Other Site	Sleeping	**Geographic**
Ruin	Camping	Hazard
Skiing	**Transport**	Lighthouse
Swimming Pool	Airport, Airfield	Lookout
Winery, Vineyard	Border Crossing	National Park
Zoo, Bird Sanctuary	Bus Station	Picnic Area
	Cycling, Bicycle Path	River Flow
	General Transport	Waterfall
	Parking Area	
	Petrol Station	
	Taxi Rank	

Maps ▮

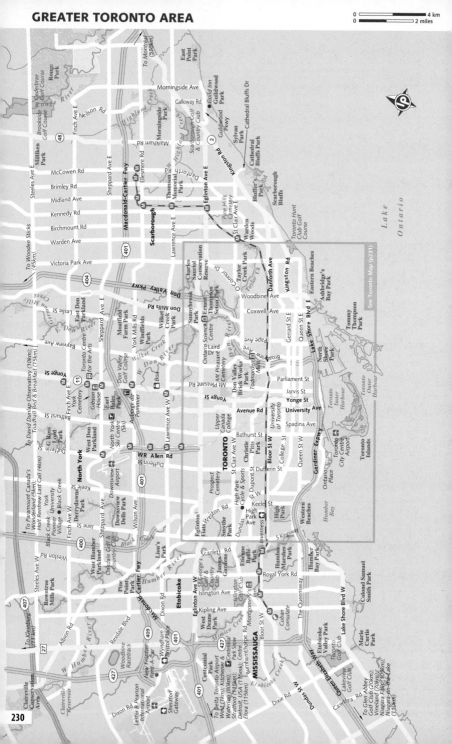

0 —————— 4 km
0 —————— 2 miles

TORONTO

0 _____ 3 km
0 _____ 2 miles

SIGHTS & ACTIVITIES	(pp45–80)
Baldwin Steps	(see 2)
Beach Fairway Golf Course	1 F2
Casa Loma	2 B2
Colbourne Lodge	3 A3
Dish Cooking Studio	4 C2
Exhibition Place	5 B3
Fort York	6 B3
High Park Animal Paddocks	7 A2
High Park Municipal Pool	8 A2
High Park Tennis Courts	9 A2
Hillside Gardens	10 A2
Joe Rockhead's Climbing Gym	11 B3
Molson Amphitheatre	(see 12)
Ontario Place	12 B3
Ontario Science Centre	13 E1
Princes' Gate	(see 2)
Scadding Cabin	(see 2)
Spadina Museum	14 C2
Sunnyside Gus Ryder Pool	15 A3
Sutherland-Chan Clinic	16 C2
Todmorden Mills	17 D2
Todmorden Mills Wildflower	
Preserve	5 B3
Toronto Swing Dance Society	18 A2
Toronto Windsurfing Club	19 D4

ENTERTAINMENT	(pp115–35)
Academy of Spherical Arts	34 B3
Cinesphere	(see 13)
Docks Drive-In Theatre	35 D3
Docks Nightclubs	(see 35)
Dream in High Park	36 A2
Hugh's Room	37 A2
Matador	38 B2
Omnimax Cinema	(see 12)

SHOPPING	(pp147–63)
Bark & Fitz	39 C1
Bark & Fitz	40 A2
Boj Décor	41 D1
Common Cloth	(see 42)
Made You Look	42 B3
Sleuth of Baker Street	43 D1

EATING	(pp91–113)
Celestin	20 D1
JOV Bistro	21 D1
Julie's	22 B3
Mildred Pearce	23 B3
North 44s	24 C1
Scaramouche	25 C2
Vanipha Lanna	26 B1

DRINKING	(pp118–25)
Addis Ababa	27 B3
Amsterdam Brewing Co	28 C3
Ciro's	29 B2
Gladstone Hotel	30 B3
LCBO (Old North York Train	
Station)	31 C2
Rebel House	32 C2
Social	33 B3

SLEEPING	(pp165–78)
Allenby	44 E2
Beaconsfield	45 B3
Bonnevue Manor	46 A3
Candy Haven Tourist Home	47 D1
Castlegate Inn	48 C2
Coach House	49 C2
Drake Hotel	50 B3
Feathers B&B	51 D2
French Connection	52 B1
Grayona Tourist Home	53 A3
Havinn	54 C2
Terrace House Bed & Breakfast	55 C2
Vanderkooy Bed & Breakfast	56 C2

TRANSPORT	(pp209–15)
Dupont	57 C2
Parking	58 B3

INFORMATION	
Dental Emergency Clinic	59 C1
New Zealand Consulate	60 C2

Warden Ave
Victoria Park Ave
Danforth Ave
Kingston Rd
LAKE ONTARIO
RC Harris Filtration Plant
Balmy Beach
The Beach
Beaches Park
See The Beaches Map (p246)
Queen St E
Kew Beach
Woodbine Beach
Woodbine Ave
Little India
Coxwell Ave
Greenwood Ave
Donlands Ave
Dundas St E
Eastern Ave
Leslie St
Jones Ave
Carlaw Ave
Gerrard St E
Queen St E
Lake Shore Blvd E
Tommy Thompson Park
See East Toronto Map (pp244–5)
Greektown
Pape Ave
Broadview Ave
Don Valley Pkwy
Cabbagetown
Parliament St
Sherbourne St
Front St E
Harbour St
Castle Frank
Eglinton Ave E
Don Mills Rd
Charles Sauriol Conservation Reserve
Edwards Gardens
Overlea Blvd
Millwood Rd
Laird Dr
Bayview Ave
Mt Pleasant Cemetery
Mt Pleasant Rd
St Clair Ave
Summerhill
Rosedale
Davisville
Yonge St
Avenue Rd
Bloor-Yorkville, University of Toronto & Yonge Street Strip Map (pp237–9)
Yorkville
Bay St
Bloor-Yonge
College
ROM Museum
Queens Park
University Ave
Dupont
St George
Spadina
Chinatown
St Patrick
Osgoode
St Andrew
Union
King
Entertainment District
Harbourfront
See Downtown North Map (pp240–1)
See Downtown South Map (pp242–3)
See Kensington Market Queen West Map (pp240–3)
Kensington Market
Little Italy
College St W
Ossington Ave
Bathurst St
Davenport Rd
See The Annex & Little Italy Map (pp242–3)
Dufferin St
Dundas St W
Queen St W
Gardiner Expwy
Lake Shore Blvd W
Hanlan's Point Beach
Toronto Inner Harbour
See Toronto Islands Map (p247)
Eastern Channel
Eastern Gap
Lansdowne Ave
Dundas St W
Roncesvalles Ave
Keele St
Bloor St W
Jameson Ave
Grenadier Pond
Eglinton Ave W
St Clair Ave W

231

SIGHTS & ACTIVITIES (pp45–80)
Art Gallery of Ontario (AGO).......1 B3
Campbell House.......................2 D5
Canada Life Building................3 D5
Chum/Citytv Complex..............4 C5
Church of the Holy Trinity.........5 F4
Church of the Holy Trinity
    Labyrinth........................6 E4
City Hall.............................7 E4
Elgin & Winter Garden Theatre
    Centre...........................8 F5
Elmwood Spa.......................9 E3
Grange..............................10 B4
Gray Line Tours..............(see 82)
Great Cooks on Eight.............11 E5
Henry Scadding House............12 F4

Mackenzie House.................13 G4
MuchMusic Studios...........(see 4)
Nathan Phillips Square...........14 E5
New Tribe..........................15 C5
Old City Hall......................16 E5
Ontario Specialty Co.............17 G5
Osgoode Hall.....................18 D5
Speakers Corner..................19 B5
Textile Museum of Canada......20 D3

EATING 🍴 (pp91–113)
Baldwin Naturals.................21 C2
Balkan Bistro......................22 C3
Barberian's Steak House.........23 F3
Bright Pearl.......................24 A3
Café Crepe........................25 C5

Commensal........................26 E3
Dumpling House Restaurant.....27 A3
Furama Cake & Dessert Garden..29 A4
Fujiyama...........................28 B2
Goldstone Noodle Restaurant...30 A4
John's Italian Café................31 B2
Matahari Bar & Grill..............32 B2
Midi................................33 C3
Phở Hu'ng.........................34 A3
Queen Mother Café..............35 C5
Richtree Market Restaurant......36 F5
Saffron Tree.......................37 E2
Senator Restaurant...............38 F4
Swatow............................39 A3
Terroni............................40 F5

DRINKING 🍷 (pp118–25)
Village Idiot.......................41 C3

ENTERTAINMENT 🎭 (pp115–35)
Canadian Opera Company.....(see 43)
Canon Theatre....................42 F4
Cinematheque Ontario.........(see 1)
Four Seasons Centre for the
    Performing Arts...............43 D5
Grossman's Tavern...............44 A2
Horseshoe Tavern.................45 A5
Massey Hall.......................46 F4
Music Gallery.....................47 B4
National Ballet Of Canada.....(see 43)
Rex................................48 C5

Rivoli...............................49 A5
Rivoli Pool Hall.................(see 49)
Sonic..............................50 A3
T.O. Tix............................51 F3
Top O' The Senator..............52 F4

SHOPPING 🛍 (pp147–63)
Black Market Megawarehouse...53 B5
Black Market Vintage Clothing..54 B5
Boomer............................55 B5
C-Squared.........................56 B5
Change Room......................57 A5
Eaton Centre......................58 F3
Eko................................59 B5
Friendly Stranger..................60 C5

Get Outside........................61 A5
John Fluevog......................62 B5
Kiehl's.............................63 A5
Mendocino........................64 B5
Muchstore.........................65 B5
Pages Books & Magazines.......66 B5
Sam the Record Man..............67 F3
Sears Department Store...........68 F3
Second Vinyl......................69 C5
Showroom.........................70 B5
Silver Snail Comic Shop..........71 B5
Steve's Music......................72 A5

SLEEPING 🛏 (pp165–78)
Baldwin Village Inn...............73 C2

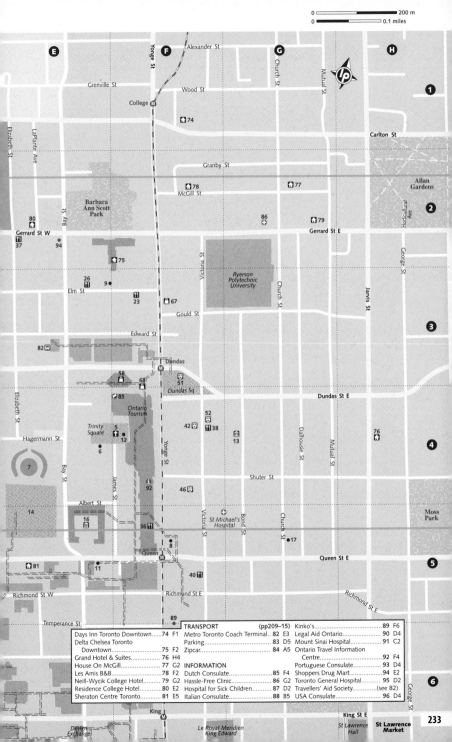

TRANSPORT	**(pp209–15)**	Kinko's	**89** F6
Metro Toronto Coach Terminal..	**82** E3	Legal Aid Ontario	**90** D4
Parking	**83** D5	Mount Sinai Hospital	**91** C2
Zipcar	**84** A5	Ontario Travel Information	
		Centre	**92** F4
INFORMATION		Portuguese Consulate	**93** D4
Dutch Consulate	**85** F4	Shoppers Drug Mart	**94** E2
Hassle-Free Clinic	**86** G2	Toronto General Hospital	**95** D2
Hospital for Sick Children	**87** D2	Travellers' Aid Society	(see 82)
Italian Consulate	**88** B5	USA Consulate	**96** D4

Days Inn Toronto Downtown.....**74** F1
Delta Chelsea Toronto
  Downtown.....**75** F2
Grand Hotel & Suites.....**76** H4
House On McGill.....**77** G2
Les Amis B&B.....**78** F2
Neill-Wycik College Hotel.....**79** G2
Residence College Hotel.....**80** E2
Sheraton Centre Toronto.....**81** E5

Bulwer St

Soho St

Queen St W

Pullan Pl

Osgoode

A   B   C   D

Spadina Ave

1

72

79

Richmond St W

Duncan St

90

88

82

71

Nelson St

1

39

University Ave

104

100

66

Entertainment
District

John St

118

Adelaide St W

Adelaide St W

36

48

122

York St

3

Oxley St

69

Pearl St

See Downtown North Map (pp232–3)

10

Charlotte St

2

103

96

125

105

78

81

98

85

St Andrew

95

52 93 68

Peter St

56

45

King St W

26

12

70

89

108

Mercer St

Emily St

58

86

Metro
Hall

84

112

Wellington St W

113

30

Clarence
Square
Park

Windsor St

6

3

73

Simcoe
Place

92

100

121

6

Front St W

31

19

Station St

Metro
Convention
Centre

Blue Jays Way

111   63

8

Simcoe St

4

Spadina Ave

Navy Wharf Ct

24

Bremner Blvd

Bobbie
Rosenfeld
Park

York St

Lower Simcoe St

29

Harbourfront

Rees St

Lake Shore Blvd W

5

Lower Spadina Ave

Gardiner Expwy

Harbour St

Queens Quay W

25

32

22

110

76

Spadina
Ave
Slip

Peter St
Slip

Reest
St
Slip

34

Robertson

Simcoe St
Slip

35

4

33

14

Cres

21

17

49

75

15

20

80

Tourism
Toronto

York St
Slip

6

13

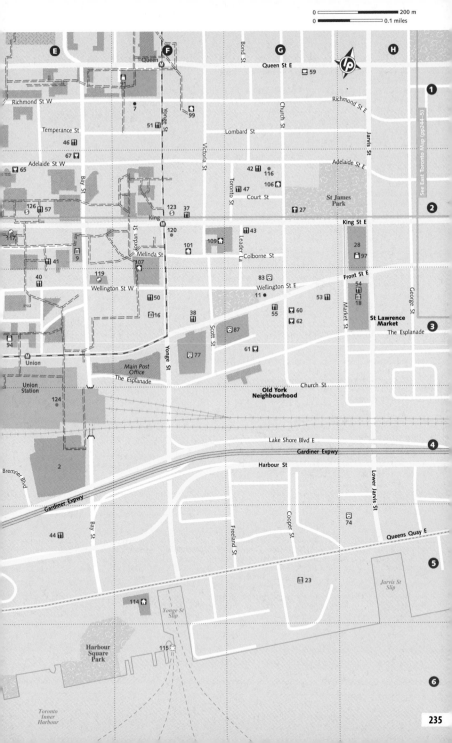

0 ————— 200 m
0 ————— 0.1 miles

E **F** **G** **H**

Queen

Queen St E

🖥 59

1

Richmond St W

Richmond St E

Temperance St

Lombard St

🏥 51 Victoria St

46 🍴

99

Church St

Jarvis St

67 🏥

Adelaide St W

Adelaide St E

🖥 65

Bay St

42 🍴
116

St James
Park

Toronto St

106 🏠

126 57

47

Court St

🖥 27

King

123 37

King St E

120

43

28

🏠 97

101

109 🏠

117

9

Leader La

41

Melinda St

107

Colborne St

Front St E

54

119

Wellington St W

83

18

40

Wellington St E

Market St

St Lawrence
Market

George St

50

11

53 🍴

3

16

38

55

The Esplanade

60

62

94

Scott St

87

Union

61

Yonge St

77

Union
Station

Main Post
Office

The Esplanade

Church St

124

**Old York
Neighbourhood**

Lake Shore Blvd E

4

Gardiner Expwy

Harbour St

Bremner Blvd

2

Lower Jarvis St

Bay St

Gardiner Expwy

Freeland St

Cooper St

74

44 🍴

Queens Quay E

5

🏛 23

Jarvis St
Slip

114 🏠

Yonge St
Slip

Harbour
Square
Park

115

6

Toronto
Inner
Harbour

See East Toronto Map (pp244–5)

235

BLOOR-YORKVILLE, UNIVERSITY OF TORONTO & YONGE STREET STRIP
(Map pp238–9)

Walmer Rd

A

B

C

D

Tranby Ave

Kendal Ave

1

Madison Ave

Huron St

Admiral Rd

Bedford Rd

Boswell Ave

Elgin Ave

Avenue Rd

73
16

Lowther Ave

St George St

Lowther Ave

Bedford Rd

85

82

Yorkville

101

15

31

2

28

Prince Arthur Ave

Cumberland St

87

50

St George

84

Spadina

81

37

2

Bloor St W

See The Annex & Little Italy Map (pp242–3)

9

Devonshire Pl

Varsity
Stadium

14

7

75

3

Washington Ave

Huron St

Museum

Charles St W

Sussex Ave

83

55

Robert St

Sussex Mws

Spadina Ave

Gln Morris St

Hoskin Ave

Queen's Park Cres W

4

Harbord St

21

Queen's
Park

Classic Rd

20

Tower Rd

New College

Willcocks St

St George St

University of Toronto–
St George Campus

5

Bancroft Ave

King's College Cir

13

Queen's Park Cres E

Spadina Circle

Spadina
Circle

Russell St

103

Robert St

See Downtown North Map (pp232–3)

King's College Rd

Huron St

6

5

89

Spadina Ave

18

Ross St

College St

Henry St

McCaul St

107

Queens Park

University Ave

Toronto
General
Hospital

SIGHTS & ACTIVITIES (pp45–80)
Anshei Minsk Synagogue..........1 H2
Calphalon Culinary Centre.......2 H6
Coupe Bizzarre..........................3 D4
Downward Dog Yoga Centre....4 E5
Museum Of Contemporary Canadian
Art......................................5 B4
Trinity Bellwoods Park Ice Rink..6 C3
Trinity Bellwoods Park Tennis
Courts................................7 C4
Way Cool Tattoos....................8 F5
Zen Buddhist Temple...............9 H1

EATING (pp91–113)
Akram's Shoppe.....................10 G2
Dufflet Pastries.....................11 D5
El Trompo...............................12 G2
Fressen..................................13 G4
Full Moon Vegetarian
Restaurant.......................14 G3
Global Cheese.......................15 G2
Gypsy Co-op..........................16 D5
Irie Food Joint........................17 F5
Jumbo Empanadas.................18 G2
Le Gourmand.........................19 H5
Red Tea Box...........................20 E4
Rice Bar.................................21 G1
Rodney's Oyster House...........22 H6
Siddhartha.............................23 F6
Susur......................................24 F6
Swan.....................................25 C4
Terroni..................................26 B4

DRINKING (pp118–25)
Crush....................................27 H6
Czehoski................................28 E4
Louie's Coffee Stop................29 G2
Moonbean Coffee Company...30 H2
Red Room..............................31 H1
Supermarket..........................32 G1
Wheat Sheaf Tavern...............33 F6

ENTERTAINMENT (pp115–35)
Big Bop.................................34 F5
Bovine Sex Club.....................35 F4
Cameron House......................36 H5
Comfort Zone........................37 H1
El Mocambo Lounge...............38 H1
Factory Theatre......................39 F5
Free Times Café.....................40 G1
Graffiti's................................41 H2
Healey's.................................42 F5
Holy Joe's..........................(see 34)
Hooch.................................(see 16)
Kathedral...........................(see 34)
Reverb................................(see 34)
Silver Dollar Room..................43 H1
Theatre Passe Muraille...........44 F4

SHOPPING (pp147–63)
Annie Thompson Studio..........45 E4
Bungalow...............................46 G1
C-Pub....................................47 G2
Cabaret.................................48 E4
Capri Boutique.......................49 E5
Chatelet................................50 E5
Come As You Are....................51 E5
Cosmos Records.....................52 F5
Courage My Love....................53 G3

Exile......................................54 G3
F/X..55 G5
Fleurtje..................................56 D4
Fresh Baked Goods.................57 G1
Fresh Collective......................58 E4
Girl Friday..............................59 D4
Grreat Stuff...........................60 B4
Heel Boy................................61 E4
Japanese Paper Place.............62 D5
Lilith.....................................63 G5
Magic Pony.........................(see 20)
Polka Dot Kids.......................64 C5
Preloved................................65 F5
Red Indian Art Deco...............66 F5
Response...........................(see 58)
Suspect Video & Culture.........67 E5
Timmie Dog Outfitters............68 D5
Tin Taj...................................69 C5

SLEEPING (pp165–78)
Lakeview Victorian.................70 A1

TRANSPORT (pp209–15)
Community Bicycle
Network.............................71 F5
Parking.................................72 F5
Wheels 4 Rent.......................73 G2

Shaw St

A | **B** | **C** | **D**

SIGHTS & ACTIVITIES	(pp45–80)
Alliance Française	1 H1
Christie Pitts Park	2 C2
Christie Pitts Park Pool	3 C1
Miles Nadal Jewish Community Centre (Bloor JCC)	4 H2
Native Canadian Centre of Toronto	5 H2
Shiatsu School of Canada	6 D6
Sivananda Yoga Vedanta Centre	7 H4
Tengye Ling Tibetan Buddhist Temple	8 H2
Twist Yoga Studio	(see 22)

EATING	(pp91–113)
65 Degrees	9 C6
Bar Italia	10 D6
By the Way Café	11 G2
Chiado	12 A5
Cora Pizza	13 H3
Future Bakery & Café	14 G2
Harbord Fish & Chips	15 G4
Hodo Kwaja	16 D2
Insomnia	17 F2
Latitude	18 G4
Leão D'ouro	19 G6
Mars Food	20 F6
Mel's Montréal Delicatessen	21 F2
Noah's Natural Foods	22 H2
Papa Ceo	23 H4
Phil's Original BBQ	24 A5
Real Thailand	25 G2
Serra	26 G2
Supermodel Pizza	27 B5
Tacos El Asador	28 D2
Victory Café	29 E3
Xacutti	30 E6

DRINKING	(pp118–25)
Ciao Edie	31 E6
Kalendar	32 D6
Labyrinth Lounge	33 G2
Madison Avenue Pub	34 H2
Päaeez	35 D6
Tranzac	36 G3

ENTERTAINMENT	(pp115–35)
Andy Poolhall	(see 31)
Bloor Cinema	37 F2
Brunswick House	38 G2
Cineforum	39 F6

Dance Cave	(see 41)
El Convento Rico	40 B5
Lee's Palace	41 F2
Mod Club	42 B5
Royal Cinema	43 C6
Sneaky Dee's	44 F6
Tafelmusik	(see 45)
Toronto Consort	(see 45)
Trinity-St Paul's Centre	45 G2

SHOPPING	(pp147–63)
A Different Booklist	46 E3
Balfour Books	47 D6
Ballenford Books on Architecture	48 E3
Beguiling	49 E2
Clay Design	50 G4
David Mirvish Books	51 E3
Dragon Lady Comics & Paper Nostalgia	52 C6
Girl Friday	53 B5
Good For Her	54 F4
Grassroots	55 F2
Honest Ed's	56 E2
La Maison de la Presse Internationale	57 C6
La Maison de la Presse Internationale	58 F2
Little Chloe's Chic Boutique	59 G4
Outer Layer	60 F2
Parentbooks	61 F4
Secrets From Your Sister	62 F2
Seekers Books	63 F2
Soundscapes	64 D6
Suspect Video & Culture	65 E2
Things Japanese	66 F6
Toronto Women's Bookstore	67 H4
Touched By An Angel	68 F6
Trove	69 F2

SLEEPING	(pp165–78)
Annex Guest House	70 H1
Casa Loma Inn	71 G2
Global Guesthouse	72 H2
Madison Manor	73 H2
Palmerston Inn Bed & Breakfast	74 E5
Posh Digs	75 E4

INFORMATION	
Kinko's	76 G2
Shoppers Drug Mart	77 G2

Christie Pitts Park

Bickford Park

Manning Ave

Euclid Ave

Harbord St

Ossington Ave

Roxton Rd

Shaw St

Harbord Park

Ulster St

Little Italy

Beatrice St

Manning Ave

Euclid Ave

Concord Ave

12

24

53 27

40 42

College St

Shannon St

Roxton Rd

Shaw St

Crawford St

Cinder Ave

Beatrice St

See Kensington Market & Queen West Map (pp240–1)

9 57 43

10 64

32

52

47

35

6

Gore St

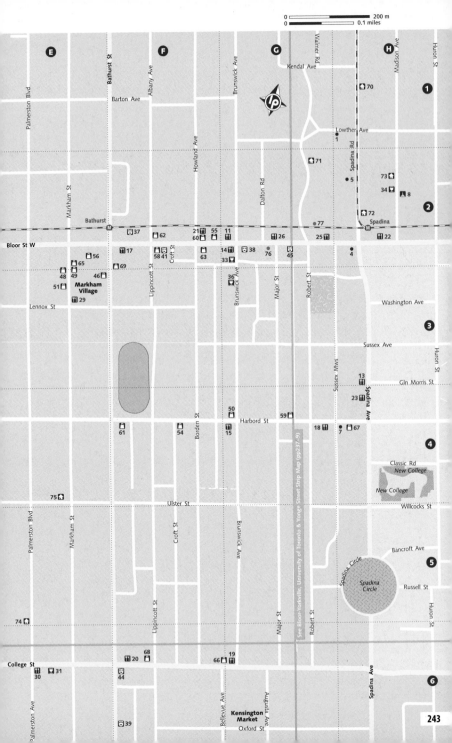

Elm Ave **A** Maple Ave
48
Rosedale Valley Rd
N Sherbourne St

Nanton Ave **B**
Dale Ave
McKenzie Ave

Castle Frank Rd

Cambridge Ave **C**
Broadview Ave
Bloor St Viaduct Broadview

D
Playter Blvd
Hurndale Ave
1

Bloor St E
Sherbourne

Castle Frank
Castle Frank Cres

Dearbourne Ave
Fairview Blvd
Wolfrey Ave
Hogarth Ave

Bowden St
44

26

Selby St
47 50 52
Liuden St
Howard St
Isabella St

St James
Cemetery
5
2

Rosedale
Ravine
Park

Don
River

Rosedale Valley Rd

Sparkhall Ave
Bain Ave
Withrow Ave

2
Wellesley St E
Earl Pl
Sherbourne St
Bleeker St

St James Ave

Rose Ave

Bayview Ave
Don Valley Pkwy

See Bloor-Yorkville, University of Toronto & Yonge Street Strip Map (pp237-9)

51
54
38

Homewood Ave

Prospect St

21
12
Metcalfe St
39

Winchester St
Broadcast Lane
28
Millington St
Sackville Pl

Aberdeen Ave
Carlton St

49 56 27 25
15

Ontario St

Wellesley
Park

Amelia St
Salisbury Ave

Sackville St

Rawlings Ave

Toronto
Necropolis
8
4

Geneva Ave
Spruce St

Riverdale
Park

Riverdale Ave
Langley Ave
Victor Ave
Simpson Ave

Gerrard St E
First Ave

3
Horticultural Ave
1
Gerrard St E

55

Seaton St
Bleeker St

Oak St

River St
Dundas St E

Allen Ave
Dundas St E

Munro St
Broadview Ave

4
Jarvis St
53
George St

Pembroke St
Sherbourne St

Parliament St
Regent St

Shuter St

Sackville St
Tracy St
Teflann St

Wascana Ave

Bayview Ave
Don Valley Pkwy
Carroll St
Hamilton St
Thompson St
20

Grant St
De Grassi St
Boulton Ave

Moss
Park

Queen St E
Richmond St E

Berkeley St

Power St

King St E
Bright St

7
22 37

Lewis St
Saulter St
McGee St
Queen St E

St
James
Park
9

Adelaide St E

46 35

5
King St E

St
Lawrence
Market
36

See Downtown South Map (pp234-6)

Derby St
Erin St
3

Princess St
Front St E
33

George St
Frederick St
Lower Sherbourne St

6
The Esplanade
Longboat Ave

Hahn St

Eastern Ave

Trinity St

Cherry St
Mill St

34 29 40
42
43

Distillery
District

Overend St

Richmond St E
Adelaide St E

King St E

6
Lower Jarvis St
Market St

Gardiner Expwy
Queens Qu E

Gardiner Expwy

Villiers St
Saulter St S

Don Roadway

31

Toronto
Inner Harbour

See Toronto Islands Map (p247)

SIGHTS & ACTIVITIES (pp45–80)
Allan Gardens Conservatory......1 A3
Chapel of St-James-the-Less.....2 B2
Elissa Gallander Yoga Studio..(see 11)
Enoch Turner Schoolhouse........3 B5
Riverdale Farm.............................4 A5
St James Cemetery......................5 B2
St Lawrence CRC.........................6 A5
Toronto Climbing Academy........7 D4
Toronto Necropolis.....................8 C2
Toronto's First Post Office..........9 A5

EATING 🍴 (pp91–113)
Bar-Be-Que Hut.......................10 H3
Big Carrot...............................11 D1
Chapter Eleven........................12 B2
Edward Leveque's Kitchen........13 G4
Joy Bistro...............................14 E4
Lennie's Whole Foods..............15 B3
Leslie Jones...........................16 F4
Myth.......................................17 E1
Ouzeri...................................18 E1
Pan On The Danforth................19 E1
Pop Bistro..............................20 D4

Pure Spirits............................(see 34)
Raashna.................................21 B2
Real Jerk...............................22 D4
Siddhartha.............................23 H3
Toast....................................24 E4
Town Grill..............................25 B3

DRINKING 🍺🍷 (pp118–25)
Allen's...................................26 D1
Brass Taps.............................27 B3
Jet Fuel.................................28 B3
Mill Street Brewery.................29 B5
Tango Palace Coffee Company.30 F4
Waterside Sports Club.............31 A6

ENTERTAINMENT 🎭 (pp115–35)
Bad Dog Theatre.....................32 D1
CanStage (Canadian Stage
   Company)............................33 B5
Dancemakers..........................34 B5
Dominion On Queen................35 C4
Lorraine Kimsa Theatre for
   Young People.......................36 A5
Opera House...........................37 D4

Phoenix.................................38 A3
School of Toronto Dance
   Theatre...............................(see 39)
Toronto Dance Theatre.............39 B2
Young Centre for Performing
   Arts....................................40 B5

SHOPPING 🛍 (pp147–63)
Another Story Bookshop............41 D1
Auto Grotto Automobilia...........42 B6
Carrot Common.......................(see 11)
Case Goods Building.................43 B6
El Pipil..................................44 D1
Grassroots..............................(see 11)
La Di Da.................................45 D1
Librarie Champlain..................46 B4

SLEEPING 🛏 (pp165–78)
1871 Historic House B&B...........47 A1
Ainsley House.........................48 A1
Amsterdam..............................49 B3
Au Petit Paris..........................50 A1
Banting House Inn....................51 A2
Clarion Hotel and Suites...........52 A1
Comfort Suites City Centre........53 A4
Homewood Inn........................54 A3
Pimblett's Downtown Toronto....55 A3
Toronto Townhouse B&B............56 B3

THE BEACHES

0 ——————————— 400 m
0 ——————————— 0.2 miles

SHOPPING 🛍️ (pp147-63)
Arts on Queen.................21 E2
Boa, Bark & Fitz..............22 D2
Froosh...........................23 D2
Kids at Home..................24 D2
The Naked Sheep............25 D2

SLEEPING 🛏️ (pp165-78)
Accommodating the Soul..26 C2

INFORMATION
Changing rooms..............27 C3

DRINKING 🍸🍷 (pp118-25)
Castro's Lounge..............15 D2
Kaffeehaus Konditor........16 B2
Lion on the Beach...........17 C2
Remarkable Bean............18 E2

ENTERTAINMENT 🎭 (pp115-35)
Alliance Atlantis Cinemas..19 A2
Fox Cinema....................20 E2

EATING 🍴 (pp91-113)
Akane-ya........................8 E2
Ali's Tandoori Curry House..9 E2
Beacher Café.................10 D2
King's Table...................11 E2
La Tea Da Salon de Thé...12 D2
Nevada.........................13 C2
Spiaggia........................14 E2
Wholesome Market........(see 20)

SIGHTS & ACTIVITIES (pp45-80)
DD Summerville Pool..........1 B3
Kew Gardens Lawn Bowling
Club............................2 C3
Kew Gardens Skating Rink...3 C3
Kew Gardens Tennis Club....4 C2
RC Harris Filtration Plant....5 F2
Tat-a-Rama.....................6 D2
The Beaches CRC..............7 D2

246

TORONTO ISLANDS

0 ——————— 500 m
0 ——————— 0.3 miles

SIGHTS & ACTIVITIES	(pp45–80)
Beach Volleyball	.1 C4
Boathouse	.2 D4
Centreville Amusement Park	.3 C3
Frisbee Golf Course	.4 E3
Gibraltar Point Lighthouse	.5 B4
Hanlan's Point Tennis Courts	.6 B3
Hedge Maze	.7 C4
St Andrew-by-the-Lake Church	.8 D4
Tram Tours	.9 C4

EATING 🍴	(pp91–113)
Rectory Café	.10 E3

SLEEPING 🛏	(pp165–78)
Barb's Island Loft	.11 F2
Smiley's B&B	.12 E3

TRANSPORT	(pp209–15)
Airport Ferry Dock	.13 B1
Bathurst St Ferry Terminal	.14 B1
Centre Island Ferry Terminal	.15 C3
Hanlan's Point Ferry Terminal	.16 B2
Toronto Islands Bicycle Rental	.17 C4
Toronto Islands Ferry Terminal	.18 D1
Ward's Island Ferry Terminal	.19 E2

INFORMATION	
Changing Rooms	.20 C4
Fire Station	.21 E3
First Aid & Lost Children Area	.22 C3
Lockers	(see 20)
Seasonal Tourist Information Booth	.23 C3

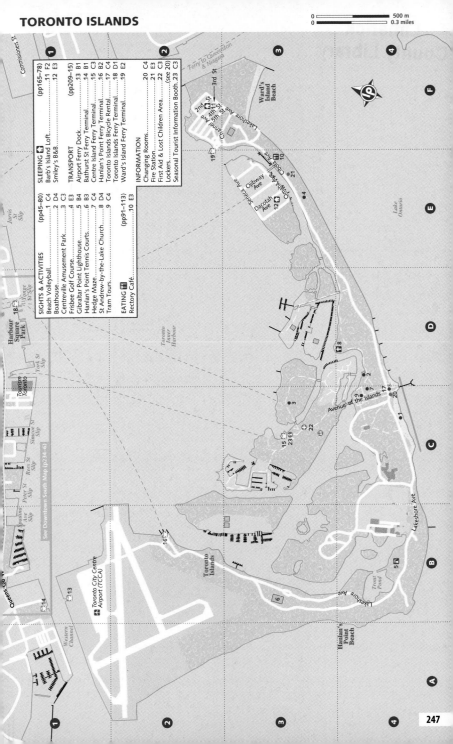

247

Limerick
County Library

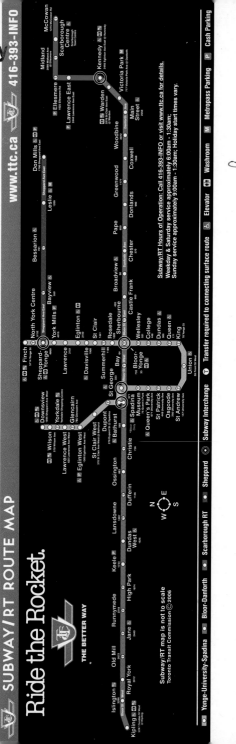